The Making of Contemporary Africa

Capital and Labour in the Nigerian Tin Mines

The African Worker

Insiders and Outsiders; The Indian Working Class of Durban
1910–90

# THE MAKING OF CONTEMPORARY AFRICA

## The Development of African Society Since 1800

### Second Edition

BILL FREUND

LYNNE RIENNER PUBLISHERS

BOULDER

First published in the United States of America in 1998 by
Lynne Rienner Publishers, Inc.
1800 30th Street, Boulder, Colorado 80301
www.rienner.com

ISBN 978-1-55587-806-1 (pbk. : alk. paper)

Printed and bound in the United States of America

The paper used in this publication meets the requirements
of the American National Standard for Permanence of
Paper for Printed Library Materials Z39.48-1992.

10  9  8  7

# CONTENTS

*List of Illustrations and Tables*                                    viii

*Preface to the Second Edition*                                          x

*Preface to the First Edition*                                         xii

*List of Abbreviations*                                                xvi

**1  Africanist History and the History of Africa**                     1

**2  Material and Cultural Development in
    Africa before the Nineteenth Century**                             14
*Hunters, Gatherers and Cultivators*                                   16
*The Formation of States*                                              21
*Some Major African States*                                            24
*Modes of Production, the State and Class Society*                     30

**3  The European Intrusion in the Era of
    Merchant Capital**                                                 34
*The Portuguese Epoch*                                                 35
*The Atlantic Slave Trade*                                             40
*The Foundations of South Africa*                                      47
*The Age of Merchant Capital*                                          49

**4  The Era of Legitimate Commerce, 1800–70**                         51
*Abolition and Legitimate Commerce*                                    51
*Class and Trade in Coastal West Africa*                               56
*Nineteenth-century East Africa*                                       58
*The Era of Informal Empire*                                           63
*South Africa in the Age of the Great Trek*                            65

**5 The Conquest of Africa** 73
*Imperialism: Theory and Practice* 73
*The Build-up to Conquest* 79
*The Partition of Africa* 84
*Resistance, Collaboration and Contradiction in African Society* 91

**6 The Material Basis of Colonial Society, 1900–40** 97
*The Era of Force and the Chartered Companies* 100
*Mines* 103
*White Settlers* 106
*Lords and Chiefs* 109
*Peasant Production* 111
*The Colonial State* 118

**7 Culture, Class and Social Change in Colonial
Africa, 1900–40** 125
*Class Relations in Colonial Africa* 125
*Culture and Social Organisation* 132
*A Changing Faith* 135
*The Modalities of Resistance* 140
*Thuku and Chilembwe* 145

**8 Industrialisation and South African Society,
1900–40** 149
*Reconstruction and Union* 151
*An Era of Confrontation* 155
*Pact and Fusion* 158
*The Crisis of the 1940s* 163

**9 The Decolonisation of Africa, 1940–60** 167
*The Second Colonial Occupation* 168
*Social Confrontation and Class Struggles* 176
*The Political Setting* 183
*Independence for British West Africa* 184
*The End of British Rule in East and Central Africa* 189
*Decolonisation in French Africa* 195
*The Congo Crisis* 198

**10  Tropical Africa, 1960–80: Class, State
    and the Problem of Development**                    204
*Neo-colonial Myths and Realities*                      204
*The Ruling Class in Contemporary Africa*               209
*Class, Party and State*                                213

**11  Southern Africa in Crisis**                       220
*The Nationalist Party Victory and its Implications*    220
*The Armed Struggle in Southern Africa*                 230
*The Challenges of the 1970s and 1980s*                 237
*The End of Apartheid*                                  243

**12  The Age of Structural Adjustment**                247
*Intensifying Contradictions in the 1970s*              247
*Crisis after 1980*                                     253
*Structural Adjustment in Ghana and Uganda*             256
*Decay of the State; Drive for Democracy*               260
*A New Africa Struggles into Being*                     266

*Annotated Bibliography*                                269

*Index*                                                 317

# LIST OF ILLUSTRATIONS AND TABLES

**Plates**

1 Merchant capital: hide and skin merchant with his goods, Kano (Nigerian savanna)
2 Merchant capital: ivory caravan on march to the coast (mainland Tanzania)
3 Pre-capitalist ruling classes: the Timbo *almamy* and his retinue (Futa Djallon, Guinea)
4 Pre-capitalist ruling classes: Haile Selassie's ministers prior to the Italian invasion of 1935 (Ethiopia)
5 Imperialist conquest: Asante, 1896. The perspective of a 'master race'
6 Imperialist conquest: Asante, 1896. 'A sketch from life' showing the Asantehene, his mother and the Ansah brothers of Kumasi
7 Colonial agriculture: white settler cultivation, Delamere estate at Njoro, Kenya Highlands
8 Colonial agriculture: cocoa production in a rich peasant household, Gold Coast
9 Colonial society: diamond workers in iron 'mittens' being examined for stolen gems, Kimberley (South Africa)
10 Colonial society: Missionaries and staff, Nanzela, Barotseland, Northern Rhodesia
11 Decolonisation: The Congo crisis begins, Patrice Lumumba at a press conference following the intervention of Belgian paratroopers (1 September 1960)
12 Decolonisation: The Congo crisis continues, Tshombe's troops recapture a North Katanga town and American weaponry, February 1962.

**Maps**

1 Pre-colonial Africa: Places and People     23
2 Nineteenth-century Africa     66

3   The African Colonies in 1914                          120
4   Independent Africa, 1982                              206

**Tables**

6.1  Expansion of export cash crops from tropical
     Africa in '000 tons                                 123
8.1  Percentage of total population urbanised            164
9.1  Pre-war and post-war population of the largest
     African cities, c.1955                              168
9.2  The growth in the European settler population       169

# PREFACE TO THE SECOND EDITION

The direct reason why I have written a new edition of this book is that so many teachers of African history who have found it helpful and stimulating as a text have asked me to bring it up to date. The result, apart from editing changes, has been a rewritten eleventh chapter and a new twelfth chapter. For most of Africa, independence now goes back some thirty years and more, and post-independence no longer means 'contemporary'. The experience of the 1960s and 1970s increasingly has to be understood as part of the past. I have also wanted to bring the bibliography up to date in order to introduce readers to newer books and themes. In certain areas, for example the Horn of Africa or the analysis of pastoral societies, it seems to me that the literature is very much stronger than it was fifteen years ago.

Looking back at my efforts to try to understand Africa along lines that I call materialist in the Introduction, I am fairly unrepentant. Some of my friends have urged me to take cognizance of the bold and wonderful world of the post-modern. I suppose I think that I anticipate some of the deconstructive energy of the post-modern in the original edition of this work. In fact, I feel that the influence of Marxism on me, amongst many others, as an essentially subversive set of ideas already embodied much of this force. Of course, for yet others, Marxism was simply another cate-chism in which to believe, which contained comprehensible answers to life's problems. The fall-out over the end of the Cold War has made mincemeat of that approach to Marxism as a new orthodoxy. It was already fairly clear to me in the early 1980s that there was no royal road to development and the good life obvious to all right thinkers but perhaps post- modernism deserves credit for putting the accent on such a criticism of positivist thinking. Certainly my assessment of the southern African region and the real and potential shifts in it has become very much soberer and more conservative over time.

I also think that post-modernity and its avatars have had a salutary effect in pushing us to become more aware of our own biases and of our own sources as writers. How different people have exchanged and understood knowledge, a basic necessity for developing a sociology of knowledge, has entered far more clearly into Africanist debates thanks to the influential writing of such scholars as Achille Mbembe, Jean-François Bayart, Bogumil Jewsiewicki and Luise White. It is seductive and fascinating to explore means of communication less direct but perhaps more expressive than the written, or even the spoken, word. I am less enamoured of that side of post-modernity which poses as a justification for crude forms of relativism (my view is OK, yours is OK, so long as they can be experientially pursued) that make the study of history a nonsense or simply a search for 'discourses'. Spokespersons for this approach are rarely very interested in interrogating their own biases and contradictions. Discourses do not come from thin air or from disembodied categories such as 'gender' or 'ethnicity' and the search for a common grasp of the world around us cannot be abandoned. There is still space for a viable materialist (as opposed to economistic) understanding of the world despite postmodernism.

One important development that influences me, often indirectly, is the emergence of a significant philosophy in Africa which embraces serious debates about what Africa is or means. I would refer readers here particularly to the following impressive studies: Kwame Appiah, *In My Father's House*, Methuen, London, 1992; Paulin Hountondji, *African Philosophy; Myth and Reality*, Indiana University Press, Bloomington, 1983; V. Y. Mudimbe, *The Invention of Africa*, Indiana University Press, Bloomington, 1988.

I would finally like to acknowledge some institutional debts. In recent years, I have been able to widen what has become a heavily South African knowledge base through first trips to Mali, Senegal and Madagascar thanks to conferences, the first two under the auspices of CODESRIA, the crucial organisation for African social scientists. The chance to serve as external examiner for our sister department at the University of Zimbabwe has enabled me to travel in and understand that country far better. The University of Natal Research Fund allowed me to make a short exploratory visit to Uganda in 1994 where I was a guest of the Centre for Basic Research, Kampala. Awards from the university and the Human Sciences Research Council of South Africa permitted me to catch up with international research at African Studies Association of the USA meetings in St Louis and Toronto. They, and additionally the Oppenheimer Trust and the CNRS of France, also helped to support a 1995 sabbatical spent at Oxford and at the Ecole des Hautes Etudes en Sciences Sociales in Paris which was partially devoted to this project.

# Preface to the First Edition

It takes some temerity to attempt a synthesis of the field one studies and teaches, particularly if one is a younger scholar. The first chapter of this book endeavours to explain the problems of African historiography as it has developed and I will not anticipate the points that I make there, except to say that my dissatisfaction with earlier syntheses in the light of the scholarship of the past decade or so and the irrelevance of much earlier writing to the current mood in Africa itself seem to justify the attempt.

This work is introductory. It assumes no previous knowledge of the history of Africa and is intended for the intelligent general reader. Unlike most textbooks, however, it avoids blandness and does not attempt to appeal to every point of view. It is an extended essay that considers, for various periods since the beginning of the nineteenth century, a few general themes: broad social and economic developments, the relationship of African social forces to outside interventions and the interplay of classes within Africa. Against these themes the main political events of African history are set.

In my view, the web of social and economic relations that emerges from human satisfaction of material needs forms the core of historical development. This book is therefore a *materialist* interpretation of history, in terms of how events are explained. This is generally to be preferred in usage to *Marxist* history which I feel has an unnecessarily sectarian ring, although it is largely to Marx and his followers that I turn for inspiration. Class struggle, with the classes defined ultimately in terms of their relationship to the labour process determines the form of history for Marx. He brilliantly showed at varying levels of abstraction the one fundamental class contradiction that mattered to him politically, that between capital and labour in capitalist development. Classes are not unique to capitalism and forms of domination can precede or succeed true class societies. In the African continent there is a great range of historically specific social and economic relationships that, with some imagination and flexibility, can be discussed in class terms. One should not apply too mechanically the well-known terminology of domination and appropriation that comes out of the study of other parts of the world. Yet class certainly cannot be left out of African history.

For those interested in, but totally unfamiliar with Marx's historical categorisation, this book cannot hope to fill the gap. The reader is referred to works introductory (say Leo Huberman, *Man's Wordly Goods*) or systematic (say Paul Sweezy, *The Theory of Capitalist Development*). There are many of both. My own approach, moreover, involves a selection from a large range of interpretations of what Marx most emphasised in his work and of what a materialist history ought to be.

To the extent that the available format and information allows, this book tried to adopt the point of view of the ordinary cultivators and wage-earners of Africa. Yet at present it seems there is no single appropriate political line to be followed that can shape this perspective precisely. I therefore make my own political judgments, breaking with most previous radical (and indeed liberal) writing on Africa in trying to consider nationalism in modern Africa critically, rather than taking automatically a nationalist point of view.

Today, considerable debate rages among intellectuals of the Left concerning the relative explanatory merits of internal class forces and external pressure and influence in the development (and underdevelopment) of contemporary Africa. The two are, in my view, so closely related that this is much like the question of the primacy of chicken or egg. However, I feel strongly that, until very recently, the pendulum has swung too far *politically* towards subsuming all Africa's problems as being the result of alien forces. The explosive power of capitalist penetration is often reduced to an imperialist conspiracy theory. This is why I lay so much emphasis on social rather than national relationships, whose character was *never* entirely determined, even under colonial rule, by imperialism.

Much radical writing on Africa has tried to ignore or to sidestep Marx's emphasis on the dynamism and qualitative transformation induced by capitalism. At one extreme, it has even been claimed that Africa was conquered in order to forestall its economic development under indigenous auspices. I believe that it was conquered to open it up for capital in the one way that was historically possible. This resulted in the extraction of wealth which went overseas, but also in the genuine development of productive forces in Africa. From this perspective colonialism had both progressive and regressive features, as will be seen from a more detailed analysis; it cannot be understood in a purely linear way. Materialist history cannot possibly be reduced to anti-colonial polemic. The complex interrelationship between capitalism and colonialism in Africa is the central theme of the second half of this book.

Contemporary Africa suffers from extremely unequal power relations in the world and contains many features that can be *described* as 'economically dependent'. Unlike many radical writers I have become convinced, particularly during the last couple of years working on this book, that 'dependence' is a vague indeterminate quality that *explains* by itself rather little and belongs for most purposes to a nationalist, not a Marxist, point of view. There are many places in the pages to come where I deliberately criticise the 'dependency' perspective because it is so often confused with a class-conscious one and has acquired great currency among left-wing considerations of the 'Third World'. In 1974 the editors of the first issue of the *Review of African Political Economy*, which has played such a major role in the development of Left thought on Africa, wrote that:

> We are...at odds with a position, claiming the mantle of Marxist orthodoxy, which holds that the distortion of so-called peripheral capitalism is no more than the natural and inevitable concomitant of all capitalist development, and that the potential of peripheral capital is only as limited as the potential of capitalism itself.

Their position is now much less universally held and, on the whole, the perspective adopted here is not far from 'Marxist orthodoxy'.

A few rather more specific points about this book are also in order here. I have virtually excluded from these pages the history of Egypt and the Maghreb – Tunisia, Libya, Algeria and Morocco. These countries are as African as any other, but they are served by a large specialised historiography primarily in languages other than English, including Arabic which I do not read. It is on grounds of my ignorance and for the sake of convenience that I exclude them. As the first chapters stress, in reality the Sahara never formed an effective barrier to human, economic or cultural movements.

Other emphases reflect the state of my knowledge and the quality of available work. The detailed bibliographies, intended as guides to further reading, indicate my predilections, strengths and weaknesses while no doubt unintentionally omitting much excellent work. I have made an effort to consult and to consider material in languages other than English, particularly French, but my command of the literature is certainly far less extensive. The ex-British colonies have pride of place in this volume as one result. However, they do include Africa's largest (Sudan), most populous

(Nigeria) and most productive (South Africa) countries. I use many examples from two countries where I have lived and done research, Nigeria and Tanzania. A third, South Africa, was my first field of research and seems to me so important, compelling and distinctive that I treat it separately and very generously, from the point of view of space, for the twentieth century. Those whose background is in other parts of the continent should learn more about it.

The spelling of African proper names presents a great problem to the scholar. There has been an increasing tendency towards the use of more phonetically correct usage which, however, only serves to confuse the general reader. The spellings chosen here represent a personal compromise between accuracy and custom which can never satisfy all.

I should like to thank those kind enough to read and criticise drafts of parts of this book: Jane Guyer, Chris Saunders, Charles Stewart, Gavin Williams and especially Fred Cooper, who has been a great stimulus and friend to me during the period at Harvard when it has been written. Chapter 1 received valuable criticism when given as a paper at Boston University, the Canadian African Studies Association annual meeting and the University of Cape Town. The bibliographies exclude material which is unpublished but in some cases has been of considerable impact on my ideas. I should like to thank particularly these friends and scholars who made work of their own available to me which fits this category: Karin Barber, Babacar Fall, Vincent Farrar, Dave Hemson, Martin Legassick, Jay O'Brien, Dan O'Meara, Mary Rayner, Bob Shenton, T. V. Satyamurthy, Bonaventure Swai and Mike Watts. I also wish to record my gratitude to Boston area friends: Bill Hansen, Brigitte Schulz and Jordan Gebre Medhin who has taught me about the Horn of Africa; to Masao Yoshida who prepared a bibliography on Uganda for me, to Sid Lemelle and Chris Allen, to my patient editor Chiu-Yin Wong, and to the first person who suggested that I try to write a book of wider general interest, my mother Elisabeth Grohs Freund.

*Bill Freund*
*Cambridge, Massachusetts*
*October 1982*

# LIST OF ABBREVIATIONS

This list includes abbreviations used in the Notes to Chapters and the Annotated Bibliography (see pages 269–316). It does not include abbreviations used in the main text which are defined at the first mention.

| | | |
|---|---|---|
| *AA* | – | *African Affairs* |
| *AB* | – | *Africana Bulletin* |
| *AEHR* | – | *African Economic History Review* |
| *AHS* | – | *African Historical Studies* |
| *BIFAN* | – | *Bulletin de l'Institut Fondamentale d'Afrique Noire* |
| *CEA* | – | *Cahiers d'études africaines* |
| *CJAS* | – | *Canadian Journal of African Studies* |
| *CSSH* | – | *Comparative Studies in Society and History* |
| *EAPH* | – | *East African Publishing House* |
| *EHR* | – | *Economic History Review* |
| *HJ* | – | *Historical Journal* |
| *HWJ* | – | *History Workshop Journal* |
| *IJAHS* | – | *International Journal of African Historical Studies* |
| *IRSH* | – | *International Review of Social History* |
| *JAH* | – | *Journal of African History* |
| *JAS* | – | *Journal of the African Society* |
| *JBS* | – | *Journal of British Studies* |
| *JDS* | – | *Journal of Development Studies* |
| *JHSN* | – | *Journal of the Historical Society of Nigeria* |
| *JICH* | – | *Journal of Imperial and Commonwealth History* |
| *JMAS* | – | *Journal of Modern African Studies* |
| *JSAS* | – | *Journal of South African Studies* |
| *KHR* | – | *Kenya Historical Review* |
| *MERIP* | – | *Middle East Research and Information Project* |
| *RH* | – | *Rhodesian History* |
| *RLIJ* | – | *Rhodes-Livingstone Institute Journal* |
| *SS* | – | *Science and Society* |
| *THSG* | – | *Transactions of the Historical Society of Ghana* |

# 1

# AFRICANIST HISTORY AND THE HISTORY OF AFRICA

Africans have been conceptualising their lives and social relationships historically since the advent of agriculture and stockherding gave importance to questions of origin, genealogy and property long centuries ago. As state mechanisms and class contradictions evolved in many parts of the continent, historical interpretation became increasingly formalised in the hands of specialists. Informal traditions frequently survived in a masked form reflecting subversive interpretations and societal conflicts. The issues that mattered to such historians, the lineage of kings, the point of origins of peoples, the coming of an ecological disaster or a political defeat, belonged to a problematic that stemmed from prevailing material and social conditions. Although presented as objective truth, the tales of praise-singers, diviners and court officials were actually ideological in purpose. They represented the appropriation of social knowledge by particular groups for particular ends.

In much of Africa historical knowledge was conveyed purely by word of mouth in poetic, musical and dramatic settings. However, in some regions, such as the Ethiopian highlands, the East African coast and the West African savanna, the spread of literacy created the possibility of written history as well. The chronicles of Ethiopian monks and Timbuktu scholars were not simply royal commission work: they expressed the outlook of the class of men who wrote them, a class whose world-view was closely linked to specific traditions of Christian and Islamic knowledge.

With the conquest and partition of Africa by the European powers and its forcible incorporation into a world system of exchange based on capitalist production, the possibility of an autonomous development of intellectual activity in Africa was cut off as surely as the guillotine severs a

1

head from a body. The praise-singers continued to chant, but what they had to say ceased to have the same relevance.

The colonial masters of Africa took a keen interest in the territories they ruled, of course. They were as concerned as any African king had been to appropriate knowledge about Africa, for the purpose of effective administration and the promotion of capitalist enterprise. Much of this knowledge was historical; quantities of historical material were amassed and collected in colonial archives and libraries. However, the colonial period produced very little in the way of overtly historical publication. The dominant colonial science was anthropology. From the time of Sir Harry Johnston, writing in 1899, it was a full half-century before a European again wrote a general history of Africa. What most interested Europeans in Africa was themselves: a history of trade and diplomacy, invasion and conquest, heavily infused with assumptions about racial superiority that buttressed colonial domination. For the period following conquest, colonial writing focussed on the progress of administrative structures, transport networks and business enterprise in an heroic spirit. Yet it was in the colonial context that for the first time 'Africa' as an entity from the Cape to Cairo, from the coastal lagoons of the West to the Horn of the East, could be conceived. Attached to this concept there could be as well specialists, continental experts, 'Africanists'.

There are certain exceptions to this generalisation that deserve notice. First, in some parts of Africa, notably South Africa, imperialism brought in its wake large and internally complex settler communities, sections of which began to produce their own histories. The intellectual thrust of Afrikaner nationalism in South Africa was marked first by the publication of an anti-imperialist history of the country in the Afrikaans language. Jan Christiaan Smuts epitomised the antagonisms between the settlers of the South African Republic and the major imperialist power, Britain, in a famous pamphlet on the eve of the Boer War, *A Century of Wrong*. This historiography gave little consideration to the African masses of the country; its subject was the settler community.

As an African working class in the South African cities became stronger, more developed and a potential threat to the state and to capital, historical conceptualisation bifurcated along two lines of analysis. One increasingly posed racial conflict as a central theme, celebrating a racially defined society and re-expressing imperial oppression largely in terms of foreigners meddling with the appropriate racial ground rules of the 'South African way of life'. This line continued to take as its subject the 'white' community. The other, or liberal school, generally pro-imperialist, developed the new themes of 'racial conflict and co-operation' and 'race relations' in propounding more enlightened means of managing the black masses of South Africa. Within these limits a relatively richly documented and lively historical literature arose before World War II.

Secondly, in those parts of Africa where the indigenous petty bourgeoisie shared in some of the fruits of colonialism and were sufficiently self-conscious as a class to seek an historical view of their own, local histories and traditions were collected, sometimes with great assiduousness, and published locally. They reflected the outlook of their authors, often championing the interests of a particular pre-colonial state, ethnic entity or important family of chiefs and were generally under the heavy influence of a Christian mission education. A famous, early and relatively accessible example is the Revd. Samuel Johnson's *History of the Yoruba*, written in Nigeria before the turn of the twentieth century. In many parts of Africa such histories came virtually to displace earlier oral traditions in popular knowledge.

Finally, intellectuals of African origin, both West Indian and North American, became fascinated in their ancestral continent, whose rescue from obloquy and oblivion in the eyes of their enemies ranked high on their own programme of national liberation. Like the colonial writers they conceived of Africa as a whole, but their outlook was pan-African and closely tied to their own nationalist reaction to American society. Unlike the colonial writers, they stressed an historical perspective, romanticising a grandiose African past and condemning its colonial present. A distinguished scholarly and sometimes stirring example in this category is W. E. B. DuBois' *The World and Africa*.

In the 1940s all this changed rapidly. Under the impact of wartime pressures and a deteriorating living standard, African labour insurgency and peasant movements seriously challenged colonial strategies. Given a global perspective of growing Soviet power and more developed anti-imperialist movements in much of Asia, the West was under pressure and on the defensive. As a result, Britain, France and then Belgium moved towards restructuring colonial relationships and devolving political authority within Africa. The 'new nations' of Africa were conceived.

Within the West itself there were strong motives for creating a framework in which African history could be studied and taught. One was the practical requirement of developing history departments in the universities founded in Africa during the late colonial period. Another was the need for a better comprehension of an insurgent Africa. Most important, though, was engagement in struggle on the ideological plane in order to capture it for a new synthesis, a new form of collaboration between Western political and economic interests on the one hand and the dominant class within the new Africa on the other hand. One important part of this synthesis was the fleshing out of 'Africanist' history, which dominates the ideas in books on the history of Africa in libraries everywhere in the world.

In Britain much of this development took place in the School of Oriental and African Studies in London, which Lord Curzon had once described in the planning stage as 'part of the necessary furniture of empire'. The first African history conference in Britain took place there in 1953 as the West African colonies were moving towards self-government. In the USA, overwhelmingly the most important capitalist state, academic knowledge of Africa was sparse and African studies centres were created: the first at Northwestern University with Carnegie money in 1948; the second at Boston University in 1953 with Ford money. Others soon followed and attracted scholars from the old colonial powers. In France the first professorships in African history were funded in 1960, the same year as French West and French Equatorial Africa were dismantled and accorded independence. Such institutions could be the base, not so much of historians of Africa, but of 'Africanists' who interpreted 'Africa' both to the West and to the African intelligentsia itself.

As the introduction to the published papers of an important conference in 1961 began:

> Every self-conscious nation looks back upon its past to revive former glories, to discover its origins, to relate its history to that of other parts of the world and to arrive at a knowledge of the development of its political, social, economic and other systems.[1]

What is a self-conscious nation? What glories? What relations to the rest of the world are relevant? All of these questions tended to be side-stepped in Africanist writing.

In general the new synthesis aimed at flattering nationalist sensibilities. Again and again, 'Africans' were progammatically placed to the fore without the issue ever being raised of which Africans or why? An overwhelmingly foreign group of scholars felt confident that they could express the 'African point of view'. The new writing was heavily dependent on material already available through colonial amateur history writing, travelogues, local histories, ethnographies and collected traditions, but it received a new ideological impetus through its central tenet: that Africans had a history. This could be pitted repeatedly against the racist and anti-historical synthesis of the colonial point of view which reflected, as it had created, 'common wisdom' about Africa in the West. Each subject in the history of Africa was reinterpreted (to borrow the words of Terence Ranger) in terms of 'African activity, African adaptation, African choice, African initiative', whether it was the slave trade, peasant cash crop economies, the formation of states or religious change: 'a straight line of initiative from human evolution at Olduvai to the modern period'.[2]

The Africanists' most indisputable achievements lay in the study of pre-colonial Africa. Here there was a welter of unsubstantiated but densely woven preconceptions in existing sources on the primacy of foreign contacts and foreign invaders, which have gradually been sifted out and corrected in the name of an Afrocentric approach. Moreover, there has been a tremendous advance in the accumulation of evidence and information. Indeed, for many Africanists, despite their frequent insistence that they were addressing relevant current issues, pre-colonial history *was* African history.

This approach contained fundamental limitations. The most significant was the reification of *method*, defined as the technical collection and sifting of data, as opposed to *content*. This has created a

mystique of method, conceived as the application of ever more refined techniques to ever larger quantities of facts, which is one of the means by which the social sciences – including history – cover up their theoretical impoverishment and contradictions.[3]

Secondly, the writing of much pre-colonial African history has been dependent on uncritical borrowings from the sophisticated and insightful writings in social and cultural anthropology, a field that developed with colonial domination of non-Western peoples. Anthropologists, focusing on small communities over a limited period, usually dealt with their subject peoples as residents of a 'timeless present' abstracted from history. The 'timeless present' could be extended back into the past at will and high-lighted as the essentialist core of social relations whatever the twentieth century might be bringing in its wake. At the same time, anthropologists frequently underplayed or neglected material factors in the lives of their 'tribe'. Many (not all) Africanists sold a view of Africa at bottom tribal, changeless and *essentially* unified in a spiritualised entity that defied rational penetration.[4] Such social phenomena as slavery in Africa are thus assessed as timelessly 'African', rather than in terms of real historical categories.[5]

For Africanists the economy was a factor in society to be discussed separately from (if it received much attention at all) political or social developments. Analysis consisted of a history of trade at the expense of production, domination, sexual relations and other, more fundamental, aspects. Trade was ideologically cast as the bringer of good news and progressive change from long distances, the outside agent that made African history possible.

The essentialist cast of Africanist history was strongly enhanced by the influence of Islamic Orientalism. Orientalism combined a learned scholastic appreciation of the Islamic classics with a tradition of contempt for the people of the modern Middle East and an assumption that the categories of Islamic thought overruled any need for historical investigation of social and material change. The dead hand of the Islamicists, and their successful self-marketing to the needs of Western power politics, has been dissected brilliantly by Edward Said:

> None of the innumerable Orientalist texts on Islam, including their summa, the Cambridge History of Islam, can prepare their readers for what has taken place since 1948 in Egypt, Palestine, Iraq, Syria, Lebanon or the Yemens. When the dogmas about Islam cannot serve, even for the most Panglossian Orientalist, there is recourse to an Orientalized social science jargon, to such marketable abstractions as elites, political stability, modernization and institutional wisdom, all stamped with the cachet of Oriental wisdom.[6]

The annexation of many parts of African history by the learned but self-contained, arid discourse of Islamicists with their assumption of a timeless Islamic 'civilisation' that can never really alter but only flourish or decay has had a crippling effect on serious historical study.

If Africanist history focused on an idea, it was that of state formation. It glorified state power in African empires of the past whose 'scale' steadfastly 'expanded'. These were held out self-consciously as worthy and relevant predecessors of contemporary African states replete with 'lessons' for the current ruling strata.[7] This idealist and moralist strain has in fact been fundamental to the Africanist synthesis.

More recent African history, the subject of most of this book, has also been touched by the magic wand of 'African initiative'. The subject and content of imperialism was discreetly abandoned to survivors from the older colonial school, a small academic establishment that continued to thrive, if not to grow, in the former colonial countries. Modern Africa was almost entirely interpreted in the light of the nationalist movements that came to power around 1960. Thus there is now a substantial literature on 'primary' anti-colonial resistance movements, focusing on religious and military aspects or on leadership and pointing to the more 'modern' secondary resistance that would bring about independence. The colonial period itself is usually cast in terms of a rags-to-riches saga for the African petty bourgeoisie that it engendered, the self-styled 'educated élite'. Book after book built up to the happy ending: national independence.

This very brief summary does not do justice to many variations and does not attempt to qualify the work of individuals. Africanists include men and women of profound learning as well as charlatans who might fail to pass muster in established fields. Some have drunk deeply from the Africanist well while others have remained relatively sober. Certain broad variants can be pointed out. In the USA the substitution of method for ideas has, until recently, been especially marked while the 'African initiative' message is often flashed in neon. Even the study of the colonial period was left largely to political scientists and there were few to challenge the self-evident truths of romantic nationalism or marginal economics. The situation in Britain has been more complex, partly because British Africanists have perforce been less insulated from changes in the African universities and current events in Africa generally. In France until recently no serious examination of the colonial period was possible in the universities, while history has been much less influential in the spectrum of African studies (truer yet for other European countries).

Within Africa itself the distinctive outlook of African historians can to some extent be delineated. Nigerians, notably the so-called Ibadan school, have until recently been overwhelmingly orientated to the study of administration, pre-colonial and colonial, and to their own class antecedents, reflecting their self-confidence as Africa's wealthiest would-be bourgeoisie. In programmatic statements, they have laid especial weight on purging Nigerian history from what is still seen as too great an emphasis on foreigners. Yet African historians, including Nigerians, have always stressed material forces in history more than their mentors, as witness the work of Professors K. O. Dike or B. A. Ogot, the pioneer academic historians of British West and East Africa respectively.

West African history in general experienced a slightly earlier development than elsewhere and has remained remarkably self-satisfied within the Africanist paradigm. Whereas it was clearly the most developed historiography in the early 1960s, today it must be noted as the most backward. In contrast, in East and Central Africa the shakier situation of the new ruling classes and the potential for social revolution demanded a more protest-orientated and radical history with greater emphasis on the twentieth century. The tides of Africanist history swept at the cliffs of South Africa, but never have succeeded in establishing dominance. Typical Africanist monographs on protest and resistance, biographies of pre-colonial chiefs and an elevation of Africans as a blanket category to what Leonard Thompson (the doyen of South African liberal historians by the 1960s) called the 'forgotten factor' in southern African history, all made headway. However, it was patently impossible to explain South Africa in terms of African initiative or other Africanist techniques; too many fundamental questions were conveniently shelved thereby.

Is it true then that an 'Africanist is a specialist whom we employ to get the better of Africans?'[8] Not entirely. African history is a more complex and contradictory terrain than a simple conspiracy theory allows for. In the context in which it arose, African history (and African studies) had a radical edge to it. The founder of African studies in the USA, the cultural anthropologist Melville Herskovits, had first spent many years defending the existence and dignity of surviving aspects of African culture among New World Blacks within an intensely racist general milieu. His work, and that of many other Africanists, raised the issues of African pride, integrity and regeneration. At present this defence, with its attendant faith in what Herskovits called 'cultural tenacity' may seem romantic not to say reactionary, but it cannot be dismissed as such in the context in which it arose historically. Two seminal British Africanists, Thomas Hodgkin and Basil Davidson, came to their African work from Left political commitments and an engagement in anti-colonial struggle, what Hodgkin himself called 'the radical anti-colonial tradition'.[9] Even much of the smuggest and most dubious Africanist material is not so much worthless as an attempt to deflect important questions that are raised in the form of struggles in Africa with which specialists must come to terms.

In the 1978 synthesis, *African History*, produced by the most influential historians of Africa in the USA (Philip Curtin, Steven Feierman, Leonard Thompson and Jan Vansina), the virtues of the discipline are uncritically celebrated. The introduction begins by assuring us that 'African history has come of age'! In fact, coming of age has hastened the destruction of the synthesis. During the 1970s the new wisdom of 'African initiative' came under increasingly effective attack, notably from Africans themselves. An examination of some relevant collections based on key conferences, *The Historian in Tropical Africa*, published in 1964, *Emerging Themes in*

*African History*, published in 1968 and *African Studies since 1945*, published in 1976, shows an initial self-confidence, a progression of divergent views and ultimately, in the final volume, an acute sense of crisis in the field.[10]

In the middle volume, the editor, Terence Ranger, while sustaining the basic Africanist hypotheses, prophetically referred to a potential enemy who had not yet made his appearance, the 'radical pessimist'. In the mid 1960s radicals still generally followed the anti-colonial tradition of Hodgkin and Davidson, supported a nationalist line and were relatively optimistic about developments in the newly independent African states. A remarkable exception was the West Indian psychiatrist, Frantz Fanon, who saw a little of life in independent West Africa while in the service of Algeria. The result was his blistering attack on the new order in *The Wretched of the Earth*. However, it was quite some time before this was translated into historical writing.

By the end of the decade, though, dissent began to show its head in a number of directions. One of the few economic historians of Africa, C. C. Wrigley, wrote an important article criticising the positivist nature of Africanist history for going to the extreme of celebrating the slave trade for strengthening and expanding the scale and bureaucratic sophistication of African kingdoms. In the radical academic atmosphere of Dar es Salaam (Tanzania) at roughly the same time, political economist John Saul wrote an important consideration of Tanzanian history-writing which attacked the positivism and class bias of East African historiography. In 1973 a Kenyan historian, William Ochieng, in a controversial article, openly wondered about the celebration of the past, in particular of politically salient Kenyan tribal entities projected backward into time, so characteristic of Africanist scholarship. He proposed that historians concentrate rather on investigating the roots of underdevelopment and the oppressed conditions of the masses.[11]

The causes of dissent lay fundamentally not in the internal dialogue of scholars, but in the genuine contradictions and instability of the 'neo-colonial' social and political relations that dominate Africa. The obvious calamities which plagued African states were poverty and dependence, but underlying them were the gradual decay of the colonial economies in many areas and the increasing difficulties experienced by the ruling strata in holding the line and effectively controlling their own populations. The intensifying struggle for independence in the Portuguese colonies, which involved relatively concrete socialist goals and fighting on class, as much or more than, national lines highlighted related but unresolved issues everywhere on the continent. In this context, celebrating African achievement began to appear patronising, undercutting its own anti-racialist claims, as well as irrelevant.

The stage was now set for the 'radical pessimists' to enter the scene and they brought with them a powerful set of tools from elsewhere, conceptions of the 'development of underdevelopment' as part of the world process of capital accumulation which had been posed among radical South Americans and the North American Marxists Baran and Sweezy and were welded into a strong polemic by Andre Gunder Frank. Samir Amin, an Egyptian economist based in Senegal, began to bring this line of thought to African subjects and to reinterpret African history with reference to the roots of dependence and underdevelopment. In 1972 the Guyanese Walter Rodney, himself one of the most critical and far-ranging of Africanists, published *How Europe Underdeveloped Africa*. Although, as the title indicates, Rodney's polemic was continental (and by implication, radical) and he betrayed much of the influence of the earlier idealist and romantic Afro-American nationalist understanding of Africa, his book represented a powerful and effective break with the positivism of the Africanists.

During the 1970s the historiography of South Africa was rapidly transformed. At first the origins of reconsideration among writers on South Africa lay in the patent failure of liberal analysis to reflect adequately the realities of the apparently invincible apartheid state. To see capitalist development as steadily undermining the racial order, to advocate publicity for the 'African point of view' in the interests of managing better 'race relations', the stock-in-trade of South African liberals of the day, was transparently unconvincing. At the same time the failure of nationalist movements on the lines of those elsewhere on the continent to topple the regime brought a corresponding lack of nerve to Africanist interpretations of history. Historians began to penetrate the ideology of *apartheid* to search for social and economic structures and ultimately for a class-conscious comprehension of the logic of capital accumulation in South Africa.

These tendencies were intensified in the wake of renewed labour insurgency from 1971, the collapse of Portuguese colonialism in 1974 and the urban risings associated with the Johannesburg township of Soweto in 1976. A growing number of young historians (among others) searched for understanding in diverse currents: radical British social history, Marxist structuralism associated with the theoreticians Louis Althusser and Nicos Poulantzas, labour history as well as neo-Marxist concepts of underdevelopment. The most influential within an extensive new wave of writing have been self-consciously Marxist authors. If South Africa at the end of the 1960s appeared at the dead end of African history writing, twenty years on it appeared to be the cutting edge.

In France the impact of underdevelopmentalism was at first felt in social sciences rather than in history. However, one major historian, Catherine Coquery-Vidrovitch, has collaborated closely with Amin and directed research to bear upon the economic structures of colonial West Africa. She and other French historians have also felt the impact of the important French school of economic anthropologists who have revived the materialist analysis of pre-capitalist social formations first proposed by Marx. Some of these, notably Emmanuel Terray, have on this basis, begun the re-examination of major themes of pre-colonial African history from the perspective of the dominant mode of production in African societies. There are clear indications also, from Kenya, Tanzania, Nigeria, Senegal and elsewhere, that the new generation of African intellectuals is no longer content to have ancient 'civilisations' glorified and African initiatives of whatever stripe and regardless of content, vacuously applauded. Professor Ranger himself has noted the 'widespread feeling of artificiality and distance from real issues' in Africa about Africanist history.[12]

As Marxist analysis of Africa deepened, the underdevelopmentalist hypothesis itself came under attack. The complete assimilation of African social conditions to those of Asia and Latin America as part of a deliberately, almost conspiratorially, underdeveloped 'Third World' failed to explain the immense range of variety in the patterns of economic and social life. It also obscured specific and concrete historical developments in particular areas while illuminating some widespread patterns. The affinities between underdevelopmentalism as an historical catch-all explanation and radical (but bourgeois) nationalism were multifold. In much of the writing on underdevelopment internal social contradictions were passed over or treated superficially while actual relations of production were subordinated to the problem of 'unequal exchange'. In reaction, Marxists began to insist that class categories and class analysis be raised instead as the fundamental tools for understanding African historical development.

There has long been a Marxist tradition of writing on Africa, stemming from the European Communist parties. Its strength lay in a resolute anti-colonialism, an interest in economic structures and an emphasis on protest and labour activity. However, it was unable and unwilling to challenge Africanist verities when couched in nationalist phraseology; and it was inept at conceptualising class relations and social change in Africa widely divergent from the European model with which writers in this tradition were familiar. After the 1920s Marxist writing was itself dominated by a crude positivism, despite the example of Marx himself, which prevented it from convincingly cutting through the Africanist paradigm. In the words of Raymond Williams:

> Marxism, as then commonly understood, was weak in just the decisive area where practical criticism was strong: in its capacity to give precise and detailed and reasonably adequate accounts of actual consciousness: not just a scheme or a generalization but actual works, full of rich and significant and specific experience.[13]

In the last twenty years, however, a variety of currents from throughout the world, including the impact of Maoism, the revitalisation of Trotskyism and other directions of Marxist thought, have made a revival possible.

This revival is central to the erection of a new problematic, the posing of new questions in Africa as elsewhere. Marxist historians of Africa are now beginning to go beyond the idealist framework of asking whether trade, state formation, or colonialism was 'good' or 'bad' to question where their significance actually lies. They are more conscious as well of writing within a particular perspective, a class perspective, comprehending 'Africanism' as a particular ideological construct, rather than aspiring to achieve an 'African point of view' while dealing with their subject, 'Africa'. Africanist historiography has not lost its vigour entirely; the writing done within the 'Africanist' camp cannot be totally rejected without cost. It continues to yield significant analysis and information; indeed, the content of the best work produced belies the impoverished theoretical basis of their programme. What is important to perceive, though, is that Africanist history can no longer seriously be taken as read; the synthesis once envisioned by nationalists in Africa and their would-be managers in the West is in disarray.

This book, therefore, does not start with the old arguments about Africa having or lacking a history, with hypotheses about 'enlargement of scale' or balance sheets of good and bad in 'contact' with the West. It tries to adhere to the new critical tendencies emerging in Africa and elsewhere. The central themes which dominate the modern history of Africa are the penetration of capital with its relationship to political and economic imperialism and the resultant transformation of class and class struggle. The limits of transformation, the network of social forces other than class, are also fundamental. On this basis my reconceptualisation of the history of Africa attempts to proceed. In this I align myself to an early programmatic statement by Basil Davidson, so largely forgotten in the Africanist enterprise, of trying to present 'the essential unity of the people of Africa with the peoples of the rest of the world' in a materialist context.

## Notes

1. Jan Vansina, Raymond Mauny and L.-V. Thomas, *The Historian in Tropical Africa* (Oxford University Press, 1964).
2. Bonaventure Swai, 'Antinomies of Local Initiative in African Historiography', Historical Association of Tanzania, pamphlet 12, 1979.
3. Henry Bernstein and Jacques Depelchin, 'The Object of African History: a Materialist Perspective', *History in Africa, V* (1978), *VI* (1979).
4. Sometimes this kind of mystification is even apparent in a title such as Jacques Maquet's *Africanity*, (Oxford University Press, 1972).
5. Frederick Cooper, review article on African slavery, *JAH, XX* (1979). New directions in anthropology there have certainly been, but they have often continued to lack an historical dimension. This is true for Marxist studies among others. As the field diversifies, moreover, it loses any central coherence.
6. Edward Said, *Orientalism* (Random House, 1978), p. 109.
7. See, for instance, Ivor Wilks, *Asante in the Nineteenth Century* (Cambridge University Press, 1975).
8. Christopher Fyfe, ed., *African Studies since 1945* (Longman, 1976), p. 4.
9. Ibid., p. 11.
10. Vansina *et al.*; Fyfe; T. R. Ranger, (ed.), *Emerging Themes in African History*, (Heinemann, 1968).
11. C. C. Wrigley, 'Historicism in Africa: Slavery and State Formation', *AA LXX* (279), (1970); John Saul, 'Nationalism, Socialism and Tanzanian History', in Peter Gutkind and Peter Waterman, *Africa: a Radical Reader* (Heinemann, 1977); William Ochieng, 'Undercivilization in Black Africa', *KHR, II*, 1973.
12. Fyfe, p. 17.
13. Raymond Williams, *Problems in Materialism and Culture* (New Left Books, 1980), pp. 18–19.

# 2

## MATERIAL AND CULTURAL DEVELOPMENT IN AFRICA BEFORE THE NINETEENTH CENTURY

'Accept the chief, fear him. May he also fear you.'

Daniel Biebuyck and Kahombo Mateene, eds, *The Mwindo Epic* (University of California Press, 1969)

Colonialists and nationalists, radicals included, have generally accepted the historical centrality of race and an identity of race, language and culture which defines the history of Africa as a history of black people. Of course, at a practical level, most Africans living south of the Sahara are and have been black, so the connection seems obvious and demonstrable. Yet race, to the limited extent that it has a scientific classificatory value at all, is purely a biological term that can only express relationships between physical characteristics. It has nothing whatsoever to do with culture or any cultural traits such as language. Semitic languages, for example, have for many, many centuries been spoken in Asia and Africa both by people whom we might call 'white' and others whom we might call 'black'. Our twentieth-century world is so race-conscious, with racial divisions such a powerful force for antagonisms and oppression, that this fairly obvious point is difficult to keep in mind. If the notion of a black or African people has a justification today, it is as the result of a contemporary sensibility and a consciousness formed within the capitalist world economy that has been gathering strength during the past five centuries. To apply such a framework to the more distant past, which this chapter examines, makes no sense.

Stripped of racial determinism, African history quickly loses the unity which common prejudices, positive and negative, assume for it. There is no foreordained African cultural oneness that has been convincingly defined that suggests otherwise. The broadest themes of African history do reflect continent-wide developments precisely because they are themes that belong to the basic stock of social and economic developments of mankind everywhere. The more detailed history, which belongs to another volume than this one, can best be treated on a region-by-region basis. African regions were not watertight compartments isolated from one another.

Trade goods, ideas and popular migrations moved in ways which historians can reconstruct only very hazily. They were not limited by the Sahara Desert or the oceans that surround Africa. Such interconnections, however, are not a sufficient basis for unity in our analysis. What must strike any student of Africa is, in fact, the immense variety among its peoples, cultures and institutions.

Closely associated with Western racial stereotypes is the assumption in common wisdom of the historic backwardness of Africa. At one time this backwardness was defined largely morally, in terms of decadent and barbaric customs. In the commodity-laden world of the twentieth century the term is used in general to refer to economic backwardness. Africanist historiography has placed an obsessive emphasis on reversing this perspective through haphazardly celebrating the African achievement, often creating an implausibly idealised and romanticised old Africa. Where does the truth actually lie?

It is undeniably the case that, in technological terms, no part of sub-Saharan Africa during this millennium has been among the most advanced regions of our planet. Human developments, both social and technical, have proceeded most unevenly. This is true not only between continents but within Africa itself. The most developed regions, the West African savannas and forests, the middle Nile valley and the Ethiopian highlands, have been the scene of class societies that show many parallels with the Middle East, India, China and medieval or early modern Europe. In other regions material advance proceeded more slowly.

Only from the coarsest perspective of power politics, however, can history be reduced to a horse race. Even while accepting the centrality of material progress as an historical force, one people deserve as much respect, consideration and study as the next. Studies of the few surviving hunters and gatherers, the most technologically 'primitive' Africans, suggest that their human qualities, their ideological perspectives and their forms of aesthetic expression such as music and drawing, are in no whit 'inferior' to twentieth-century industrial civilisation.

Moreover, it is quite wrong to assume that Africans organised stable 'civilisations' or 'cultures' that suited their needs and then stagnated within given limits. The more recent centuries that precede the colonial occupation of Africa witnessed dynamic change rather than cycles of stagnation and decay, although these can of course be found in Africa as elsewhere. Two epochal events in the history of Africa, the *Mfecane* in the far south, which resulted in a first great wave of state formation in what is today South Africa, and the Islamic holy wars (*jihads*) which transformed society and culture in the central savanna of West Africa, both took place in the first quarter of the nineteenth century. This was late enough to allow for virtually first-hand European descriptions, but neither has been explained successfully through European influence or cause.[1] Both represented major new developments of internal contradictions and forces. This dynamic, if increasingly influenced in the nineteenth century by the commercial expansion of Europe, was still clearly active until decisively cut off by conquest, largely in the final quarter of that century. Even then, intense external influences had to work through internal social processes and structure. The following two chapters will consider these influences; this one, in somewhat artificial isolation, is particularly concerned to recapture some facets of internal dynamism.

## Hunters, Gatherers and Cultivators

For most of mankind's long history on the African continent, as elsewhere in the world, man was a hunter who gradually learnt more and more about his natural environment while refining his stone and bone tools. Along with man the hunter lived woman the gatherer and it was she who secured most of the food consumed as well as succouring the offspring. She acquired a knowledge of botanical lore that matched man's awareness of the animal world. The tropical grasslands that cover much of Africa were an attractive environment for foraging populations. This may help to explain why our species seems to have evolved in eastern Africa originally and why foraging communities persisted in many parts of the continent long after knowledge of agriculture was widespread. Even into the twentieth century a few such communities survived in a variety of natural environments. Most were the descendants of agricultural peoples, so far as we can ascertain from their languages and customs, but there are examples – notably the Hadza who lived in north-central Tanzania and the so-called San of the Kalahari Desert of southern Africa – who may well be descendants of ancient foraging communities.[2]

Studies of surviving hunters and gatherers, combined with physical remains uncovered by archaeologists, help to recreate a little of the life of ancient Africa. To the extent that environment limits their way of life, it has been argued that such a transposition is quite legitimate. The !Kung San of the Kalahari are organised into small bands, numbering up to several dozen people. Band membership is informal, shifting and based on little more than personal preference within the ecological limits. There is no systematic institutionalised leadership among them apart from what natural ability throws up; relations between men and women are relatively egalitarian. The evidence of cave paintings and travellers' accounts suggest that the !Kung San and similar peoples have long been accomplished artists and musicians who have found extensive and impressive forms for articulating their emotions. They have a remarkable command of knowledge over the flora and fauna of the Kalahari ecosystem.

The most remarkable facet of Richard Lee's important study of the !Kung San is his convincing refutations of the usual clichés about the short, nasty and brutish life of savages. For a small population (and the !Kung San are very careful to practise a system of long child-spacing), foraging provides a relatively secure and leisured life. Lee's subjects contained a larger elderly population than is typical in agricultural Africa and producing adults are able to support a substantial number of 'pensioners' and children. The !Kung San understand agricultural techniques from neighbouring populations perfectly well but they have no reason or desire to adopt them. Indeed, from his evidence, historians find a serious problem in explaining why Africans ever did turn to agriculture.

For this, several explanations can be offered, however inconclusively. One lies in the systematic emergence of that unique type of hunting which allows for a large stationary population – hunting for fish. The archaeologist J. E. G. Sutton has, in fact, suggested that a large section of the African savannas between the Sahara and the forests, together with a swathe of East Africa, experienced an important transitional 'Aquatic Age' which allowed new skills and populations to build up. At the same time, it is possible that Africans began to acquire domesticated animals, especially cattle. Cattle-keeping allows for much larger populations than foraging, but it is also much more susceptible to the problems of climate and, particularly, drought or irregular rainfall. It is the irregularity of rainfall which to this day sets the parameters of the possible for agriculturalists in much of Africa.

A third consideration, not necessarily separated from the first two, revolves around the impact of more long-term climatic changes on foragers, in particular in the region of the Sahara Desert which crosses the African continent from the Atlantic to the Red Sea. It has frequently been asserted that the Sahara became notably drier five to six thousand years ago, pushing out a numerous population who could not adapt to the change without moving. Much African agricultural innovation apparently occurred during this period and in regions not too far removed from the desert.

It is much easier to imagine how, rather than why, agricultural knowledge developed and it may be guessed that much of the advance was pioneered by women. Foraging populations became aware of the nutritional value of particular wild crops, especially grains, mastered the art of preparing and cooking them and took to camping on sites where they were plentiful. Observation led to experimentation in planting seeds; gathering began to give way to systematic sowing and harvesting of crops. Such at least is a logically schematic reconstruction of what happened, not one based on direct knowledge.

The classic African savanna grains are millet and sorghum, but other grains were developed where suitable just as different varieties of millet and sorghum, appropriate to particular soils or rainfall belts, were developed. In the Ethiopian highlands, teff became the staple. In the western portion of West Africa, perhaps beginning in the marshlands known as the Interior Delta of the Niger River in present-day Mali, a type of rice was widely cultivated. East Africans may have initiated the planting of ensete, a root crop related to the banana. This would have disposed them to accept the banana, believed to have been introduced at a later date from Asia. Root crops enabled agriculturalists to penetrate the forests. The yam was the most significant, although the native oil palm of West Africa also provided a multi-faceted fundamental asset. In forest and savanna regions cultivators learnt to balance grain or root staples with vegetable crops such as the cowpea which perhaps was first cultivated in northern Nigeria.

Irregular rainfall, poor soil and relatively light population densities all encouraged the persistence of so-called slash and burn techniques which gave the soil a long time to recover from usage and reflected a satisfactory response to ecological possibilities. Yet in certain regions denser populations developed intensive techniques such as stall-feeding cattle, hill terracing, manuring of fields and irrigation. In grain-growing zones, the perfection of storage facilities was crucial to provide for the hungry season.

Some writers have claimed that after agriculture the greatest innovation of early Africa was the production and working of iron. Iron was first smelted in western Asia, the technique spread slowly to Egypt and then was taken up with amazing rapidity throughout Africa in the centuries immediately before and after Christ. Iron hoes allowed for much more efficient agricultural exploitation, although in many regions iron was too rare to be used in this way and farmers continued to make do with wooden digging sticks until very recently.[3]

Agriculture transformed social and cultural life in Africa. It allowed for vastly greater population densities and for the consistent production of a surplus beyond immediate consumption needs. Social organisation took on new complexities, the most fundamental being the intensified concern with property rights over resources. Whereas surviving foraging bands emphasise natural phenomena like the sun, moon and stars in their religious beliefs, agriculturalists devised earth cults and ritualised their ancestors, claiming that descent entitled them to possess the land they worked. Ancestor worship is closely linked to social ideas based on kinship networks. Lineage groups tracing a common origin from a real or legendary ancestor became the fundamental building blocks of social organisation.

A conventional term for a social or political group defined in genealogical terms is *tribe*, a word that goes back to Roman lineage terminology. In principle, there is nothing wrong with its appropriate application to African conditions, but in practice the word has been abused so systematically that it is preferable to avoid it entirely. 'Tribe', in the African context, has become a kind of second-class term for ethnic group, especially where so-called traditional ethnic rivalries are assumed to be the natural basis for modern political life. It is then applied backwards sloppily with historical reference to states or language groupings as in the so-called Asante or Yoruba 'tribes'.

'Tribe' also implies a primordial unchanging character which is far from the shifting and conflicting realities of lineage-based African communities. Lineage formation was as much or more ideological as it was a true reflection of literal prevailing social pattern. In reality lineages expanded through absorbing unrelated individuals such as captives or migrants who were incorporated through devices that anthropologists call 'fictive' kinship.

Within lineage groups, inequality could and did develop. Elders, the closest living men to the all-powerful ancestors, secured control of aspects of production and the distribution of foodstuffs for consumption. The head of the household was able to exploit the labour of junior members. Eventually juniors might succeed as heads, but they could not all do so and this was a major reason for internal tensions and the hiving off of new households.

Equally important, if not more so, was the potential for exploiting both the labour and the reproductive capacity of women, which alone made possible the growth of the household and the lineage. The desirability of control over women for elders encouraged polygamy as social ideal and reality. Marriages largely represented alliances between male lineage heads in which women were redistributed. The condition of women in lineage societies varied considerably however. In some places women retained a large proportion, if not all, of the product of their labour while evolving situations which enabled them to function independently of a husband's household. In other areas, women had the entire burden of bringing up children added to agricultural labour and were exploited harshly. This was frequently the case where the absence of the tse-tse fly allowed for the keeping of cattle which generally became entirely the province of men. It has been argued that women's rights were greater in those societies that reckoned descent through the mother (*matrilineal*) rather than the father (*patrilineal*), but research is inconclusive.[4]

Lineage-based households were not geographically static. Migrations over great distances are attested as historical events in many regions, particularly within Bantu-speaking Africa. Migration is a response to changing environmental or social conditions; it may largely have represented a means of seizing upon new opportunities or a reaction to the scourge of drought. In the region of modern Angola, the Imbangala were migrants who terrorised their neighbours as a predatory response to the commercial lure of the Portuguese slave trade. This was the basis for their 'tribe'. Nineteenth-century migrants in an adjoining area, the Chokwe, responded to new post-slaving international trade possibilities by migration, raiding and absorption of surrounding populations who could participate in Chokwe commercial operations.

Marriage, migration and expansion could bring about both friendly and hostile links between lineage societies. In addition, and from a very early date, they established networks of inter-regional trade. The two classic items of early African trade were iron and salt. Both could be found very widely but some natural sources were much richer than others and encouraged the emergence of long-distance trading networks. Dried fish as a preservable source of protein was another standard early trade good. Apart from iron, metals worked in early Africa included tin, gold and copper. Some of the technology involved in their processing is likely to have been derived from iron smelting and smithing. The resultant artefacts were highly prized but scarce, luxury goods *par excellence*. Mining developed on an important scale in many areas. It was largely alluvial or shallow open-pit work which agriculturalists could pursue in the course of the dry season. Craft production, such as bead and basketwork, carving and pottery, sometimes became the speciality of particular villages who found a wide regional clientele.

Lineage organisation has shown a remarkable strength, adaptability and staying power in Africa as in farming villages throughout the world, but it rarely existed as the only community form. Other social linkages that cross-cut lineages were virtually universal and extremely varied. The most straightforward were village assemblies and associations that could embrace villagers of different lineages. Disputes between villages could sometimes be settled by cult authorities who enjoyed a wide prestige; their protection often helped to further trade over long distances. Boys (and sometimes girls) were initiated into community-linked age-sets that included representatives of different lineages. Age-set affiliation united generations over substantial territorial zones. In addition there existed other forms of societies which were not necessarily generational. Title and secret societies, for instance, initiated a minority of the community, practised secret rituals and could adjudicate disputes. All such non-lineage organisations sprang out of the interaction of lineages and related to the contradictions and tensions that arose within them. Their emergence reflected the growing scale and complexity of agricultural communities which expanded through migration, peaceful interchanges and conquest.

## The Formation of States

At some point such contradictions led further to the development of the state. The origins of the African state have been disputed extensively by historians. Into the 1960s it was commonly held that Africans had a common pattern of 'divine kingship' which had diffused as an idea, perhaps from Egypt. Few hold such views anymore for there is increasing evidence that states arose from internal forces prevailing in various parts of the continent. For, after all, if these forces were not called to bear what sense would it have made for people to accept a foreign concept?

The ideology of royalty in Africa typically contained an important dimension of reciprocity, of mutal obligation between the subject and his ruler. The ruler protected his people and brought them prosperity through good harvests and his healing touch. A ruler had to be seen to be a generous giver who could play host to the needy. This is not, however, to suggest that the relationship thus evoked was simply reciprocal. Reciprocity hid systematic appropriation of the goods produced by cultivators and had the potential thus to generate the reproduction of a ruling class.

The historical materialist concept of the state goes back to the work of Friedrich Engels, *The Origins of the Family, Private Property and the State*. For Engels the secret of state formation lay in the activities of a nascent ruling class. Such a class could achieve success in containing some controls over the production and reproduction of society as a whole through the imposition of a state apparatus and state ideology. The internal logic of the association is impeccable but the reality is clearly more complicated. In particular, African states often seem to have exerted little control over the production of cultivators. They continued to co-exist with lineage organisations, the two apparently articulating only through the collection of tribute from villagers.

One of the first contemporary Marxists to re-examine the question of the state, Catherine Coquery-Vidrovitch, suggested in a provocative article at the end of the 1960s that Africa was the seat of the original 'African' mode of production in which the kings, or ruling classes, were sustained largely through their control over long-distance trade in luxury goods. The principal problem with such a formulation is that it fails to explain why the mass of cultivators should accept such a state in their midst. Control over trade does seem to be an important aspect of the origins of the state in many but not all parts of Africa. In most cases traders were not highly taxed, as they could find alternative routes for their goods rather than pass through the domains of an overtly greedy ruler; nor were rulers effective generally in controlling the production of traded goods.

What they generally did control effectively were the means of destruction and protection. The capture of individuals through warfare and raids could enlarge the lineage unit. It also allowed, particularly in the first generation of captives, for a large, dependent force that could be used either in battle to sustain the power of a particular household or as labour to support a homestead that might evolve into a court. In much of the West African savanna, royalty particularly prized their stables and cavalries which only a wealthy minority could maintain. Horse ownership allowed for sustained raiding and warfare. Even when, as would generally have been the case, captives were only a small proportion of the total population, they would have formed the forces required to allow states to collect tribute from villages of free cultivators.[5]

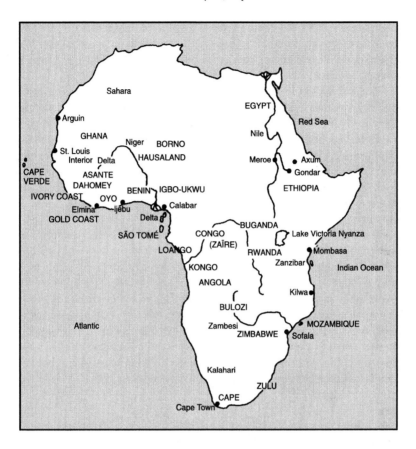

Map 1. Pre-colonial Africa: Places and Peoples

One problem which bedevils much of the literature on the state in Africa is that authors of all persuasions tend to accept the arbitrary definitions of social anthropology which propounded a rigid distinction between states and 'tribes without rulers' or 'stateless societies' in the interest of easing colonial administrative problems. The existence of a state was often assumed to equate to the presence of a 'chief' and in other respects the state was confused with the tribe. African states were conventionally distinguished from lineage-based communities as 'tribes *with* rulers'. The state needs to be assessed more broadly and historically in terms of the development of a ruling class and wide-ranging state apparatus rather than the mere presence of a monarch or leader. In most areas this was no doubt the product of a long process rather than an overnight change. Only at a late stage in this process could states effectively establish a national culture or entirely transcend earlier forms of social organisation.

Much of the history of African states that can be reconstructed revolves around tensions between royal and lineage principles. Rulers were concerned to establish their own lineages in a special situation or to create a super-lineage basis for their own authority. Their 'divinity' was a means of distinguishing themselves from the human, the normal social chains that tied ordinary men and women to one another. They attempted to appoint their own men to tribute-collecting offices in order to supercede the control of lineage heads; here lay the seeds of a royal bureaucracy. In some cases, they were quite successful.

The *obas* of Benin ruled an area in south-central Nigeria which was an old-established state when first encountered by the Portuguese in the late fifteenth century. In Benin lineage organisation had become attenuated and of limited importance. Villages paid tribute to office-holders who owed their power to the *oba*. The court sponsored a large amount of artisanal activity and commerce, providing the focus for a well-ordered capital city with several tens of thousands of inhabitants. The religion of Benin orientated people towards a hegemonic national, court-centred structure of belief. The state had become an inherent part of Bini political culture and it is not surprising that it survived until the British conquest of 1897.

## Some Major African States

The Ethiopian highlands were probably among the earliest centres of African state formation. The first Ethiopian state that can be identified was Axum, with its capital in the province of Tigre near to the Eritrean border. Axum controlled ports on the Red Sea and traded with the Mediterranean world in the Roman era almost two thousand years ago. The Semitic speech of many of the highlanders attested to the antiquity of human movements that linked them with the far side of the Red Sea in Asia. In the fourth century the Axumite rulers accepted Christianity. They followed the doctrinal view of the Coptic Egyptian church combined with earlier elements of Jewish belief probably derived from the Jewish Himyarite culture of South Arabia. A new state culture, identified with Axumite kingship, spread through much of the highlands. This is often mistakenly identified with Ethiopia as a whole. In reality other states with interpenetrating cultural and linguistic traditions arose in the central and southern highlands, whose history is much less known. Eventually Axum's power collapsed. A state based in the north-central area of the highlands where the local language was Amharinya arose in the thirteenth century and succeeded in conquering both the old Tigrinya-speaking region further north where Axum had been located and other regions. This state, explicitly laying claim to the heritage of Christian Axum, was the expression of an expanding land-owning class that knew its greatest epoch in the fourteenth and fifteenth centuries.

A succession of states going back at least as far in time centred in the valley of the middle Nile and particularly the region where the Blue and White Niles meet, far enough south of the Sahara for rain-fed agriculture to flourish away from the river while irrigation provided rich harvests adjoining its banks. Meroe, as the Greeks called it, was a prosperous centre before the rise of Axum. The physical remnants of Meroe suggest a culture that borrowed much both from the Greeks and the Egyptians, while creating a distinctive synthesis. Meroe's successor-states adopted Coptic Christianity as the court faith. While a Christian Abyssinian state thrived in the Ethiopian highlands Christianity was replaced, apparently peacefully, by Islam as the state cult on the middle Nile. In the sixteenth century the kingdom of Sennar reunited a large area which gradually became Islamised. As in Ethiopia the mass of peasantry in Sennar paid heavy taxes to subsidise their rulers' households. This was the one region of sub-Saharan Africa where literate skills were effectively put to the uses of tax collecting. A large, literate merchant class made its home in numerous towns and played a crucial role in deepening Islamic cultural influence in what is today the Republic of the Sudan.

The formation of states in the savannas of West Africa may also go back some two thousand years. The first to which written outside sources refer was Ghana, old at the time of the earliest Arabic reference in the tenth century. In general it is identified with the ancient dispersal point that Soninke speakers call Walata. Archaeological evidence in southern Mauritania, where its capital was located, suggests that Ghana may have had its predecessors. What we know of Ghana comes primarily from Arab travellers who were interested in its commerce, especially in gold. These sources, like those for other early West African courts, provide little information on aspects of West African society of less commercial significance. Its location in arid southern Mauritania, more or less on the far northern edge of cultivation, points to Ghana's crucial position controlling the 'port' from which gold could be carried north over the desert by caravan. There is scattered early evidence of other very old states in the Senegambian region, further to the south-west and on the middle Niger, which cannot have been so orientated to the desert trade. In the fifteenth century Arabic sources begin to refer to a strong state called Borno, south-west of Lake Chad in what is today northern Nigeria. There is a connection between Borno and Kanem, an even earlier state near the desert edge in modern Chad. Borno, which produced no gold, was far less likely than Ghana to have had trans-Saharan trade as its social basis. If Kanem's location suggests a trading entrepôt function, this southward shift in the centre of gravity reveals a deepening control by a dominant class over a population of cultivators.

From the sixteenth century, the most dynamic region in the entire savanna was the Hausaland plain west of Borno. Here a high water table and numerous river valleys that permitted year-round irrigated cultivation provided the basis for an exceptionally dense population which established a thick network of walled settlements and extensive specialised commodity production, particularly of textiles. In this region the economic foundation for the division of labour and production of a substantial surplus was surer than in lands further west where the gold-trade states of Mali and Songhay in their time succeeded Ghana.

It was the trans-Saharan trade which introduced Islam to West Africa by the tenth century at the latest. In time West African traders, like their North African colleagues, found the faith a firm bond along the chain of commercial routes and towns where business transactions, above all credit, depended on personal trust and affiliations. Rulers also turned to Islam as an additional source for re-enforcing their own power. It bound them to distant centres of culture with which they sought good relations while creating a new role for themselves as protectors of a universal faith. In most of the West African savanna before the nineteenth century, however, the peasantry remained deeply involved in earlier rituals and wore Islamic garb lightly, if at all.

Some of the pastoral peoples of both desert and savanna took Islam to themselves with more passion. Certain pastoral lineages became specialists in Islamic learning and increasingly committed to the wider propagation of Islam and its establishment as the juridical basis of the state. Such lineages among the Moors of Mauritania, the Tuareg of the middle Sahara and the savanna Fulbe, who appear through linguistic evidence to have originated in the present-day republic of Senegal and ranged eastwards to Nigeria and beyond, interacted easily with one another and were the crucial factor in initiating *jihads* from the late seventeenth century onward. Their heads established themselves as the focal point of a new ruling class in the many regions of West Africa where the *jihads* triumphed.

Islam brought literacy, as had Christianity even earlier in north-eastern Africa, and with literacy came in time a stratum of clerics whose surviving chronicles help us to recreate the history of the savanna region. Without literacy, as is the case in the forest regions of West Africa, the history of state formation is far more difficult to retrace. It has already been pointed out that the Benin state had reached a high level of maturity by the end of the fifteenth century. The wonderful bronze work unearthed in various parts of southern Nigeria and dated even earlier can be associated with a substantial social surplus and leisured class. One set of finds, just to the east of the Niger River at Igbo-Ukwu, contained a treasury of finely worked objects. We still have no idea as to the specific political or socio-logical context of these spectacularly beautiful handicrafts which specialists have dated variously to between the ninth and fourteenth centuries.

Further west sizeable states developed later. Their growth has been ascribed to the intrusion of long-distance trade that corresponded to the systematic exploitation of gold deposits in the forest region of modern-day Ghana. Why gold mining should have led to state formation here when it did not in goldfields further to the west, has been a contentious issue. The Muslim traders who organised the commerce did not themselves seize power and rulers could not tax them severely for fear of their re-routing their caravans. It has been suggested by Emmanuel Terray that gold production, involving control over slaves and thus linking up to slave raiding and trading, was fundamental to the authority of the ruling class of warriors among Akan-speaking peoples. Yet most of the gold produced came from dry-season, spare-time labour from ordinary free households. Of all the states in the region the most powerful was the confederacy under the Asantehene, the ruler of Asante. During the eighteenth century the Asantehenes succeeded in obtaining tribute from most of what is today Ghana. With the decline of gold mining the commerce of Asante expanded to take in the sale of slaves and the purchase of guns, cloth and manufac-tured goods on the coast and the export of kola nuts to the savanna.

Elsewhere in Africa there are a number of major state clusters. None is likely to be very ancient. The vast majority of the population in the southern half of the continent speak closely related languages, grouped together by linguists under the name Bantu. Bantu languages are believed to have a common origin in a dialect of the widespread Niger-Congo family of West African languages spoken in the Nigerian-Cameroun borderlands some two to three thousand years ago. The similarity of Bantu languages suggests a dramatic process of migration or cultural adaptation. Various ingenious efforts to explain the spread of Bantu have been made but none are entirely satisfactory. It may be surmised, though, that the establishment of well-peopled agricultural communities did not long precede the Christian era in eastern, southern and south-central Africa.

At some stage a process of state formation involving the mixture of pastoralist and agricultural peoples began in the region of the East African Great Lakes. The best-studied state is Buganda, whose heartland lies on the fertile plains north-west of Lake Victoria Nyanza. In the eighteenth and nineteenth centuries Buganda's *kabaka* extended his authority over a vast territory in modern Uganda. This was coupled with flourishing trade and handicraft production and increasingly successful efforts by royalty to bypass the prerogatives of Ganda lineages.

Rwanda, to the south-west of Buganda covering most of the territory of the contemporary republic of that name, was comparable in size and population to Buganda. Here the population was sharply demarcated between pastoralists and cultivators. The physical differences between the cattle-keeping Tutsi and the agricultural Hutu have generally suggested to Europeans the presence of two different stocks or 'races' of people. Yet both speak the same language and their appearances may in fact reflect different diet rather than ancestry. The royal lineage stood at the head of the great Tutsi cattle-keeping lineages who collected tribute through clientage relations with poorer herdsmen and farmers. Cattle-keeping was reified as the essential part of the national culture; actually there were wealthy Hutu agricultural households as well who themselves controlled the surplus labour and product of the poor while cattleless Tutsi were dependent on the households of the great to gain access to the means of production. Thickly-populated Rwanda was a crowded land; the poorest cultivators were forced to hire themselves out as day-labourers.

Another belt of states came to stretch across much of the southern savannas south of the equatorial forest of Middle Africa. South of the mouth of the river Europeans called Zaïre, or Congo, lay the Kongo kingdom from whence the river had derived the name. When the Portuguese first arrived in the late fifteenth century it had already existed for at least several generations. Another node of political centralisation lay far inland in a basin particularly favoured by salt and iron deposits for the development of long-distance trade. This may have been a basic reason for the rise of the Luba kings in present-day Shaba province, Zaïre, Other states of the southern savanna of Zaïre, Zambia and Angola associated their founding legends with the Luba. This includes the upper Zambesi floodplain region of western Zambia unified as the Lozi state – Bulozi – in the nineteenth century.

Bulozi occupied a zone of remarkable fertility and suitability for cattle-keeping where control over the flood-waters by a class that could command the labour of many workers profoundly affected the quality of life. Such control came from a strong nineteenth-century monarchy. Canal construction and corvée labour gave the Bulozi state a direct interest in production and required a high intake of exploitable captives from the surrounding region.

Other states flourished in various parts of southern and eastern Africa. People ancestral to modern-day Shona speakers in Zimbabwe, another early source of gold deposits, created the massive stone tower ruins which have given their name to the modern state. In the far south of Africa, however, there appears to be little precedent for the great state-forming events of the early nineteenth century. Ecological pressures may have been responsible for the intensification of rivalries between small chiefdoms in the region between the Drakensberg mountains and the Indian Ocean. The most successful contender, Shaka, used an exceptionally aggressive and predatory army, which he developed through distorting the age-grade system so as to force an entire generation of warriors to fight for him while the women of the nation worked to produce the food to support them. This forged the Zulu state. Following its creation yet other armies, desperate to re-acquire cattle stolen by the Zulu, exploded through the interior grasslands of modern South Africa and far beyond, creating new political formations in Zimbabwe, Malawi, Mozambique, Zambia and Tanzania. In so doing the marauding warriors showed a constructive, progressive side, but it was also a brutal destructive process. The Zulu word '*Mfecane*', meaning 'crushing' or 'breaking' is often used by historians to refer to this historical era attracted by the writing of John Omer-Cooper.

A striking feature of African states and peoples was how little they looked to the oceans surrounding their continent. Men went out past the Atlantic breakwaters in West Africa to fish and established canoe networks along the lagoons that fringe the ocean, but they did not sail the seas. One exception was the east coast, so favourably situated with prevailing winds for transit across the Indian Ocean and the Arabian Sea during the monsoons. The antiquity of the trade can be attested from a navigator's handbook that survives from Egypt in the first century after Christ. Trading ports, most typically located just off the coast on islands, formed an important part of the commerce of the East. Of the rulers of the stone-built coastal cities that we know about the most powerful were those of Kilwa in modern Tanzania who controlled caravans bringing gold dust from the interior mines of Zimbabwe. Neither they nor their compatriots north or south ever appear to have ruled states of any continental compass. Class societies orientated to commodity production and overseas trade, while assimilating the Islamic faith that arrived with the dhows from across the Indian Ocean, had taken root in these entrepôt states before Vasco da Gama first laid eyes on them in 1498. A common denominator of coastal culture was the Bantu language rich in Arabic borrowings spoken in the towns and on the islands – Swahili.

### Modes of Production, the State and Class Society

Within the Marxist tradition there lies an assumption that behind the façade of various forms of pre-capitalist society, a hidden basis exists for the state and state authority riveted to material conditions and the form of surplus extraction that a ruling class secured from the masses. Marxist writers have therefore concerned themselves on this basis to establish a classificatory system for comprehending the phenomenon of the African state. They began with the scheme that Marx had worked out, sometimes rather impressionistically, for other parts of the world. In Europe, according to Marx, what may be called the lineage mode of production (last of great significance among the Germanic tribes) gave way to the ancient mode of production based on slavery and then to the feudal mode of production, characterised by the relationship between lord and serf. In Asia the relationship between a despotic state and the undifferentiated village community held in communal rather than personal servitude, determined a distinctive Asiatic mode of production. One attempt at a rigorous definition of 'mode of production' considers it '... an articulated combination of relations and forces of production structured by the dominance of the relations of production.'[6]

A materialist conception of history lays emphasis on technical forces and social relations of production, but the value of simple characterisations of the type that can be derived from formulations like the one given is strictly limited. Raymond Williams has suggested that 'some of the best Marxist cultural analysis . . . is very much more at home in what one might call epochal questions than in what one has to call historical questions'.[7] Technological capability, the forces of production, can determine political forms only in such an immensely broad framework as to be but a starting point for discussion. Social relationships and cultural forms can show remarkable variety. Discussion on the rights of office-holders over peasants, the significance of slavery and the relation of town and country has sharpened the questions historians ask about relevant parts of Africa. Yet each system, when examined closely with the aim of recreating its social and cultural life, has a uniqueness and fluidity that the classification scheme fails to reveal.

A particular problem that has affected most efforts to apply the mode of production concept is the overtly easy identification of the mode with the state. More thought might instead be focused on the character and workings of class rather than the state with relation to production. To what extent we can speak of class societies and struggles in pre-capitalist Africa has barely been addressed by historians, yet it is a fundamental question.

Africa provides fascinating examples of areas which produced substantial surpluses, organised trade, consumed and exchanged luxury goods and witnessed extensive social inequalities without the development of centralised state mechanisms. The Igbo country of south-eastern Nigeria is a major case in point. The Igbo and other 'stateless' Africans were hardly at a more primitive material state than their king-ridden neighbours and they represented a large proportion of sub-Saharan Africans in the nineteenth century and before.

Igbo villages have been described by historians and anthropologists as democratic communities where each household head is capable through individual effort of earning coveted title, position and wealth. However, Igbo communities did not lack for inequality, slavery and forms of social oppression. Title societies functioned as agencies of the richest and most powerful forces and as such contained an incipient form of class rule. The imaginative recreation of Igbo society by such novelists as Buchi Emecheta and Chinua Achebe spotlights the intensity of contradictions and conflicts within superficially undifferentiated African communities. These went on not only beneath the façade of political events; they lay at the heart of social change and material developments that marked the history of Africa.

The Igbo notwithstanding, state formation very broadly appears to have intensified the articulation of class relationships in Africa. Class societies formed most unequivocally and consciously in parts of Africa where state forms developed most intensively. There is little question that the Hausa-land plain had by the nineteenth century witnessed a remarkable conver-gence here. A clearly demarcated minority enjoyed leisure and consumed surplus without working with its hands. Its legitimacy was linked to close association with the state and the state in turn with the defence and propagation of the Muslim faith. Despite the extent of commoditised production and commerce the important class of rich merchants relied on the protection and patronage of the state; they aspired to no autono-mous political role. The Hausa language distinguished between free and slave, rich and poor, office-holder and commoner while the proverbial wisdom of the Hausa is rich in its consideration of these social distinctions:

*Mai abu shi ne da bara.* (There is no rich man without clients.)
*Abokin sarki, sarkin ne.* (The friend of the ruler is a ruler.)
*Dan halas ake zargi, bawa sai sanda.* (The free man needs only a reproach; the slave must be beaten.)

The Hausa stressed above all the contradiction between two groups, the office-holding, horse-riding heads of great households whose existence defined the state – the *masu sarauta* – and the common folk – the *talakawa*. Throughout Hausa community life, among women's organisations, in villages and trade guilds, the standard names for the hierarchy of principal office-holders, chief, treasurer and so on were repeated. Such a structure lent linguistic legitimacy to the architecture of subordination. In fact the picture was greatly complicated by the other distinctions – the varying degrees of slavery, the situation of strata living off the surplus unproduc-tively without being office-holders (for instance the Islamic teachers), stratification within the household, the trade guild and between the sexes and surviving lineage linkages – all require much deeper elucidation than is justifiable in these pages.

Even here class consciousness was generally masked by established relationships of clientage and reciprocity and by local and religious iden-tities. To an outsider, this suggests superficially a world of organic com-munity and wholeness that seems now to have been lost both in the West and in Africa. This is an illusion. The task of historical materialism, at least, is to uncover the unfolding richness of the cultural and social contra-dictions that typified change in Africa as elsewhere.

## Notes

1. However, in recent years, the historian Julian Cobbing has reinterpreted the destructive aspects of the Mfecane as being largely the product of some kind of imperial or white agency. While generating a great deal of ink, this perspective has seemed unconvincing to his peers. Carolyn Hamilton, ed. *The Mfecane Aftermath* (University of the Witwatersrand and Natal University Presses, 1995).
2. The hunting and gathering peoples whom Europeans called Bushmen and Khoi Khoi pastoralists called San actually had no generic name for themselves. San has recently become the preferred scholarly term.
3. Since the 1970s, as archaeological knowledge has increased, the sequence for the spread of iron use has been thrown into confusion. The complexity of smelting technology implies diffusion from one or certainly only a small number of centres of invention but, although many would argue to the contrary, there is no evidence that iron was not smelted somewhere in Africa without techniques borrowed from elsewhere.
4. Scholarship with a feminist orientation should eventually allow for generalisations on a securer base. At present though, feminists have opened up the question in forms which have invited intense ideologically determined disagreements which make a synthetic treatment difficult. It should be made clear that the issue of female subordination cannot be linked directly to the form of inheritance characteristic in particular societies. Many determined inheritance through females and are considered matrilineal rather than patrilineal or double-descent form. However, this gave power to maternal uncles not to fathers. Nor does double-descent imply especially sexually egalitarian communities. For a feminist study that asserts otherwise, see Karla Poewe, *Matrilineal Ideology* (Academic Press, 1981).
5. Such evidence as the existence of a slave trade across both the Sahara and the Red Sea attested for many centuries confirms that slavery long pre-dated the Atlantic slave trade at least in some areas of Africa, although doubtless on a relatively modest scale.
6. Barry Hindess and Paul Hirst, *Pre-Capitalist Modes of Production* (Routledge & Kegan Paul, 1975), p. 9.
7. Williams, *Problems in Materialism and Culture* (New Left Books, 1980), p. 38.

# 3

# THE EUROPEAN INTRUSION IN THE ERA OF MERCHANT CAPITAL

'Peace prevailing in these four kingdoms, one cannot hope for many captives.'

> Louis Charbonneau, seventeenth-century traveller to Senegal (author's translation), in Boubacar Barry, *Le Royaume de Waalo*, pp. 155–6

'We depend entirely on selling slaves and palm-oil for our subsistence, suppose then the slave trade done away with, the consumption of palm-oil in England to stop, the crop to fail, or that the English ships did not come to Bonny, what are we to do? We must starve, as it is contrary to our religion to cultivate the ground.'

> Secretary to Anna Pepple, Bonny house head, 1839, in Thomas Hodgkin, *Nigerian Perspectives*, p. 304

Between the fifteenth and eighteenth centuries European traders, missionaries and soldiers arrived in sub-Saharan Africa establishing economic and, to a much lesser extent, political relationships, that led ultimately to the colonial expansion of an industrialised, capitalist society. Before the impact of the Industrial Revolution in the late eighteenth century the dominant form of capital in Europe was merchant capital, capital originating from individuals or companies of traders. At its most sophisticated, long-distance commerce could begin to call on joint-stock companies, chartered ventures protected through royal monopoly and pioneer insurance firms. The colonial slave plantation was the great innovation of this pioneering phase of capitalism. But merchant capital's ability to transform productive relations was limited. This was to depend on the gradual

34

development of a world market, its tentacles stretching to every continent including Africa.

The most notorious aspect of this early contact period was the trade in men and women which brought millions of Africans across the Atlantic to the plantations of the New World. It is known that during this era Europeans in Africa did not establish territorially significant colonies. So what was the significance, scale and impact of their intrusion? Can we trace clearly features of this period which fatally hooked Africa into a relationship of 'underdevelopment' or 'dependence' on an emerging capitalist world order, as has frequently been claimed? Where does the slave trade fit into this? In order to pursue a more systematic account of Africa in the nineteenth and twentieth centuries we must first consider these questions with reference to an earlier period.

It is convenient to divide the long phase of early European contact into two chronological eras. For two centuries, from the mid-fifteenth to the mid-seventeenth, the Portuguese were overwhelmingly the most important European presence in Africa. Their pre-eminence deteriorated rapidly in the second quarter of the seventeenth century giving way to the Dutch, French and British in particular. From then the slave trade came to dominate European interest in Africa, which was not the case earlier.

## The Portuguese Epoch

Portuguese ambitions during the first two centuries of contact with Africa were diffuse. One was to secure manpower to exploit in Brazil and the island colonies, but the Portuguese state and Portuguese merchants were equally interested in the spice trade, in precious metals, particularly gold, and in forging strategic alliances aimed against Mameluk Egypt and then the Ottoman Empire. By the early sixteenth century these interests began to mesh into a structure of strategic and economic considerations of world dimensions and complexity. Portuguese imperialism was *not* a consequence of the particularly advanced state of the Portuguese economy. The manufacturing sector in Portugal was weak. Much of the early wealth of the Portuguese ports originated rather from the trans-shipment trade between the North and Mediterranean Seas, and most of what the Portuguese had to sell in Africa originated from other parts of Europe. This gave a particularly sharp edge to the Portuguese search for gold and silver which could be used to buy other commodities.

The lack of desirable items for sale posed a dilemma to the Portuguese (and later other Europeans) in the Asian trade opened up by Vasco da Gama's fleet sailing around the Cape of Good Hope into the Indian Ocean. Europeans had little to sell Asians in exchange for the silks and cottons, tea, porcelain and spices of the East. Their greatest strength still lay not in superior techniques of manufacture but in their advanced weaponry and sailing skills. As a result there was a very strong element of force in the character of Portuguese commercial intrusion. This was the essential context for Portuguese involvement on the East African coast of what is today Kenya and Tanzania and in Ethiopia as part of a broader Indian Ocean strategy. The Swahili coast towns were either forced into submission or accepted alliances with Portugal. Occasional attempts to convert ruling houses to Catholicism invariably failed miserably and in general the Portuguese contented themselves with collecting tribute and imposing a close strategic watch on the ocean by means of strong forts, of which the most impressive was Fort Jesus in Mombasa which still stands. There is little to suggest that internal social or economic relationship changed notably during the era of Portuguese dominance.

Strategic considerations also informed the relationship established between the Portuguese and Ethiopia. From early in the fifteenth century there was speculation in Europe concerning the project of an anti-Egyptian and/or anti-Turkish alliance with the highland Christian kingdom of which they held vague but increasing knowledge. This interest was reciprocated by several Ethiopian rulers whose relations with Egypt were sometimes poor and who were impressed by what they began to learn of European military technology. By the fifteenth century the Islamic world was feeling the growing pressure of expansionism fuelled by European merchant capital but put forth as part of a crusade to push back Islam. This, it has been suggested, gave to the politics of the Horn of Africa, a Christian versus Islamic cast that had been a very minor element in previous centuries. In the early sixteenth century an Islamic religious teacher serving in the Harari state on the edge of the Ethiopian plateau, named Ahmad ibn Ibrahim or Ahmed Grañ, 'the Left Handed', organised a successful holy war through the plateau. He was assisted by Ottoman weaponry, the first intrusion of firearms into the region.

However, before an Islamic Ethiopia could be consolidated, a Portuguese fleet cruising the Red Sea in pursuit of Turks made contact with refugees from the Christian kingdom. Vasco da Gama's grandson and several hundred Portuguese soldiers were despatched and proved crucial in turning the tide against Ahmed Grañ, who was killed in battle with a new Christian ruler in 1543. Thereafter, for almost a century, the Portuguese maintained some presence in Ethiopia. This took the form primarily of several generations of determined Jesuits who wished to win the Ethiopians away from heresy and became embroiled in the factional politics of the Ethiopian ruling class. They succeeded in converting one emperor, Susenyos, whose thirty-year rule was weakened partly as a result of the hostility this engendered among clerics and notables. His successor, Fasilidas, expelled the Portuguese entirely in 1634.

So in Ethiopia the Portuguese intrusion was followed (much as in Japan during the same years) by a policy of exclusion and elimination of European influence. During the sixteenth and seventeenth centuries European artisans had made their way to Ethiopia and enjoyed considerable prestige, one surviving consequence being the construction of the castle-palaces of Gondar, but these techniques were not widely diffused and did not lead to significant long-term economic change. With the decline of Portuguese (and Ottoman) sea power in the Indian Ocean, European interest in Ethiopia and East African coast faded until the nineteenth century.

Nothing in Africa fascinated the Portuguese more than the prospect of gold. Everywhere they went they inquired after it. In two regions this developed into a strong, permanent interest. One was on the stretch of the West African coast that became known to Europeans as the Gold Coast. Here the Portuguese erected a great medieval fort at Elmina in 1481. To Elmina came caravans that diverted gold from older trade routes established throughout West Africa. During the sixteenth century this trade was a jewel in the Portuguese crown, a source of as much as one-fifth of its income in good years. The Portuguese rarely interfered in local politics and, so far as is known did not consistently attempt to control gold production anywhere. From the beginning of the seventeenth century the Elmina officials suffered from the competition of private European traders who could offer African merchants better prices for higher quality goods. By the time the Dutch threw the Portuguese out of Elmina in 1637 its gold trade was in a state of irremediable decline.

The other gold-bearing region of Africa of which the Portuguese became aware was the plateau zone of south-central Africa now known as Zimbabwe. As soon as they reached the East African coast the Portuguese ascertained that this gold was exported to Asia via Sofala, a port on the coast of modern Mozambique under the control of the city of Kilwa. Sofala was quickly seized and an attempt was made to redirect the trade to Mozambique island where the Portuguese built their fort and town in

1507. This tactic proved unsuccessful and, for reasons that are not entirely clear, the gold trade quickly dried up. It has been suggested that the gold supplies were in any case petering out at this time.

However, the Portuguese persisted. They found a highway to the interior in the form of the Zambesi River which they followed inland, establishing forts and trading settlements in strategic locations. During the sixteenth century Portuguese soldiers and priests established themselves in market centres and became a factor in internecine politics in the plateau region south of the Zambesi valley. They may have been partially responsible for the collapse of the Rozvi state then dominant on the Zimbabwean high veld. Commercially their intrusion was a complete failure. The amount of wealth that could be drawn from scattered alluvial pockets of gold mined by women during the dry season was very limited and the prospect of rich trade that lured the Portuguese into the interior never materialised. In 1693 a revived state on the plateau under the Changamire dynasty smashed the last remnants of Portuguese military force in the area.

However, the Portuguese remained in the lower Zambesi valley. Here the Crown granted land to Portuguese women in an unusual tenure arrangement that established property rights for the course of three lives heritable through the female line. The intention was to create a class of Portuguese landowners. The *prazos* were much too large to function as estates. Their owners survived primarily as traders and tribute-gatherers who amassed considerable retinues of slaves but exerted a generally rather tenuous authority with some tribute rights over the free population of *colonos*. Some *prazeros* gained a kind of acceptance as chiefs, and by the eighteenth century the large majority were predominantly of African and Indian origin. This transformation has been described as an 'Africanisation'. Although the Portuguese state could exert little authority over them the *prazeros* clung to a cultural identification with Portugal and with Roman Catholicism that reflected their continuing business as middlemen-traders caught up in ocean commerce. During the eighteenth century they turned to the burgeoning ivory trade to build their fortunes.

The only region other than Zambesia where Portuguese involvement had some lasting significance lay across the continent where the savanna that stretches south of the Congo basin reaches the Atlantic. Here the Portuguese encountered the one powerful African state that fronted the sea coast in the fifteenth century – the kingdom of the Kongo. Impressed by the state of order and control and the more open terrain which made possible physical penetration into the interior, the first Portuguese quickly established an alliance with the Kongo state. The Kongo rulers, particularly the early sixteenth century monarch usually known by his Portuguese name of Dom Afonso I (Mbemba-a-Nzinga), were in their turn immensely impressed by the material paraphernalia of Portuguese culture and attempted to secure aid for the introduction of techniques of all kinds into their state. Instead, they got priests. Dom Afonso, his successors and the Kongo ruling class in general accepted baptism and a veneer of Catholic practice diffused widely while the Catholic Church, in Rome as well as in Portugal, came to accept the Kongo as a nominal, if backsliding, Catholic state to which it had certain commitments. Over the centuries many priests were sent out who did succeed in training Kongo priests. Apart from this aspect, however, Kongo was a grave disappointment to the Portuguese. It proved very remote from the Indian Ocean trade and lacked any precious minerals. Even before the death of Dom Afonso I, Kongo became a state that exported slaves.

According to the testimony of the king himself this initially had a very destructive impact, including, it may be imagined, on his own authority. Therefore Kongo is often taken as the classic model of an African state whose autonomous development was destroyed and power laid waste by European commercial influence and the slave trade in particular. But the case is not very convincing. Kongo remained a strong state for almost two centuries after its 'discovery' by the Portuguese and its power was eventually broken through the revolt of a major provincial lord. After initial devastations the slave trade was largely redirected outside the kingdom's borders to raiding and trading networks deeper in the interior. Recent research has tended to refute the earlier stereotype of slavery-caused depopulation in Kongo.[1]

There was one notable change, however; this was in agricultural production. The cultivation of African grains and rootcrops gave way relatively early to American cassava (manioc) and maize, crops which spread far inland but otherwise had no parallel in scale of adaptation elsewhere in Africa.[2] Cassava can be grown in poorer soil and with less labour than practically any other crop; it thrives where other plants will not take root. This may have freed women from agricultural labour and perhaps allowed populations to build up that might otherwise have diminished. However, the evidence for this is very limited.

The Kongo kings failed in their efforts to spread new craft techniques among their subjects. Instead, the ruling class became enthusiastic consumers of imported textiles and other goods. Although several priests produced written Kongo in dictionary form, no written culture emerged.

Thus the Kongo ruling class came to depend on the consumption of goods available only through import from Europe in exchange for the sale of gathered natural products or human labour-power in the form of slaves. After their initial attempts the Portuguese did not do much to spread manufacturing techniques to the region. This was, of course, their policy towards other potential rivals, European as well. The dominant economic philosophy of European society at the time, mercantilism – the ideology of merchant capitalism – emphasised commercial secrecy and monopoly.

Yet other rivals persevered and were able to copy and ultimately to innovate. Kongo society, for reasons that related to its own internal dynamic, remained relatively impervious to innovations that could not be fitted readily into the existing mode of production. The resulting interrelationship has been considered one of unequal exchange or dependence by those writers searching to find early roots of underdevelopment. This is a very simplified way of describing a complex of class and commercial interconnections engendered through contact, but it is significant that those commanding means of coercion in the Kongo preferred (they could not be forced) to sell people or products of the bush rather than to intensify the application of forces of production.

South of the Kongo state the Portuguese presence intruded markedly in the area that became known after the title of a local ruler: Angola. Angola was a particularly early focus for the slave trade and the one place other than the Zambesi valley where the Portuguese tried consistently to sustain a territorial empire in the course of wars in the seventeenth century. They eventually undermined the power of those Mbundu-speaking rulers nearest the coast, but others further inland continued to control, and indeed to fatten upon, the slaving operations. Mulattos or culturally 'Portugalised' African armed traders known as *pombeiros* served as the vital intermediaries.

### The Atlantic Slave Trade

The Portuguese had an effective base for the penetration of Kongo and Angola in the island colony of São Tomé. During the first generation or two of contact it was here that most slaves were sent and here that a sugar plantation economy arose. Another group of islands, much further north, served as a parallel base. These were the arid Cape Verdes, unsuitable for plantation agriculture but the site of a cotton textile industry used for the varied trade, including one in slaves, pursued by Portuguese settlers along the West African coast from modern Senegal to Liberia. Cape Verdeans included a bigger component of immigrants from Portugal and they, like their São Tomé compatriots, played a crucial role in providing personnel to man the commercial networks on the mainland.

São Tomé proved to be only one in a chain of land-exhausting sugar plantation centres which the slave trade serviced. In economic terms the organisation and evolution of the sugar plantation, demanding large inputs of firmly controlled, hard-worked human labour, determined the history of the trade. The first European-run sugar plantations were in Crusader Cyprus. The focus then moved westwards through the Mediterranean to Sicily and southern Portugal, then to the Atlantic islands of Madeira and São Tomé. São Tomé at the end of the fifteenth century was the earliest slave plantation colony to rely overwhelmingly on African labour. From the Atlantic islands the focus of sugar production then shifted to the tropical colonies of the New World whose vast lands required settlers to be exploited effectively. It was Portuguese initiative which created the important original plantation nucleus in north-east Brazil.

The very weakness of Portuguese power, political and economic, was ironically a factor in the spread of the plantation. During the 1630s the Dutch temporarily succeeded in conquering part of Brazil and, in so doing, mastered the art of sugar-milling. They introduced the system into the Caribbean region and seized upon the growing importance of the Portuguese slave trade in providing a vast coerced work force. To this end they captured and held for a time the Angolan capital of Luanda, although during this period they failed to export large numbers of slaves. In 1654 a Brazilian force under Salvador da Sá, representing a revival of Portuguese power, threw the Dutch out of Angola.

By this time, under Dutch inspiration, the sugar plantations had begun to spread through the Lesser Antilles, and later extended to the larger British island of Jamaica, with the French island colony of St Domingue (Haiti) the greatest eighteenth-century exploiter of African slave labour. The merchant fleets of France, and especially industrialising Britain, overtook the Dutch to become the major slaving powers of the eighteenth century. The Portuguese, too, expanded their slave trade and remained the third most important agent while most of the other European powers, as well as Brazil and New England, were active participants.

Men have long associated the cruelties of the slave trade with unimaginably great profits and tainted wealth. In truth, the slave trade was immensely profitable for European merchants during the seventeenth century in that the price of goods bought in Europe for sale to Africa was very low compared with the money value of slaves sold in the Caribbean. The business was a risky one, though, subject to European wars, piracies, shipwrecks and disease. Throughout the slaving period voyages could be extremely remunerative, but during the eighteenth century, despite the insatiable demands of the plantations which were prepared to pay ever higher prices, profits on average appear to have diminished as African traders improved their bargaining power in this repellent business.

The slave trade was a factor in the accumulation of capital which helped to fuel the Industrial Revolution. The causal link cannot be traced directly for the trade itself (and Euro-African commerce in general) was just one element in a great complex of economic activities: the plantations, their exports, their consumption of foodstuffs and textiles from Europe, North America (and, on a small scale, Africa) and the general development of shipping, to name only the most obvious. Slaving played its part in laying the foundations of capitalism within this broader structure made possible by the expansion of world commerce.

At its height the slave trade overtook or entirely replaced other forms of commerce between Europe and Africa. Regions such as the Swahili coast and Ethiopia which appeared to be less likely major slave exporters were neglected, although a slave trade arose in the late eighteenth century from Kilwa and the off-shore island of Zanzibar to service the plantations founded by the French on the fertile, previously uninhabited islands of Mauritius and Réunion in the Indian Ocean. The gold export trade of Elmina virtually disappeared in the eighteenth century as the Gold Coast too became a major slave exporter.[3] The Senegambian region, largely transformed into an exporter of gum arabic, was an exception, as was the extreme south of Africa where a colony of settlement developed under Dutch rule and into which the slaves were imported. (This will be considered separately towards the end of this chapter.) However, it is generally fitting to treat the period of contact from the mid-seventeenth to the early nineteenth century as the era of the slave trade.

The Europeans did not introduce the slave trade to sub-Saharan Africa. The very first slaves purchased by the Portuguese at Arguin, on the desert shores of modern Mauritania, came from the diversion of caravans which carried a not inconsiderable ancient slave trade across the desert. At Elmina the Portuguese at first bought gold through the sale of Angolan slaves to African merchants. While the treatment and use of slaves in

Africa was very different from the commercially orientated plantations of the New World, nevertheless Africans were sometimes being seized violently, captured and made available for exchange purposes as commodities. But the Atlantic slave trade did increase enormously the amount of slaving in Africa.

In recent years there has been considerable research into quantifying the slave trade. Philip Curtin inaugurated this tendency with his 'census', published in 1969, which estimated that between eight and nine million slaves were despatched from Africa to the Americas. Subsequent studies have raised these figures by some twenty-five to fifty per cent to include those who died before reaching the African coast or on the coast waiting to be sold.[4]

It is virtually impossible to gauge the social significance of the slave trade in quantitative terms. Our knowledge of the historical demography of Africa is, and will probably remain, virtually nil. It is often assumed that such a huge number of people lost to Africa must have had a severe effect on the population, but there is little hard evidence to back such a claim. A larger number of Europeans, some 20 000 000, crossed the Atlantic to settle voluntarily in the New World in a single generation before World War I with, it is usually argued, a generally beneficial effect on the economies of the countries left behind. Slaves were despatched from Africa over a period of almost four centuries (although mainly from 1750 to 1850) from an entire continent. Some of the most heavily slaved areas, such as the hinterland of the Niger delta, are today among the most densely populated parts of Africa, while thinly peopled districts, once thought to have been denuded of people under the slave trade, are ecologically unattractive and presumably were underpopulated in the past. The impact of such crucial factors as the preponderance of males among the slaves exported cannot be measured either. It has sometimes been suggested that the spread of new American crops, especially cassava, neatly countered the demographic impact of the losses, but this seems unlikely because of their limited adaptation outside a zone radiating from Angola and Kongo.

The qualitative loss of slaves to Africa is even harder to measure. It may best be imagined in terms of land not cleared, settlements not established, cultivation becoming cruder or more laborious but, like any other counterfactual view of history as it might have been, this cannot be assumed to have been the case. What is more sure is that the increase in insecurity and violence brought by slaving affected the quality of life.

For Africa the trade involved the import of new commodities as much as the export of human beings. In exchange for slaves Africans accepted from Europeans a wide range of goods, the most important being Indian and European textiles. These and a range of others, notably metalware and salt, replaced domestically produced goods that were highly valued, traded for centuries and scarce in many regions. From Ijebu in Yoruba-speaking country, Benin and the Ivory Coast, African-woven textiles were purchased for sale to the Gold Coast. Where inter-African trade had existed European merchants attempted to participate and control. Contrary to later stereotype only a moderate amount of alcohol was sold to Africans; it became *par excellence* a ruling class token of hospitality and prestige. Guns and ammunition became increasingly significant trade items as their quality improved. At first, primitive European muskets had been valued largely for their symbolic fright value. They were often depicted on decorative plaques in Benin but there, as elsewhere, were probably used in fighting only occasionally. In the eighteenth century, however, the sale of guns belonged to the brutal cycle through which the slaves were produced for the market.

A noteworthy item in the trade was the cowrie shell of the Indian Ocean, brought in perhaps as replacement for local shell currencies that had already existed in parts of West Africa. A number of other durable trade items such as bolts of cloth and brass manillas became widely diffused bases for exchange. The slave trade gave a fillip to a vast expansion in the exchange economy and the role of commodities in African life. The geographic scale of slaving at its height was astounding; by the end of the eighteenth century slaves were coming for sale on the coast from such remote regions as the Hausa states and the centre of south-central Africa in the later Katanga (Shaba) province of Zaïre.

Europeans rarely ventured far from the coast in pursuit of slaves, less so than the Portuguese had done earlier on. In some regions they established forts for which they paid a rent to the local authorities who saw them as guarantees for the steadfastness of the trade rather than as threats to local sovereignty. The Gold Coast numbered some two dozen on a 200-mile coastline where the savanna interrupted the West African forest and swept down to the sea, creating relatively healthier conditions for foreigners to the tropics. Off-shore islands were often ideal trade bases. In other regions, such as the Loango coast of modern-day Gabon and the Congo Republic, or the Niger delta, Europeans generally spent the nights on their ships. The forts contained barracks to hold the slaves and small garrisons but were generally ineffectual at repelling assaults by sea and changed hands often. African rulers sometimes tried to establish permanent alliances with parti-cular European companies or states, but usually were anxious to permit as much competition as possible in the interest of favourable exchange rates.

The trade was thus an African trade until it reached the coast. Only very rarely were Europeans directly involved in procuring slaves, and that largely in Angola. Particularly in savanna regions, long-distance caravans brought slaves from hundreds of miles in the interior. In forest regions such as the modern Ivory Coast 'stateless' communities passed on slaves like a baton in a relay aimed at the sea. Slaves generally appear to have been sold several times before reaching the point of shipment.

Powerful ruling classes were never so foolish as to sell their own manpower in any significant numbers. Slaves from say, Asante, were generally procured either through tribute or through raiding expeditions on the frontiers and this seems to hold as well for Kongo, Benin and Dahomey. Some slaves were debtors, prisoners or the victims of famine, but the majority were obtained through violence: wars, raids and kidnapping. It was the small-scale societies unable to resist either systematic or random violence of this kind that suffered the most and were obliged, in order to survive, to retreat to remote and defensible locales.

A peculiar consequence of the efforts of the 'African initiative' school to promote the historic grandeur of African kingdoms has been a consistent attempt to play down the transparently enormous importance of slaving for the forest states of West Africa: Oyo, Dahomey, Benin, Asante and others. Undoubtedly major wars between these states continued to have political rationales; their foreign policies cannot be reduced to manhunts. Victims, though, were systematically sold as slaves and all such states engaged in bloody and deliberate raiding which, when successful, provided booty that justified the participation of the soldiers. When occasionally Europeans were in a position to foment armed violence they were not averse to doing so. Major wars invariably resulted in the arrival of large numbers of captives on the coast.

The most successful states retained many slaves. For domestic purposes African households preferred to absorb women; the Atlantic trade demanded male labour. Male slaves in Africa were used as soldiers, and thus as sustainers of class or state power, a practice that intensified under the slave trade. The armies of bravoes that typified nineteenth-century Yoruba states and the class of *tyeddo* warriors, or royal slaves, that served the rulers of the Senegambia were partly created by the trade. In some areas, notoriously in Dahomey, women were also used extensively as warriors, perhaps reflecting the population imbalances caused by the slave trade.

So-called stateless societies sometimes found effective ways of participating in the trade too. Existing institutions could be altered to streamline involvement without actually establishing kings on thrones. For instance, the Igbo-speaking country behind the Niger delta was a major source of slaves. Much of the trade down to the delta ports was organised through the Aro society, operating under the protection of a sacred oracle who could both demand slaves in notional human sacrifice and protect a long-distance marketing system that traversed often warring village communities. Another group, particularly associated with the Nike region, became the armed procurers of the slaves in alliance with Aro. It is not surprising that twentieth-century anthropologists in Igbo-land have described 'democratically' ordered communities of autonomous households that nonetheless placed great value on wealth, contained secret societies with extensive punitive powers and held slaves and other dependents.

The commercial opportunities of slaving sometimes encouraged remarkable migrations and social and ideological changes to accommodate new material opportunities. In the Angola hinterland a new people, known as the Imbangala, formed out of bands attracted to slave-hunting and trading. Predatory and terroristic in their seventeenth-century heyday, the Imbangala defied the norms of kinship, absorbed huge numbers of unrelated recruits and attracted Mbundu households of the area into alliance. The slave trade largely created the Imbangala as a corporate entity.

All along the African coast there arose intermediary strata whose way of life centred on negotiation between European and African traders. These children of the slave trade formed what may be described loosely as a class of *compradores* by analogy with those powerful Chinese merchants who controlled the contemporary trade at the Chinese ports between Europe and the Celestial Kingdom. Sometimes they were Europeans, particularly Portuguese, who had become half-absorbed into African society. More often they were the descendants of Europeans and their 'country' wives, perfectly situated to mediate exchange relations between different modes of production. Speaking European languages, most often a form of Portuguese, and adhering at least nominally to Christianity, they could communicate perfectly with whites. Their African background similarly equipped them to function among those with whom they had been brought up. Such communities arose all the way from Angola north to Saint Louis, the principal French settlement at the mouth of the Senegal River. There was some seizing of local political power by European-descended compradore families like the Cokers and Roberts of the 'Southern Rivers' region of the present-day Sierra Leone coast. But purely

African compradores were more successful at this. Such were the house heads of Calabar in the Niger delta who transformed the elder-dominated lineage inheritance system to establish 'houses' organised to absorb large numbers of slaves and to sell others. Within the houses power was often unstable and trading slaves sometimes seized power. In Calabar wealth brought political authority.

At the economic heart of compradore relationships lay ties of credit. The trust system of the Guinea Coast was essential to the functioning of a trade where the captain of the ship did not have a local bureau to administer his business, to hold on to his unsold goods or to collect slaves in advance for him. Corresponding to trust was the comey, through which Europeans paid a 'customs' duty to African political authorities so as to be able to proceed with their affairs. Comey and trust relationships formed a class of considerable wealth and sophistication whose most successful members often sent their children to Europe for schooling and who were most tightly committed to, and dependent upon, the trade with the West. They generally commanded numerous slaves to minister to their household needs, to protect their masters and to engage in productive activity. Some, for example, had large farms manned by slaves which produced foodstuffs for the slave voyages.

Thus a major consequence of the slave trade was the creation of a class that depended for its existence on Euro-African commerce. More broadly, in many parts of Africa those who could appropriate surplus and command force developed a general orientation towards the hunting and sale of people, rather than the systematic production of exchange values through agriculture or crafts as a means of acquiring desirable commodities. The slave trade did not introduce predatory ruling classes to Africa, who indeed could be found in areas relatively untouched by it, but intensified internal slavery, violence and what the radical West Indian historian Walter Rodney aptly called 'social oppression' without any corresponding development of the forces of production. From a class perspective, this was its principal significance to the African continent.

## The Foundations of South Africa

It was at the height of the slave trade that a different, directly colonial, form of European penetration crystallised at the southern tip of Africa. Ships *en route* from Europe to Asia and back had taken to calling at Table

Bay to purchase fresh meat from the resident Khoi Khoi pastoralists and to make extended stops for repairs or convalescence. In 1652 the Dutch East India Company established a permanent base at Cape Town to regularise this contact as a useful staging point in its Asian commerce.

Within five years the Company began to permit individuals to retire from its service and to settle permanently at the Cape. Relatively few settlers emigrated to South Africa, but those who did flourished and by the end of the eighteenth century they numbered approximately 25 000. The Company hoped they would perform a useful service on its behalf by providing agricultural produce for passing ships and the garrison stationed at Cape Town. In fact the settlers quickly discovered that their best prospects were first in the cattle and sheep trade with the Khoi Khoi and then in founding their own herds and ranging far into the interior with them.

Pastoral competition led to quarrels over trade and raids for stock, bloodshed and colonial expansion. While the Company was uneasy at spreading its resources and expenses further into Africa, it lent occasional support to the *veeboers*, the cattle farmers, and gradually annexed more and more territory. The *veeboers* themselves organised fighting commandos who often effectively dislodged Khoi Khoi populations in raids. Gradually the Khoi Khoi were pushed far to the east or north of the Cape or pressed into clientage relationships with the *veeboers* who appropriated most of their stock. Without the stock, Khoi social organisation dissolved.

Nearer to the Cape something like a plantation economy developed. Land was granted in freehold to farmers who cultivated European grains such as wheat, and vineyards. The Dutch East India Company imported slaves from Mozambique, Madagascar and Asia to work the fields. In contrast with the classic plantation colonies of the Caribbean, the dominant economic element at the Cape was the passing ship trade and its purchases of liquor and animal products. Even the slaves, who came slightly to outnumber the free colonists, were used in large numbers as artisans and hired servants, particularly in Cape Town itself, the 'Tavern of the Seas'. The Company aspired to initiate an export-orientated agriculture but the Cape produced no tropical luxuries or staples to sell.

Through the seventeenth and eighteenth centuries the Cape settlers, a *mélange* of Dutch, French, Scandinavians and Germans, evolved an African (or *Afrikaner*) society of their own with a distinctive dialect that moved away from standard Dutch. They ranged from a few wealthy individuals owning large numbers of slaves and controlling exclusive contracts to provision the Company to landless discharged soldiers. It was upon this settler community that Dutch rule depended and operated, however much metropolitan officials might fulminate against the impoverished and undeveloped character of the colony and the troublesome inhabitants from an imperial point of view. At the lowest level of authority the Afrikaners commanded effective political, military and judicial power. They in turn depended on the imperial economy to sell their produce and on imperial arms for the possibilities of further expansion.

The racism that accompanied European imperial expansion in the age of plantation slavery prevailed at the Cape as a concomitant of the high level of social stratification and the realities of conquest and slavery. However, class society at the Cape was less racially determined than the typical Caribbean plantation colony. The crucial relationships of domination were those between slave owner and slave, master and servant. Intermarriage and concubinage were very common, particularly between poorer whites and Asian slave women, and legal distinctions were made over status (freedom versus 'unfreedom') rather than race. Many of the offspring of mixed unions were accepted into the Afrikaner community. The small stratum of 'free blacks' held a shadowy and insignificant social position. Spreading over 100 000 square miles (256 000 square km) by the opening of the nineteenth century, the Cape was mainland Africa's first real colony. In time it was to witness the most intense form of capitalist exploitation and development on the continent, but this was in long years to come.

## The Age of Merchant Capital

At the beginning of this chapter it was suggested that during this era the foundation for a world economy was laid. In the fifteenth and sixteenth centuries Africa's participation was limited and intermittent. But with the development of the slave trade the significance of Africa as a source of labour and as part of the great global commercial network grew markedly. A crucial difference between merchant and industrialised capital is that the former generally depends on interconnections between existing productive and social systems and the profits which can be obtained through mastering the interstices between them, while the latter derives from an actual transformation in a productive system as a whole. Merchant capital characterised and dominated world enterprise before the Industrial Revolution of the late eighteenth century. During this period corresponding productive changes occurred only to a limited extent, especially in Africa. Only at the Cape did a socio-economic system form that was in any way comparable with the intensification of unfree labour exploitation that merchant capital engendered in some parts of the world, notably the slave plantations of the Americas. Where European penetration of Africa went deepest, in the Kongo kingdom, Angola and Mozambique, it did so by adapting to the existing political and social ideologies and relationships.

A consistent materialist analysis of the period suggests that while ruling classes in Africa sharpened their predatory character and orientation to trade in imported manufactures, it is not really satisfactory to see Africa as simply 'dependent' on the West as a 'periphery' within a neatly articulated world economic structure. Within African societies, surplus-appropriating classes and strata in non-class societies actually reinforced their own positions through their command of trade objects and the violence accompanying the slave trade. In the merchant capital era European commerce could not, and in general did not even try to, conquer African peoples and to reorient African societies forcefully. Thus 'dependency' could develop only as part of the logic of the needs of dominant strata and classes in Africa. It is important to remember this point when examining the history of the greater part of the nineteenth century, as the next chapter will show.

## Notes

1. In fact there was significant depopulation in the nineteenth century. This is argued in John Thornton, 'Demography and History of the Kingdom of the Kongo, 1550–1750', *JAH, XVIII* (1977).
2. From the nineteenth century, however, these crops became far more prevalent and often assumed the status of staples. They were very widely cultivated on a secondary basis earlier as a result of their introduction by the Portuguese.
3. See the discussion in Walter Rodney, 'Gold and Slaves at the Gold Coast', *THSG, X* (1969).
4. Number-crunching historians attracted by the slave trade have been so pleased with their recent quantitative exercises as to claim that their work puts in the shade all previous considerations on the slave trade. In fact, taking the last qualification into consideration, many estimates of the slave trade from the 1960s or earlier (for instance, those of K. O. Dike) are not far from the mark.

# 4

## THE ERA OF LEGITIMATE COMMERCE, 1800–70

Even the merchants themselves, finding that the quantity of goods thus sent for sale into the interior had a sensible influence in curtailing their own store trade, by preventing in great measure the resort of the Ashantees to the coast, were obliged to yield to the current and to carry on their business principally by means of agents employed in the same manner...

All was now cheerful bustle and activity. There was not a nook or corner of the land where some enterprizing trade had not led him. Every village had its festoons of Manchester cottons and China silks, hung up upon the walls of the houses or round the trees in the market-place, to attract the attention and excite the cupidity of the villagers.

Brodie Cruickshank, *Eighteen Years on the Gold Coast of Africa* (Hurst and Blackett, 1853), II, pp. 32–3

### Abolition and Legitimate Commerce

In the final quarter of the eighteenth century the movement for the abolition of the Atlantic slave trade gathered force in Britain, the premier European slaving nation, and culminated in a ban from 1807. The British then pressured other nations to sign anti-slave trade treaties. In 1833 slavery in the British plantation colonies was entirely abolished to be followed in time by the French, Scandinavian and Dutch colonies, the South American republics, the United States (in the course of its Civil War), Spanish Cuba and finally, in 1888, the empire of Brazil.

There is substantial controversy among historians over the causes of the abolition movement and its relationship to broader trends within the world economy and capitalist society. In the floodtide of colonialism the freeing of the slaves was frequently and fatuously underlined as the ultimate paternalist symbol of European moral superiority and good will; abolition helped to justify colonial conquest. One man at first, the West Indian historian Eric Williams, attacked this view. In his famous study *Capitalism and Slavery* he tried both to delineate the relationship of the slave system to the process of capital accumulation which made the Industrial Revolution possible and to demonstrate that its abolition had equally sound economic causes, particularly the declining profitability of sugar plantations on the British West Indian islands and the rivalry of free labour production interests elsewhere. Britain thus turned against slavery because it was expensive, not because it was immoral.

More than forty years after its appearance Williams' work appears powerful in outline but too narrowly economic in focus. There is no question that the importance to British colonial trade of the worn-out sugar isles was declining from the late eighteenth century, but Williams had no justification for assuming that the continuation of the slave planta-tions would actually have been unprofitable. Cotton plantations in the southern USA continued to prosper throughout the slave era past the middle of the nineteenth century. Fertile virgin lands for the expansion of British-grown sugar-cane beckoned in newly conquered Mauritius, Guyana and Trinidad at the very time of abolition. The trade itself continued to be profitable if less consistently so than a century earlier.

Moreover it is impossible to reduce the anti-slavery movement to narrow economic foundations alone. In France, for example, the debate on the future of the slave trade and slavery was an integral part of the radicalising process of the Revolution. France abolished slavery before Britain, although this liberation was reversed later by Napoleon. The fervour and moral emphasis of British 'humanitarianism' had the support of some self-interested investors in free labour but cross-cut specific inter-est-group politics.

Abolitionism was part of an ideological transformation in Western thought that in turn reflected the growing dominance of the capitalist mode of production and the capitalist conception of labour. For the capitalist, who finally came into his own with the British industrial revolu-tion of the eighteenth century, the ideal worker is one who has been torn from the land, lacks any claim on the landlord or employer beyond his wage and is obliged to sell his or her labour on the market. Slavery ties down capital and immobilises labour; it stands in the way of genuine free enterprise as a form of labour monopoly. That passionate insistence on liberty which gave to the great bourgeois revolutionary movements in the USA, France and elsewhere a cast of social radicalism could not tolerate the idea of institutional slavery. As a result, to a certain extent, the short-term interests of specific slave-holding bourgeoisies in the colonies could be and were pushed aside by the broader demands of capitalism.[1]

Practical critics of slavery also appreciated the possibility that slave disaffection and revolts could in time lead to outright rebellion. In the richest of all the West Indian colonies, the French half of Hispaniola now known as the republic of Haiti, such a generalised slave revolution did take place in 1791, leading to the extinction both of French authority and of the entire plantation system. The Haitian revolution and the fundamentally backward nature of slave systems were the frequently repeated themes of colonial abolitionist reformers in the early nineteenth century. Their arguments frequently pointed at the future not only of the plantation colonies but also of the African continent where slaving seemed to limit, if not to stifle, all other forms of commerce and industry. How could this situation be reversed so as to transform the continent into a hive of industrious activity for the benefit of European commerce?

Out of this problematic came the slogan of 'legitimate commerce' which could oust the horrors of the slave trade to the benefit of all parties, an ideology which dominated the intensifying European penetration of nineteenth-century Africa, the creed of explorers and missionaries as well as traders. While the Industrial Revolution in Europe gained breadth and complexity the demand for new products in industrial processes and consumption increased and some of these could be found readily in Africa – beeswax, wild rubber, ivory and, above all, the vegetable oils derived from palm, palm kernel and ground-nuts. All of these were relatively peripheral to the industrial needs of Europeans, yet they provided the basis of what has often been described as a commercial revolution due to the enormous increase in Afro-European trade.

Palm oil began to be exported from West Africa long before the start of the nineteenth century. The trade arose initially from the provisioning of slave vessels. The real stimulus for its massive expansion (150 ton average per annum in the 1790s, 3000 tons in 1819, 8000 tons in 1829, 25 000 tons in the mid-1850s, all from the Bight of Biafra), came from the British demand for oil for use in soap, candles and industrial lubrication.[2]

Ground-nut exports took off in the late 1830s in Senegambia. After several years France became the principal consumer.

In the era of legitimate commerce what Africa imported was perhaps more vital than what she exported. During the nineteenth century Europea shipped to Africa enormously increased quantities of goods: alcoholic beverages, arms and, above all, cloth, whose European price fell precipitately to the advantage of African producers of oils and other products. 'The quantity of cotton goods (measured by the yard) exported from the United Kingdom to West Africa increased thirty times in the short period between 1816–20 and 1846–1850.'[3] It was, moreover, industrialising Britain that secured the lion's share of nineteenth-century commerce. At first glance it does indeed seem that the good coin of legitimate trade succeeded in driving out the bad coin of slaving. A closer look suggests that this misses the fundamental link between the two.

First, it must be pointed out that the Atlantic slave trade did not simply end as a result of British abolition. For as long as the market was good in Cuba and Brazil slaves continued to be shipped over the ocean in amazingly high numbers. It has been suggested that the years after 1807 actually brought record numbers of slaves to the New World. Only when slaves could no longer be marketed in the plantation economies there did the trade finally peter out and this is generally equated with the decade of the 1860s in West Africa. It should be noted, however, that in certain areas such as the Gold Coast, the slave trade had practically died out much earlier.

Yet this important qualification is only a chronological revision. Other issues might occasion more surprise. For instance, the new forms of commerce proved relatively compatible with slave trading. In a number of regions, notably the Niger Delta and Dahomey, both trades flourished simultaneously during much of the second quarter of the nineteenth century. The commercial mechanisms created by slave trade (credit, units of exchange, commission systems) continued.

Even when slaves were no longer exported the impact of legitimate commerce was to increase slaving and the holding of slaves *within* Africa. The demand for new articles for sale to international markets was indeed a spur to intensified commodity production in Africa but, given African social conditions and the slaving heritage, there was no reason for this to lead to free labour production. Much of the newly applied labour was the task of dependents – women, clients, youths but, above all, slaves. Male labour, no longer transportable overseas, continued to be seized in raids by the predatory forces the trade had engendered, but now was available relatively cheaply for local use. Another expanded category of work for slaves was the porterage of enhanced quantities of goods.

Domestic slavery could be nicely fitted in to the expansion in oil products. In the West African savanna, caravans from deep in the interior had brought slaves to the coast. Now enterprising traders took their domestics and slaves down with them to the vicinity of the sea and had them grow ground-nuts. This was the origin of the so-called 'strange farmers' of the Gambia valley and migrant *navétanes* of Senegal. In Dahomey there are reports of actual plantations where palm oil was produced by the slaves of the king and perhaps other officials and merchants. Some authors suspect similarly systematic cultivation (and certainly collection) of kola nuts in Asante for sale northward to the Sokoto caliphate region.

The expansion of slaving was very marked in the eastern half of Africa during the nineteenth century. During this era the *prazeros* of the Zambesi valley sold off large numbers of subject African *colonos* unable to flee their bands of armed retainers. Many of the slaves wound up on the sugar islands of the Indian Ocean. It was only after 1800 that most of the East African interior was 'opened up' by the expansion of trade in slaves and ivory. Some of the slaves were sold to Arabia and other parts of the Islamic world outside Africa, but many were retained in the great new commercial entrepôt of Zanzibar where there emerged a class of Arab plantation owners specialising in the production of cloves who required a massive importation of labour from the mainland.

Thus the main change between the eighteenth and nineteenth centuries was not the difference between slave labour and free but simply the quantitative intensification and significance of commerce. Increasingly improved weaponry arrived in Africa and assisted the expansion of hunting both animals and men and made warfare more murderous. Firearms made access to European traders of vital importance to African rulers if they hoped to keep up with their neighbours and rivals. They highlighted the growing dependence of African ruling classes and others, such as lineage elders who could appropriate surplus, on trade goods that were entering the continent on all sides. The slave trade prepared the way for the triumph of 'legitimate trade'; it may have been a necessary precedent for the smooth West African ascendancy of the latter. At the same time, despite prevailing philosophy in Europe, the intensification of commodity exchange required not the proliferation of 'free' labour but of slavery and other direct forms of labour coercion under African social conditions.

## Class and Trade in Coastal West Africa

Ancient African state formation is often shakily ascribed to long-distance trade. One reason for this may lie in an unthinking extrapolation from the nineteenth and twentieth centuries. For the nineteenth century there can be little doubt of the great significance of the penetration of the world market, although it was not always the existing ruling class that secured the greatest benefit from it.

The compradore acquired an unprecedented importance in this era. It was in West Africa, where commerce expanded so markedly from such a strong historic base, that he came most fully into his own. On the Gold Coast he was apt to be an active Methodist layman, anxious to educate his sons as far as possible, including if possible schooling in Britain, and eager to participate in the recreation of many aspects of respectable European society on the Guinea Coast. Such a man was James Bannerman, the 'great man of Accra, wealthy, liberally educated and a gentleman.'[4] The gum trade in St Louis and the ground-nut trade in Gorée island spawned an equivalent class that looked to France for their cultural reference point. Charles Heddle, the wealthiest West African coastal merchant of the second half of the nineteenth century, came from a Gorée background, settle in Sierra Leone where he amassed landed property, and spent his final days in gilded *nouveau riche* retirement with a pretty young wife on the French Riviera.

The slave trade had depended on the trust or commission system whereby Africans were granted goods as capital to procure slaves between the visits of the European ships. Legitimate commerce required a great expansion of trust with credit made available to African traders on a considerable scale. Yet the sometimes grand life-style of the coastal merchant was rarely matched by capital resources; he was ultimately dependent for lines of credit on a small number of merchant firms – Brazilian in Angola, Bordeaux-based in the Senegambia, Liverpool-orientated in the Niger Delta and the Gold Coast. Control over small armies of slaves enabled him to provide for personal needs and further his business. To only a limited extent did the compradores turn their slaves to systematic plantation cultivation for commercial sale, although examples do exist. Never do they seem to have effectuated any transformation in local productive forces.[5]

Little bourgeois fish in a vast non-capitalist sea, they lacked the social wherewithal to initiate capitalist production and the essential accompanying state framework. This had the effect of increasing their dependence on

European state power; if a crisis raised the necessity of transformation, they had to seek sustenance from one or another European state. Their struggle was one for recognition as the foremost agents of European commercial, political and cultural penetration.

An important section of compradores consisted of new strata issuing directly from the activities of the anti-slave trade movement. In 1787 the Province of Freedom was established under British authority on the Atlantic peninsula known as Sierra Leone, a home for Maroons who had escaped into the interior from the slave plantations of Jamaica, Black Loyalists who had come from the USA to Canada during the American Revolution and migrants from Britain itself, where slavery was already illegal, a disparate group of free blacks. The British philanthropists first organised the Sierra Leone Company to further commerce and free labour. Their overbearing conduct, together with poor administration, led to sharp conflict and Sierra Leone had a turbulent history before the British state assumed power in 1808. Under Crown Colony status Sierra Leone throve and its population grew as 'recaptives' were released from liberated slave vessels and brought to the capital of Freetown where the anti-slavery squadron and court was headquartered.

The Sierra Leoneans, or Creoles, rapidly welded together a distinctive colonial culture characterised by the Krio dialect they spoke. Some Creoles, of recaptive origin, were Muslim, but the majority were Christian Protestants, and Christianity became their most distinguishing cultural feature, much as it did for the *trekboers* of South Africa. Within a generation the Creoles had produced their first ministers of the gospel; within two their first doctors and lawyers. Early British hopes for Sierra Leone as an agricultural export colony soon died. The wealthy Creoles of Freetown were often landlords, but above all merchants who established trading networks deep in the interior. Many of them returned to their places of origin in other parts of Africa, particularly present-day southern Nigeria, and here they occupied a major role in the spread of commerce, Christianity and European customs. The Yoruba called the Sierra Leone returnees 'Saro' and the Saro formed a decisive wedge of Western cultural influence and commercial innovation among them.

In Lagos the Saro met with another distinctive group, the Amaro or Brazilians. In Brazil, particularly Bahia, it was not uncommon for African slaves to acquire their freedom within their own lifetime and a significant number began to return to West Africa in the early nineteenth century. The most influential and historically significant were associated with the kingdom of Dahomey, where some were themselves important slave traders while the trade survived. Others engaged in 'legitimate' trans-Atlantic commerce as Africans continued to be good customers for the sugar-cured tobacco of Bahia. Amaro remained as Catholic as the Saro were Protestant and were less often merchants than artisans, skilled craftsmen in the new techniques demanded in the burgeoning West African ports. Significant as the compradores were, they must be measured with other new classes that expanded: artisans, wage labourers, for which a regular pool began to exist in the Gold Coast by mid-century, and soldiers who were prepared to fight for pay in cash. The *tirailleurs* or sharp-shooters of French Senegal were the most famous example, raised on a regular basis by the 1850s.

Several hundred miles down the Windward Coast from Sierra Leone a parallel community was founded under the auspices of the American Colonization Society which sought to establish a home for free American blacks. This was Liberia, whose capital, Monrovia, named for the American President Monroe, was established in 1822. Other settlements were amalgamated into the unified republic of Liberia which became a sovereign state in 1847. The USA had no interest in assuming here the authority that Britain did in Sierra Leone. There were West Indian immigrants and recaptives in Liberia, but the dominant settler element was the 'Americo-Liberian' population, immigrants from the USA impelled to Africa by the growing harshness towards free blacks there. Although the Liberians recognised no foreign authority their values were those of a colonial middleman society expanding among hostile 'natives'. On the coast below Monrovia lived the Kru people. They were, *par excellence*, the sailors of West Africa and as such formed another key layer in the overall expansion of capitalist commercial interests.

## Nineteenth-century East Africa

On the eastern side of Africa the mixture of intensified commerce, slaving and the import of firearms was more explosive than in West Africa because the slave trade had been so much less significant earlier. With the exception of the Zambesi valley and its ancient gold trade, links between coast and interior south of the Horn of Africa had been fragmentary. In the eighteenth century long-distance trade in ivory and slaves, as a symbiotic commercial complex, spread north of the Zambesi. By the end of the century great caravans began to criss-cross what is today mainland Tanzania from the Indian Ocean shores to Lake Tanganyika and across into the very centre of Africa. The Nyamwezi people of the Tabora region specialised as caravan leaders and porters. Commercial networks extended rapidly through the corridor between Lakes Tanganyika and Malawi, into the copper-mining district of present-day Shaba province, Zaïre, and north to the interlacustrine states, notably Buganda. The country around Lake Malawi suffered intensely from slave raids as the junction point between the coastal trade and the explosive force of the *Mfecane* chiefdoms.

Banditti with guns succeeded in establishing new power foci, the nuclei of states, at places where trade could bring an accumulation of wealth and command over the means of destruction. Msiri, a Nyamwezi from western Tanzania, established such a centre in Shaba. Further north around the headwaters of the rivers feeding into the Congo lay the headquarters of the great Zanzibar trader and marauder, Tippu Tip. Within Nyamwezi country itself, astride the principal route from the ocean to Lake Tanganyika, Mirambo was the most famous nineteenth-century power broker. Several Arabised Muslim states-in-formation flickered around Lake Malawi. However brutal the process of state-building noted by early European travellers as they approached the new domains being carved out by the great traders, they generally remarked on the prosperous and orderly conditions prevailing near the capitals where the new power was fitfully being born.

The Nyamwezi at least partly acquired their identity as a people from their characteristic commercial role. Traders from their region began to reach the coast around the opening of the nineteenth century and, by mid-century, the economy of north-central Tanganyika depended upon porterage wage-labour and other side-effects of trade. If the slave and ivory business devastated some regions, it brought prosperity to others in the form of markets for crops and cattle and generalised surplus accumulation. Access to trading routes and to firearms brought about great imbalances in power between regions and peoples. From the mid-nineteenth century the feared Maasai pastoralists lost their grip on the plains of central Kenya while the Kamba people, who traded extensively with the coast, became stronger, as did the Kikuyu agriculturalists south of Mount Kenya. Charles Ambler has rightly pointed out that these ethnic or tribal categories were not necessarily in place in the nineteenth century; in fact, the development of new commercial niches may have helped them to begin to congeal.

Quite unlike any other contemporary East African state, however, was the island sultanate of Zanzibar. The impact of firearms and the caravan trade gave Zanzibar, an important slave trade centre at the opening of the nineteenth century, a special attraction to the rulers of Oman in Arabia who had established suzerainty over the old coastal ports with the collapse of Portuguese authority. In 1840 Seyyid Said (ruled 1804–56) moved his capital to Zanzibar island where a city of stone-built mansions with great carved wooden doors sprang up. Seyyid Said established excellent relations with the naval masters of the Indian Ocean, the British; it was under their aegis that his commercial empire prospered in close relation to the commerce of British India. It was largely to India that Zanzibari-grown cloves were shipped. The lush, well-watered island proved to be an exceptionally well-favoured growing spot for this rare spice tree and by the middle of the nineteenth century Zanzibar had become its major world producer. Clove trees (and, to a lesser extent, coconut palms) formed the agricultural basis of a plantation economy which attracted a community of Arab and Arabised merchants into land-ownership while depending on the finance of Indian capitalists. From Zanzibar's mainland port of Bagamoyo caravans, fitted out by Indian merchants and often led by the dependents and sons of Zanzibari planters, headed inland. True Zanzibari authority did not extend beyond a very limited coastal zone but, as far west as the lakes, the Sultan retained esteem as protector of long-distance commerce.

The clove and coconut plantations of Zanzibar, partly equipped through staple food-producing estates on the mainland coast, responded to a process of intense commercialisation that led to total transformation in relations of production, an extreme example in Africa of the impact of nineteenth-century commerce. Yet the planters and merchants of Zanzibar did not have the makings of a capitalist class. Older, pre-capitalist values, emphasising an integrating Muslim culture and paternalistic clientage relationships, inhibited the emergence of a full-blown, wage-labour dependent, capitalist society on Zanzibar, whose plantation economy led to no further structural evolution. It had a basically dead-end character. The Zanzibar state was also slow to develop the administrative and military apparatus which might have given it more strength to fend off the pressure from European imperialism that built up dramatically in the 1880s.

Both in the Great Lakes region north of Buganda, and further north on the coast, in the Benadir of modern Somalia, travellers under the auspices of Zanzibar brushed against counterparts from another and far more politically ambitious Islamic state, Egypt. The attempt by the Egyptian Muhammad Ali (ruled effectively 1807–48) and his successors to forge a powerful regime, in good part through African expansion, is one of the epic stories of the nineteenth-century history of the continent. Muhammad Ali's most forceful economic and military measures frightened Europeans who felt their commercial position in the Near East threatened and pressed him at knifepoint to compromise. Yet the process of commercial penetration and state aggrandisement begun by Muhammad Ali continued until the bankruptcy of Egypt on the eve of the scramble for Africa.

Military expansion proved inherent in the logic of the state Muhammad Ali established. Under Muhammad Ali Egyptian armies succeeded in seizing control of the middle Nile valley and the adjacent Red Sea coast. Later Kordofan and Dar Fur, far to the west of the river, were added. A somewhat expanded version of this territory, the modern Republic of the Sudan, is territorially the largest country in Africa, covering almost 1 000 000 square miles. The search for slaves, who fed the Cairo luxury market, the state army and the expanding cotton fields of the delta, formed a major facet of the Sudanese conquest. On the frontiers, armed merchants, the 'Khartoumers', led countless expeditions searching for elephants and men.

The ambitious Cairo authorities looked as well at the region of the Horn, establishing several coastal bases and penetrating the Ethiopian plateau on a number of occasions. In 1875–6 the financially over-extended Egyptians launched an ill-fated, three-pronged invasion of Ethiopia which failed disastrously. If the mercantile forces emanating ultimately from industrialising Europe were the motor pressing Egypt forward into Africa, the ambitions of the Egyptian state lacked a solid economic basis in empire or elsewhere. Instead, grandiose imperial dreams led to grandiose expenses that helped to bankrupt Muhammad Ali's successors.

The third African power to emerge in a kind of pre-partition of eastern Africa was the Ethiopian monarchy. In mid-century a nobleman-bandit named Kassa took the throne as Emperor Tewodros (Theodore) and essayed the recreation of a unified imperial power in the highlands with an unprecedented importation of firearms. Tewodros failed to control the strong centripetal tendencies that worked against monarchy in Ethiopia. His inept dealings with Europeans led to the imprisonment of missionaries and others at Meqdela (Magdala) fortress, their rescue by the British Napier expedition in 1868 which met with little resistance from Ethiopians, and the emperor's suicide.

However, Tewodros had successors who followed his efforts to base a new power in Ethiopia on firearms and a partly remodelled state apparatus. One was the great Northern lord, the Tigrean who took the throne-name of Yohannis (John) IV and achieved wide acceptance in the northern and central highlands as emperor after his coronation in 1872. His principal rival was the ruler of Shewa, Sahle Silasse, and Sahle's heir, Minilik. Shewa was so well-situated, on the one hand for the firearms trade to the coast, and, on the other hand for commerce with the south (from whence slaves, ivory and coffee could be procured), that in the long term it made a more logical pivot to the new empire that would in time share in the imperialist partition of Africa.

Up to a point, another major beneficiary of the new forces operating in Africa was the kingdom of Imerina, which acquired control of most of the island of Madagascar in the late eighteenth and early nineteenth centuries under its rulers Andrianampoinimerina ('my paddy fields stretch to the sea') and his successor Radama I, who used commerce to acquire guns. A major slaving power, Imerina agreed to cease participation in the maritime slave trade while continuing to raid on the island for its own purposes. It was not only slaves who were put to work for the kings and queens of Madagascar. Intensive labour requirements foisted on the mass of commoners led to the diffusion of irrigated rice paddies where suitable and (for a time) to the development of an industrial base which could produce armaments as well as allow for a large standing army to be created. For a significant phase, the Imerina state opted to isolate itself from most contacts with Europe while trying to continue a partial economic modernisation. At its peak, the kingdom of Madagascar had diplomatic relations with a number of European powers and accepted Protestantism as the state religion. Yet fear of imperial conquest always prevented the development of a modern transport system, notably over the escarpment from the ports of the east coast to the royal capital of Antananarivo. Internal tensions inherent in its incomplete modernisation coupled with the declining ability of Malagasy rulers to balance the hungry ambitions of different European powers led to the state being seriously crippled in a war with the French in 1883–85 and finally to its conquest in 1896.

In the conditions of eastern Africa the characteristic results of the age of legitimate trade were both the expanding African empires of Zanzibar, Egypt and Ethiopia and the predatory new state creations of Mirambo, Tippu Tip and their like. Existing states experienced variable fates. Buganda was at first strengthened by the sweep of new commercial forces after 1850. The great powers of the *kabaka* could only be enhanced by the possibilities of firearms and the sale of ivory. Yet, it can be argued from hindsight, social forces within the ruling class were beginning to consider action aimed at freedom from royal control, based on the new contacts with outside. In Bulozi, on the Zambesi floodplain, the expansion of commerce in the second half of the nineteenth century enabled the *litunga* to strengthen and greatly expand slavery, allowing for state-based water control works that in turn formed the basis for a much more rigid and harshly articulated class society than any known before.

It might be expected that the well-established states of West Africa would be more likely to absorb the press of commerce to themselves with their ruling aristocracies and kings best fit to take advantage of opportunities for new wealth. It has been claimed, for instance, that Asante handily enough adjusted the focus of its trade from slaves sent south to kola nuts sent north. No great new empires that can be linked closely to the changing economic developments paralleled the scale of Asante, Oyo or Benin. One major forest state, Oyo, collapsed in the 1820s as a result of internal revolt, slave risings and the pressure of the *jihad* in the north. Over the next seventy years various new political units arose in the territory of old Oyo and tried to seize its mantel, but none succeeded. The issue of access to Western arms, which largely meant access to the lagoon port of Lagos, often determined the balance of power in the lengthy series of wars that raged through Yoruba-speaking lands. Each contender depended on Saros and other contacts in Lagos to procure arms.

## The Era of Informal Empire

The first seventy years of the nineteenth century witnessed significant, but still very limited, extension of actual European colonial power in Africa. It has been called the period of 'informal empire', particularly on the part of Britain, whose commercial ascendancy in the overseas trade of Africa became more and more marked. So long as trade expanded satisfactorily under existing conditions there was little reason for Western regimes to plan military expeditions and colonial adventures that cost money and were unlikely to yield immediate results of any profit.

On the east coast the British consul in Zanzibar watched discreetly over British interests and the general conduct of commerce. The abolition of the slave trade in Zanzibar in 1873 was due largely to British pressure. In the Egyptian empire European influence became ever more important: Europeans in the service of the government were among the highest civil and military officials in the conquered areas south of the Sahara. But before 1870 the different nationalities tended to cancel out one another's influence.

A parliamentary select committee in 1865 virtually called for the complete withdrawal of the British state from West Africa, following the demise of the Atlantic slave trade. This commission, however, which envisioned a continued role for traders and missionaries of compradore background, took place at a period of particularly striking downturn in the palm-oil trade when there was good, if short-term, reason for commercial pessimism. Its recommendations were almost entirely ignored.

In fact throughout this period both Britain and France tended gradually to increase their stake in Africa. The era was one of exploration, so much of which consisted of probing for commercial and political information. In West Africa Europeans discovered the course of the Niger and made direct contact with the savanna states. By 1870 the sources of the Nile were known and the mountains and lakes of East Africa seen by Europeans. The one great mystery remaining was the character of the central equatorial basin and the course of the Congo, which Stanley would solve soon afterwards.

Colonial expansion consisted largely in the seizure of points here and there along the coast which appeared most appropriate for controlling long-distance commerce, often under the cover of suppressing the slave trade. Like wary wrestlers, agents of European states sought out pressure points that could be used to lay effective hold on the trade of the African interior. In addition to Sierra Leone the British established themselves at the mouth of the Gambia (Bathurst, founded 1816) and, in 1851, on Lagos island, ideally situated to tap the commerce of Dahomey and Yorubaland. British political influence rose steadily along the Gold Coast where the old forts were directly ruled by the state again from 1850, after a period of purely merchant control. In the Niger delta British treaties allowed increasing intervention in the political and commercial affairs of treaty-signing states. This was the most productive palm-oil export zone of all and British traders began to dream, once the course of the river was known, of the possibility of direct commerce with the interior. This was anathema to the whole middleman character of the delta ruling class and their dependents, but despite all their efforts steamships began to penetrate up the Niger (after the Baikie expedition of 1854) and then the Benue and to establish, towards the end of this period, permanent commercial relations with the southernmost *jihad* emirates yielding allegiance to Sokoto. Equivalent French finger-holds were established at Grand Bassam and Assinie on the Ivory Coast and at Libreville in Gabon. More solid was the foundation in the 1850s of a territorially extensive colony in Senegal. After the retrocession of St Louis, at the mouth of the Senegal River, to the French by the British following Napoleon's defeat, Baron Roger became the soul of a French attempt to establish a slave-based plantation colony in the valley of the Senegal River, an attempt which proved premature historically. Moorish raids, the inability to control a labour force and inept administration led to the collapse of the plantations after several years. The Roger initiative indicates the depth of French commitment to Senegal and its historic use as a precedent in capitalist penetration for West Africa.

In the 1850s, under the energetic leadership of General Louis Faidherbe (governor 1854–61, 1863–5), the French pursued a deliberate policy of expansion as a means of building commercial prosperity. Cape Vert, on which was built the new town of Dakar, the Petite Côte (Little Coast) to the south and the kingdom of Waalo behind St Louis were annexed directly to the French Empire, which already had another base of territorial control on the African continent in Algeria on the Mediterranean. The French decisively beat the most energetic *jihad*-leader of the region, al hajj Umar, at the battle of Medina in 1858, and he turned back towards the east to found his new state. French power was applied systematically to prevent the formation of a hegemonic Islamic power in the Senegambian region. By 1870, with greatly increased commercial interests and knowledge of Africa, with potential available armies of cheaply paid Africans, improved arms and awareness of how to cope with tropical health conditions, the conquest of Africa by Europeans, if not inevitable or predictable for the immediate future, was no longer impossible.

## South Africa in the Age of the Great Trek

In the extreme south of Africa colonial expansion had already reached a significant stage before the nineteenth century. The expansion of the exchange economy and capitalist productive forces had generated a complex class society at the Cape. In 1806 the last Dutch government at Cape

Map 2. Nineteenth-century Africa

Town surrendered to a British army. The British had already occupied the Cape for several years previously (1795–1803), but were now determined, for strategic purposes, to retain the colony. Thus the Cape came to be situated within the context of a far more dynamic economic system than that of the Dutch. Within a very short time British merchants dominated commerce at the Cape.

The principal goal of the Cape's new rulers was to establish a basis for progressive prosperity on capitalist lines to the advantage of Britain. This involved finding a commodity for the world market which could be produced locally. At first Cape wine exports prospered, thanks to admission without tariff payments into Britain, but they suffered from the gradual imposition of free-trade regulations on wine. Only in the 1830s did the eastern Cape begin to export wool on a significant scale, beginning a twenty-year boom that at last made the colonial South African economy modestly viable, allowing for transport improvement and giving a capital value to pastoral land.

The government was anxious to eliminate slavery and establish a free labour market, yet social stability at the Cape rested on the position of land-owning slave-holders who stood to lose most of their capital in the wake of slave emancipation. A succession of laws shifted back and forth between more and less coercive solutions to the problem of labour control (Hottentot Proclamation of 1809, Ordinance 50 of 1828, abolition of slavery of 1833), while the community of masters became mistrustful. Although fearful of consequent military involvements leading to unremunerative expenditure and unknown political consequences, the British army intervened with increasing decisiveness to secure proclaimed frontiers and push back the Xhosa in the east from the regions where *trekboers* had established farms. This was insufficient to solve the needs of the pastoral economy. Frontier districts became overpopulated while the state appeared to threaten the basis of farmers' control over labour, especially those too poor to procure workers through competitive wages.

Between 1795 and 1815 frontier farmers engaged in several rebellions against the Dutch and British colonial government. The last of these – the Slagters Nek rebellion – was the most easily quelled. Direct resistance to the British appeared hopeless. Instead scouts began to explore the possibilities of a leap beyond the colonial frontier to the north. The *Mfecane*, clearing populations off fertile areas which could serve as corridors for armies, greatly increased prospects of success.

In 1834 the first parties of some 10 000 emigrants initiated the Great Trek from the colony, establishing themselves through much of what has become the Republic of South Africa. This is not to say that, despite the advantage of firearms, the trekkers instantly conquered all the Africans of the region, but they did succeed in winning several crucial military victories that allowed for the establishment of zones where they controlled land and a limited amount of local labour. Throughout this period hunting, trading and transport-riding remained very important in the trekker economy, perhaps more so than farming and stock-herding, especially north of the river Vaal. Only in the 1860s did the political centres there consolidate into one South African Republic. Even then the most northerly section, the Zoutpansberg, had to be abandoned with the revival of a powerful Pedi state. South of the Vaal, after 1852, the British acknowledged the independence of the Orange Free State, smaller, more compact and more commercially integrated with the Cape.

In one area, Natal, the trekkers were pursued and beaten back by British expansion. The trek to Natal put the emigrants directly in conflict with the Zulu state. After the Zulu massacre of an advance party, the trekkers won revenge at the battle of Blood River in 1838. The British feared both regional destabilisation and rival overseas links that the trekkers could establish on their newly-acquired sea coast. An imperial force defeated the trekkers of Natal in 1842 and the territory became a second British South African colony.

By mid-century South Africa was the scene of several colonial or colonially derived societies with somewhat different economic and social forces in ascendence, depending on the strength of capital penetration. British merchant capital in South Africa held the Cape as its base with its ports and nascent finance facilities. In 1853 a constitution vested powers of self-government in an assembly elected on the basis of a low property qualification and no racial discrimination. The patronage that white politicians and merchants established over black wage-workers and farmers laid the foundation of 'Cape liberalism'. In the eastern Cape a prosperous class of labour-employing, plough-using, market-orientated black peasantry responded strongly to the advance of the market and accepted white merchants and professional men as political representatives; the successful amongst them were still able to call on the labour of extended families, although poorer families were more likely to be producing simply in order to pay their tax and survive. Cape society was the strongest of the colonial and colonially-derived states in relation to its African neighbours and it had a moderate basis of agricultural prosperity in wool.

Towards the end of its heyday the Cape liberal outlook was expressed graphically by one of its leading spokesmen in the Cape, John X. Merriman:

The Cape ministry are not, as you know, Solomons; but they do heartily oppose and detest Mr. Froude's and Lord Carnarvon's native policy. We are gradually educating the natives. We are introducing individual tenure of land and European implements. We have four thousand natives at work on our Railways. Gradually the power of the Chiefs is being broken up, and our laws introduced, and I hope this session to get a measure for the modified municipal government of locations. Lovedale has three hundred native boys and seventy girls, very many of whom pay for their own education...They learn trades and...may earn forty shillings a week as printers.[6]

Natal was a vastly weaker unit, particularly as measured against its Zulu neighbour to the north. In Natal, settlers (mainly from Britain) struggled to find a profitable basis for economic exploitation. Much land became tied up in speculative ventures orientated in fact towards the collection of tribute or cash from African peasants, at least until a higher level of capitalisation could be achieved. In the 1850s it became apparent that there was a future for sugar plantations along the coast, but the settlers lacked the coercive power to obtain African labour under plantation conditions at low wages. They turned to indentured labourers from India, who began to arrive in 1860 and made the fortunes of the lowland sugar planters. The Natal system had no room for the ideal of a liberal society; in theory a non-racial franchise was evolved but in practice, the Natal vote from its creation in 1856 was a white vote. Natal controlled extensive and populous African 'locations', upon which pressure could be exerted to draw labour and cash, a system associated with Theophilus Shepstone, Secretary of Native Affairs (1845–76) and self-proclaimed Great White Chief of the Natal Zulu. The South African historian David Welsh has argued that if a model of segregation in later South African society existed, it lay in Natal, a theme recently taken up by Mahmood Mamdani looking for a historic model of rural colonial administration in Africa. The weakness of colonialism in Natal encouraged the cult of African 'tradition', sustaining a system of indirect rule through the chiefs and extracting small amounts of labour and goods from African farmers through the modest application of force that was systematically feasible.[7]

The trekker states, and especially the South African Republic, were yet slower to acquire commercial coherence. The newcomers awarded themselves huge landed estates, but their control over local labour, now officially considered to be squatting on private property, was more nominal than real. African squatters provided little labour and less cash to landlords, who in turn found the establishment of commercial agriculture a difficult process. Among the trekkers acute distinctions between rich and poor developed fairly quickly. A small class of notables whose commercial linkages gave them command over labourers and firearms dominated trekker society.

Within all these formations and well beyond their borders some Africans turned with alacrity to new economic possibilities created by the penetration of commodity relations. In the eastern Cape, Natal and else-where, petty accumulators sprang up as a class among African cultivators and supplied much of the agricultural surplus of the colonies. It was often such farmers who were enthusiastic propagators of mission Christianity. From the 1850s the first African professional men returned to the Cape from Britain, contemporaries of an equivalent generation of West African coastal compradores.

Some of the extension of wage-labour represented immigration and proletarianisation. In this category belonged the less fortunate *Mfecane* refugees of the eastern Cape, or Mfengu, who remained farm labourers, together with Xhosa ruined by the takeover of land or the destruction of stock commanded by the prophetic movement known as the cattle killing, in 1857. This does not entirely explain the spread of migrant labour in southern Africa, however. Initially wage-labour could be quite advanta-geous to the worker, Mfengu included, who might return home with shotgun and cattle and supply the bridewealth that would enable him to found a new homestead.

By the 1860s migrants were coming to the Cape in large numbers from as far as the Pedi state in the north of the claimed territory of the South African Republic and what is today southern Mozambique. While major African states such as Lesotho, the Zulu kingdom, the Pedi state and others retained political independence quite effectively and were if any-thing a threat to their colonial neighbours, rather than the other way around, exchange relations connecting Africans into circuits that ulti-mately linked back through the Cape to Europe had achieved a remark-able importance even beyond colonial frontiers.

On a much smaller, but still significant scale, capitalist forces encour-aged new social relationships in Angola. The fishing fleets off the coast of southern Angola as well as the thriving coffee estates of Cazengo, inland from Luanda, depended heavily on slavery, which remained legal under the Portuguese flag until the 1870s. From the slave trade era a small class of local capitalists, of varying racial origin but including an important number of both mulattos and Africans, arose. Inland the rapid extension from mid-century of the ivory and then the rubber frontiers brought advantages to two trading peoples, the Chokwe of the interior, who absorbed vast numbers of slaves, and the Ovimbundu of the central highlands, intermediaries *par excellence* in 'legitimate commerce' between the Portuguese on the coast and the interior peoples. They forged an identity as trading peoples that may be readily compared with the Nyam-wezi and Kamba across the continent.

Southern Africa provides the most complex and far-reaching examples of class formation and economic change brought about through the extension of trade in nineteenth-century Africa, an extension that reached widely indeed. Through the century African ruling classes expanded their interests in the acquisition of commodities they could not produce through a social order increasingly dependent on firearms and trade goods. Defence and exchange goods equally must have extended their significance for the mass of cultivators.

However, there is little reason to think that this era brought about a correction to the direction of change and the abuses of the slave trade. To accept this is largely to accept the propaganda of the old 'humanitarian' imperialist lobbies. The magnetic attraction of commercial enterprise to Africans did not often lead to change in the social and technical relations of production. This seems characteristic of merchant capital, based as it is on the interstices between productive systems, in exchange. Nineteenth-century Europe was industrialising rapidly, but in its relations with Africa the form and impact of merchant capital remained little changed. By mid-century, cheap, industrially produced cotton goods from Europe were reaching so remote a region from the sea as the central savanna of West Africa in large quantities across the Sahara, but it is not at all clear that any new political or social consequences ensued. In fact, this chapter has undoubtedly exaggerated such consequences by generalising from those zones where they were notably significant. In consequence, the real meaning of 'legitimate commerce' for the African continent lay in an intensification of social and economic processes already initiated in the slaving era.

## Notes

1. This approach to abolition is influenced by the ideas of Frederick Cooper, who has himself used the work of David Brion Davis, *The Problem of Slavery in the Age of Revolution* (Cornell University Press, 1975).
2. The figures are from David Northrup, 'The Compatibility of the Slave and Legitimate Trades in the Bight of Biafra', *JAH*, XVII (1976).
3. A. G. Hopkins, *Economic History of West Africa* (Longman, 1973), p. 128.
4. Cited by Susan Kaplow, 'The Mudfish and the Crocodile: Under-development of a West African Bourgeoisie', *SS*, XLI (1977), p. 318.
5. See the case-study by Agneta Pallinder-Law, 'Aborted Modernization in West Africa? The Case of Abeokuta', *JAH*, XV (1974).

6. From Stanley Trapido, 'The Friends of the Natives; Merchants, Peasants and the Political and Ideological Structure of Liberalism at the Cape 1854–1910' in Shula Marks and Anthony Atmore, eds, *Economy and Society in Pre-Industrial South Africa* (Longman, 1980), p. 254.
7. David Welsh, *The Roots of Segregation: Native Policy in Colonial Natal 1845–1910* (Oxford University Press, 1970).

# 5

# THE CONQUEST OF AFRICA

'But as for us, our Lord is Allah, our Creator and Possessor. We take what our Prophet Muhammad, (upon him be peace) brought to us.'

> Abd-al-Rahman, Caliph at Sokoto to the Royal Niger Company, ?1900, in R.A. Adeleye, *Power and Diplomacy in Northern Nigeria* (Longman, 1971), p. 335

'If I were received by the Queen . . . nobody would ever think of attacking me.'

> Moshoeshoe of Lesotho, in Peter Sanders, *Moshoeshoe, Chief of the Sotho* (Heinemann, 1975), p. 318

'One thing only has checked the development of these rich regions – native misrule.'

> A.F. Mockler-Ferryman, 'British Nigeria', *JAS*, II (1902), p. 169

## Imperialism: Theory and Practice

Within the last quarter of the nineteenth century the slow process of European political penetration of the African continent gave way to a scramble for colonies that resulted in a partition of all the lands south of the Sahara apart from the Republic of Liberia and Ethiopia. A materialist assessment of imperial conquest will necessarily consider how this process related to the contradictions within capitalist economy and society in

73

Europe as well as events in Africa. For more than sixty years the terrain of discussion has been dominated by one long pamphlet, *Imperialism, the Highest Stage of Capitalism*, written during World War I by the leading figure of the Russian Revolution, Vladimir Ilyich Lenin.

As the title suggests Lenin considered that capitalism had advanced in the late nineteenth century into a qualitatively distinct phase of development through the formation of national oligopolies, particularly in the heavy industries such as coal and steel and in the most rapidly industrialising countries like Germany and the USA. This followed logically from processes of concentration and centralisation of capital about which Marx had already written when they were in an early stage. All intelligent commentators of the world scene knew this, but many believed that concentration would lead in turn to an internationally interlocked and pacifist-minded capitalist class, increasingly uninterested in war or aggressive competition. Lenin disagreed: the monopoly stage did not bring about an end to capitalist competition. Rather it placed competition on a ruthless and gigantic scale in which the monopolies could harness the apparatus of militarised states to enforce their demands.

The trend towards monopoly dovetailed with Marx's predicted decline in the rate of profit within the industrialised capitalist states. Finance, unable to find profitable outlets for investment at home, required in order to survive new overseas outlets which could be guaranteed only through the economic and political conquest of hitherto non-capitalist societies elsewhere in the world. Lenin realised that there was a wide range of economic advantages potentially accruing to expanding imperialist states in this era. It included the creation of privileged markets through tariff barriers for national monopolies; the extension of trade and the acquisition of raw materials such as rubber and tin for new industries. He gave pride of place, however, to the imperative of investment outlets, following in this respect the arguments of the English anti-imperialist social reformer, John Hobson.

One result was the partition and threatened re-partition of the world by the great powers. Propagandists pressed forward imperialism as an idea through chauvinist slogans which won over the support of a 'labour aristocracy', a sector within the working class who thrived on imperialism and formed its principal domestic prop. Imperialists demanded armaments and pressed national regimes in Europe from crisis to crisis, leading ultimately to the catastrophic World War I.

Lenin's analysis was exaggeratedly compressed; he aimed at fitting together all the principal phenomena of his time into one clear-cut statement about imperialism. If he had a focus historically it was the question of the causes of World War I. The partition of Africa was incidental to his treatment. His analysis combined a Marxist framework with ideas plucked from bourgeois reformers and pacifists such as Hobson.

Hobson had expressed only admiration for genuine capitalist entrepreneurs and feared that the new dominance of the banks and investment interests was destroying wholesome capitalism in Europe. What Hobson deplored were 'coupon-clippers', the class of shareholders who could live in idleness off their investments and pressurise the state to act in their interests abroad. In his work *Imperialism*, written in direct reaction to the Boer War, Hobson painted an artistically compelling portrait of capitalism gone soft and decadent. Lenin was contemptuous of Hobson's hopes for capitalist reform, but seized gladly upon his ill-defined notion of decadence and parasitism.

Some elements of Lenin's synthesis, such as his theory of a labour aristocracy and the origins of the war, require a critique elsewhere than in these pages. Here discussion will be confined to those aspects of his analysis relevant to the history of Africa. Anti-Marxist writers often attack Lenin (and by implication other Marxist writers) for exaggerating or inventing the economic side of imperialism. It is pointed out correctly that African trade never became crucial to European industry and that investment by capitalist firms in Africa (apart from South Africa) never developed very far. Lenin, it is claimed, ignored the non-economic motives which imperialists both in Europe and on the spot in Africa considered as justifying their own actions.

The thrust of this critique depends largely on a crude misreading of Lenin. Lenin appears from a few remarks in his pamphlet to have been quite aware of the inadequate treatment he had given the wider, non-economic context of imperialism. Imperialism was not simply a state economic strategy; it became a climate of opinion, linked to militarism, racism and nationalism, that blanketed Europe like a dark cloud. Mass right-wing movements emerged in the late nineteenth century among hard-pressed peasant proprietors and petty bourgeois who, unable to accept socialist ideas about class and property, turned to nationalism, racism and imperialism as a means of solving their problems. Leading elements nurtured imperialist ideology explicitly as part of a propaganda campaign to woo workers to their causes; state-school systems and the press endlessly reiterated patriotic and militarist rhetoric. For the German Empire the historian Hans-Ulrich Wehler has stressed that the imperialist banner was one under which an otherwise divided and internally antagonistic bourgeoisie could potentially be united by political brokers.

The new 'scientific' racism, built around a vulgarised interpretation of Charles Darwin's theory of the survival of the fittest as the key mechanism in human (and biological) evolution, suffused European culture. Acceptance of supposed objectively defined 'races' as fundamental human categories became the common wisdom of Europe. Black 'Negroid' Africans were assigned virtually the lowest place on the human pecking order, fit only for rule by their white 'Caucasian' superiors. The white conquistadores of Africa viewed themselves as the possessors of racially and culturally superior ideas and behaviour patterns – bearers of a 'civilising mission' first and foremost – rather than economic exploiters. However, all this does not so much refute Lenin's assessment as amplify and enrich it.

Where Lenin erred was in his acceptance of Hobson's impressionistic and moralistic picture of capitalist decadence. From the vantage point of the 1990s it is clear that in 1915 capitalism was not on its last legs nor was it entering a 'final' stage. It would continue to know periods of great vitality and unprecedented expansion.

Most contemporary Marxists (and non-Marxist observers), however, agreed with Lenin and Hobson. The period of extended crisis that economic historians consider the great depression of the nineteenth century, extending from the 1870s to the 1890s, portended to be a final one for the capitalist system. N. I. Bukharin, on whose thinking about imperialism Lenin very much depended, saw imperial conquests as a consequence of a neo-mercantilist outlook. Rejecting the buoyant confidence in economic growth and free trade typical of the middle nineteenth century, the ruling class now held the grim conviction that the golden days of capitalist accumulation were over forever and that competition must henceforth be a struggle for advantage in a no-growth, zero-sum game. There was more than enough economic evidence pointing towards both Hobsonian decadence and Leninist catastrophism.[1]

However, in trying to explain the conquest of Africa by the European powers, the evidence suggests exactly the opposite, stressing the vitality and hunger for new spheres to appropriate by capital. Lenin underscored the link between overseas investment and imperialism. Africa received little of this investment before World War I, but it can be argued that conquest was part of the necessary process of creating social and political conditions under which capitalist investment would ultimately pay off. Such an argument follows readily from Marx's own view of the expansive and absorptive character of the capitalist mode of production and assumes fundamental continuities in capitalist development from the era of so-called free competition.

This is not to dismiss entirely that side of the scramble for Africa that stemmed from the intensified competition between economic rivals. The great depression of the 1870s brought about demands for protected markets and supplies while British dominance in world manufacture and export gave way to an effective challenge from Germany and the USA especially, with business turning ever more to the state for assistance in competition. But this tendency must be seen in conjunction with one that stemmed directly from conditions within Africa and the interaction between Western capitalist enterprise and pre-capitalist African societies.

As the previous chapter suggested, the volume of commerce between Africa and Europe had increased greatly during the middle decades of the nineteenth century, that era of cheap manufactured exports and expensive tropical imports. One result was the increasing importance of the trade to African societies and the greater diffusion of trade goods. Imported guns helped to forge entire new empires, like that of Samori Toure in the West African savanna or Tippu Tip on the upper Congo. The accessibility of weapons strengthened some ruling classes while challenging others. Never were the strata of middlemen who connected the trade-routes and linked African commerce to the coast more important.

Yet the extension of the new commerce made apparent to interested Europeans the barriers ahead before new qualitative advances could be reached. Europeans had to contend with paying off networks of middlemen and helping to sustain ruling classes and merchants who skimmed off profits and increased the price of commodities. States fought wars to increase their territory and command over labour, a tiresome impediment to commerce that often blocked important trade-routes. Abolition of the slave trade had failed to bring about the attenuation of African slavery which was held to stultify economic initiative and to cause warfare and social instability. Thus African society badly needed reform in order for the ambitions of Western commerce to be realised. Governments were required which could smash the power of ruling classes, construct telegraph lines and railways, impose uniformly peaceful conditions and permit coastal traders direct access to free peasant producers.

Colonial advocates often spoke of the need to 'open up' Africa, to protect the roads into the interior and to circumvent the middlemen. The trade depression of the early 1870s made this vision of Africa an increasingly urgent one. As oil prices fell, creditors foreclosed on coastal merchants and steamship lines undercut shippers; tensions mounted in West Africa. Cowrie and other local currencies suffered from an intensifying devaluation compared with European coin. The result, to borrow A. G. Hopkins' phrase, was a destabilisation of political as well as economic and social relations. The ensuing political crises contained a logic of their own which invited military intervention in response to the clamour of both local and European commercial interests. In the countries which traded most with Africa – Britain, France and Germany – the chambers of commerce of such major business centres as Liverpool, Manchester, Lyon and Hamburg demanded the extension of direct control to growing parts of the world outside Europe.

Special conditions in South Africa made the urge for intervention uniquely compelling. From 1867 the discovery of minerals brought to the fore the question not merely of trade, but of capitalist production. The British Union Jack flew ever further in the southern African interior in response to capitalist demands for creating social conditions favourable to cheap and efficient large-scale mineral production. Once colonial rule was established production-related imperatives were increasingly crucial to the policy of the new regimes throughout the continent.

Late nineteenth-century imperial conquest can be related also to other aspects of what the American economic historian, David Landes, has dubbed the Second Industrial Revolution. The capitalist quest for raw materials, of which a bigger range were needed in more quantity than ever, enhanced interest in the tropics. New technology immeasurably cheapened the cost of expansion and conquest in Africa. Medical discoveries enabled Europeans to live there far more safely, avoiding the sacrifice in lives so typical of early attempts at colonisation. Precision arms, which in turn depended on advances in the European machine-tool industry, presented European-led armies with an enormous new advantage over Africans. When they took elementary tactical and strategic precautions tightly formed 'squares' of troops so armed could easily mow down infantry or cavalry charges aimed at them from so far away that they were virtually invulnerable.

It was significant too that the commercial expansion of the era of legitimate trade had as one by-product the rise of European-controlled armies of African troops prepared to fight for small wages and the prospect of loot. By the 1870s the so-called Hausa troops, ancestral to the West African Frontier Force and the French *tirailleurs sénégalais*, or Senegalese sharpshooters, were well in formation. They and other African

forces spared European governments the expense and political complexities contingent on the dispatch of European armies overseas.

The relative cheapness of expansion allowed European officers in
Africa, avid for glory and promotions, room for considerable initiative
and permitted the conquest of many regions whose commercial appeal
was severely limited. The scramble thus proceeded with a speed and a
geographic spread that went far beyond the boundaries which can be
directly explained by crisis in existing trade relations. Yet the need to
expand these relations provided a solid economic base for the diplomatic,
political and strategic aspects of the scramble.

This helps to elucidate one obviously central fact of the conquest. It was
Britain and France, with their long-established vested interests in Africa,
who although least affected by the global tendencies towards industrial
monopolisation and capital concentration among the major Western
powers, took the lion's share of Africa.[2] In addition it underscores a
dimension which African nationalists have long pointed out: the Partition
had a strong co-operative and collaborative side to it, symbolised by the
handshake over new African boundaries at European conference tables.
For all serious capitalist interests, occupation by some efficient colonial
power, if one's own regime was not able to assume control, was better than
none. In this regard it is noteworthy that, despite much fighting talk, no
European state went to war with another during the scramble era over a
favoured chunk of Africa.[3]

## The Build-up to Conquest

During the 1870s several significant manoeuvres in West Africa projected
colonial build-up. They occurred in just those zones where commercial
relations with Europe were most developed. On the Gold Coast the forts
controlled by the Dutch and the British (the Danes having sold out in 1850)
were rationalised geographically by agreement in 1867. This introduced a
period of uncertainty as old alliances, commercial and political, were called
into question. Asante had preferred to establish links with the Dutch rather
than the British and was especially concerned. When complete withdrawal
by the Dutch began to be considered, the old dream of achieving hegemony over the coast seized the imagination of the Asante court.

Those westerly coastal states which most resented the sudden imposition of Dutch hegemony were instrumental in forming the Fante

Confederation in 1868. In part the confederation aimed at meeting the threat of the Dutch and of Asante, but it represented as well the political aspirations of the compradore merchants and chiefs of the Gold Coast. They conceived of the confederation as the bare bones of a Western-type state that would promote English education, road construction and commerce with a unified legal code, military force and political representation beneficial to the Anglicised merchants of the coastal towns. Despite the name a number of non-Fante communities belonged to the confederation.

The weakness of the compradore stratum, which failed to organise an efficient fighting force or systematic revenue collection, brought about the collapse of the confederation after several years. Yet it was also subverted by British hostility. The British, for the first time, preferred to cut out the compradores from any potential role as a national bourgeosie and to deal directly with the chiefs. As the Fante Confederation collapsed, British political involvement on the Gold Coast increased. In 1871 the Dutch were bought out of the western forts. Asante threatened to restore its old hegemony over most of the coast. The British were not prepared to tolerate such a development and organised an invasion expedition. This resulted not only in a decisive British victory, but in profoundly destabilising the Asante state. Effective alliances were made with various previously subordinate rulers who now refused to support the Asantehene. Some had been enriched and strengthened by the new direction and volume of 'legitimate' trade over the past half-century. The sack of Kumasi in 1874 heralded the end of the Asante Confederacy, cutting it off from the coast and depriving it of all its tributaries. Its authority now extended only some thirty to fifty miles from Kumasi. Shortly afterwards the Crown annexed the coastal territories as the Gold Coast Colony.

Some two years later the arrival of Colonel Brière de l'Isle as governor of the French colony of Senegal marked a radical new advance movement in the region where French commerce predominated. The French systematically developed a policy of transport and communications deployment: the construction of a railway from St Louis to the new port of Dakar through Cayor (which was essential for the expansion of ground-nut production and export), and of a telegraph line to Futa Toro in the interior valley of the Senegal and, most ambitiously, the extension of the railway to the upper Niger. The French move into the interior followed the great trade routes along which slave caravans had made their way.

For Brière de l'Isle and his henchmen, African rulers were so many impediments to the extension of a commercially viable French empire.

Their taxes and marauding armies prevented the realisation of a great potential surplus production from the peasantry and their rule stood in the way of the establishment of the necessary transport network. Lat Dyor, the Damel of Cayor, formerly dependent on the French for his power, at first agreed to the laying of the railway but then reneged as he came to realise that the old forms of social authority might not long survive its construction. Through the early 1880s he harassed the French forces with guerrilla warfare that represented a major phase of the wars of conquest in Senegal.

By this time, however, expansion into the interior had proceeded apace. In 1883 the advanced military stood at Bamako on the Niger, poised to wage a major attack on the Tukulor empire founded by al hajj Umar that controlled most of the western half of the modern republic of Mali. French expansion had come under the virtually autonomous direction of military officers who conceived of an unlimited strategically orientated expansion all the way across West Africa to Lake Chad, linking the Sahara with French Algeria. From a business standpoint there was little to recommend colonial expansion into ever more thinly peopled and barren regions. Indeed, as the advance columns were increasingly forced to live off the newly conquered, they became brutal and rapacious marauding bands.

The third great region of commercial interest to Europe on the West African littoral, together with Senegambia and the Gold Coast, was the Niger delta, the heartland of the palm-oil trade. The delta experienced an intense version of the pressures caused by profits squeeze and new technological development in Europe. The arrival of the steamship allowed new firms entry into the area through buying cargo space and thus threatening old arrangements and trade-share agreements. It was a British entrepreneur, George Goldie, who, through fair means and foul, succeeded in amalgamating firms and eliminating rivals to create the United Africa Company in 1879. He was particularly concerned to drive out of the area new French arrivals. By 1884 the delta trade had become a virtual monopoly with Goldie an increasing political as well as economic force.

Hundreds of miles further to the south lay the mouth of that other great river flowing into the Atlantic, the Congo. This region experienced a rapidly growing trade in palm oil, ivory and wild rubber which, by the late 1870s, was beginning to approach the value of the trade of the Niger delta. Yet Europeans knew almost nothing of the interior beyond the river rapids not far inland until Stanley descended the Congo from the east to reach the coast in 1875, successfully crossing central Africa from shore to shore. He revealed to the West the existence of a vast navigable river system through which the equatorial forest could be penetrated and the trade middlemen who controlled stretches of the water could be circumvented and subordinated. Here was a potentially wealthy no man's land to attract capitalist cupidity.

The British had dominated overseas trade of the Congo region but they were never to establish colonies here. Instead Leopold II, king of the Belgians, who had devoted his energies and fortune to a feverish world search for an appropriate colonial sphere to carve out and eventually transfer to the Belgian state, successfully made it the focus of his attention, thus ensuring the European continent's first industrialised country its long-term place in the sun. The initial indifference of the Belgian bourgeoisie, coupled with the presumed jealousy of the British, stimulated the king to try a complex con trick. In 1876 he formed an International Association supposedly dedicated to opening up the Congo Basin to the benefits of free trade for all. Aware of the importance of British benevolence, or at least neutrality, he won or bought to his side the services of many figures on the British imperial scene, including Stanley himself and the British missionaries already active in the Lower Congo.

Seeing through Leopold's schemes, but unwilling to advance into the interior, the British government chose to support Portugal's shadowy rival claims to the area. Portuguese expansion in Africa was pursued fitfully and with more or less through the nineteenth century. The very economic weakness of the Portuguese bourgeoisie, given its old ties to, and knowledge of, the African trade lent a particular practical weight to imperial expansion creating a sphere of commercial monopoly. Britain was inclined to favour the claims of this backward state because British commercial influence was strong in Portugal.

However, for those Britons who took the promise of a commercialised Congo seriously, the extension of Portuguese control, with its tolerance of slaving and its protectionist customs barriers, was entirely unwelcome. Within the interested sectors of the British bourgeoisie, Leopold could count on support as an alternative to Portugal. Leopold had as well to count on the French factor. An Italian in the French service, de Brazza, had travelled overland to the Congo from the French trading posts in Gabon to the site of modern Brazzaville, and the treaties he signed, particularly the 'Makoko treaty' with a Teke ruler, were ratified by the French Chamber of Deputies in 1882. As Leopold realised, this placed the question of a political partition directly to the fore and his Association was now reconstituted as a framework for the 'Congo Free State'. With the advancing claims of France, Leopold and Portugal, the characteristic pattern of the scramble began to emerge.

The next major crisis began in Egypt in 1882. The 'Urabi movement, which overthrew the Egyptian ministry and was linked to massive riots against Westerners in Alexandria, was a classic response to one of the most important destabilising consequences of the great depression. Egypt's cotton production, its strategic location *vis-à-vis* both the eastern Mediterranean and the Suez Canal and the general scale of Western business interests involved, made its future a matter of great concern to the European countries. It was Britain who moved in alone to establish effective control over Egypt, a control which would bring great economic and strategic advantages although the policy of sole intervention was not at first intended. As a result the other European states were encouraged to make moves on the chess-board that would counter the new British advantage. So long as the British state was committed to some balance of powers arrangement in Europe, concessions were in order.

Egyptian intrusion into north-eastern Africa meant that the collapse of the Egyptian state had direct ramifications elsewhere. Parallel to the 'Urabi movement was the Mahdiyya movement in the Nilotic Sudan. From 1881 this movement of Islamic revival under a new prophet, or Mahdi, whose coming it was said Muhammad had predicted, aimed at the elimination of Egyptian control and swept from victory to victory leading to the fall of Khartoum, commanded by General Charles Gordon, an Englishman in Egyptian service, in 1885. For more than a decade the new Muslim commonwealth encountered no serious threat from any Western state. The British contented themselves with controlling effectively the desert approach to Egypt.

Further south, along the Red Sea coast, they were disposed to accept the new imperialist claims of Italy in place of Egypt. Italy seemed too weak to challenge British military or commercial interests. The real goal of Italian policy was domination over the highlands of Ethiopia and the first stage involved intrigue and arms sales to the most powerful Ethiopian provincial lords. It was with British complaisance also that in 1890 Italy established the colony of Somalia on the Benadir coast. If Italian intrusion into north-east Africa was not unwelcome to the British, there was a growing disquiet, still not leading to any definite policy, over European rivals' control of the valley of the Nile and its sources.

In 1884, Germany, a far more significant European power than Italy, suddenly entered the colonial scene. German capitalism had made giant strides forward and by the 1880s was becoming a more serious commercial and industrial rival to Britain than France. German business interests in various parts of Africa were growing rapidly, although nowhere predominant, and from the late 1860s the chambers of commerce of the major coastal ports began to demand colonies. In the past the German chancellor Bismarck had always found such demands pointless and unappealing.

Then towards 1884 he suddenly changed his mind. The Egyptian crisis appeared to create particularly favourable circumstances for the proclamation of colonies from the point of view of international rivalries. Political considerations seemed to make it advisable to do a favour for the commercial ports and manufacturing interests. Moreover there is considerable evidence that Bismarck, once a great proponent of free trade, had gradually come to the conclusion that Germany required the protected markets and raw materials which colonial barriers could create. Very discreetly he lent approval to several expeditions that set out for Africa to make treaties and hoist the flag. Within a few months the foundations were laid for the establishment of four German colonies in Africa – Togo, Cameroun, South-West Africa and East Africa (Tanganyika).

At this juncture Bismarck hosted a grand conference in Berlin which in 1884 considered the outstanding issues concerning Africa from the point of view of the main European regimes involved. The German move became a kind of model for the proclamation of protectorates and colonies that all the powers could recognise. To Portugal's discomfiture, Leopold's Free State won control over a vast region in Central Africa, while French claims north of the Congo River were recognised. The Rivers Congo and Niger were declared zones of free trade. Goldie's position on the latter ensured who would turn this to benefit. Scholars have disputed which of the events of the late 1870s and early 1880s actually set off the scramble for Africa, but nobody would deny that by the time the Berlin Conference broke off it was well under way.

### The Partition of Africa

The French conquered most of the territory of West Africa, establishing control over the interior savanna, the Sahara and three new coastal colonies: Guinea, the Ivory Coast and Dahomey. British West African policy, perhaps in response, also became more aggressive. French occupation deprived British stations on the Gambia and in Sierra Leone of an economically significant hinterland, but this mistake was not repeated further to the east. Goldie's company received a royal charter and proclaimed a protectorate over much of the Niger delta while the British state assumed control over the remainder. The coastal middlemen were forced into dependence upon the renamed and chartered Royal Niger Company. Attempts by the most prominent, Ja Ja (a former Brass slave who created his own state in Opobo), to organise palm-oil shipment direct to Europe in league with some of the Company's rivals, led to his seizure by treachery, and deportation in 1887. Company treaties gave a legal cover to further penetration within the Sokoto caliphate and the French agreed to accept a demarcation line which granted to the British what became Northern Nigeria.

Commercial interests were equally concerned to establish a viable economic hinterland for the British coastal port of Lagos. To this end the British engaged in a 'race for the Niger' to push back the French and preserve most of the Yoruba states as a British sphere of influence. In 1893 the Lagos regime provoked war with the most commercially effective Yoruba middlemen state, Ijebu, whose power was quickly smashed, an adventure that followed hard upon the French expedition to nearby Dahomey. As a result the British were able to secure as a colony the most populous region of West Africa, Nigeria. Simultaneously, pressure from Gold Coast commercial interests to destroy and annex Asante was becoming intense. It was the more attended by the state as the prospect of French moves in the area became likely. In 1896 the British found an excuse for war, Asante was conquered and the Gold Coast acquired a suitable hinterland.

Perhaps more surprising, given the relative weakness of developed economic interests, was the growing British commitment to intervention inland from the east coast of Africa. Two regions particularly fixated propagandist attention and ultimately became British colonies – Buganda on the shores of Lake Victoria and the lands west and south of Lake Malawi. In both cases Christian missionary penetration had begun in the 1870s and missionaries established strong lobbies to advocate new political arrangements that would further commerce with Europe and allow their own proselytising work to go ahead. In the powerful kingdom of Buganda, destabilisation took a unique form. Ambitious strata in the ruling class turned to the rival claims of Islam, Protestantism and Catholicism in their struggles against the throne. Buganda's purportedly strategic position on the headwaters of the White Nile may also have provoked intervention. In

1887 the British-sponsored International British East Africa Company established itself in Buganda and set up posts on the route inland. In 1890 Germany recognised a northern border for its new East African colony which acknowledged a British sphere of control in what became Kenya and Uganda.

Around Lake Malawi Scottish missionaries had established bases from the late 1870s among populations that had suffered raids from the *Mfecane*-derived Ngoni chiefs and from new, expanding state formations drawn into the commerce in ivory and slaves with the coast. The Portuguese controlled access to the sea via the Zambesi River. The missionaries saw them as a blight on Protestant commercial and religious influence. But it was only through the influence and money of Cecil Rhodes' British South Africa Company that the British government finally asserted control over the region after 1890, pushing aside Portuguese claims.

Through the 1890s control over the upper Nile became the great question of the partition for European rivals. Leopold was extremely anxious to push the borders of the Free State to a navigable section of the river. The French organised advances towards the Nile east from Lake Chad and west from the Red Sea with the partial collusion of Minilik, the Ethiopian emperor. It was this threat to the waters and the rear of Egypt that finally led to a gradual organised British advance against the Mahdist state. By the time the Marchand expedition planted a French flag at Fashoda in 1898, it was confronted with a large British army that had destroyed the strength of the Mahdists at Omdurman and was constructing a railway and telegraph system that efficiently linked the upper Nile to Egypt. The French were forced to withdraw while Leopold had to be satisfied with the lease of a small portion of land on the river. The British then controlled the entire Nile valley, apart from the source of the Blue Nile in Ethiopia.

The Ethiopian situation was unique. This was the only sub-Saharan state which succeeded in maintaining sovereign independence throughout the scramble. Indeed, Ethiopian expansion southwards has justifiably led to the conclusion that Minilik was himself a major participant in the imperialist advance. Even before he secured the throne of the whole country, Minilik had been most energetic in procuring modern arms, from the French and, ironically enough, the Italians. Through the 1890s Italian determination to subdue Ethiopia became increasingly clear and the British had effectively recognised their pretensions in the region. However, by 1896 Minilik was able to summon an immense army of perhaps 100 000 men with guns to meet an Italian military advance from coastal Eritrea. The Italians lacked seasoned local troops and made foolish tactical errors; the result was a spectacular victory for Minilik at the battle of Adwa. Italy was not prepared to continue the war and Minilik agreed to recognise Italian control over Eritrea, thus blocking his own advance to the sea. On this basis, and as a result of delicately balanced diplomatic strategies, the Ethiopian state was able to survive, an issue which will be pursued in another context below.

The greatest prize for European capitalism in all Africa was the southern section of the continent. The discovery of mineral deposits of great wealth in the South African interior represented a potentially strong asset to Britain but created complex problems of transport, supplies, organisation and, above all, labour control, which required an appropriate state apparatus to be solved to the satisfaction of capital. The expansion of diamond mining at Kimberley from 1867, attracting a vast array of fortune-seekers of all races who descended on the arid countryside north of the Orange River, immediately engendered a piecemeal imperial response. The British engineered land claims to justify the proclamation of Griqualand West, a territory that enclosed the diamond fields. In 1868 the kingdom of Lesotho was incorporated into the Cape Colony for fear that the Orange Free State Boers, who had just defeated it in war, might annex it.

Then piecemeal schemes gave way to grander dreams of amalgamation and control. These were particularly associated with Sir Theophilus Shepstone, the Natal Secretary of Native Affairs. The continued independence of the last strong African kingdoms of southern Africa, such as the Zulu state, prevented the satisfaction of expanding demands for labour. Shepstone felt that it was time for a reckoning with these states. Yet war with Zululand was beyond the capacities of Natal, while the South African Republic was unable to challenge the Pedi state within its claimed borders, the Zulu, or the Ndebele north of the Limpopo. For Shepstone and other would-be enlightened British labour managers, the marginal market economy of the Boer republics, concerned only to procure farm workers, militated even more than Natal's weakness against any efficient regional system.

Shepstone's influence on the Governor, Sir Bartle Frere, and the Colonial Secretary, Lord Carnarvon, helped bring about British intervention and annexation of the South African Republic in 1877. In the next years the dominant aspect of British policy lay in the subjugation of African states. The Pedi of the northern Transvaal were finally beaten and brought under control. War was provoked with the Zulu. The Zulu won a famous victory at Isandhlwana in 1879, but the British were determined to pursue their object and finally crushed Zulu resistance, exiling the king, Cetewayo. Zululand was broken up into thirteen separate chiefdoms, the strongest of which were controlled by notorious labour-recruitment agents. Following a brief restoration of Cetewayo under conditions that led to a civil war, a second abolition of the monarchy and the proclamation of a British protectorate followed in 1881.

Yet confederation failed. In 1881 the Boers north of the Vaal rose in rebellion and defeated a British force at Majuba. This, and the expense of the African wars, strengthened the hand of the Little Englanders in the British Liberal Party who had been dubious of the extravagant forward policy pursued by Carnarvon. W. E. Gladstone, who made successful political capital of the issue, returned to power in Britain and restored the South African Republic to independence on condition of a British veto over its foreign affairs.

The policy of retrocession was profoundly undercut by the discovery of gold within the territory of the South African Republic in 1886. If Kimberley destabilised the South African status quo, the imperatives demanded by the rise of the new city of Johannesburg, on the ridge of white water, the Witwatersrand, were shattering. The sheer scale of gold discovered was spectacular by any standard, an impressive Gold Rush ensued rapidly. As geologists and engineers set to work it became increasingly clear, moreover, that seams of gold, not very rich but extremely reliable, stretched enormous, deep-level distances, seams which could form the basis of a gigantic, long-term industry requiring both vast numbers of workers and capital investment.

As surely as though an earthquake had shifted the angle of the terrain, the centre of gravity in the political economy of southern Africa moved towards the Republic and the Rand. Within a few years Johannesburg had overtaken Cape Town as the largest city in the region. The Cape Colony, together with its weaker sister, Natal, could no longer serve as effective imperial instruments. The annexation of the Tswana chiefdoms west of the Republic and the establishment of the domain of the British South Africa Company north of the Limpopo in 1890 apparently hemmed in the Transvaal from three sides, but this was not necessarily sufficient to destroy its autonomous development. Men of talent and ambition from the Cape and Natal re-directed their interests and orientation to servicing the mining economy. The 'Cape Dutch' intelligentsia which had begun to emerge, perceiving the increasing contradiction between the republics and British imperialism, began to articulate an Afrikaner nationalism that crossed the existing frontiers and posed itself as an alternative to the imperial system. President Paul Kruger was determined to use the rapidly growing revenues of the South African Republic to break away from the British stranglehold. Yet he, himself a participant in the Great Trek as a child, was also the prisoner of a social system which was not easily transformed towards meeting the requirements of capitalist mining. The Randlords objected to the high tariff rates of the Netherlands railway company that connected the Rand to the Portuguese port at Lourenço Marques in Mozambique, the nearest outlet to the sea. They objected to the high charges of Eduard Lippert, the concessionaire who controlled the dynamite monopoly. They objected to the state dependence on liquor revenues which resulted in an intoxicated and inefficient labour force. Most crucially they objected to the incompetence of the republican state in procuring the huge, cheap and disciplined African labour force they required. For the Boer notables who controlled the Volksraad, or parliament, the creation of the requisite giant labour procurement system was not only beyond their technical capabilities, it also militated against what control they had over their farm workers. It was not that the Transvaal state was opposed to the gold mines. Kruger was only one notable who had made a small fortune through subsequent land speculation while the most energetic men, such as Louis Botha, the future South African premier, were turning their hand to 'progressive' farming to feed the urban population. The changes were slow in coming, however, too slow for those Randlords poised to make huge investments in the new deep levels of the goldfield.

Cecil Rhodes, who had cornered the Kimberley diamond fields, was a crucial actor in the shift in imperial strategy towards confrontation in the Transvaal. Rhodes, as premier of the Cape, had stood for a policy of collaboration between Boer and Briton. His confidence in the course of events and the future of the Cape was shaken by his own rather unsuccessful financial interventions on the Rand, where he failed to capitalise on the deep-level discoveries. In 1890 his British South Africa Company sent the Pioneer Column into the lands of Lobengula, the Ndebele ruler, where they established 'Southern Rhodesia' and then quickly extended control over a vast swathe of Central Africa, making of Rhodes the only European capitalist to have an African colony actually named for him. Rhodesia was meant to be the setting of a 'Second Rand', but Rhodes' advisors were misinformed; his Rhodesian adventures were anything but a boon to his pocket-book.

It was Rhodes, in collusion with Alfred Beit of the great deep-level firm of Wernher, Beit & Co. and the secret support of the British government, who hatched the conspiracy to take over the Transvaal. As a propaganda ruse, the British were inclined to defend the claims of the immigrant *uitlanders* to the vote in the South African Republic. Not surprisingly, faced with such a flood of new immigrants, the Boers had enacted tough laws to make the acquisition of citizenship a lengthy business. Almost believing their own propaganda, Rhodes and his henchmen hoped that the *uitlanders* of Johannesburg would rise in revolt if a small party of armed men crossed the frontier raising the British standard. This they failed to do. The Jameson Raid of 1896, launched from Bechuanaland, was a fiasco.

The raid eliminated Rhodes as a major factor in South African politics, but the British government, now dominated by Colonial Secretary Joseph Chamberlain, was determined to gain its object. The new high commissioner in Cape Town, Sir Alfred Milner, was a hawk determined to smash the republics. A crescendo of increasing demands, followed by the stationing of troops along the border, finally led to the outbreak of war in 1899.

The Anglo-Boer War was Britain's greatest imperial war fought on African soil. At great expense, some 300 000 armed men were required to subdue the Boers. The sheer weight of numbers turned around the initial advances of the republican commandos, and by mid-1900 the Boer capitals of Bloemfontein and Pretoria were conquered. The Boers, however, then determined on a strategy of guerrilla warfare which exhausted British efforts at control. In order to destroy the commandos, their families were rounded up into concentration camps, fields were burnt, homesteads looted and destroyed and a blockhouse sweep system inaugurated. Perhaps ten per cent of the Afrikaners in the republics, particularly children, died as a result of these policies.[4] It took until May 1902, at the peace of Vereeniging, to bring the fighting commandos finally to a negotiated settlement which extinguished the independence of the republics. This gigantic war effort was the greatest and most costly episode of the scramble. With Britain's victory the City of London could rest assured of its position with respect to control over world gold supply and Milner could get on with the task of reconstruction to provide a political and social basis for mining production after the peace.

By 1902 Africa was partitioned. There continued to be talk of re-partition, particularly with regard to King Leopold's dubious Free State and the rich territories 'wasted' on the Portuguese, but these plans came to nothing. In the end, in 1918, the most energetic proponent of re-partition, Germany, found itself eliminated from the board as a result of World War I.

### Resistance, Collaboration and Contradiction in African Society

Samori was able to take all the traditional resources of the African leader, adapt them to his needs and even occasionally transform them to meet some new requirements. He bowed to the social and technical customs of his background, but at the same time he had an instinctive feeling for terrain and a rapidity of reflex.[5]

In West Africa Samori was the greatest of all military resisters, not only because of his personal skills and his willingness to adopt extraordinarily mobile guerrilla tactics, but because he was not a 'traditional' ruler but a forger of empire with new weaponry and support, a man of the nineteenth century much like Mirambo or Tippu Tip. Through the 1880s and 1890s he fought the French in the lands between eastern Guinea, southern Mali and the northern half of the Ivory Coast. His admiring biographer, the French historian Yves Person, devoted a magisterial three-volume study to his career which nevertheless concludes that his 'Dyula' empire was doomed through its technical backwardness compared with the European powers that determined to crush him.

No historian of Africa disputes this technical inferiority and its importance in the defeat and conquest of African states, but it is often forgotten that technical inferiority was imbedded in a social context that could not easily be altered from within. The threat of conquest brought out to the full the contradictions within African states which were a contributing cause of their conquest. It is at this level that a class perspective illuminates what otherwise can only be the story of unequal fights and one-sided diplomacy. In practice conquest only sometimes constituted a sudden overwhelming threat to African sovereignty. More typically, it was a process. The intensification of commercial relationships created conditions whereby access to trade goods had become the top political priority. After initial treaties and commercial arrangements, it was that much more difficult for African states to resist the next stage of penetration or effective control.

Only very fitfully or late in the day did African ruling strata acquire a sense of 'Africanness', a view of a shared common confrontation against the force of powerful new enemies. Rulers and ruling classes alternated so deftly (and at times desperately) between strategies of collaboration and resistance that it is difficult to classify them along a sharp divide between the two except where circumstances clearly offered them little choice. They generally perceived the scramble in terms of their own specific class interests, much as ruling classes anywhere, as well as, more narrowly, in terms of older strategic and diplomatic objectives. There are certain examples of rulers who called for a common front of action. In the 1840s Moshweshwe, the creator of Lesotho, negotiated with other southern African kings, proposing an anti-European alliance. Minilik, the conqueror of Adwa, at one point proposed an alliance to the Khalifa, the successor to the Mahdi in the Sudan. Yet both these men, like Samori himself, pursued collaborative strategies as well. Moshweshwe often worked with the British and, at yet another point in his career, tried to organise an alliance against them with the highveld Boers. Samori was by no means always prepared to hurl defiance to the French and, towards the end of his career, rejected an alliance with Asante and sought actively for a British protectorate. Minilik's policies included deals with Italians and Frenchmen at various stages.

Where ruling classes were divided, the situation was most complicated. Buganda is a classic example. The very successes of the kingdom in the nineteenth century had thrown up ambitious men who were restive under the grip of the *kabaka*. Unable, as upstarts, to take a position on the basis of the old lineage structure of an earlier historical phase, they were consequently very strongly drawn to the economic potential of expanding trade connections and the ideological attraction of new religions introduced by Muslim traders and Christian missionaries. Mutesa, the greatest nineteenth-century *kabaka*, was for a time inclined to become a Muslim, but he held back for fear of the threat to the basis of his own power that such a conversion might bring. From 1884 his successor Mwanga, alternately favoured and then turned against Islam, Catholicism and Protestantism while around each religious banner congregated a committed sector of the ruling class. The British intervention, which ultimately dethroned Mwanga and replaced him with an infant and a regency, enshrined a balance of these factions under an Anglican ascendancy. Only when it was too late did Mwanga take up guerrilla warfare and make common cause with his great former rival and fellow refugee, Kabarega of Bunyoro.

In the Yoruba states of the Lagos hinterland the British had to engage in only one major military operation, that against Ijebu Ode in 1893. After the power of Ijebu was smashed, the other Yoruba states were willing to conclude agreements with the British that gave considerable social power to the ruling classes, particularly those who were involved in the Lagos trade. Lagos merchants came from, and traded with, virtually every Yoruba state which thus acquired vital firearms. The basis of economic and military power had already tilted powerfully towards reliance on these networks. Under these circumstances, if 'resistance' meant upholding the fundamental material interests of a class, collaboration itself became a logical, if discreet, form of 'resistance'.

Nor were African societies especially cohesive in the shadow of conquest. The impact of intensified commercial penetration under more favourable exchange terms through the middle years of the century created a variety of different new interests already undercutting the authority of the state in many regions. The economic basis of the Asante Confederacy, for instance, gradually altered with the decline of the slave trade and the rise of 'legitimate' commodity trade to the coast, upsetting the balance of control over many of the Asante tributary states. Every large state preyed on and raided its small neighbours who were often prepared to welcome European influence and power. Oppressed classes within the state also did not invariably support their rulers when given a choice. Philip Igbafe has noted that, following the conquest of Benin, plans by the *oba* and his court to organise resistance in the countryside were cut short abruptly by the British threat to emancipate all the slaves forthwith.

In South Africa the defeat of the republican Boers, who presented the strongest single challenge to imperialism, was in large measure due to their inability to garner any significant African support. Their commandos were hemmed in by Swazi and Zulu to the south-east, Tswana to the west and Pedi to the north-east, decisively limiting their scope of action. They fought for a particular way of life that depended on control, even if slacker than what was to follow, over African labour and land, that militated against establishing solid alliances with Africans. Even among the Boers a considerable number fought with the British. These were drawn disproportionately from among the underprivileged non-landholding *bywoner* class with nothing to gain from the notables' struggles. Class interests prevented the formation of a wider, anti-imperialist movement, typifying the limitations of resistance in many parts of Africa.

In order for African states to have resisted conquest effectively, they would have required to put up not merely a very substantial military effort, but to move towards an economic and social transformation, the creation of a milieu for the reproduction of technology that could have met the depredation of the Europeans on their own terms. Samori and Minilik were able to procure weaponry, obtain training for many of their troops in its use and even organise simple repair work on materiel. Yet even they could not compete with the precision-arms factories of Europe. Moshweshwe, a particularly far-sighted individual, remarked in his wars with the Free State that what even the Boers, let alone the British, could potentially command was economic power and infrastructure, the capacity to supply and feed troops with which the social structure of his kingdom could not compete. What was required was transformation – social as well as technological. One place where attempts in this direction were relatively sustained and impressive was the Imerina kingdom that dominated nineteenth-century Madagascar. Imerina rulers encouraged Christianity and the spread of literacy. A few Malagasy acquired technical training and the state made use of occasional resident Europeans to establish the beginnings of a military-orientated manufacturing sector just as had Peter the Great's Russia or Muhammad Ali's Egypt. Yet such efforts were resented in many quarters and pushed aside during 'traditionalist' reigns. Attempts by the monarchy to extract more surplus from the masses and create a new basis of ideological support for the state met with powerful resistance. A first war with the French in 1883–5 led to peasant and slave risings that undercut the strength of the monarchy to resist the final onslaught a decade later.

Some African states were not prepared even to contemplate the necessity of such a transformation. The Sokoto caliphate, probably Africa's most populous country in the late nineteenth century, was a prime example. There was little 'collaboration' in Sokoto and its emirates until the actual conquest, but the resistance to Lugard's occupying armies was pitifully inadequate. When the British took Kano they seized large amounts of modern arms that no soldier had ever been taught how to use. Each emirate that fought did so separately with mounted cavalry attempting to charge squares of men armed with repeating rifles. When Sokoto was taken the last caliph, Attahiru, escaped to the east, requesting in writing to the British that he be allowed to make his way towards Mecca in peace. At the battle of Burmi in 1903 he and his fellow refugees, men who 'knew how to die when facing the enemy', were annihilated, but only British determination to prevent the flight occasioned their fierce resistance.[6] It is especially remarkable that states such as Asante and Benin, with such long direct and indirect experience of Europeans, were so technically unprepared to cope with the intensified pressure of the scramble.

Yet the survival of independence might conceivably have been more feasible were the European power not so determined to extinguish it. In all of Asia, only one state, Japan, witnessed an effective transformation under a section of its ruling class that made it rather quickly an industrialising, capitalist society. At the same time other states – Persia, Afghanistan, China and Siam – remained independent as a result of balancing the rivalries between potential occupying powers. A parallel case can be made for Ethiopia. Minilik did not transform Ethiopian society root and branch. He concentrated on building up military strength, purchasing armaments through the expansion of the Ethiopian state into the central and southern highlands, where resources could be plundered and loyal soldiers rewarded with grants of land. This enabled him to confront one of the weakest potential conquerors, Italy, with Africa's largest army, 100 000 men, considerably more than the Transvaal and Free State Boers ever assembled. After victory in battle Minilik benefited enormously from the reluctance of the Italian government to pursue the war further. He could with excellent effect play off one foreign power against the other, while gradually taming the autonomy of the provincial lords and creating the beginnings of a national bureaucracy. The transformation of Ethiopia was a very slow process; strong elements of older social relations, what revolutionaries called 'feudalism', were still evident at the time of the overthrow of the monarchy in 1974. Nor was imperial rule a pleasant experience for the mass of peasants, who bore its expenses and whose exploitation made possible some transformation, or the diverse peoples of Ethiopia who were forced to accept a Christian Amharinya ascendancy in the first stages of 'nation-building'. Even for Ethiopia there was no question of using independence to renounce change and pursue purely 'indigenous' historic patterns of development; it had to live within a world which was rapidly moving ahead. This dilemma would have faced other African states had they retained independence.

Imperialist domination marked more than a phase in the history of Africa. It was the precondition of the emergence of African society as it now exists. Indeed, Africa as a meaningful concept owes itself primarily to the predatory instincts of the new conquerors and then, with time, to opposition to them.

The most interesting resistance struggles were not really those fought by African states to retain their sovereignty, for this type of resistance tended to be the class struggle of dominant elements who had themselves a strongly predatory character. More historically resonant were those popular risings against the imposition of colonial control which represented a reaction to new and oppressive demands on the masses that began to call up new kinds of leadership. Some, like the Herero war in South-West Africa in 1905–6 and the Bambatha rebellion among the Zulu in Natal soon afterwards, were sad affairs because they were largely a desperate response to extreme provocation by colonial and settler authorities. The Chimurenga risings of Zimbabwe and the Maji Maji fighting that swept southern Tanzania had a more forceful and original thrust. They form part of the social and political dialectic of the colonial era which the next chapter begins to investigate.

## Notes

1. The critique of Lenin made in these pages owes much to V. G. Kiernan, *Marxism and Imperialism* (St Martins, 1975), Anthony Brewer, *Marxist Theories of Imperialism: A Critical Survey* (Routledge & Kegan Paul, 1980) and Bill Warren, *Imperialism: Pioneer of Capitalism* (New Left Books, 1981).
2. Even more surprising was the expansion of Portugal, an extremely backward capitalist society, as a colonial power. W. G. Clarence-Smith has convincingly explained this in terms of the particular needs and background of the Portuguese bourgeoisie rather than, as had become traditional, 'despite' economic rationality, in 'The Myth of Uneconomic Imperialism: The Portuguese in Angola', *JSAS*, V (1979).
3. For instance, during the Boer War, while popular sentiment in Germany and the USA was strongly pro-Boer, those forces that represented big money and political power strongly backed the British war effort.
4. And an equally high percentage of the many African refugees placed in camps.
5. Yves Person in Michael Crowder, ed., *West African Resistance* (Hutchinson, 1971), p. 140.
6. Quote from a British officer, cited in R. A. Adeleye, *Power and Diplomacy in Northern Nigeria, 1804–1906* (Longman, 1971), p. 310.

# 6

# THE MATERIAL BASIS OF COLONIAL SOCIETY, 1900–40

It is given to few men to think clearly on the Africa question. One of these few men is Sir George Goldie. He has said Africa should be divided up into that region which white men can colonize in the true sense of the word – a region so admirably represented by South Africa; then a region which white men can colonize to much the same extent as they can in India – the highlands of British Central Africa; and then that region which white men cannot colonize at all in the true sense of the word – West Africa. This is politically the Africa we must keep in our mind, remembering England wants markets as well as colonies; and so West Africa, the richest raw-material market in the world, is as much use to her as a colony and she can hold it easily by a garrison of Englishmen as a feeding ground for her manufacturing classes here at home.

Mary Kingsley in the Liberia Bulletin, no. 14, 1899, p. 48

The imperial conquest of Africa was undertaken to tap African resources in order to help resolve the economic problems of Europe. Yet the circumstances of the conquest brought the colonial rulers to grips with a basic contradiction: only a long, intensive process could create conditions within Africa that could bring about substantial opportunities for invest-ment, sales and profits. Beneath the surface of *colonial* political and admin-istrative policy lay the unfolding process of *capital* penetration, a process that was far from reaching full fruition in the colonial era.

Anti-colonial writing tends to view the conquest and foreign rule of Africa as systematic plunder. While naked robbery plays a role in capitalist development, the remarkable feature of capitalism, which if ignored obvi-

97

ates the point of distinguishing it as a system or mode of production, is its ability to feed upon itself and to expand directly through the production process. Slavery, by contrast, is a system which has almost invariably required endless fresh inputs of labour from raids and conquests of other societies and other modes of production, off which it lives parasitically; it is not self-sustaining. Capitalism begins with an initiatory process of what Marx called primitive accumulation of resources and labour. It comes into being 'dripping from head to foot, from every pore, with blood and dirt' through 'the expropriation of the mass of the people by a few usurpers'.[1] However, once an expropriated population, divorced from the means of production, is available for the 'free' sale of its labour to the highest bidder (which, since the owners of capital have probably been able to erect a suitably efficacious state apparatus is not likely to be an impressive offer), expropriation becomes a daily part of the work process, not merely plunder of the people's resources. It is then no longer an *ex*propriation but a systematic *ap*propriation.

Colonial rule began with an act of political expropriation, with the use or threat of force, to extract surplus from Africa in the form of either direct labour or the product of labour which could then be commoditised. The state acted as a tribute-taker rather than an organising agency for capitalist producers as in a developed capitalist society. This was indeed plunder pure and simple, but it could not yield any great wealth. Capitalism demanded the further development of commodity production and the circulation of goods from which firms in the metropolitan countries could benefit. Where possible colonialism was about pressing forward the social and economic conditions, the development of class forces, that could lead to capitalist production in Africa itself. The tribute-taking stage had some significance throughout the period covered in this chapter, but was particularly important before World War I. In certain parts of Africa, particularly those with a long history of slave and 'legitimate' trade, commodity production was already well advanced at the time of conquest and now took off far beyond the level for which forced labour or crop plantings could have allowed. South Africa was the one place where capitalist production became generalised during this period and, for this reason, it is discussed below in a separate chapter.

Yet elsewhere the remarkable feature was the limited impact of capitalism in transforming economy and society at the root. In an important recent study, Anne Phillips rightly sees this as the 'enigma' of colonialism. Pre-capitalist social forms, showing extraordinary flexibility and powers of adaptation, survived to a remarkable extent. One reason was the resistance to transformation, to the expropriation of material, social and cultural values, by a resilient population of cultivators. The task taken on by capital, that of mastering an entire continent, demanded time, personnel and capital investment that two generations of colonialism did not have in sufficient quantity. This was so precisely because the slave trade, and even the far more extensive 'legitimate' trade, had *not* evoked the irrevocable dependency upon the West that the dependency school of writers have claimed. The high tide of colonialism in Africa came between the two world wars, an era when capitalist trade growth internationally was fitful and often problematic.

The result was the dual economy of 'tradition' and 'modernity', in the terminology of bourgeois economists. Marxists generally speak of the articulation of different modes of production in which Western-based capitalism becomes increasingly dominant. This takes into consideration the important additional factor of power. Such structural formulations help somewhat to describe social change, but are at such a high level of abstraction as to prevent the observation of a myriad of interconnections, of transitional forms, class relationships and human adaptations that make up the thread of twentieth-century African social history (and the next two chapters).

At the heart of the economic task of the colonial state lay the problem of labour. To open Africa to effective capital penetration, the most central issue which underlay all others, and which to some extent explains the need for conquest itself, was to prize open the labour resources of the continent, to redirect them functionally, socially and geographically in order to create a surplus from which capital could benefit. Even the basic requirement of improved transport, road and railway construction, was ultimately related to the urgency for releasing human labour used in porterage to other forms of productive labour. Coupled with this was the objective of attacking local manufacturers to substitute a taste for imported commodities and to reorient established trade routes and sometimes entire populations to the coast-interior trajectories. Much of the surplus production of Africans had passed through the hands of the dominant elements within Africa: women's surplus into the hands of men, youth's surplus into the hands of elders and, in many areas, the surplus production of the peasantry into the hands of ruling classes and merchants. The conquest enabled this to be made available to the benefit of Western business and the sustenance of the colonial administration.

### The Era of Force and the Chartered Companies

The first two decades of the twentieth century have some unity in African history as the era of force, a period of raw and brutal intrusion by the developing colonial state into the lives of Africans. The use of force must be stressed first in the establishment of colonial domination politically. If the 1880s and 1890s were *par excellence* the era of wars against powerful African kingdoms: Buganda and Bunyoro; Asante and Dahomey; Benin and the Yoruba states; the realms of Samori and the Mahdi; the states of the Hehe and Ngoni; of Kazembe and Lobengula and the Merina, then the period up to World War I was one of smaller-scale operations against people without regular armies and structured states. Such peoples rarely surrendered to colonial authority without a fight and required to be conquered one by one, often only to reject authority repeatedly. Innumerable expeditions were sent through the forests, hills and broken country of central and south-eastern Nigeria, western Kenya, the Nuba Hills and southern savanna of the Sudan and the central Ivory Coast to name a few. When the people could not fight they fled, so colonial forces tended to adopt a scorched earth policy, stealing stock, destroying crops and burning huts, to bring them to their heels.

It cannot be said that force was new to African history, but in the course of establishing colonial control a new purpose can be discerned. Such expeditions had as their goal not only recognition of a flag of sovereignty, but the systematic payment of tribute in the form of taxes and labour. They were as much economic as political in character. By 1914, when World War I broke out, colonial expeditions had generally accomplished their goals, but the war itself had led to renewed resistance, notably in French territory, where authorities demanded the 'blood tax' of young men for the army in 'pacified' areas. The most difficult Africans to conquer were pastoralists, particularly in desert country. The Italians effectively established their rule in the northern part of Somalia only in the late 1920s, while it took until the early 1930s for the French to break the resistance of Saharan peoples between Mauritania and northern Chad. Throughout Africa, but particularly in such regions, colonial administration had a strongly military cast in the earlier phases.

The economic system of early colonialism in Africa rested on compulsion in most regions. In virtually every territory the 1900s and 1910s were the most intense phase of forced taxation, forced cultivation and forced labour. It was only through the widespread use of forced labour that the characteristic essential requirements of the colonial system could at first be met. Men were needed everywhere to construct and maintain roads and railroads. Until a transport network could be developed, wherever animal power could not be utilised, porters were required on an immense scale to bear commodities in and out. Conditions in African construction camps were appalling. A notorious case (and a late one) was the line of rail that linked the French side of Stanley Pool on the Congo River to the sea, the Congo-Ocean, which was completed in 1930. Some 20 000 conscript workers lost their lives as it made its course through the forests.

Nowhere in Africa was the regime of force so raw and dramatic as in the Congo Free State of Leopold II. King though he was, Leopold ran the Free State like a capitalist of the robber-baron era. The Leopoldine system had its roots in the king's pursuit of quick profits to create a capital base needed for large-scale investment, especially in transport. The forests of the Congo basin were rich in low-grade rubber, conveniently excluded from the free-trade provisions of the Berlin Conference, and rubber found a buoyant market in the West as the use of bicycles and then automobiles developed. It was rubber which, from the middle 1890s, made the Free State pay.

The king handed out most of the forest zone to concession companies, keeping a large zone, the *domaine de la couronne*, as his personal fiefdom. The companies enjoyed administrative as well as political power and their agents had orders to force the Congolese to bring in as much rubber as possible for a minimal price. Collection on the scale demanded required people to travel far from their homes, to work under sometimes dangerous conditions and to neglect normal domestic obligations. It was enforced through mass terror: armed expeditions, the use of hostages, especially women and children, mutilations and killings. Resistance evoked countless brutal expeditions and the flight of Africans away from the rivers of the Congo system to less ecologically favourable areas. The consequent devastation and depopulation approached a genocidal scale and probably outdid in horrors anything ever perpetrated by the slave trade. The era of 'red rubber' will always be associated with Joseph Conrad's great novella, *Heart of Darkness*, which linked the Congo Free State terror to the 'horror of it' – the hideous, unacceptable face of European civilisation.

Conrad was associated with a group of reformers who exposed conditions in the Congo in the early years of the twentieth century. Their writings excited the self-interested concern of those non-Belgian Europeans who realised that Leopold had duped them in selling the world on the freetrade character of his 'International Association' in 1884–5. As a result, for fear of foreign intervention, the Belgian state took over the

Congo in 1908, an object long intended by Leopold. The Free State regime was not changed substantially at first. Forest exhaustion and the flooding of the market with cheap, high-quality South-East Asian plantation rubber cut into the rubber-gathering system. What really ended it, though, was the fruition of Leopold's real work: the establishment of the transport system that permitted the export of large quantities of minerals from the interior, which by 1914 formed the basis of the economy of the Belgian Congo.

The ruthless application of force gave way to a particularly effective, concentrated system of exploitation, admired by Belgium's fellow colonial powers and attracting investment funds from the biggest Belgian monopolies, of which one, the industrial-financial consortium of the Société Générale, controlled half the commoditised economy of the interwar Congo. A complex and occasionally changing system of regional zones subdivided the Congo for economic purposes into areas that produced particular cash crops, migrant labour or food crops for the mines and towns. Forced cotton cultivation, to the benefit of the Belgian textile companies, was widespread in savanna regions from the 1930s. The mineral wealth of the Congo furthered new investments and helped finance a river-rail network of great length. The size of the wage-labour force passed 500 000 before 1930, the highest total in tropical Africa. Not without justice, the Congo system has been described as an edifice resting on three pillars: business, the Catholic church and the state, institutionally associated and intermeshed with remarkable clarity.

Elsewhere in the African forest zone conditions at first resembled those in Leopold's realm. Rubber regimes operating in much the same way dominated south of the Congo frontier in parts of Portuguese Angola, across the river in French territory and into southern German Cameroun. The French system was, if anything, even more brutal, and it survived into the late 1920s, despite the poor prices earned by wild rubber on the international market.

When the Belgian state assumed control of the Congo in 1908, concessions companies lost their administrative authority. Belgium was following a pattern noticeable in most of the African colonies. In many parts of Africa the crude commercial motives for conquest had brought the grant of charters to private firms for all administrative and economic authority. They then did the dirty work of subjugating the territory. Bismarck originally favoured this system in all four German colonies. The French granted most of French Equatorial Africa to concessions companies at first. More than half of Mozambique was chartered by the Portuguese.

Kenya and Uganda were initially administered by the International British East Africa Company and the Rhodesias by the British South Africa Company, while the Royal Niger Company at first represented British rule in eastern Nigeria.

Such a system proved unworkable on the whole and many of the charters (such as the IBEAC in British East Africa and that of the Deutsch Ost-Afrika Gesellschaft in German East Africa) were quickly withdrawn. The companies were unable to function profitably while maintaining and extending an administration. European governments were not initially delighted to assume the running costs of African territories that might bring trouble with home legislatures, but by 1900 or soon after it was understood that there was no practical alternative. The concession system survived in French Equatorial Africa until the 1920s; the British South Africa Company was dismantled as a political operation as late as 1924, to the profit of its shareholders. Only in Mozambique, where the concessionaires were foreigners who held the Portuguese state to the full term of original agreements, did company rule persist in one section until 1942.[2]

## Mines

For Western capital, especially big finance capital, by far the most attractive prospect held out by the conquest of Africa, was its mineral resources. In the pre-World War I era, stock market booms and speculative rushes centred around a mythical second Witwatersrand in Southern Rhodesia, then the gold fields of the Gold Coast and finally the tin deposits of the Jos Plateau and environs in Northern Nigeria. However, the greatest mineral development in tropical Africa during the interwar years came in the Belgian Congo. Leopold II had pressed his agents to extend the Katanga Province of the Congo in a deep salient that pushed like a great dagger into the Rhodesian reserve of Cecil Rhodes' British South Africa Company. Katanga was quickly ascertained to contain very rich copper deposits. Katanga copper was developed entirely by one company, the Union Minière du Haut-Katanga. UMHK, once divested of minority British interests, itself was controlled by the Société Générale, the largest Belgian financial and industrial trust.

The problem of obtaining labour in a sparsely peopled area, poor in water supply, in the southern savannas of Africa was great. In the earliest phase of development the state coerced men, most of them 'freed' from slavery, to the mines. Later the UMHK experimented with a series of recruitment schemes that brought in migrant workers from hundreds of miles away in northern Katanga, Maniema Province and even the Trust Territory of Ruanda-Urundi carved from German East Africa for the Belgians after World War I. Partly because of the strong position of British recruitment agents the copper mines then came to depend on the labour of British Central Africa – Nyasaland and especially Northern Rhodesia – as well as Portuguese Angola.

During the 1920s, however, technological development and geological research made it clear that an even greater copper supply could be exploited west of the frontier within Northern Rhodesia. The Northern Rhodesian Copperbelt went into full production in the middle and later 1930s. Two giant firms dominated it, the South African finance house of Anglo-American and (the genuinely British and American) Rhodesian Selection Trust. The British South Africa Company continued to enjoy huge royalty profits in its capacity as 'landlord' on the basis of concessions from Rhodes' time.

Labour from the British colonies now mainly stayed in Northern Rhodesia. UMHK turned largely in response to Congolese labour and consequently initiated a policy of labour stabilisation. Until the late 1920s the calculations of mining management everywhere in Africa assumed that the African labourer could be denied a family wage even at subsistence level. Brought in on a short-term contract basis, he was housed in a compound under conditions of extreme social control and deprivation while his family on the homestead were expected to look after themselves. UMHK continued to expect 'redundant' or retired workers to return to the bush, but they now encouraged mine-compound family life, engaged the Catholic church to supply elementary education for the children and basic health care, and provided plots so that wives could cultivate food on a small scale. Skilled jobs reserved for immigrant European labour in other territories were done far more cheaply in Katanga by Africans, who were nevertheless much better paid than the unskilled mass of workers. Even before formal stabilisation policies were initiated, Africans had the option of settling in the shanties of the new city of Elisabethville, which allowed them a certain margin of freedom and enterprise. From the 1920s the appalling disease and accident rates on the Copperbelt fell rapidly. The poor conditions of rural life in south-central Africa on both sides of the frontier, Belgian and British, led to a flow of workers to the mining towns. In Northern Rhodesia this occurred well before the formal establishment of stabilisation policies.

In the 1920s other mining enterprises also flourished in the Belgian Congo, notably in the production of tin and industrial diamonds, of which south Kasai became the foremost world producer. Minerals dominated the Congo economy and led to its remarkable and close integration with all the biggest trusts of metropolitan Belgium on a scale beyond any comparison in Africa. UMHK relied on African peasant production from up the line of rail, especially Kasai Province, to feed the miners; this proved to be the cheapest system and was initiated through a massive forced cultivation and requisition system. From the 1930s Northern Rhodesian administration and economy too was entirely suborned to copper production. Here, however, food came from European settler farmers along the Rhodesian Railways line.

It is instructive to compare the Central African Copperbelt with the Northern Nigerian tin fields, which began to export on a substantial scale at about the same time as Katanga. Early tin production was in the hands of numerous small producing companies, of which most represented the financial interests of a range of inter-investing mining finance houses. The dominant power on the local scene, however, was the Niger Company, which had secured exclusive prospecting licences, partly through its close links with the Lugard regime, and transferred them to producing firms for handsome considerations. Like the BSAC it had 'landlord' rights securing an income from royalties and rents. The Company also handled local financing and cash needs, supply provisions and transport of men, equipment and tin. It guaranteed a British Treasury loan for the construction of a railway, thus putting the burden on the state to procure forced labour to build it and exert its land right. Profits, as divided among many producing firms, were small. Mechanisation on the open-cast pits was at a low level, especially before the introduction of hydroelectric power in 1925. Production control largely took the form of forcing African miners to turn over ore to the European holders of exclusive leases, required for the export of tin from the ports. Only in the late 1920s did a large trust, Anglo-Oriental, which sought to corner the volatile world tin market, extremely vulnerable to the trade cycle, move in and assert control over half of total production. Based on control of access to mechanised equipment, their profits became quite handsome in the late 1930s once workers' wages had collapsed in the depression.

In the early phase of development there was much informal forced labour, arranged through the system of Native Authorities, colonial officialdom and mines managers. The managers wanted a system of intensive state-organised recruitment, both to assure their labour supply and to reduce its price, but the state could never make up its mind to back schemes along these lines. The highly commercialised peasantry of Northern Nigeria and immiserated people from over the borders in Cameroun, French West and Equatorial Africa, fleeing from taxes and conscription, threw up a huge labour force (approaching 40 000 averaged monthly on the eve of World War II) without compulsion. In Nigeria labour recruiters and skilled workmen were often African. The number of European employees was tiny in comparison with Central Africa and confined largely to management and petty stake-holders.

Where mining operations held sway they invariably played a central role in the process of capital penetration in colonial Africa. In none of the cases described above did full-scale capitalist production relations come to prevail before World War II, however. A wage-labour force came to the mines through its need for cash, rather than through direct compulsion, but even where it was 'stabilised' men did not earn a family wage or one that allowed for social reproduction without the survival of the peasant household.[3] Workers had to go to the countryside and, in the case of commercialised Nigeria, the enormous trading sector that ultimately fed off peasant production, when their digging days were over. The mines, especially before 1940, did not so much proletarianise the peasantry as intensify the conditions through which the cash nexus and market demands penetrated the countryside.[4]

## White Settlers

In the absence of mineral prospects, colonialism and capitalism had to turn to agriculture and the African peasantry for the production of wealth. Before the beginning of the twentieth century African producers had sold gathered and hunted products for the world market in large quantities, but only to a much lesser extent cultivated crops. At first the colonialists were gloomy about their prospects of doing so. Plans for agriculture were generally linked to plans for the settlement of planters from the metropole.

White settlement colonies and plantation agriculture had a lengthy and profitable history in other parts of the world. Settlers from the mother country were likely to retain a myriad of ties to it and they shared deeply internalised capitalist values that might radiate out to the conquered African population. Colonial governments had a natural sympathy for what seemed to them to be the most efficient, progressive, European-like production techniques which settlers were likely to initiate. Ideal colonial collaborators, settlers could share in the tasks of local administration, justice and defence, easing burdens of state. Rich settlers often had excellent connections at home, notably in Britain. In British Central and East Africa, moreover, settlers were often part of a spill-over from South Africa, from where they emigrated willingly without special encouragement from the state.[5]

However, there also proved to be considerable negative aspects to settlers from the colonial point of view. They required large-scale infrastructural expenditures in the form of social services and economic assistance. Their total dependence on colonial political domination and their tiny numbers created among them an intense and uncompromising racism that outdid that of administrators or merchants and deeply antagonised Africans. Settlers rarely came to Africa intending to live from their own and their families' labour alone, although there were a few exceptions in the Portuguese and Italian colonies. Elsewhere they aspired to be capitalist farmers requiring vast outlays of land and the subordination of a great deal of cheap, initially coerced labour. In the production of most crops, unless economies of scale were of great weight, 'modern' settlers could not in fact compete economically with African peasants. They consequently required subsidies and price supports from the state that drained the colonial treasuries. This was so especially during the great depression.

Kenya is often seen as the classic 'white man's colony'. When originally conquered, the colonial budget had a large deficit and the British were anxious to find a way to make it pay quickly, especially after the expensive construction of the Uganda Railway from the Indian Ocean to Lake Victoria which passed through its heart. There appeared to be large tracts of vacant arable land in high, healthy country only sparsely inhabited by Maasai pastoralists and ideal for handing over to settlers. Appropriate and gigantic land grants became policy from 1903. The largest number of settlers were South African or connected with South Africa. Their viability depended on state authority to enforce their property rights and state expenditure to support their agricultural endeavours. In the Kenya highlands farmers could raise many temperate climate crops with which Europeans were familiar, but it took a generation of expensive experimentation to gauge the effects of local plant and animal diseases and, even then, Kenyan wheat, bacon or dairy products were not competitive on the world market. The middle and lower reaches of Kenyan commerce came into the hands not of white settlers but of immigrants from India. Largely to prevent Indian competition the settlers persuaded the British government to reserve large sections of central Kenya for whites only, creating the infamous 'white highland' policy.

In order for the highlands to achieve any viability, settlers successfully demanded the stifling of any African enterprise that might affect their needs of cheap labour. In fine quality *arabica* coffee, the settlers found an apparently ideal export crop, but it could be grown just as well on a smaller scale by Africans and indeed already was south of the frontier in Tanganyika. Thus settler pressure imposed upon Kenya a policy of 'whites only' coffee-growing. In fact only a small proportion of the reserved 'white highlands' were effectively farmed, less than ten per cent on the eve of World War I and never over twenty per cent in the interwar era. Labour and especially land policies engendered by the settler system led quickly to organised and intense African opposition, even in circles that might have been expected to support colonial rule. So it is hardly surprising that for many officials in Britain the white settlers seemed to hang like a weight around the neck of colonial development in Kenya, both on political and economic grounds.

In a consideration of the most easterly part of Northern Rhodesia abutting Nyasaland, which the British intended to be a settler zone, Leroy Vail has pointed to the potential ecological deterioration inherent in settlerdom. The Ngoni people of this region were herded onto a tiny, insufficient section of land and obliged to migrate for cash on unfavourable terms. The lower country in the valley of the Luangwa River was given over to wild animals as a game reserve, which in turn allowed trypanosomiasis (sleeping sickness) to spread like wildfire since it uses wild game as a carrier. This disease makes it impossible for domestic cattle to survive. The land alienated in large quantities in higher country around Fort Jameson was hardly used by settlers who had no convenient transport outlet and failed to establish a profitable basis for agriculture. As a result this land also reverted to bush, game brought trypanosomiasis and the cattle population was permanently decimated. Small wonder then, when faced with such examples, that finance capital in the Belgian Congo, where it was dominant beyond any other African colony, allowed little scope for settlers and that by the 1920s the mines decided to rely on African farmers for their needs in foodstuffs.

Despite their tiny numbers in Africa before 1940 in numerous colonies, the settlers had acquired an important position as a pressure group and, in a few places, formal representation within the government. The state resisted the demands of Kenya settlers for political domination in the territory, but granted them innumerable favours. In one colony, Southern Rhodesia, the British South Africa Company administration gave way in 1924 to a settler-dominated local government under Crown Colony authority. The Company linkages combined with the proximity of South Africa to bring about the special circumstances there.

In certain parts of Africa corporate plantations run by European managers took shape. Some major examples were the Firestone rubber estate in Liberia, the Unilever palm-oil properties in the western Belgian Congo and the Tanganyika sisal estates. Unilever effectively purchased palm oil tapped by peasants who were forced to sell to them at monopoly prices, thus paralleling the ground monopoly of the capitalist tin-mining firms in Nigeria. On the sisal estates migrant labour from poor parts of Tanganyika and Ruanda-Urundi did the work with a recruitment system much like that in the mines of southern Africa. Migrant labour combined with a strong element of direct coercion to produce the work-force on the northern Mozambique sugar plantations. This type of agriculture only partly fitted the settler pattern.

## Lords and Chiefs

Where they appeared as obvious alternatives to settlers in certain parts of Africa, the colonial regimes dreamt of transforming native aristocracies into capitalist farmers and improving landlords. Such aristocracies had often been able to command tribute, tax and labour from a dominated population in the past. In sub-Saharan Africa the potential for pursuing such a strategy lay largely within British domains, which included the most populous and stratified social formations in Africa as a whole. A classic case was the island of Zanzibar where the sultans presided over a class of Arab or Arabised landlords whose wealth derived from the slave-based production and export of cloves. The British, after proclaiming a protectorate in Zanzibar, were anxious that this high-value export crop should continue to flourish. They therefore buttressed the rights of landowning aristocrats and attempted to transform the slaves into a class of docile, proletarianised, agricultural labourers.

Another apparently propitious locale for the pursuit of such a goal was Buganda, where British conquest had been assisted by the scheming of ambitious chiefs who eagerly seized upon European religion, literacy and culture as tools in conspiring against the *kabaka*. The Uganda Agreement of 1900 apportioned much of Buganda to them in the form of large landholdings. Ultimately there were some four thousand such *mailo* estates. It was hoped that the landlords would persuade a peasantry, transformed into trusty tied labourers, to produce valuable export crops by fair means or foul. Lord Lugard, the conqueror of northern Nigeria who had earned spurs in Uganda earlier, at first wished to turn the emirs and their officials into landowners there. As in Buganda this was an area where a ruling class had enjoyed control over a substantial surplus, but without any obvious commercial commodity sought after in Europe.

On the whole the strategy of working through an African aristocracy failed and was fairly swiftly abandoned. The basis of authority, political and economic, of the African ruling classes over the free peasantry was very different from that of improving European landlords and they were unable to enforce a transition to capitalist agriculture, particularly when it was coupled with the abolition of slavery. The Uganda Agreement initially appeared to be a great success as the Ganda peasantry began to grow cotton for export in appreciable quantities, with the *mailo* owners commanding various means of coercion and taking a share of the produce for their own benefit. However, as early as 1911, production began to stagnate and other areas of Uganda overtook Buganda as cotton producers. Social tensions within Buganda deepened, bringing with them administrative headaches. The colonial state began to turn against the landowners' prerogatives after World War I. In northern Nigeria policy was totally the reverse of what Lugard at first envisaged: land was declared to be state property and all private ownership disallowed. The 'aristocracy' became a class of venal state functionaries.

Only in Zanzibar, where the landowners held a monopoly over both land and clove trees, could the colonial regime keep faith with an African ruling class. Yet even there the landowners' appeal lay far more in their political hold than their economic efficiency as producers. For much of the colonial era they were hopelessly in debt to Indian merchants. Where conditions for class control were less propitious, on the old slave estates in the hinterland of Malindi (Kenya) or the Pangani river valley (Tanganyika), plantation agriculture did not long survive the end of slavery.

Abolition had a profoundly negative effect on the power of the old ruling classes which had so generally depended on unfree labour to sustain and fight for their great households. At first colonial regimes gingerly went about abolishing 'domestic' slavery. Ex-slaves formed a major part of the coerced labour force of mining areas and the 'villages de liberté' of French West Africa became notorious for French labour coercion of the liberated populations. Yet with time and state encouragement the developing cash nexus brought about a slackening or disappearance of the old bonds that held captives and outsiders to their dependent roles in households. Clientage continued, but it too came to function on a cash basis. With this disappeared the power of African ruling classes, where they existed, to command labour and production.

## Peasant Production

The real motor force of capital penetration in colonial Africa, mining excluded, proved to be peasant-grown cash crops. Given the alternatives the African cultivator faced during the first half of the twentieth century, this was generally the most attractive. In comparison with settler agriculture the development of peasant commodity production required much less effort and social outlay from the colonial regimes. Peasants were actually more productive in per-acre use of the land.

The cash-crop phenomenon is still not very well understood by historians, but there are two widely prevalent stereotypes concerning it which are clearly incorrect: that peasants produced crops simply as rational 'economic men' responding to cash incentives like businessmen, and that they were or became an undifferentiated class or community of producers.

The capacity of pre-colonial African cultivators to produce a surplus for storage or exchange and to adapt their lifestyle to take advantage of new opportunities or to avoid ecological catastrophe was very considerable, if variable from place to place. Sometimes African producers responded with alacrity to new market opportunities after conquest. In Southern Rhodesia, for instance, despite the seizure of half the land by settlers, peasants produced most foodstuffs for the towns and mine camps until in the 1920s the settlers seriously began to turn to capitalist agriculture and to block peasant access to the market.

This peasant response has been characterised mechanically in terms of a 'vent for surplus': the new roads and railways (coupled with Pax Britannica, Germanica, Belgica and so on) yielded produce from hitherto idle peasants. Celebrating the virtues of the enterprising peasant had been the contribution of economic historians to the Africanist school. What actually occurred was exceedingly complex. Social and cultural, if not technical, aspects of the production and reproduction relationships changed substantively to allow for the cash crop phenomenon. The simplest way to explain these changes is in terms of capital penetration, the investiture of commodity relationships ever deeper within the necessary transactions of life. Extended families and communal work obligations gave way to more individual relationships, or at least became ever more nakedly conducted in cash terms. Often peasants intially produced cash crops in response to the regime of force and its tax demands. Chiefs, notables and household heads pressed those under their control to produce. This gave way to production that operated more freely in terms of the market mechanism: producers sold to traders because they needed cash to survive. They could no longer withdraw from commercial interchange. A man's productive and reproductive capacity depended on marriage, marriage depended on bridewealth payments and bridewealth had to be produced in cash. Crudely speaking, over much of Africa, this development accelerated after World War I.

World War I was more of a landmark in the social and economic, rather than the political history of Africa. The principal political consequence was a repartition of the colonies with the Germans eliminated from Africa. In three German territories (Cameroun, South-West Africa and Tanganyika) heavy fighting caused great hardship to the vast numbers of African soldiers and porters drafted into service. The French, moreover, pressed into service a large conscript force on the European front. South-West Africa passed to South African rule. Cameroun and Togo were split between Britain and France with France gaining the bigger share. Britain acquired German East Africa, now renamed Tanganyika, apart from Ruanda-Urundi which went to Belgium and a small corner handed over to Portugal. In theory the ex-German territories were all under the trusteeship of the League of Nations, but this had very little practical effect; the smaller units were largely absorbed into bigger neighbouring colonies and all were run in the manner of the previously established systems of domination.

The sufferings of Africans during the war probably marked the last high-point of the reign of crude force. During the interwar years a surplus was increasingly produced in Africa through the play of already powerful market forces. In the first years of the century the population probably declined, and in some places was devastated, in most of sub-Saharan Africa apart from the already heavily commercialised zones of West and

South Africa. With new social and economic conditions there was a trend towards an increase in population.

This, of course, imposed new kinds of presure on peasant reproduction as land became scarcer, but it is also an important reminder that the intensified cash nexus brought both opportunity and oppression. The lure of money suggested, by no means unrealistically, that the client, the slave, the youth, the woman, had some chance to earn his or her freedom. Depending on family circumstances and the terms of trade, the household head could aspire to be a petty commodity producer.

Every African peasant community ever studied has shown striking differentiation among households between the (relatively) rich and the poor. Yet the remarkable feature reproduced in so much of the continent was the failure of class lines based on production to cohere firmly among the peasantry. The successful producer did not long remain a 'kulak'; he used his success to buy his way out of production entirely, not to buy more land or equipment. He invested in lorries or in town property that could bring in rents. In some regions he bought ploughs and oxen and rented them at a profit, in others he took to moneylending.

What so sharply characterised the colonial era in Africa was the continued dominance of merchant capital, acting now entirely in harness to financially consolidated, cartelised and concentrated industrial capital in Europe. Calling into being this massive outpouring of peasant surplus, capital did not thrust towards the immediate dissolution of existing productive forms, but instead intensified the web of traders' and middlemen's activities on an unprecedented scale.

The human links in this dense chain of traders and middlemen were very often foreigners. The colonial economies attracted commercial pioneers from throughout the world: Greeks in the eastern half of Africa, Jews in southern Africa, Lebanese in West Africa and Indians everywhere, particularly in East Africa. With their strong kin networks, extending through the caste system (in the case of Hindus), the Indians rapidly developed trading systems which played the central role in the commercialisation of rural Uganda, Kenya, Tanganyika and, to a lesser extent, Nyasaland, Mozambique, Madagascar and other territories. In West Africa, African traders, middlemen and purchasers of crops were very significant, despite Lebanese competition. Here there was an Asian-like bazaar economy. Elsewhere Africans aspired enviously towards advance on the commercial rungs, despite their weaker position.

Most of the profits creamed from the surplus of peasant production, however, accrued to a small number of monopoly firms who generally controlled the credit of the smaller traders. The economy of French West Africa was dominated by Compagnie française de l'Afrique Orientale (CFAO) and Société Commerciale de l'Ouest Africain (SCOA) in particular. The third powerful firm there was the Anglo-Dutch house of Unilever which based its finances on control of palm oil sales and soap manufacturers. Unilever absorbed the Niger Company and its smaller rivals, previously amalgamated into Lever Brothers, and had the lion's share in the economy of British West Africa as a general trading firm, as well as an important one in the French colonies. Colonial banking was also controlled by a small number of rivals. Until the mid-1920s it was monopolised in the Gold Coast and Nigeria by the Bank of British West Africa, integrated with the shipping monopoly of Elder Dempster. In British East Africa commercial houses often represented Indian-based imperial firms.

While the formation of such firms as Unilever apparently belonged to the most sophisticated trends in world capitalist development, their continued hegemony in Africa depended on commercial, rather than productive relations, on peasant individuation and the intensified cash nexus. The conditions under which the peasant household and oligopolies established relations varied enormously. In fact those areas in West Africa where a high level of commoditisation had preceded conquest were also very important cash crop areas. There and elsewhere cash cropping relied on the articulation of a great network of labour migration. Such variables can best be understood through surveying the export crop zones.

Only to a very limited extent did the African colonies export basic foodstuffs to the world market. The cash crops were largely discretionary items of consumption such as coffee, tea and cocoa or industrial crops such as oil-bearing nuts and kernels, cotton and sisal. Therefore a major consideration in their acceptance by Africans was the extent to which they cut into food production. The ideal cash crops were what the French called 'rich' crops – tree crops that allowed for continued self-consumed staple production with a relatively limited input of labour. Cocoa was an ideal example and a remunerative one. At the opposite end of the scale was cotton, which greatly interfered with food crop agriculture and offered the peasantry pitifully low prices for a large amount of labour time. Because most of the colonising powers were anxious to control a supply of cheap cotton for their respective textile industries its cultivation was often pressed, but state compulsion was in general essential throughout this era for its systematic development.

The cocoa export production of West Africa makes a striking contrast. In what was the Gold Coast it is said that a labourer brought back the first pods from the plantations on the Spanish island of Fernando Póo (now called Bioko) in the Gulf of Guinea. Its cultivation was furthered by the Basel Missionary Trading Company, which successfully combined the Gospel with business, as well as by coastal middlemen merchants who knew the prices and potential value of the crop in Europe. From the 1890s enterprising cocoa-tree cultivators often travelled deep into lightly settled forest country and obtained land cheaply from communities there. At first they could count on the labour of subordinated household members, youths and women and perhaps also slaves for the initial hard work of clearing. In western Nigeria twenty years later the labour of slaves and pawns, who were engaged to work for a household head to fulfil a debt, appears to have been fundamental to the original cocoa plantings.

In all Africa the southern Gold Coast and western Nigeria were the most commercialised zones before conquest. In part this reflected the development of internal productive forces, but clearly it must also be related to the intensity of commercial contact with Europe from the days of the slave trade. Neither colony collected head-or poll-taxes as in most of Africa; revenue sufficient to balance the colonial budget could be derived from customs income alone – in Nigeria mainly from spirits imports. Thus commerce in cocoa, already preceded by the trade in rubber, timber and palm oil in the nineteenth century, was not originally or merely a response to taxation. By World War I the Gold Coast was becoming the main world producer of cocoa.

Gold Coast cocoa production depended upon tens, then hundreds of thousands of migrant workers who obtained a share of the crop for their labour. Through the 1920s, as cocoa farming spread further east in Nigeria and north in the Gold Coast, migrants still hoped to acquire cocoa plots of their own eventually. This became less and less possible and their situation more marginal as time went on. Within the cocoa-tree owning population there was a concentration in the hands of bigger producers. Beyond the zone of cocoa farming there developed rural communities devoted to producing foodstuffs in which the cocoa forests were now deficient. Fewer yams were grown and more people ate cassava, a protein-poor but relatively easy to grow root crop, as their staple. Cocoa trees also flourished to the west of the Gold Coast in the Ivory Coast and here too migrant labour was a crucial component in the economy.

The great export crop of the West African savanna was ground-nuts, an annual growth long cultivated and consumed by Africans. It was less soil destructive and less demanding than cotton and could be intercropped with grains. One great centre of ground-nut production was northern

Nigeria. Ground-nut cultivation for export was largely induced through both administrative and economic pressures by the local merchants and ruling class whose agents demanded cash taxes and bought crop advances. The sudden surge in ground-nut sales that followed the completion of the railway to Kano in 1912, plus a major drought, led to a severe famine. As a result ground-nut production fell off for some years, only to rise again after World War I.

The other great ground-nut-growing zone was in Senegal and Gambia. Here, much as in the southern Gold Coast, the historical conditions included a background of commercial production and transport aimed at overseas sales. Ground-nuts were cultivated with such intensity as to affect foodstuff production and, under French auspices, Senegal became a major importer of Asian rice and therefore sub-Saharan Africa's first food-deficient territory. Much of the expansion of ground-nut production related to the control over a great labour pool of youthful adepts by Islamic orders, particularly the Senegalese-originated Murids. To work for a holy man was among the highest obligations enjoined by the Muridiyya. The *shaykhs* could order new settlers in a community to produce ground-nuts and make over the harvest for a period of some years before granting the land to them. The most intense ground-nut production in Senegal occurred in the Murid 'new territories' opened up by the French-built railway on land previously limited to pastoral activity. In other parts of Senegal ground-nut production relied upon the labour of seasonal migrants from the French Sudan and Guinea – the *navétanes* (or strange farmers, as the Gambians called them).

Across Africa in Buganda there was a new spurt in cotton production during the 1920s, linked to the use of massive migrant labour from Ruanda-Urundi and intensifying commercial pressures and inducements. This went hand in hand with a diminution in the legal power of the *mailo* landowners for here smallholders directed the advance. Elsewhere in Uganda cotton production was associated originally with pressures from administratively appointed chiefs who garnered the lion's share of the profits.

The greatest cotton zone in Africa, however, was just south of the Sudanese capital of Khartoum, in the land between the Blue and White Niles called the Gezira. The 'Gezira scheme' relied on a special agreement between the British state and a corporate consortium which shared the profits. The state erected a series of waterworks and irrigation facilities upon which the peasantry depended. Within the Gezira, under the umbrella of state coercion, a class of moneylenders and rich farmers, pressed the poor to produce cotton while a bottom layer of migrants from northern Nigeria and other parts of Islamic West Africa supported the heaviest burden of exploitation. Elsewhere in the Sudan religious orders organised the growing of cotton in circumstances not dissimilar to Senegal. Most of the examples considered above cannot be comprehended entirely on the basis of pressures affecting the local household. It is true that the labour of youths, women and other dependents within the household was crucial for the efflorescence of cocoa in south-central Cameroun or coffee on the slopes of Mount Kilimanjaro among the Chagga of Tanganyika. Elsewhere, as indeed with mining and settler agriculture, 'peasant' export agriculture depended fundamentally on migrant labour. Labour migration came to involve millions in every section of the continent. Workers circulated within the more commercially developed colonies such as Nigeria, Kenya and the Belgian Congo and elsewhere crossed borders to where they could find the source of cash they needed.

Labour migration developed at the intersection of two powerful tendencies. On the one hand it initially offered to the migrant the possibility of returning home having achieved a particular target in cash, whether under compulsory or voluntary circumstances; youths could escape from exploitation by elders and grasping chiefs. On the other hand it appealed enormously to capitalists of all sorts who were able to procure a wage force without paying for long-term subsistence costs or family support; all they needed to offer was a wage to cover the immediate survival needs of the individual worker while on the job together with a cash sum to be introduced into the rural household. Under these circumstances the social obstacles that obstructed the introduction of capitalist production could be profitably evaded. The extent to which labour migration disrupted (or actually assisted) the viability of household production varied enormously, not the least on the specific conditions of each individual. Whether or not agricultural labour was women's work was an important factor. Cattle-owning communities where the migrant worked to buy stock seem also to have been able to sustain a higher rate of migration. Workers became experts at knowing the conditions in different distant labour markets and the fortunate could sometimes accumulate cash to begin a petty business or acquire land. Others, however, were trapped in a cycle of stagnation and decline where the viability of rural communities became affected, notably in southern Africa.

Many colonies became informally divided into 'rich' export-producing zones and 'underdeveloped' reservoirs of migrant labour. Apart from Nigeria, where the north absorbed much of its own wage labour force, the West African savanna away from the coast was such a reservoir for the southern forest belt. Rural Northern Rhodesia and Nyasaland, southern Mozambique and Ruanda-Urundi, were others. In those colonies and, above all, in and immediately around South Africa where the demands of capital for labour were truly voracious, peasant production suffered most drastically and African lands were virtually synonymous with migrant zones. Parts of Kenya and especially Southern Rhodesia and South-Weat Africa also approached such conditions.

It has been suggested earlier that capital penetration in Africa through the nineteenth century had a real but fairly limited impact. The colonial era, however, marked a watershed. Dramatic evidence came with the onset of the great depression which by 1930 was felt in severity throughout the continent. Obliged by the tax system and by their own dependence on cash Africans in many regions responded to catastrophic declines in the price of produce by growing more, not less, cash crops. They could no longer simply withdraw from the market when prices were poor. The regimes in settler colonies such as Northern Rhodesia and Kenya actually turned increasingly to the encouragement of African production as the peasants so clearly best sustained the new harsh conditions of the international market. The depression also revealed that migrant labour could no longer be summoned or dismissed at will; Africans were not always able or did not choose to leave town and return to the bush as jobs became scarce. A process of proletarianisation had begun which helped to sustain the first serious waves of strikes by workers in the late 1930s (Copperbelt strike of 1935; Thiès, Senegal railway strike of 1938; Mombasa dock strike of 1939) as more prosperous conditions returned and portended a new era.

## The Colonial State

Colonial administration was shaped to the needs of the material conditions of the African colonies as seen from the metropolis. Initially after the conquest the administrations had a strongly military character. Individual officers had enormous discretionary powers and were often eccentrics and adventurers. In time the systems became increasingly bureaucratised with larger and more specialised services emanating from the colonial capitals. Yet in the countryside a small number of all-purpose local administrators, those the French called the *rois de la brousse* (kings of the bush), still retained a great deal of authority, especially in assessing politically the balance of social forces. The British referred directly to a 'political' service at the local level.

From the pages above it should be clear that the state intervened crucially and repeatedly to promote capitalist enterprise through policies regarding labour, taxation, land and business; this after all was its main purpose in Africa where it cannot be said to have stemmed from the interplay of local forces. The state never simply represented the interests of a firm, however. It mediated between the needs of a variety of metropolitan interests, occasionally conflicting. This is where it differed from the chartered companies that often had done the dirty work of conquest.

More surprisingly, the colonial state often acted to limit or even to block capital penetration in the course of dissolving existing social relationships. This was largely for reasons of expediency. Resting on a small military presence, which was small because home treasuries had limited patience with expenditures on African adventures, local interest groups had to be appeased and balanced against one another. Social conflicts had to be avoided when possible. Indeed, the state often acted as a brake for capital through conservative policies meant to shore up existing African institutions which seemed to form an essential prop of the system as a whole. At the same time, as the era of force began to fade in most regions, military regimen began to give way to bourgeois normality and the rule of bourgeois law; this also limited the sway of colonial despotism.

The colonialists saw themselves as paternalist, bureaucratic dictators, yet they relied on creating a class of intermediaries who could effectively intervene in the daily lives of Africans. This meant, in the countryside, the recognition (or creation) of the colonial chiefs whose primary function was to collect taxes and to preserve administrative control. Sometimes chiefs were members of old royal families carefully selected for their subservience and at first frequently removed when they failed to serve their purpose. Sometimes they had no traditional legitimacy at all, occasionally having been interpreters or even servants to the first generation of Western conquerors. The latter were particularly frequent in regions where no hierarchial political authority had previously existed.

Traditional legitimacy was often irrelevant so long as patrimonial ties in society continued to be salient. Upstarts in such areas as south-eastern Nigeria (the warrant chiefs) and northern Uganda proved very effective at exerting their authority and incidentally used their administrative situations to form the lynchpins of a new class. However, the British in particular were often convinced that, when possible, it was worthwhile to establish the appearance of a 'traditional' government as a means of securing effective overall control, particularly where the very low level of economic development did not disrupt the superficial workings of such

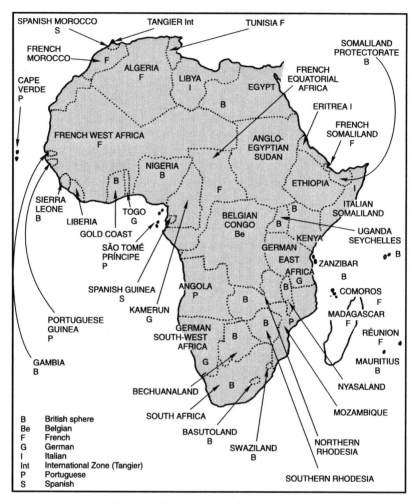

SPANISH MOROCCO
S

FRENCH
MOROCCO

CAPE
VERDE
P

TANGIER Int

TUNISIA F

SOMALILAND
PROTECTORATE
B

F

ALGERIA
F

LIBYA
I

EGYPT

FRENCH
EQUATORIAL
AFRICA

B

ERITREA I

FRENCH WEST AFRICA
F

NIGERIA
B

ANGLO-
EGYPTIAN
SUDAN

FRENCH
SOMALILAND
F

B

F

ETHIOPIA

I

SIERRA
LEONE
B

LIBERIA

TOGO
G

GOLD COAST

SÃO TOMÉ
PRÍNCIPE
P

SPANISH GUINEA
S

KAMERUN
G

BELGIAN
CONGO
Be

GERMAN
EAST
AFRICA
G

B

KENYA

ZANZIBAR
B

ITALIAN
SOMALILAND

UGANDA
SEYCHELLES

B

B

PORTUGUESE
GUINEA
P

GAMBIA
B

ANGOLA
P

GERMAN
SOUTH-WEST
AFRICA

B

B

B

B

P

G

COMOROS
F

MADAGASCAR
F

RÉUNION
F

MAURITIUS
B

BECHUANALAND

B

NYASALAND

B   British sphere
Be  Belgian
F   French
G   German
I   Italian
Int  International Zone (Tangier)
P   Portuguese
S   Spanish

SOUTH AFRICA

BASUTOLAND
B

SWAZILAND
B

MOZAMBIQUE

NORTHERN
RHODESIA

SOUTHERN RHODESIA

Map 3.   The African Colonies in 1914

'traditions'. Indeed social science research of the period, largely under the rubric of anthropology, was directed to finding the real chiefs, the 'legitimate' older forms of social and cultural authority, in the service of fine-tuning colonial domination.

This policy is generally known as 'indirect rule' and is particularly associated with Lord Lugard and northern Nigeria, in part because of the ideologically efficacious propaganda of Lugard and his wife, an imperialist publicist. Under indirect rule the British claimed to interfere as little as possible with the regime of the emirs whose 'native authorities' were buttressed by 'native treasuries'. Thus Africans could advance along 'their own lines'. In reality, while the emirs could use their positions to extort substantial incomes, their freedom to rule was very circumscribed. The original ruling emirs were almost all deposed while their allegiance to Sokoto was largely nullified. In one emirate, Daura, the pre-Sokoto *jihad* ruling family was 'restored' to the throne as a prospective lesson to other notables. The treasuries went largely to the sustenance of the indirect rule bureaucracy and emirs, although the very biggest also supported public works, thus subsidising the colonial administration as a whole in which the 'native authorities' had absolutely no authority. Undoubtedly, though, they were as a result able to become crucial in the maintenance of colonial power and in the conduct of political intrigues within the context of colonial northern Nigeria.

The indirect rule model was copied elsewhere. Lugard, after unifying northern and southern Nigeria, used it to reintroduce the monarchy to Benin in 1916. In the 1920s the Asantehene was restored to the Golden Stool in the Gold Coast while a strange, deeply resented attempt was made to resuscitate the Oyo Empire after a century of eclipse in Yoruba country, Nigeria. Other classic locales for indirect rule were Swaziland and Basutoland in southern Africa, Barotseland in Northern Rhodesia and Buganda in Uganda. The first three were migrant labour reserve zones, a condition that went well with the depredations of 'traditional' authority reinforcing its own controls while acting in the colonial economic interests.

In contrast the continental European powers tended from an early date to humble the prerogatives of most local aristocracies. Their relative disinterest in indirect rule partly reflects the extent to which so many of the strongest and most coherent nineteenth-century African states lay in the areas of commercial importance that the British managed to reserve for themselves. Yet the French and the Belgians too made an effort to utilise the old ruling strata when it seemed advantageous and the difference in colonial policies on this score is sometimes overdrawn.

Colonial success in making use of African authorities in this manner varied, often with the particular social and political circumstances of the territory involved. Undoubtedly in some areas the mass of people were caught up sufficiently in apparently traditional systems that continued to maintain real patrimonial force locally so as to blunt effectively the development of an anti-colonial consciousness. On the other hand, the 'native authorities' system aroused the anger of any Africans of weight excluded from them, notably among the trading and clerical class of coastal British West Africa. Now thoroughly subordinated economically to the monopoly firms, but increasing in numbers and sophistication, this class found limited outlet for development or accumulation in a system dominated by the concept of indirect rule. In West Africa a few representatives of this class became elected members of legislative councils and municipal officials, but their powers were purely advisory.

The French colonies were as despotically ruled as any, but they contained the anomaly of the *quatre communes*, the four towns of Senegal – Dakar, Saint Louis, Gorée and Rufisque – where all locally born residents had the legal rights of French citizenship from 1871 and were represented in the French Chamber of Deputies. A small number of Africans outside the communes, through the administrative evaluation of a variety of criteria, could obtain a similar status. Such representation existed also for Angola in the Portuguese parliament under the republic (1910–26). An imitative system of individual assimilation was also created then. This eventually covered perhaps one per cent of the Angolan population with a smaller proportion in Guiné or Mozambique. The legal rights of Africans in the French and Portuguese systems (including the existence of a free press) were at times significant, but varied depending on the vagaries of metropolitan democracy. Such democratic rights as existed diminished under Vichy France (1940–4) and in Portugal after the overthrow of the republican regime in 1926.

Nevertheless African intermediaries of the old compradore type were deliberately rejected by the colonial powers as principal bearers of intruding capitalist values, political or economic. In the economic sphere they were outdistanced by Indians, Lebanese and other immigrants who carried little political weight while the framework of indirect rule was deliberately designed to exclude them. Yet all the other potential agents of a new society – accumulating peasants, white settlers, old ruling classes – also presented problems as much as opportunities for capital, a situation the next chapter explores.

### Notes

1. Karl Marx, *Das Capital*, I, chs 31–2.

2. The weakness of Portuguese capitalism meant that national interests were unable to compete very effectively within Portuguese colonies in many spheres and that different regions of the colonies were never integrated into one coherent economic unit. British interests predominated in the plantation sector of the Zambesi valley of Mozambique while South African and Rhodesian interests affected the entire colony. Belgian capital, according to W. G. Clarence-Smith, predominated in the economy of northern Angola.

3. With the exception of a minority of skilled workers, European or South African whites in southern Africa, Africans from the coast in West Africa.

4. The size of the mines work force in cases discussed (1937): UMHK mines, Belgian Congo, 8166 averaged monthly; Northern Rhodesia mines, 19 304; Nigerian tin mines, 36 142.

5. Europeans in tropical Africa in 1935–6; the largest settler communities:

1. Southern Rhodesia    55 419    5. Belgian Congo    18 680
2. South West Africa    31 049    6. Kenya    17 997
3. Angola    30 000    7. Mozambique    10 000
4. French West Africa    19 061    8. Northern Rhodesia    9 913

From Lord Hailey, *An African Survey* (Oxford University Press, 2nd edn, 1945), p. 109.

TABLE 6.1.  *Expansion of export cash crops from tropical Africa in '000 tons*

| | 1895 | 1905 | 1920 | 1928 | 1934 | 1938 | 1941 |
|---|---|---|---|---|---|---|---|
| *Coffee* | | | | | | | |
| Angola | | | | | 16.4[s] | | |
| Belgian Congo | | | | | 17[s] | | |
| Ivory Coast | | | | | 1.3[t] | 10.1[x] | 28 |
| Kenya | | | 3.5[f] | 7.9[q] | | 17.7[y] | |
| Tanganyika | | 1.1[b] | | 6[k] | 14.8 | 13.7 | |
| Uganda | | | 0.2[g] | | | 12.6[y] | |
| *Cotton* | | | | | | | |
| Belgian Congo (fibre) | | | 0.02[h] | 9.6[l] | | 42 | |
| French Equatorial Africa | | | | 0.8[l] | 5[u] | 9[z] | |
| FrenchWest Africa | | | | 4.2[m] | | 3.9[aa] | |
| Nigeria | | 1.9[c] | | 6[n] | 4.6[v] | 8.3[bb] | |
| Uganda | | 0.2[d] | | 36[o] | | 80[cc] | |
| *Cocoa* | | | | | | | |
| Cameroun | | | 2.5 | | 21[w] | 31 | |
| Gold Coast | 0.01 | 5 | 125 | 225 | 230 | 263 | |
| Ivory Coast | | | 2.5[i] | 16[l] | 26[t] | 55[aa] | |
| Nigeria | | 3.9[b] | | 45[n] | 63[v] | 96[bb] | |
| Togo | | | | | 8.6[s] | | |
| *Bananas* | | | | | | | |
| Cameroun | | | | | | 17[dd] | |

| | 1895 | 1905 | 1920 | 1928 | 1934 | 1938 | 1941 |
|---|---|---|---|---|---|---|---|
| Guinea (French) | | | 0.1 | $4.0^l$ | $22^u$ | 53 | |
| *Ground-nuts* | | | | | | | |
| Gambia | | $58^e$ | | $75^m$ | | $50^{dd}$ | |
| Nigeria | | | $41^j$ | $109^n$ | $189^v$ | $250^{bb}$ | |
| Senegal | | 220 | | $410^p$ | $520^m$ | 601 (French West Africa)$^y$ | |
| *Palm kernels* | | | | | | | |
| Belgian Congo | | | | | | 85 | |
| Cameroun | | | | | | 36 | |
| Dahomey | | | | | | 52 | |
| French Equatorial Africa | | | | | | 13 | |
| Ivory Coast | | | | | | $36^{bb}$ | |
| Nigeria | $121^a$ | $174^c$ | | $255^n$ | $275^v$ | $334^{bb}$ | |
| Sierra Leone | | | | | | 78 | |
| Togo | | | | | | 13 | |
| *Palm oil* | | | | | | | |
| Belgian Congo | | | | | | 66 | |
| Cameroun | | | | | | 8.9 | |
| Dahomey | | | | | | 16.6 | |
| Nigeria | 54 | | 78 | 125 | | 122 | 139 |
| *Sisal* | | | | | | | |
| Kenya | | | $5^f$ | $15^q$ | | $31^y$ | |
| Tanganyika | | $21^b$ | | $18^k$ | 73 | 107 | |
| *Tobacco* | | | | | | | |
| Southern Rhodesia | | | | $1.6^i$ | $9.6^r$ | $9.2^{aa}$ | |

| | | |
|---|---|---|
| a 1900–4 average | k 1925 | u 1933 |
| b 1913 | l 1929 | v 1930–4 average |
| c 1910–14 average | m 1930 | w 1935 |
| d 1905–6 | n 1925–9 average | x 1937 |
| e 1910 | o 1925–6 | y 1936–8 average |
| f 1920–2 average | p 1924–8 average | z 1938–9 |
| g 1923–5 average | q 1927–9 average | aa 1939 |
| h 1917 | r 1927 | bb 1935–9 average |
| i 1922 | s 1934–8 average | cc 1937–8 |
| j 1915–19 average | t 1932 | dd 1936 |

*Sources*: diverse statistics

# 7

## CULTURE, CLASS AND SOCIAL CHANGE IN COLONIAL AFRICA, 1900–40

'The white man had indeed brought a lunatic religion, but he had also built a trading store and for the first time palm-oil and kernel became things of great price, and much money flowed into Umuofia.'

Chinua Achebe, Things Fall Apart (Fawcett Crest, 1969 printing), p. 162

'Immediately white men came justice vanished.'

Testimony of a chief in Okigwi Division, Nigeria, as reported in A. N. Afigbo, The Warrant Chiefs (Longman, 1972), p. 283

### Class Relations in Colonial Africa

From the social perspective the development of capitalism tends towards the increasing dominance of two antagonistic classes: the capital-holding and investing bourgeoisie and the landless and resourceless working class or proletariat. However, the operative word here is 'tends'. Even in the most advanced capitalist society at present, the picture is far from being so simple. Technological needs create new strata who are part-managerial, part-worker in outlook and function; increasingly elaborate state mechanisms need manning. The classic division of capitalist/proletarian is in any event the historic product of centuries of economic change and class struggle in Europe. In Africa the classic tendency began to take shape during the colonial period but, in accordance with the limited economic development of capitalism achieved only a modest social purchase.

In Europe capitalist development determined a process of growing privatisation of land rights with the dominance of capitalist social, legal and economic arrangements on the land. There was little of this in colonial Africa. Even where settler agriculture predominated, as in the highlands of pre-World War II Kenya, the 'landless' squatters continued to have extensive access to land and stock through the inability of the settler landlords to control the situation. As we have seen, attempts to turn African aristocracies into progressive landlords generally failed and private land tenure developed only very fitfully. In most of the continent, population densities were not high enough to prevent continued cultivators' access to basic resources. Where pressure on the land occurred it took the form of tilling increasingly less favourable soils or the decline in the amount of fallow time to which the land had exposure.

Instead of straightforward capitalist farming, a bewildering and rich variety of transitional forms between pre-capitalist and capitalist social types arose, depending on a host of specific circumstances. Of uniform weight as a cause of change in rural life was the greatly increased role of cash transactions, infesting all the ceremonial rituals and essential interactions that marked the community. Social reciprocity linking large households and villages gave way before the smaller household and this in turn provoked greater emphasis on the need to secure money and to buy services and goods.

Many researchers have followed the lead of K. W. J. Post in taking the increasing subjection of a more individuated peasantry to the cash nexus and the economic demands (and political controls) of the state as part of an historic process of *peasantisation*. Such a process would require qualification for those parts of the continent where either a sharply articulated class structure had long existed (Hausaland or highland Ethiopia) or commodity exchange had become extremely important by the nineteenth century (the Niger delta or southern Gold Coast). Lugard, for instance, saw the British, in conquering northern Nigeria, as frankly replacing an earlier ruling class through making demands upon the *talakawa*, the mass of poor commoners. 'Peasantisation' may also obscure the great variety of situations which came to prevail depending upon the sexual division of labour, prevalence of pastoralism, existence of a 'rich' cash crop and so on.

Peasantisation, for instance, could lead to both immiseration or modest prosperity. In the first generation of colonial rule the evidence of warfare, disease, famine and depopulation in much of sub-Saharan Africa suggested the predominance of the former. When crops brought in relatively good prices and the opening of transit routes enabled commodities to be bought and sold comparatively cheaply, the situation was reversed. Populations began to increase and living standards, from the point of view of commodity accumulation and circulation, to rise. The worst conditions never applied to some parts of Africa while the improvements characteristic of the 1920s never much assisted such backward regions as Portuguese Guinea.

Within the village peasant households differentiated into richer and poorer depending on a wide range of factors. It would be wrong, however, to overstress the development of distinct (and potentially antagonistic) *classes* among a socially exclusive peasantry. The most prosperous peasant often moved out of agriculture entirely and learnt to exploit the system commercially. It was here, rather than in agriculture proper, that profits lay. In the richer coffee or cocoa zones the peasantry as a whole tended to aspire to petty proprietorship and the accumulating drive of the little capitalist. The scale of this drive, despite the absolute poverty of Africa compared with industrialised countries, was strong. As the more important zones of cash crop agriculture attracted large migrant labour forces, the aspirations of the successful local farmer passed on to those from other zones.

Where settlers or urban-based enterprise pushed against such possibilities, peasantries were often most frustrated. Thus in southern Africa many rural zones were increasingly unable to permit the extended reproduction of peasant families. The population depended so heavily on cash flows from mines, farms and towns that they were no longer able to sustain themselves on the land, let alone export cash crops. Settler areas generally sharply demarcated 'white' and 'African' productive spheres; thus even here the extreme differentiation that followed was territorial and entire districts decayed.

The peasantry generally confronted two basic forces against whom it could strive directly: the colonial state with its agents and the merchant network. Thanks to the almost universal and inevitable use of African agency in both these spheres at ground-level, such confrontation was rarely perceived by peasants as being confrontation simply with 'colonialism', 'whites' or 'the state'. Indeed social and political conflict in rural Africa were frequently imbricated into older conflicts and cleavages. This was especially so in supposedly traditional settings. No sooner had the British restored the Asantehene to his throne in Kumasi in 1935 and the rejoicings of the Asante nation died down, than conflicts began to break out within the framework of the indirect rule system. Cocoa wealth and the end of slavery with other forms of pre-capitalist dependence made it impossible to reorder smoothly the old hierarchies. Some of the chiefs were soon in sharp conflict with the 'young men' or commoners. Some provincial notables were advantaged through the restoration of the Golden Stool; others resented the new framework through which they were obliged to operate and agitated for separation from Asante. The Asantehene had to find a way to promote the interests of his richest subjects, the large farmers and cocoa-brokers, without losing the esteem of the masses.

There were some close parallels in Buganda. The depredations of the *mailo* lords evoked intense antagonism expressed in the name of those lineage chiefs whose humbler claims had been ignored in the Uganda Agreement. The Ganda commoners often supported this agitation, having little more affection for the principal agency of the new ruling class, the *Lukiiko*, or legislature, than the eighteenth-century English artisans held for their corrupt House of Commons. They preferred to defend the prerogatives of the *kabaka*, now transformed in memory into a stern but just champion of the poor. It does not take too searching a light to see an acute class conflict operating through the veil of constitutional and cultural forms.

Retention of land rights and the strength of merchant, as opposed to industrial, relations within colonial Africa, meant that the rise of a large wage-labour force did not entirely proletarianise, or divorce from the land, the workers. Instead the cash nexus, together with pressure from the colonial state, threw up an immense migrant population while constantly pressing men (and, more slowly, women) into the towns to lead a marginal life searching for patrons and work.

Conditions in the towns (which lacked decent housing or sanitation and the most basic amenities), not to speak of rigidly-controlled mining compounds, were stark; the worker had to rely on maintaining home contacts if possible. This helps to explain the close links which often bound him to more thriving kin and neighbours who could offer lodging or an employment opening in the town and/or access to land and services in the country.

It is sometimes rather too crudely stressed that this meant that Africa developed no real working class. In fact, workers, even those not entirely committed to life on a payroll, could and did resist capital and fought it when they felt that it was necessary to their interests. However, the form of struggle tended to reflect their continued attachment to the land. It seems typical of early working-class history in colonial Africa that labourers shirked, evaded discipline or control and deserted rather than strike or establish formal industrial organisations. Yet such resistance could be most effective. According to the Rhodesian Chamber of Mines in 1905:

> from the majority of natives of the town to obtain a good day's work is an impossibility. By a system of passive resistance they are able to defeat the objects of a master who deserves value for his money.[1]

However, the relationship of worker to peasant was close and responses to rural conditions had the greatest significance for the urban workplace or mine-camp and vice versa. The extension of wage-labour was to have important consequences, economic and social, for the rhythms of rural life. It was through wage-labour, particularly when cash cropping was not a feasible option, that cash entered into the community to the benefit of the worker. Whereas cash agriculture could sometimes be a means of maintaining existing social control mechanisms, wage-labour, especially if it benefited former slaves, youths or women, tended to threaten them and destroy the patriarchal coherence of the household, lineage or village. Without placing him in the position of a pure proletarian, wage labour increasingly put the African worker in direct contact with capital and created the conditions for new forms of class struggle throughout the continent.

On the higher rungs of the labour hierarchy, though, stood a growing number of skilled workmen, generally paid far more than the unskilled and able to support a family with their wage. The railwayman and the clerk are the most important and widely distributed examples. The experienced clerk in Nigeria in the 1920s made five, six or seven times the wage of the building worker. Skilled workers often identified with some aspects of the colonial system to which their skills seemed linked. These were often derived from a mission education and they aspired to running small businesses while looking up to those Africans at the top of their hierarchies at work and outside. When they formed labour organisations their severance pay as a base for capital accumulation in trade or land was generally a much more significant demand than the pension. Often the clerk or artisan kept to his job for only a limited number of years while he planned his entrée into the petty avenues of commerce. Where women played a major role in trade he sometimes lent money to set up his wife or other female relations with goods and connections. At the same time, vulnerable to the trade cycle through dependence on wage labour and occupying a strategic position in the colony, the skilled worker had the capacity to disrupt a whole territory with a major strike and could display a strong labour consciousness.

What was barely discernible within colonial society was an African bourgeoisie. African businessmen there were, but largely in the sphere of circulation. Within the systems of production, whether in agriculture or in industry, pre-capitalist ownership of the means of production dominated or foreigners were essentially in control. Some historians stress that African businesses were overwhelmed by unfair competition from both European settlers and trading diasporas such as the Indians, with the complicity of the colonial state. It has often been noted that colonial banks were reluctant to make credit available to African concerns. It is less often pointed out that some Africans, those who had the collateral that fitted the banks' requirements, did succeed in procuring loans.

The impermeability of African social and economic conditions to capitalist transformation was perhaps as, or more, crucial than discrimination in blocking the formation of a capitalist entrepreneurial class. No native bourgeoisie seriously contested, however unequally, the conditions for capitalist accumulation in Africa with the great Western banks and industrial trusts. This contrasts sharply with conditions in much of colonial Asia, particularly British India, or in South Africa, which will be discussed in the next chapter.

It is quite wrong, though, to assume that because no African bourgeoisie existed there were not African surplus-consuming classes. They existed and grew in extent, without coming together as a unified class before 1940. Undeniably those who already commanded labour and resources were in the best position to improve upon their opportunities. Chiefs were often the ideal and premier local opportunists with a punitive corrupt power enhanced by their chance to be the first to know what the colonial administration's plans were about. This was nowhere more true than in such an authoritarian, bureaucratised colony as the Belgian Congo.

Scheming and acquisitive chiefs star equally in *Mister Johnson*, Joyce Cary's comedy on rural northern Nigerian colonial society and in the Camerounian fiction of Mongo Beti and Ferdinand Oyono. In Iteso, a district of northern Uganda where cotton farming flourished from the 1920s on the basis of plough and oxen ownership, it was a small number of local notables, made into 'chiefs' by the British, who, according to the studies of Joan Vincent, formed the basis for a powerful new class.

It was more advantageous for such figures to draw in the masses as clients through the promotion of pre-capitalist forms of social association rather than to isolate themselves as capitalist proprietors. Polygamy gave a man power over the labour of several healthy young women. The survival of extended kinship relations allowed for the establishment and spread of ties that provided both labour and commercial advantages. The capitalist 'miracle' of cocoa production in the Gold Coast did not destroy older concepts of property: matrilineal rights and obligations and traditional forms of loan were very effectively enforced by accumulators. In Western Nigeria also, cocoa did not lead to a rapid deterioration of lineage land rights. Individuals placed strategically within households could operate to their advantage through the claims of lineages.

An immense network of 'independent' traders, tied to the great firms through control of goods and credit, filled the markets of West Africa. Potentially hostile to their creditors and to capitalist firms, they had as well a deep commitment to this bazaar economy engendered by the extension of merchant capital. In both commercial and state sectors, there was also an important, if strictly subordinated component of African employees, particularly in West Africa. The United Africa Company component of Unilever and other trading firms employed considerable numbers of African agents. Their promotion was slow and they were usually under fairly direct supervision of an expatriate manager. Nonetheless many enterprising traders got their start in this way and used their connections with Western capital to good advantage, particularly given the difficulties they experienced in obtaining bank loans.

The state created a substantial class of subservient African bureaucrats whose certification depended on the acquisition of formal education. As we have seen, on the west coast from Senegal to Angola, African compradores had occupied very important positions in the administration of the nineteenth-century colonial enclaves. With the conquest of the interior these opportunities were sharply circumscribed as their ranks were hemmed in by new arrivals from Europe and formal or informal racial discrimination. Before the 1890s the leading African officials and traders of Lagos were likely to socialise at the governor's home on a familiar, collegial basis. By the early years of this century, however, they were only rarely invited to formal affairs as representatives of a class from which the new 'top brass' felt utterly distant. The occasional African continued to hold an important post. The Lagos Director of Education, Henry Carr (1863–1945), a man of more (Western) culture than most of his European colleagues, (and whose library eventually formed the cornerstone for the post-war University of Ibadan) was a paragon. Very conservative in his views, Carr despised the social atmosphere of African Lagos, especially its working class, as much as any colonial official and considered himself to have the mind of an Englishman. Erudite and devout, Carr believed that the African needed above all 'a severer discipline'.[2] Yet his career and social life were invariably surrounded by racist restriction and occasionally unpleasant incidents.

Men such as Carr were the most eminent of a growing class who formed associations, based on state service or a common schooling, that marked a growing territory-wide consciousness and a sense of belonging to a distinct interest group within the colonial sphere. In the 1920s the principal clerks and traders of Tanganyika organised an African Association, deliberately intended to represent 'the African' as opposed to Asians or Europeans. In French West Africa, association with the Ecole William Ponty as an élite-forming institution remained of the greatest significance to graduates and unified them despite origins and careers in territories that spread two thousand miles across West Africa.

Before 1940 such men did not easily come together with chiefs, especially given the efforts of British and other colonial administrators to exclude the educated from the 'Native Administrations', into a single class. The top levels of the African state employees saw these as a deliberate attempt to stymie their own ambitions. Tensions often ran high in the Gold Coast with its level of commercialisation and numerous educated men, despite the trade and family links between the two strata. The exclusion of European-trained lawyers from the 'native courts' was perhaps the most obvious symbol of this antagonism.

The 'educated élite', as they liked to call themselves, had as yet no systematic economic or political project. Their working lives were bound up in the commercial and administrative structures engendered by capitalism in its colonial guise and those structures generally bounded their imaginations and aspirations. However, this did not detract from their great importance as models, patrons and potential power-brokers within African society. Because they were at best (and indirectly only) an incipient bourgeoisie, it is tempting for those inimical to class analysis to suggest that Africa thus had no classes in colonial times, its social contradictions confined to those between ruler and ruled. In fact, social cleavages reformed and intensified in the pressures of the developing colonial economy while the class struggles abounded in many guises.

## Culture and Social Organisation

New cultural forms that arose in the colonial period betray in their tensions as in their creative spark the material forces at play underneath.

In eastern and central Africa a pervasive phenomenon that spread from town to town was the *mbeni* or *beni* dance society. *Beni* dancers sprang from peoples for whom dance had been perhaps the supreme form of musical and aesthetic expression. Yet *beni* was *par excellence* the medium of new communities of urban and wage workers. The uniformed dances imitated military gear and hierarchy within the colonial armed and civilian establishments. Dancers could express at once a pride in mastering the new techniques of survival in the land while mocking and expunging colonial symbols. In Mombasa the gang-leaders on the docks combined labour recruitment with leadership in *beni* troupes which could serve capitalist work-rhythms. Yet it was the *beni* leadership which structured communications during the first African strike on the Northern Rhodesian Copperbelt in 1935. The social and organisational uses of dance were not confined to men, but engaged the emotions and energies of women equally. The strength of the dance lay precisely in its power to represent and symbolise social tensions *and* in the absence of a more political way of resolving them.

Dance was at once a form of cultural expression and social organisation. The dance societies were one among many new organisations that multiplied in work-camps and towns, based on cultural linkages, economic interests and mutual aid. Football, which everywhere was taken up as *the* African male sport, spawned not only playing sides but sports clubs which transcended incipient class tensions while providing an outlet for leadership (and often possibilities for business) to the petty bourgeoisie. Burial and lending societies and African-run churches proliferated. Perhaps most significant was the urban tribal or home-boy association which linked countrymen who had migrated to town from the same area. It was in the towns and under the inspiration of the patterns imposed by capital penetration that 'tribalism' and tribal feeling arose.

In the greater part of Africa lineage or other kinship affiliations had certainly been of the greatest importance in the way people conceived of social organisation. However, these were not closely associated with language, ethnicity or 'race' so as to forge a tribal identity. Conquests, absorptions and migration interspersed and intermingled Africans. Pre-colonial states were often identified with a ruling house defined in terms of lineage, but they were not nations in the sense of a specific culturally-determined people.

Tribes are often conceptualised by Europeans as poor man's versions of their own nationalities and ethnicities. However, colonial tribes were not merely inventions of the conquerors. Their self-definition came out of the harshness and competitive character of economic conditions. The lucky migrant to the town could count on close kin to shelter him and to lend him access to a job or a niche in the petty marketing world. For every job there were competing work-seekers who had other friends and relations pressing for an advantage. Most had to rely on wider cultural affinities, real or invented, for establishing an ability to survive. This encouraged ethnic brokers who were able to create advantageous niches in the accumulation process through their exploitation of the patronage they could exercise. Capitalist firms and the state deliberately provoked such ethnic identifications, linked if possible to 'traditional authority' back home in the bush, in the interests of effective labour control.

Abner Cohen, writing on the Hausa trading and butchering community of the Yoruba city of Ibadan in Nigeria, provides a classic description of ethnic solidarity in practice. The ethnic leaders there were at the same time religious brokers, patrons of trade and landlords, recognised as spokesmen by the local Yoruba establishment. The 'Hausa' of Ibadan were far from all being Hausa speakers at home, hundreds of miles to the north, but in the Ibadan situation, clustered around an occupational nexus, this is what made the most sense for them to claim to be. In one way the Ibadan Hausa were an atypical example. The Islamic Hausa community of this type clearly has far deeper historical roots; this is the ethnicity of long-distance traders in agricultural societies, reminiscent of Islamic trading communities in the West African savanna centuries ago.

The choice of ethnic boundaries varied enormously and could be differently defined from place to place. In East Africa there are excellent examples of 'tribes' arising from no historical roots at all. The congeries of Bantu-speaking peoples in eastern Kenya were dubbed the Bantu Kavirondo by the British for convenience. Later their leaders chose to call themselves Abaluhyia. The biggest 'tribe' in Tanganyika, the Sukuma, were until colonial times only the varied groups designated by the Nyamwezi as 'south'. Even when self-definition had firmer roots, such as among the Yoruba of Nigeria and Dahomey, the definitions became clear-cut and functional largely in the colonial context. In the nineteenth century 'Yoruba' meant someone from Oyo. Only during the colonial period was the language standardised in written form by Christian missionaries and made the basis for a timeless and clearly-defined cultural oneness. Often tribal solidarity was situationally variable. People who identified themselves as being part of a common 'tribe' in a distant town, closer to home, where they were more numerous, split up into competitive groups that were equally considered to be 'tribes'. Whether or not you were 'Yoruba' in Ibadan required further clarification to be significant. Were you an Ibadan Yoruba or something else?

## A Changing Faith

After ethnicity religious activity has received by far the most interest of all forms of cultural expression in colonial Africa. The variety and cultural richness of African religious forms command attention while expressively infusing other facets of life.

In eastern, southern and central Africa a striking consequence of the defeat of African kingdoms was the reorganisation of resistance to conquest in the form of religious movements under the authority of oracles, prophets and doctors. The Maji Maji rebellion, which engaged a large part of the people of central and southern Tanganyika in 1906, originally focused on the healing and prophecy of a man named Kinjikitile. While it arose in an area that particularly suffered from German demands for cotton deliveries, it nevertheless required a particular local spark, a particular ideology of cultural reference. In some parts of Tanganyika Maji Maji failed to catch on because chiefs viewed it as a threat to their authority. In other areas chiefs modified and controlled it to make sure that any successes against the Germans would be theirs.

At almost the same time as Maji Maji threatened German rule in East Africa the British faced a rising in Sokoto province in northern Nigeria. People gathered around the settlement of Satiru and threatened the authority of the state in the name of an original, egalitarian and just Islamic community that represented a peasant interpretation of the *jihad* tradition of Usuman dan Fodio. They fought (and with utmost severity, were crushed) just as much or more against the Sultan of Sokoto as against the British; in fact their movement and challenge to authority antedated the British conquest.

As colonial domination became an irreversible reality, religious movements lost their political character and began to interrelate more closely with colonialism. On the eve of World War I the cult of Mumbo arose on the eastern shores of Lake Victoria in Kenya. Mumbo particularly affected the Gusii-speaking people although it seems not to have originated with them. Mumbo first appeared to its followers in the guise of a giant snake come from the lake to repair the damages in the cultural fabric of rural life. It first attracted serious attention when the British briefly evacuated the border town of Kisii, fearing German invasion in 1914. Mumbo prophesied the more or less violent disappearance of Europeans and the colonial apparatus through supernatural means and a future good life of leisure and plenty without labour. The empty town was looted and burnt and on their return the British investigated the cult members as potential subversives. However, if anti-colonial in form, Mumbo was quietist in content. God, not man, would cleanse the world of injustice. In Mumbo's visions, Christian and material ideas occupied an important place. Mumbo attacked 'traditional' customs like circumcision, challenged elder and male authority and was particularly hostile to chiefs. It was in no real sense a simple return to the old ways, but rather a synthetic movement subsuming both criticism and admiration of changing values.

Much the same could be said of the crusade against witches led by Mwana Lesa (the son of god) who roamed through eastern Northern Rhodesia and Katanga Province of the Belgian Congo in the early 1920s. Mwana Lesa sniffed out evil in the form of witches and arranged for mass killings of the accused before the British government caught up with him and had him executed in 1925. A number of writers have suggested that witchcraft accusations intensified in the early twentieth century in response to social tensions and differentiation within the community. While previously they were part of a more integrated cultural and social system and often under effective control of the chiefs, witchcraft accusations now occurred in the context of sudden enthusiastic eradication movements that could for a short time promise to rid the community of evil. Rarely did they lack for Christian symbolism or borrowings.

It was in the wake of the failure of great movements against early colonial authority like the Chimurenga (Southern Rhodesia) or Maji Maji and prophetic cults that the Christian missionaries followed, gathering up unprecedented mass support. Few Africans had shown much interest in Christianity before conquest. Ardent African converts of the nineteenth century were to be found largely in the colonial enclaves of the West African coast and in South Africa. It was a striking feature of the Americo-Liberians and particularly the Sierra Leonians that they emphasised Christian credentials as part of their validation within the capitalist commercial nexus and in association with their trading ventures, much as Afro-Portuguese commercial communities in an earlier era. Only in a few spots (Buganda, Madagascar) had nineteenth-century social changes paved the way for early mission success.

Conquest brought a quickening tempo to mission activities and in some areas mass conversions by the 1920s. Some of this may be comprehended as part of a desire by Africans to succeed in, and be accepted as part of, the new regime. In all the colonies where schools were common the missionaries completely dominated the new formal education and insisted on conversion as part of the price of schooling. So an ardent Christian faith became a part of the cultural baggage of many African accumulators. Missions were often of great significance in the acceptance of new commodities, commerce and crops and the source of technical and artisanal skills. They were *par excellence* the vehicle for capitalist values in much of the continent.

There was a certain degree of irony to this. The missionaries were typically products of declining classes and regions in the West, such as small-town southern Germany or the North American Great Plains in the era of fascism, populism and rural radicalism. For them, taking up the mission vocation was often a reaction, through personal sacrifice and commitment, against the new industrialised, concentrated capitalism at home. Missionaries tried to spread the values of an earlier capitalism – Western family structure, individualist orientation and the self-justifying work ethic. The Catholic missions of Belgian and Portuguese Africa worked particularly closely with the state. This was far less true in French territory, although the French usually insisted that missionaries be French nationals. The British colonies permitted the activities of a great variety of mission groups who competed vigorously for African souls. It was not unusual for missionaries to fight the settler interest where this was a factor, which enormously increased respect for them among Africans. Even then, with rare exceptions, they did not oppose the essence of the colonial system: segregation, land alienation and migrant labour. Few if any missionaries challenged the political and economic imperatives of colonial domination, as opposed to specific policies, and they usually accepted the racist aspect of it fairly easily.

Becoming a Christian was more than a political choice; it was also a cultural one. Before 1940 a peasant Christianity sustained by semi-literate cultivators, who could not seriously have aspired *en masse* to clerical jobs or professions, had come into being in certain parts of Africa. The significance of this, the atrophying of older religious values, may be related to the broader changes in material life considered above in which the new faith promoted greater conviction.

For a minority of African Christians the mission-derived churches were not wholly satisfying. Independent churches split off, partly provoked by the racism of the mission churches and the domineering attitude of many missionaries. In addition African accumulators used the new sects as a means of satisfying their ambitions for leadership and making business.

Some independent churches were completely conventional in doctrine; others allowed or encouraged customs that the mission churches frowned upon. Polygamy is the most important example. No mission tolerated polygamous marriage, yet material conditions coupled with older beliefs to encourage the urge for a successful man to take additional wives.

The most notorious struggle along these lines came in Kenya in the 1920s when the Scots missionaries among the Kikuyu tried to force the abandonment of female circumcision. Most other missions tolerated the practice and encouraged it to take place in mission clinics or hospitals, but not the Scots. In Kikuyu society female circumcision was considered a gauge of a woman's modesty and had thus become a key symbol of male domination. There ensued a strong reaction leading to large-scale schism within the mission church.

In a typology put forth by the Swedish missionary-sociologist, Bengt Sundkler, such independent churches could be called Ethiopian. Another group he labelled Zionist (deriving from an American sect that focused in Zion City, Illinois, with an early influence in South Africa) because they appeared to represent a yearning for emotional and social connections that the mission churches failed to make. Sundkler felt that the Land Act of 1913 and the impact of the policies of segregation helped to spread the independent churches in South Africa. In the Zionist churches a central place was reserved for the ecstatic personal experience; messianic beliefs in a better world to come on earth through supernatural means were often fundamental. Faith healing and witch cleansing were also part of Zionist practice. In the Zionist churches it is possible to see both continuity with ancient religious forms, no longer accepted as valid without some Christian context being provided, and a response to social dislocation and deprivation.

Simon Kimbangu, who in 1921 in the lower Belgian Congo began to preach that he was the son of God, able to work miraculous cures, was the most famous Zionist prophet of all. The Catholic influence in the Congo was such as to convince the authorities to quickly seize and detain Kimbangu, who lived as a prisoner in Elisabethville for thirty years until his death. Horrified and fascinated by him, missionaries began to produce a vast descriptive literature on his life and teaching. After his departure from the scene Kimbangu's followers converted a huge proportion of the

Kongo-speaking peoples of the lower river valley to the new church, which itself frequently splintered.

The extreme Belgian reaction to Kimbangu belonged to an almost universal colonial assumption that active African religious initiatives were inherently sinister and subversive. Africanist scholars of recent times gave independent churches an enormous scholarly press, assuming that they were in some sense proto-nationalist, prefiguring fully political forms of protest in colonial Africa, like all manifestations of African 'initiative'. The truth is nearly the reverse. Few independent churches functioned as anti-colonial wellsprings. They were indeed a response to colonial conditions, not in the politics of protest but in the ideology of displacement. Much religious practice can be understood as an ideological alternative to an historical outlook. It aims to cross-cut any notion of the contradictions and historical discontinuities that mark social development with a message of timeless truth. Religion thus serves as a means of acceptance and adaptation. The apocalyptic predictions so characteristic of the Zionist churches were part of their failure to imagine a rational transformation of social conditions through struggle. Visions of the hereafter replaced assessments of the present. This is by no means to denigrate the importance of sects as social phenomena, understood for what they were and are. In some colonies they absorbed the energies of a large proportion of the population and undoubtedly their study sheds great light on changing social values.

Like Christianity, Islam has been subsumed under the anti-colonial protest heading, and with equally little justification. Certainly in strongly Muslim parts of Africa rulers tried, with varying success, to organise resistance to conquest in the name of the true faith. Samori, although not a real jihadist, played the card at times. A dramatic example, and not that of a dynast, was Sayyid Muhammad Abdile Hassan, the Somali teacher and poet who harried the British in their Somaliland enclave with great success for twenty years until his natural death in 1920.

From the Muslim point of view, however, the decisive issue was the establishment of a society that upheld Islamic precepts and supported religion, an ideology open to varying interpretations. In Senegal the *jihads* persisted through the nineteenth century and continued to be aimed at the Wolof kings and their retinues. The French may have been infidels, but they were also the source of trade goods and arms; they succeeded where the *shaykhs* failed in destroying the authority of the 'pagan' rulers. So long as they did not interfere with religious practice, Christian rulers could be obeyed.

Islam is a religion of traders and townsmen. Capital penetration brought an augmentation of market life that encouraged Muslim values while typically Muslim crafts and trades flourished. The Murid phenomenon in Senegal was discussed from the economic perspective in the last chapter. Ahmadu Bamba, founder of the order, was at first mistrusted by the French and exiled to Gabon. However, he was permitted eventually to return to Senegal and became a decisive figure in the new social and economic system. In Senegal when the old ruling class was deposed it was the brotherhoods and the *shaykhs* leading them who captured the convictions of the peasantry. On the other side of the Sudanic belt the grandson of the Mahdi (who in time became a knight of the British Empire) had his followers cultivate cotton with similar results to the religious leadership in Senegal. In some respects Islam became a cement in the colonial order. Colonial regimes generally took good care to restrain missionary zeal and keep a low Christian profile in heavily Islamic areas.

Yet Muslims could pose as cultural counterweights to the mere imitation of the colonial master. Islam was apparently a dignified and respectable social garb; Muslims built up their own schools and promoted their international language of discourse, Arabic. Within Islam, every conceivable type of reaction to colonialism and capitalism could be and was expressed. In Muslim northern Nigeria rich merchants effectively usurped the place of the ruling families as principal patrons of religion. In West Africa particularly, Islam spread rapidly under the colonial aegis, adapting itself to new social forms and economic relationships. By 1940 over half the peoples of West Africa were Muslim. In Tanganyika the figure was more like one-third, with much smaller proportions else where in eastern Africa, apart from the older Islamic predominance in parts of the Horn and the middle Nile Valley.

## The Modalities of Resistance

Much of what has been written about colonial African resistance reflects the desires of nationalists and their Africanist sustainers to discover a tradition of resistance to colonialism or white rule that provides an historical platform for the political leadership that took power with the end of the colonial era. In most of Africa the display of force by the colonialists had been overwhelming and quite effective. Pride in the fighting spirit of one's parents or grandparents did not mean that one forgot their defeats and the terrible repression that often followed. Resistance existed, of course, but it was rarely to do with either race or sovereignty in the sense that would suit the fancies of later nationalists. Rather it resulted from crises in the *material* life of Africans and was related to *class* and other social cleavages within African societies.

Two of the best-known African revolts of the early twentieth century, those of the Herero in German South-West Africa in 1905–6 and the Bambatha in Natal (South Africa) shortly after, must be considered as revolts of despair, however heroic. The German regime sought an excuse to dispossess the Herero of their herds and lands. They 'succeeded' beyond intentions – most of the Herero were driven into the desert and died, causing a severe labour shortage. Shula Marks, Bambatha's historian, described that event as a 'reluctant rebellion', largely provoked by the Natal authorities with their intensifying land, cash and labour demands. Chimurenga, now enshrined as the nationalist rising of the Shona people of Zimbabwe in 1896–7, similarly was brought about not through conflict over national sovereignty but through resistance to the increasing economic demands of incoming settlers and the British South Africa Company in Mashonaland. Maji Maji, as we have seen, began in response to the German regime of forced cotton plantings. Of course, none of these can be reduced to purely economistic actions; they all developed particular spiritual and ideological forms that convinced a variety of peoples to lend support.

There was nothing to compare with any of these revolts after World War I. For a generation military resistance to European rule was of marginal significance. Yet there was resistance to the state by the masses and its assessment invariably requires a consideration of prevailing social and economic circumstances. Through much of the central provinces of French Equatorial Africa (Ubangi-Shari and Moyen Congo) a serious armed rebellion spread during 1928–9 in response to the collapse in rubber prices and the French demands for forced labour under particularly brutal circumstances on the Congo-Océan railway. Economic decline equally provoked disturbances in the central Belgian Congo, the Pende rising, in 1931 when cultivators resisted the demands of Unilever to whom they were forced to sell their palm oil and for whom they had to provide labour. Between 1924 and 1931 the Baya war took place in Ubangi-Shari. Despite the name, it unified resisters who were classified as speaking different languages and belonging to different tribes. Tax collection inspired it. In the vision of the leader Karinou, the whites would be forced to do the work of the blacks as the world turned upside down following victory.

Struggles of this kind (like Bambatha or Maji Maji) held no interest for the rising African élite. Why should they sustain resistance to the spread and intensification of the colonial economy on which their existence depended? When the élite spoke out they tended to remain narrowly class-based in their demands and too deeply rooted in the colonial structure to question the colonial order very profoundly. Attempts at class alliance with the African masses were rare and came unstuck fairly quickly; indeed élite organisations generally did not enjoy long lives and frequently collapsed when the state applied hostile pressure.

The African petty bourgeois of the Gold Coast were exceptionally articulate and able to conduct their own case. Before World War I their most significant organisation was the Aborigines' Rights Protection Society, founded in 1897. It engaged the government over proposals to alienate forest land to the Crown which potentially threatened African property rights to the advantage of British gold-mining concessionaires. The colonial government withdrew its legislation, but despite this success the ARPS continued to sit on a very narrow social base and became attenuated. After the war a pan-territorial organisation, the National Congress of British West Africa (NCBWA), was briefly of greater weight. The Congress agitated for those class-based issues that most concerned the Gold Coast élite – improved education, especially at the higher levels, and promotion of Africans within the civil service.

During this period the rhetoric of Pan-Africanism – the regeneration of a united continent, the need for Africans to rise through their own effort – gained currency within the West African élite. Pan-Africanism, including its visionary strain that followed the agitation of the Jamaican Marcus Garvey, was a creation of black America, where Garvey, who preached a return to Africa and a black peoples' capitalism, had a great mass following through the 1920s. In West Africa Garvey's economic ideas appealed particularly to those on the margins of capitalist enterprise, resentful of the handful of big Western commercial firms and ground down by the war and the severe business crisis of 1920–2. This provided a stimulus for regional or even continental political visions. It was not carried to the point of political anti-colonialism, however.

Nor did this would-be ruling class establish a political practice that could link up to mass agitation. This is remarkable because after World War I a wave of political and economic struggles swept West Africa. On the Gold Coast skilled workers began to unionise and strike. In Sierra

Leone riots provoked by inflation took an anti-Lebanese cast in 1919. Porto Novo, capital of French Dahomey, experienced a comparable riot in 1922, while early union activity and strike action hit the crisis-ridden ground-nut economy of Senegal.

The political implications convinced the British authorities to institute elective representation in coastal West African municipal bodies and legislative councils. Sir Gordon Guggisberg, governor of the Gold Coast from 1919 to 1927, while a champion of indirect rule, conciliated the professional men of the towns through the promise of better opportunities in the civil service (a promise never kept), infrastructural investment by the state and the creation of a particularly lavish and élitist secondary school for Africans, Achimota College, which was seen as the seed from which local higher education could grow. Reform and the return of better times silenced the élite. The NCBWA virtually died of inactivity by the middle of the decade.

In the Senegal communes, where Africans had the right to elect a member of the French Chamber of Deputies, a class alliance based on African unity did occur. In 1914 Blaise Diagne, a civil servant who had spent most of his career in the West Indies, became the first African to run for deputy, pulling against the big Bordeaux firms that had previously controlled the seat. Diagne attracted the vote of poorer Africans and established an alliance with the Muslim orders; he helped to arrange for Ahmadu Bamba's return from exile. But Diagne did not establish a base for challenging the French system; indeed he backed conscription of the *Armée Noire* during World War I in return for a government pledge to retain the rights of the four communes. By the end of the war he was invariably put forward as an international spokesman defending the merits of French colonialism to the world, having made his peace with French firms in Senegal. Behind Diagne lay an electoral machine through which mass support could be garnered for an élite, using the state to carve out a small niche in the colonial economy in return for petty privileges and patronage.

The nearest British equivalent was Herbert Macauley, piano tuner, chess aficionado and tribune of the Lagosian masses. For Macauley the equivalent to Diagne's alliances with the *shaykhs* was involvement in the intrigue-ridden competition for control of the old Lagos ruling house. He also led the long fight against the raising of the water rate. He was not consistently even anti-colonial, but was extraordinarily effective at uniting Lagosians of diverse backgrounds.

In general the French system was more liberal than the British in promoting Africans within the colonial administration. It was harsher though in dealings with African businessmen. The commercial élite in Dahomey, although relatively timid politically, was crushed by state policy in the 1920s. Perhaps because its aspirations were so narrowly administrative the élite stratum in French West Africa always emphasised the call for greater opportunities for African individuals within the French system.

The deterioration in commodity prices on the eve of the depression brought a new wave of confrontations. In eastern Nigeria Igbo women attacked the canteens of the monopolies and defied state authority in a series of riots, the 'Women's War' of 1929. Hit hard by the deteriorating terms of trade, they were responding to rumours of new taxes and the elimination within the indirect rule system of political representation for women as a corporate group.

Equally dramatic and significant were the Gold Coast cocoa boycotts of 1930 and 1938. The great depression particularly threatened the interests of the more prosperous cocoa farmers who had gone heavily into debt during good times and were entirely dependent upon sales of cocoa. The cocoa hold-up centred around their efforts to hold back production and force better prices from the buying firms, a venerable commercial tactic on the Guinea coast. The boycotters won support from many chiefs and, for a time, a broad cross-section of farmers. However, they had ranged against them other factions, particularly the cocoa brokers who depended directly on the firms and needed quick sales. The poorer cocoa farmers and especially the landless labourers depended on what cash they could earn and also opposed or quickly abandoned the boycott which failed by the end of 1930.

Seven years later a more effective boycott was organised. This time, in organising a new monopoly Cocoa Pool, the firms were directly challenging the brokers' power as well, so the Gold Coast petty bourgeoisie had more capacity for unity. Moreover the price of cocoa was again falling, but had recovered from the worst phase of the depression. The Pool had to be abandoned formally after months of boycott and in response the state began to plan active intervention in the organisation of cocoa marketing, a process which became of great importance after World War II and will be discussed below in Chapter 9. The class alliance of the boycotts were sustained only briefly, but they were a more weighty harbinger of the forces to be called into play in the 1940s than the promotional demands of coastal civil servants and lawyers' associations such as the NCBWA.

## Thuku and Chilembwe

On the other side of Africa new types of regional and tribal associations formed in Kenya from the end of World War I. Most interesting was the East African Association, an intertribal group in Nairobi led by a telephonist named Harry Thuku. With the economic downturn of 1920 Kenya Africans were hit by wage cuts, settler plans for an extended pass system on the South African model and a substantially increased tax to force out labour. Despite similarities to West African agitation of the period, the activities of the EAA posed a greater threat since potentially they could tie into revolt against the entire labour system. Thuku found an audience both in Nairobi and in the countryside. His movement rapidly became political in character and took on these mass economic issues. To the horror of the settlers and the regime in the midst of Kenya's 'plural society', Thuku began to work with an Indian lawyer who had been struggling against settler attacks on the Indian community. Following what was claimed to be a demagogic speech in rural Kikuyuland Thuku was arrested and his movement suppressed. The 'Thuku troubles' melted away and the tax increase was cancelled, although land and labour issues continued to be pressed by other organisations. When released, Thuku transformed himself into a conservative capitalist farmer, but he was more closely the forerunner of a type of political leadership to come than any other East African. Even the final apotheosis resembled Kenyatta's career after independence.

What Thuku hoped to achieve in 1920–1 is not entirely certain; it does not seem likely that the EAA had the capacity to develop into a revolutionary organisation. The one attempt at revolution in the British colonies was idiosyncratic and to this day wrapped in some mystery, but it is a story all the more worth telling.

When World War I broke out John Chilembwe was an independent missionary in Nyasaland, theoretically backed by black American Baptist support, but in practice largely self-sufficient. Chilembwe was a cash-crop farmer and petty businessman. Pictures survive displaying the elegant and constricted Edwardian clothes in which Chilembwe dressed himself and his family. His Providence Industrial Mission Church was a grand new brick structure, one of the largest edifices in Central Africa. He was an orthodox Baptist preacher; there is no indication of any Zionist yearnings on his part and the photo album suggests a family modelling themselves on the European mission plan, a perfect aspiring African bourgeoisie in miniature.

As a boy Chilembwe had been the protégé of a very rare missionary, Joseph Booth, whose social radicalism was intolerable both to the colonial state and the mission societies. Booth was always associated with the notorious slogan 'Africa for the Africans'. In his search for religious sponsorship he established contact with black American Baptists. He went to America, taking the youthful Chilembwe with him. Chilembwe spent three years in Virginia at a training centre before returning to Nyasaland. (Booth eventually joined the Jehovah's Witnesses, settled in Cape Town and lost touch with Chilembwe.)

In the final months of 1914 Chilembwe planned in secret a rising against British rule in Nyasaland. Exactly why is not clear. We do know that he came into ever sharper conflict with a large neighbouring settler estate, whose manager, William Jervis Livingstone, a relative of the great Scots missionary, had forbidden Chilembwe's people to build a church on his property. Some of Chilembwe's supporters were estate workers from over the border in Portuguese Mozambique where conditions were yet more oppressive. However, Chilembwe had also acquired a chain of fellow conspirators among Nyasalanders of his own class.

It is clear that Chilembwe hoped to profit from the war; this helps to explain his timing. His motives are harder to read. One published but unreliable account suggests that he simply wanted to make a witness and turn martyr – 'to strike a blow and die'. It may be that he had more concrete plans to gain control of Nyasaland and work out some *modus vivendi* with the Germans to whom he sent a message.

In January 1915 the rising took the form of attacks on several estate owners and managers, missions and arms depots. Livingstone was killed. Chilembwe preached a sermon in the grand church the next morning, Livingstone's severed head near the pulpit, calling for resignation and courage according to the most reliable witness. None of the co-ordinated parallel risings elsewhere took place and the government reasserted itself within a couple of days. Chilembwe was killed in flight across the border. The rising had no successor.

One recent discussion of the Chilembwe rising has suggested that the place of the minister and fellow conspirators of his own class has been totally misconstrued and exaggerated.[3] What was significant was an armed rebellion of plantation labourers, abused by Livingstone and his men, who were well aware of resistance to the state still going on across the frontiers in Portuguese Mozambique. It was they who spontaneously killed Livingstone, and Chilembwe's conspiracy represented only a confused and half-hearted petty bourgeois response to their workers' militancy. This interpretation has the great advantage of accounting for the otherwise remarkable willingness of Chilembwe and his friends to take on the British Empire. The élites of colonial Africa (and most of the time, the masses) did not resist in this way. This was not only because the odds were apparently hopeless. It was also because colonialism was a phenomenon of overwhelming complexity that contained very attractive as well as repellent features for Africans. No writer has expressed this better than the Nigerian novelist Chinua Achebe, in *Things Fall Apart*. Umuofia, the village of the book, is from the beginning not the harmonious bucolic community of the romantic nationalist's imagination. It is rife with contradictions and tensions. The rich heads of households who dominate the youths, women and slaves and determine the community's fate are the sources of injustice and hardship for many. Conquest evokes in Umuofia a process of disaggregation that strains and sunders the web of familial relationships, using an already existing potential for social dissidence: 'The white man... has put a knife on the things that held us together and we have fallen apart.'[4]

Achebe shows many of the finer aspects of Igbo village life; he produces an elegy to Okonkwo, the hard-working, pious and successful household head and the way that he is humiliated and killed by the coming of colonialism and Christianity. Yet Okonkwo is also an arrogant bully. Achebe portrays equally the brutality of many Igbo customs, typified in Okonkwo's murder of a captive boy he has adopted into his household when the boy is demanded in sacrifice by the gods. This above all nauseates Okonkwo's own son who leaves the homestead and ultimately becomes a Christian minister. Achebe suggests the terror and cultural ruthlessness of the colonial impact, but also its liberating and stimulating effect, a heady brew not so different from that served to the masses by early capitalism in the land of its origins.

## Notes

1. Cited in Charles van Onselen, 'Worker Consciousness in Black Miners', in Robin Cohen, Peter Gutkind and Phyllis Brazier, eds, *Peasants and Proletarians* (Hutchinson, 1979).
2. Patrick Cole, *Modern and Traditional Élites in the Politics of Lagos* (Cambridge University Press, 1975), p. 106.

3. Suggested by K. McCracken in Leroy Vail and Landeg White, *Capitalism and Colonialism in Mozambique* (Heinemann, 1980), p. 177.

4. Chinua Achebe, *Things Fall Apart* (Fawcett Crest, 1969 printing), p. 152.

# 8

## INDUSTRIALISATION AND SOUTH AFRICAN SOCIETY, 1900–40

There are others again, and these are found among the advanced class of Europeans, who maintain that the solution of the problem will be found in segregation. They say: 'Segregate the native so as to enable him to develop according to his own lines.' But this policy cannot be successfully carried out today when the interests of both races are so interwoven, when there is no land in South Africa which is not occupied by Europeans, and when the industries of the country cannot be developed without native labour... To my mind, between this policy and that of repression there is no difference.

> R. V. Selope Thema (1922), in Gwendolen Carter and Thomas Karris,
> *From Protest to Challenge,* I (Hoover Institution Press, 1972), p. 213

While the rest of sub-Saharan Africa witnessed the expansion of merchant capital in relation to a commodity-producing peasantry, South Africa went through the early stages of an industrial revolution. Fundamental economic changes clustered around the expansion of mining whose needs had spurred the imperial thrust into the South African interior. Colonial conquest intensified dependence on the world market, but brought wide-ranging economic growth and ultimately a variegated industrial development. South Africa is one country whose history suggests that there is little truth to the assertion by dependency theory radicals that imperial conquest and economic 'dependence' necessarily leads to national poverty, the 'development of underdevelopment' or indeed any determinate set of social and political arrangements.

Instead, it is to the *particular* social and political forces within South Africa that we must look for an understanding of the form taken by

South African capitalist development. South Africa can obviously be differentiated from the remainder of colonial Africa by the depth, size and antiquity of its population of European origins, but the presence of a white minority does not necessarily answer any questions; it poses new ones. In the first half of the twentieth century class struggles were intense in South Africa and class lines were not so easily definable as race lines.

The 'white' population at the beginning of the century consisted of a widely differentiated community, ranging from the Randlords down through rich commercial farmers, state employees and independent professionals, to skilled and unskilled workers. The Boer War precipitated a rapid expulsion of poorer whites from the land to the towns, where their rural skills were useless and they formed a potentially explosive element in the population. The skilled workers attracted from Europe to the mining sites and new cities held a seemingly stronger position but were subject to the vagaries of the trade cycle and, if miners, the dangers and discomforts of underground work. Conflict with capital went raw and deep on their part.

At the start of the century Africans still often related to capitalist forces as peasant-pastoralists exchanging a surplus when available or working for wages when the cash could be usefully ploughed back again into the household. Such relations were common elsewhere in Africa, if particularly intense in the south. For capitalist penetration to move foward, the subjection of African labour on a much grander, cheaper and more violent scale was necessary and this set the stage for the application of pressures and the waging of struggles. In the Cape the labour of 'coloured', or mixed-race people, the bulk of the old colonial proletariat, formed a continuum with that of Africans and whites. In Natal and, to some extent, the newly conquered Transvaal, the children of Asian immigrants began to compete effectively against merchants of British extraction. Workers of both sexes and all races and colours jostled into South Africa's towns and cities seeking a wage. How, with what sort of ideology and under what political arrangements could capitalist forces control them? The answer emerged only after a generation of conflict.

Nor was capital itself a socially undifferentiated whole. The Randlords (not themselves always in cheerful agreement) confronted the fears and conflicting labour needs of other types of employers, notably the farmers, who could not compete with the payrolls and social control mechanisms that the mines were able to afford to hold down a work-force. From World War I on, the interests of manufacturing industry, in need of a different and differently controlled labour force than gold-mining, also became a significant force. Both manufacturers and farmers held a local financial, and thus a political, base. In time, both became skilled at using the apparatus of the South African state to advance their interests; they were in effect a 'national bourgeoisie'. However, ownership of mines stock also gradually fell more and more to South African hands and the mining interest, particularly after World War I, is also more and more difficult to characterise simply as 'imperialist'. The establishment of some kind of working arrangement (despite conflicts which even today are not entirely absent between the principal capitalist forces), the alliance, in Stanley Trapido's phrase, of 'gold and maize', came together with the fight of labour against capital to form the essentials in the historical development of twentieth-century South Africa. Those who came out on top did so through the creation of a racial order that runs right through South African society, an order far more systematic and more profitable than the equivocal racism of the nineteenth century and earlier. What must be stressed is that this order has been a *response* to intense and continuing struggle, not a pre-ordained *consequence* of different races cohabiting the same land.

## Reconstruction and Union

The conclusion of the Anglo-Boer War set the stage for the social, political and economic reconstruction of South Africa after 1902. Far from solving the mines' problems, the war had made their situation particularly difficult through the disruption of supplies and the dispersal of the labour force. Central to the social programme of Lord Milner, the British High Commissioner, was the reconstruction, on a sound, efficient basis, of gold mining.

The first years of the new century were difficult ones for the Randlords as they passed through a period of low returns, little investment interest and severe labour shortages. In 1904 the British government agreed to permit the entry into the Transvaal of a large migrant labour force from northern China. The culturally isolated and miserably paid Chinese workers were crucial in restoring profitability to the mines. White workers viewed them as a threat and demanded their repatriation from Africa, which took place after 1908. By this time, however, South African blacks were prepared to enter the mines in larger numbers and for lower wages than before the war. Yet it took almost a decade for South Africa to regain its pre-eminence among world gold producers.

Wartime propaganda had frequently stressed the role of imperial Britain as the guardian of the native peoples of South Africa against the Boer republics. In practice, Milner was careful to retain all the racist elements of Transvaal custom and constitution, refusing to alter the racially determined local franchise. The colour bar was essential to his own planning of the South African future. Under Milner's inspiration the South African Native Affairs Commission, dominated by men close to the mining interest, deliberated and made its final report in 1905. The Commission proposed reconceptualising the position of Africans in the country in terms of segregation by race, land and especially political representation. It was a member of Milner's brain trust, the so-called Kindergarten, Lionel Curtis, who in practice first systematically applied the word segregation to the South African context.

Segregation represented the fruition of 'native policy' in British Natal and, increasingly, in the Cape Colony as well. The movement had been towards reducing the black franchise and squeezing the African producer to churn out a workforce too cowed to press forward its demands. This was the intended upshot of the Glen Grey Act of 1894 concerning land tenure in Cape locations, introduced into the legislature by Cecil Rhodes during his years as premier. Now a union-wide 'native policy', operating above the petty interest of particular party factions, was wanted.

For Transvaal Afrikaners the Milner regime became a by-word for repression and enforced Anglicisation. Milner strongly favoured the large-scale immigration into South Africa of British artisans and capitalist farmers so as to deprive Afrikaners of their franchise majority. This tied in very well with the needs of mines and towns for more efficient and mechanised agriculture. In this Milner had only very modest success, as the number of immigrants at a time of relative economic stagnation in South Africa was small. But his policies helped ensure the rapid revitalisation of Afrikaner national sentiment, enflamed with bitterness about wartime death, deportations and the concentration camps.

From the time he entered Johannesburg Milner's plans included the ultimate union of all the British colonies in South Africa. The restoration of self-government to the old electorate in the Transvaal and the Orange River Colony (as the Free State had been renamed), the re-enfranchisement of Cape rebels and increasingly acrimonious bickerings over railway and customs policy made the need for union more urgent. In 1906 the weakest of the colonies, Natal, was faced with a serious Zulu rebellion generally known by the name of Bambatha, the chief who led one phase of it. It was a response to intensive land and tax pressures and the gross insensitivity of the Natal regime. Among those who fought the colonial forces were many who had worked in the urban economy and many Christian converts. Bambatha was surrounded and killed and the rebellion suppressed with the loss of several thousand lives. Brutal deeds, such as the massacre at Mome Gorge, revealed the very hard core behind the paternalist façade that normally governed 'race relations' in the colony. For observers from outside the province it highlighted Natal's weakness and incompetence at dealing with Africans.

The Kindergarten proposed the negotiations for a unified South Africa, but they were taken up by local politicians who stood ultimately for a compromise between varied South African interests and the British empire. In the Transvaal the willingness of the Liberal ministry to grant self-government in 1906 had brought into office *Het Volk* led by the defeated generals, Jan Christiaan Smuts and Louis Botha. *Oranje Unie* held an even stronger position in the Orange River Colony under another Boer War military figure, James Barry Munnik Hertzog. Hertzog's movement was considerably more militant on certain nationalist issues, especially language in education, but had no coherent ideological or class basis to challenge the imperialist system. Also crucial were representatives of the pre-war political order, John X. Merriman, premier of the Cape and opponent of Milnerism, and ex-president Steyn of the Orange Free State.

Union was achieved in 1910. One provision of the new constitution was especially noteworthy: the retention in each province of the franchise as it stood. Thus Africans and other non-whites could vote in the Cape according to the existing property qualifications, but were forbidden to sit in the Union Parliament and, in the other provinces, were entirely disenfranchised. This provision practically killed the mid-Victorian political conception applied to the Cape of incorporating the black middle class as junior partners in the political system. The Union Constitution paved the road for a strictly racially defined participation, rather than non-racial liberalism, as the politics to accompany the growth of South African capitalism.

Classic liberal judgment has tended paradoxically to see at once Britain's willingness to re-enfranchise its old enemies as magnanimous and its abandonment of any pretence at championing African interests in South Africa as a sell-out, an unfortunate lapse of conscience. Yet for British imperial interests as a whole, and for finance and mining capital in particular, Union was above all a brilliant political achievement that could begin to put down those barriers to capitalist development in South Africa that had been so prominent and crisis-provoking before the war.

It was to the black middle class that the arrangements leading towards Union did indeed seem like a betrayal on the part of Britain and what remained of the Cape liberal establishment. Their deputations, associations and protests were entirely ignored in the horse-trading atmosphere of negotiation. At the same time the economic foundations of the African petty bourgeoisie were collapsing about them. The rinderpest stock disaster of 1897 and consequent serious animal epidemics and the ravages of the war were mileposts in the overall deterioration of African agricultural production in the reserves which had been excluded from settler expropriation. Erosion, ecological decline and 'overpopulation' fed into a growing pattern of indebtedness and immiseration. Instead of emulating the African progressive farmer of yore, youth looked to labour migration for its survival. The political irrelevance of the Christian African leadership accompanied the decline of merchant capital which in an earlier period had depended upon local alliances with this class. The mine labour-tout replaced the shopkeeper as the most important white man in the location.

In the first decade of the twentieth century there was some compensation in increasing land purchases outside the reserves by African land societies, often composed of ex-wage workers and in the relatively favourable position of half-shareholders and other squatters who farmed commercially on white-owned land. However, these avenues were closed off with the passage of the 1913 Land Act by the Union Parliament. The Land Act confirmed the emphasis on segregation envisioned under Milnerism. Land ownership was divided strictly on racial lines, with the Native Reserves constituting barely seven per cent of the total area of South Africa. Squatting was outlawed and although it continued in some form until well after World War II, it did so under increasingly unfavourable and unstable circumstances. The new system was underpinned politically by the Native Affairs Act of 1920 which enshrined chiefs and tribal authorities, now no longer capable of resistance to state authority, as the intermediaries between the state and the mass of Africans.

In struggling against these catastrophes African politicians from the entire country succeeded in establishing a national forum – the Native (later African) National Congress, originally founded in 1912. Congress was an impressive step forward in its national constitution, but had severe limitations as an effective force. It had little taste for mass organisation or, indeed, representation. Political inclinations of the petty bourgeois leadership remained moderate and defensive of existing rights. At first, even opinions about segregation were divided, since much of the leadership sought to cling to its traditional modest rung on the ladder. Above all, there was no strategy aimed at power or capable of presenting an alternative consistent road of national development. Much the same could be said of the African Political Organisation, dominated by Dr A. Abdurrahman, representing the Coloured people in the Cape. The APO, like Congress, was most comfortable doing deals with white patrons, a policy with increasingly shrinking rewards.

The Indian community of Natal and Transvaal appears at first sight to represent a militant contrast, particularly under the leadership of the young Mohandas Gandhi who helped to lead the Indian struggle until his departure from South Africa on the eve of World War I. Gandhi led a remarkably dogged fight against the imposition of poll tax and several other noxious ordinances by the Transvaal government before Union. While his movement achieved some success, culminating in the Gandhi-Smuts agreement, it fell far short of achieving basic social or political rights, avoided any movement towards co-operation with other oppressed South Africans and led ultimately into a pattern of dependence on the intervention of the top Indian merchant stratum nationally and the Indian government internationally for the negotiation of specific narrow redress of grievances.

## An Era of Confrontation

From Union until his death in 1919, Louis Botha was prime minister. Jan Smuts, already a dominant figure under Botha, then succeeded him in office. Having played a major role in the British war cabinet during World War I, Smuts conceived of South Africa in a sub-imperial part as Britain's junior sibling throughout southern, central and eastern Africa. With this policy never far from his mind the Union government actively fought the Germans in Tanganyika and South-West Africa during the war and South Africa was permitted to administer the latter territory as a League of Nations mandate. Union policy consisted of initiatives designed to encourage the penetration of South African settlers and capital in the territory. Smuts also favoured the emergence of British settler communities in the territories stretching from Kenya down to Southern Rhodesia that would look to Pretoria for leadership. He sought unsuccessfully to annex much of

Mozambique and Southern Rhodesia, the latter being frustrated in a 1923 referendum when the Southern Rhodesian settlers voted instead for a separate status of self-governing colony. Smuts was a highly articulate ideologue of compromise between imperial interests, mining capital and a moderate white South African nationalism. There was little in fact to differentiate his South African Party (SAP) from the apparently more 'British' Unionist Party.

With World War I and the rapid boom and slump that followed, however, the Smuts government faced increasingly intense challenges. The war brought unprecedented numbers of rural South Africans, black and white, to the cities in an era when South African secondary industry began to develop in isolation from Europe. By the end of the decade the South African population was one-quarter urbanised. The war boom was followed by a sharp economic decline in demand that hit manufacturing severely. Pressures on the working class appeared intolerable.

The gold mines, still the heart of the economy, experienced particular problems. With lowered profit margins capitalists needed vast sums to develop new mines on the Far East Rand and new forms of labour organisation and discipline to introduce cheaper production methods. In the circumstances the Smuts government had to take up the cudgels to defend business interests. This set the stage for a phase of confrontation between the white workers who formed approximately one eighth of the mines labour force and capital, quite openly backed by the Smuts regime.

Confrontation had been brewing for some time. Among the immigrant British workmen were many who had picked up syndicalist, socialist and trade unionist ideas before coming to South Africa and, particularly after Union, the cockpit that was the Rand became a perfect venue for the expression of radical ideas. Afrikaner miners, newly arrived in the harsh urban milieu, were far from immune to such influences. White workers feared being pushed down to the living standard of the mass of African miners. In the Milner era a small mines manager, Frederick Creswell, achieved fame through his experiment with running gold-mining operations entirely on a white labour basis. The experiment proved an economic failure and Creswell resurfaced as a leader of the South African Labour Party which was organised after the grant of responsible government to the Transvaal. For Creswell and others on the Labour Right the issue was above all to firm up a colour bar and to direct a politics that aimed at protecting white labour against black and local, South African-based business against the dictates of mining capital. An unsuccessful attempt by workers to seize control of some mines in 1913 led to management recognition of a white mine-workers' union. The following year Labour won the largest number of seats in the Transvaal legislature. There is reason to believe that African miners were deeply impressed by the 1913 strike. By this time a few socialists within the white labour movement had come to see the importance of organising the mass of unskilled workers and helped initiate radical ideology among some of the most receptive Africans on the Rand. In the latter war years Africans began to engage in effective strike action throughout the country. On the Rand this culminated in the great mine-workers' strike in early 1920, which at its height brought out more than 70 000 Africans. The strikers showed impressive discipline and control and it took brutal suppression with attacks on African compounds to smash it. It was of great significance that among the African demands was a call for raises and regrading that would have challenged the existing colour bar, and of even greater significance that white labour felt deeply threatened and refused to support the strike in any way. The 1920 strike marked a watershed of different forms of resistance to capital and the state by white and black which took quite separate courses.

As slump conditions hit in 1920 the mine-owners felt it was the time to break the strength of white labour. The miners were frightened; their response was similar to that of 1913 but on a bigger scale, the Rand Revolt of 1922. Workers' councils seized power in many public installations of the Rand and openly threatened the authority of the state. Smuts responded with a full military onslaught that led to over two hundred deaths. With the Rand Revolt smashed, the mine-owners were able to reduce the size and payroll of the white workforce and to reorganise the labour process so as to enhance profits substantially.

Among Africans resistance shifted from the mines to other enterprises and other parts of the country. For the first time the ANC disposed itself to support ordinary workers and protested the violence and victimisation that followed the 1920 miners' strike and other outbreaks. One largely successful African strike occurred among the Cape Town dockers in 1919, greatly enhancing the prestige of the leader, Clements Kadalie. Kadalie was a mission-educated Nyasalander of chiefly origin with a home background and outlook not very different from that of the Congress leadership, but through chance and astuteness he rose to prominence on the tide of labour militancy. Kadalie became the spearhead of the Industrial and Commercial Workers' Union (ICU) which eclipsed Congress in size and importance among African organisations of the 1920s. The ICU had an amorphous quality which defies easy categorisation. It had some of the characteristics of a trade union, but acquired much of its strength in rural areas and almost invariably shrank from industrial action or even struggle for recognition from companies. It also had some of the characteristics of a political party and frequently placed its demands in the context of general protest at the oppression of Africans in South Africa. However, it lacked a clear ideological content or political programme to give it coherence. Kadalie and other leaders were like Congressmen in favouring alliances with influential and apparently sympathetic whites of various stripes.

The ICU was at first infiltrated by the small number of white labour radicals who increasingly despaired of the possibility of opening up the existing labour movement to African workers. If most white workers feared the potential of black working-class organisation as a threat to their jobs and living standards, these few went forward from the white labour struggle of the period leading up to the Rand Revolt towards seeing a non-racial labour movement, and eventually a movement for the liberation of black labour, as fundamental. In 1921 most of them reorganised as the South African Communist Party. In the mid-1920s, after considerable internal struggle, the CP moved towards concentrating on black membership and organisation. Some of the early African and Coloured CP militants entered both ICU and ANC. In the ICU Kadalie's attitude wavered, but he came increasingly under the influence of anti-Communist liberals and social democrats, especially after he travelled to Europe in 1926. Afterwards the Communists were expelled from the ICU. At the end of the 1920s the ICU virtually disintegrated, due to regional and factional disputes and the mismanagement of the organisation, and in the wake of popular disinterest as its militant rhetoric failed to acquire content.

## Pact and Fusion

Smuts' government was challenged by the emergent Afrikaner nationalist movement which took political form under General Hertzog's leadership. Hertzog broke with Smuts and Botha to form his own party in 1913. Milner's army of British migrants had failed to materialise. Indeed, as the skilled immigrant population aged, left Africa or died, the voting population became more and more Afrikaans-speaking. In 1915 de la Rey, Beyers and other Boer War veteran leaders attempted to stage a rising in collaboration with the Germans in South-West Africa. Hertzog steered clear of open involvement and capitalised on opposition to the post-rising suppression. The emphasis in Nationalist Party politics on the language question reflected the domination of rural ministers and school teachers, but Hertzog also gained ground from the increasingly patent identification of the regime with the Randlords. The suppression of the Rand Revolt was coupled with Smuts' brutal and spectacularly bloody actions against an unarmed religious sect of Africans, the Israelites, at Bulhoek in 1921 and in 1922 against a small section of the Nama in South-West Africa known as the Bondelswarts. Both were examples of the government's incapacity to deal with opposition. Nor did the Nationalists favour Smuts' expansionist plans in Africa which threatened to drown Afrikaners in a profitable sea of black labour coerced and dominated by imperial Britain.[1]

As Hertzog's party gained strength the Unionist opposition, with their Milnerite heritage, joined Smuts and his SAP in 1919. Hertzog astutely moved towards an alliance with the Labour Party which could carry urban seats that eluded Nationalist appeal. Indeed, he made friendly overtures to the ICU and attacked repressive features of the African policy of the government. In 1924 Smuts was thrown out of office and the Pact government took power, with Hertzog as prime minister and minority support from the Labour Party.

Some Marxist writers have fastened upon the rise of the Pact as a showcase for demonstrating the importance in South African history of struggles between factions of the white bourgeoisie. Certainly at first sight Labour and the Nationalists appear to represent very different strata than Smuts' SAP. However, the evidence suggests the timorousness of the Pact's challenge to either the British connexion (politically) or the Randlords (economically). Yet its existence highlights those strata in South African society whose practice ensured a different political, economic or social development from any we have examined elsewhere in Africa at this time. These strata – petty bourgeois, manufacturers, 'new' or employed middle class and 'aristocratic' and supervisory labour – used the Pact to forge a place for their own interests in the South African sun. In defining themselves racially (or, in the case of Afrikaners, even more narrowly) they contested control over the surplus; they eschewed questioning the basic character of capital accumulation within the Union. The Pact created the political conditions for a resolution to the disputes of gold and maize (or, in Hertzog's terms, the two streams of Briton and Afrikaner) through the more rigid application of racial segregation.

The Pact claimed to defend the interests both of white labour and of the national economy as a whole. The rapid growth of industry during World War I had been a response to local consumer needs and wartime conditions. The mining interest was partly sympathetic to protection for industry because of its own needs for cheap, regular supplies for its workers and for the urban population in general, but it opposed state intervention to create a manufacturing sector that would compete for labour and reorient the direction of the economy. Even under Smuts, however, the government had moved to create the Reserve Bank in 1920 and the Electricity Supply Commission (ESCOM), the national electric supply company, in 1923. Under the Pact a battle was successfully waged for the establishment of the Iron and Steel Corporation (ISCOR), the state steel monopoly. In the teeth of mining opposition tariffs were raised and, most significantly, the mines began to be taxed more stiffly in order to benefit other sectors of the economy. At this stage it was still agriculture rather than industry which profited, on the whole. A state support system for agricultural produce was put into motion.

The state did not interfere with the employment of cheap black labour by secondary industry or the mines, but within the state sector of the economy increasing numbers of jobs were made available for unskilled white workers, notably in ISCOR and on the railways, while a statutory colour bar was enshrined on the books for various categories of jobs. The struggle to obtain equal language rights for Afrikaans enabled more Afrikaners to enter the civil service.

The mines came to appreciate, or at least to accept, much of the logic of this reorientation. By the 1930s, forty per cent of share capital in the mines was locally owned, as opposed to fifteen per cent at the time of Union. Sir Ernest Oppenheimer's Anglo-American Corporation had become the dominant force in both diamonds (DeBeers) and gold. Oppenheimer and DeBeers took a more broad-ranging view of South African capitalist development than had the old Randlords of Rhodes' time. They themselves would invest heavily in South African industry. If elsewhere in Africa colonial mining appeared to stand in the way of the emergence of any other form of economic orientation, in South Africa it was effectively harnessed as the motor force of a wide ranging capital accumulation process.

With the growth of industry and economic decline of the African reserves the number of urban Africans increased substantially and began to include an ever larger proportion of women and children. This went totally against the grain of the segregation ideology. In 1923 the Smuts government had institutionalised the establishment of 'native locations' based on strict segregation in South African cities in the Native Urban Areas Act. There was little to differentiate the policies of Smuts and Hertzog on the use of segregation as a fundamental tool of white domination, although Hertzog was more systematic. In 1925 Hertzog introduced legislation to increase the territory available for Africans in the country as part of a final solution to the land question. In return for this he sought an end to the Cape African vote and the establishment of a special Native Council system instead that would act as a buffer between the state and African opinion. In the 1920s discussion in Parliament proceeded while legislation was passed piecemeal: for instance the Immorality legislation aimed at sexual relations between whites and Africans outside marriage and the whites-only franchise for women which at a stroke reduced by half the impact of the Cape African vote.

The late 1920s brought a remarkable decline in African militancy. The ICU became weak and localised; the ANC too was virtually moribund. For a brief period the ANC president, James Gumede, had taken a radical, if eclectic, line and strongly supported a policy of working with the Communists; but the Right ousted him in 1930 and, under his conservative successor Pixley Seme, the ANC reached the nadir of its influence. From 1929 the severity of the great depression evoked a new wave of labour militancy which led to important black labour struggles under Communist Party influence. The South African Communist Party (SACP) had adopted the so-called 'Black Republic' thesis which stressed the African destiny of the country and this appealed to a new generation of black radicals and inspired intense struggles on the Rand and in Durban. These in turn met the white terror tactics of Oswald Pirow, Hertzog's Minister of Justice. Moscow-inspired self-inflicted purges also helped to weaken the party which lapsed into virtual irrelevance in the 1930s.

The growing intensity of the depression threatened the social basis of the Pact. Pact policies had not gone far enough to change substantially the situation of its supporters. Conditions in agriculture deteriorated drastically and migrants to town met little but unemployment and short wages. Hertzog's reluctance to break with the British connection entirely and to establish a Republic made his Nationalist followers increasingly restive, while the base of the allied Labour Party shrank. It lost support in the 1929 election and thereafter split. Fearing a continued slide in his political fortunes, in 1933 Hertzog fused his party with Smuts' SAP to form the United Party, effectively a party of national unity, to meet the emergency conditions of the depression and to get South Africa off the gold standard. Many of the Cape Nationalist politicians, however, refused to accept Fusion and the following year formed a Purified Nationalist Party under the leadership of Revd Daniel François Malan.

Fusion provided the ideal basis for carrying through the legislation on Africans that Hertzog had deferred in the 1920s. The agricultural interests had never liked the extent to which African land reserves were preserved, but in the new regime they were less consequential and the segregation impetus could now be taken up in more prosperous times with widespread backing from the white electorate. In 1936 the Native bills, while slightly augmenting the scale of the African reserves (to thirteen per cent of the land area of the Union), put an end to the Cape African franchise and instead created a small representation in Parliament elected exclusively by Africans (with only white representatives) and the Native Representative Councils, which exerted no power but were supposed to reflect African opinion. At the same time the pass laws and other controls over the influx of Africans into towns were extended to reinforce the segregation system. There was little dissent to the bills; only a few Cape liberals still beholden to an older tradition of control over the African population opposed them in the House of Assembly.

By this time African opinion was more aware of how segregation hit against their interests. A new body, the All-African Convention, attempted to rally protest against the bills. In the end, however, most of the petty bourgeoisie were willing to fight for seats on the Native Representative Councils and to attempt to work within the new system.

How did segregation operate? During the course of the interwar period it was more and more systematically introduced into both social and economic spheres. Schools and churches were almost uniformly divided by race. Whites were treated in separate health systems, welfare organisations and penal institutions. In the cities sanitary needs and custom were used to justify urban residential segregation, while the rights of Africans to own and improve property, varying from one municipality to another, were in general very limited. Ideas about racial purity and the evils of miscegenation, now made illicit outside marriage, became widespread. A fourfold system of job discrimination, white-Coloured-Asian-African became standard. All this cemented the growing self-consciousness of whites as part of a racially defined South African people, with class and other differentials potentially being put in the background.

Capitalists found that in return for tolerating better conditions and wages for a minority of white workers, it was possible to collude with the state in organising controls that kept black workers poor and unable to defend their own interests. Pass laws made it difficult for black workers to find employment where and when they liked and put them under the constant, if irregular, discipline of the police. The reserve system was ever more successful in supplying very cheap labour to the farmer in particular. The system of social controls as a whole (the *exploitation* colour-bar), as Frederick Johnstone has argued, determined the 'ultra-exploitation' of black workers far more than the rather limited number of jobs withheld entirely from them by statute following the legislation of the Pact era (the *job* colour-bar):

> And non-white workers have suffered far more from the exploitation colour bars of the employers than from the job colour bar of the white workers, and their grievances have always centred not around the job colour bar and their more productive employment in the prevailing system of production, but around the forced labour system and their ultra-exploitable position in, and ultra-exploitation by, that system of production.[2]

The dilemma for capital came when times were slow and white workers had to be employed in large numbers for relatively good wages. Then business was tempted to agitate for at least a weakening of segregation. Under Fusion, however, this pressure was removed. Whites could move into supervisory positions and their children, increasingly better-educated, could jump up into a higher slot in the job market. The white worker, once terrified at being ground under between capital and cheap black labour, could then find in segregation a viable and apparently stable form of survival. Fusion, however, proved to lead to a period of more than just stability; as business expanded spectacularly the contradictions in Hertzog's segregation system actually widened.

## The Crisis of the 1940s

Fusion was linked to placing South Africa, the capitalist world's main source of gold at a time of economic collapse and dislocation off the gold standard. From the mid-1930s, as the price of gold soared it fuelled an unprecedented boom in South African industry which with few breaks continued through World War II and beyond. It was the pressures people experienced as a result that evoked a new era of challenge to the capital accumulation process in South Africa. At first the boom made segregation more feasible, but then it threatened to dismantle it.

TABLE 8.1     *Percentage of total population urbanised*

| Racial group | 1911 | 1946 |
|---|---|---|
| White | 53.0% | 75.6% |
| Asian | 52.8% | 72.8% |
| Coloured | 50.4% | 62.5% |
| African | 13.0% | 24.3% |
| All races | 25.9% | 39.3% |

*Source*: D. Hobart Houghton, *The South African Economy* (Oxford University Press, 1967), p. 239.

With the depression the mines were able to begin recruiting a larger and larger proportion of their labour force from the High Commission territories – Bechuanaland, Basutoland and Swaziland. These three protectorates had been left out of the Union deliberately by the British imperial government which thereby retained a special handle on South African affairs. Now their economy, once based on the export of agricultural produce to South Africa, was transformed into that of rural slums dependent on the remittances of migrant workers. Nyasaland also began to function as a major source of mines labour. For black South Africans the 1930s marked the beginning of the end of the viability of the reserves. Hundreds of thousands streamed to the cities, seeking work in manufacturing which began to displace mining for a central position in the economy. Industrial employment increased by more than sixty per cent between 1933 and 1939 and more than fifty per cent again between 1939 and 1945. Nearly two million Africans were living in South African cities by 1945.[3] The urban locations strained at the seams from the mass of new workers and shanty towns emerged despite attempts to limit entry into urban areas.

The situation was intensified by the entry of South Africa into World War II in 1939. In wartime conditions it was impossible to police the bounds of segregation that had been laid so carefully through interwar legislation. Smuts, again prime minister after Hertzog's unsuccessful opposition to South African entry in the war, was in any case more of a pragmatist. Strikes broke out frequently, especially on the Rand, and the government labour department moved towards unofficial negotiations with the illegal African trade unions. For part of the war years pass laws were virtually suspended and African wages rose after a long period of decline or stagnation.

Boom and war re-ignited African militancy. A new generation of labour activists such as the Durban docker Zulu Phungula (whose career Dave Hemson has illuminated) stood for the rights of the African proletariat within the urban areas, where alone they could now subsist. The African Communist J. B. Marks began to organise effectively among miners. In 1940 Alfred Xuma embarked on his decade-long presidency of the ANC which began to consider the possibility of mass mobilisation and the espousal of mass issues, thus moving away from the traditional defensive policies of the past. On the Rand, conditions in the shanty towns and inflation inspired a large, militant squatters' movement. Among coloureds and Indians also the old leadership of negotiation and defense of existing privileges was discredited and radicals took the initiative.

However, these tendencies did not all come together readily. Within the ANC an 'Africanist' tendency emerged associated especially with Anton Lembede, a remarkable self-taught intellectual originally much under the influence of Afrikaner populist nationalism. Lembede and the Africanists were in favour of a growing mass involvement in the ANC while bitterly opposing socialist influence in the form of the Communist Party, with which other ANC leaders co-operated.

By 1945 conditions in South Africa were undermining the basis for the segregation ideology. Smuts was under substantial pressure from several camps. Some industrialists were demanding a relaxation of the system of urban segregation in particular. A new 'liberalism' emerged under their patronage which insisted on the primacy of further capitalist development now threatened by antediluvian segregationist practice. Such liberals had close ties with both Anglo-American and the ANC élite through such agencies as the Institute of Race Relations, an important research centre established in Johannesburg which came to depend in part on financing from American foundation money. Most held only the vision of a new and modified form of racist hegemony, but some began to press for a genuine democratisation of society. Smuts and, in particular, his influential deputy J. H. Hofmeyr, were receptive to arguments for restructuring. At the same time, it was crucial for Smuts to smash the initiatives of African militancy that had developed all the more forcefully precisely because relative labour scarcity gave such economic force to their efforts. In this context can be seen the brutal suppression of the African Mineworkers Union strike in 1946 which had broken out under Communist leadership. The NRC representatives were so outraged by the subsequent arrogance of the government that they boycotted further proceedings, breaking down the Hertzog system of native representation.

Thus the last phase of the United Party government had a contradictory character. Repression was mixed with promises of liberalisation. Attempts to give the Indians a vote while restricting their economic activities, and the proposals of the Smit (1942) and Fagan (1946–8) Commissions to register African trade unions and extend urban rights of Africans belong to this phase. It also seems ironically fitting that Smuts, now in his seventies, proved as ineffective in coping with crisis after 1945 as he had in the post-World War I era. He ended his political career with a second crucial defeat which brought Malan and the Purified Afrikaner Nationalists to power.

## Notes

1. Hertzog continued, however, to pursue Smuts' aggressive policies towards Mozambique.
2. Frederick A. Johnstone, *Class, Race and Gold* (Routledge & Kegan Paul, 1976), p. 214.
3. D. Hobart Houghton, *The South African Economy* (Oxford University Press, 1967), p. 239.

# 9

# THE DECOLONISATION OF AFRICA, 1940 – 60

'We have been informed of your good activities. Many of our recent recruits praise you very much for equipment, guidance, help and your wife's welcome. But there is something else you should bear in mind and that is (1) You are still teaching under Beecher's Report; (2) We have been informed that our enemy Bildad Giticha lunches with you in your house and that you have been dressing his wounds helping him to recover; (3) You can not serve two masters.'

> Letter from Mau Mau fighters to schoolteacher Karari Njama, in Donald Barnett and Karari Njama, *Mau Mau From Within* (Monthly Review Press, 1966), p. 141

'One must render me this justice that during the five months the strike lasted, I did not write a single article on the question and that if I dealt with it at times in my speeches, I did so voluntarily, in measured terms. Although I affirmed the legitimacy of the principles supported by the strikers ... I advocated a compromise solution as the only one possible under the circumstances. The event proved us right.'

> Leopold Sédar Senghor on the 1947 railway workers' strike in French West Africa, cited in J. Suret-Canale, 'The French West African Railway Workers' Strike, 1947–48', in Peter Gutkind, Robin Cohen and Jean Copans, eds, *African Labor History* (Sage, 1978), p. 145

'A magical word meant to exorcise ethnic quarrels and antagonisms – and as such very precious in contemporary Africa – "nation" is a fetish-word as well aimed at abolishing class differences.'

> A. Touré, 'Paysans et fonctionnaires devant la culture et l'état', in Y. A. Fauré et J. F. Médard, eds, *État et Bourgeoisie en Cote d'Ivoire*, (Karthala, 1982), p. 242 (Author's translation.)

Table 9.1.   *Pre-war and post-war population of the largest African cities, c. 1955* (1000 persons)

| | | |
|---|---|---|
| Ibadan, Nigeria | 387 (1931) | 459 (1952) |
| Addis Ababa, Ethiopia | 150 (1939) | 431 (1956) |
| Lagos, Nigeria | 126 (1931) | 312 (1956) |
| Leopoldville, Congo | 36 (1938) | 300 (1955) |
| Dakar, Senegal | 93 (1936) | 231 (1955) |
| Nairobi, Kenya | 65 (1939) | 210 (1956) |
| Luanda, Angola | 40 (1934) | 190 (1955) |
| Tananarive, Madagascar | 127 (1936) | 190 (1955) |
| Salisbury, S. Rhodesia | 33 (1936) | 168 (1956) |
| Accra, Ghana | 70 (1931) | 165 (1954) |
| Kano, Nigeria | 89 (1931) | 130 (1952) |
| Abidjan, Ivory Coast | 10 (1931) | 128 (1955) |
| Douala, Cameroun | 28 (1931) | 119 (1956) |
| Omdurman, Sudan | 111 (1938) | 116 (1956) |
| Resident in cities with populations of 100 000+ | 901 000 | 3 149 000 |

*Source:* Marvin Miracle, *Maize in Tropical Africa* (University of Wisconsin Press, 1966), pp. 34–5.

## The Second Colonial Occupation

Two related watersheds divide the twentieth-century history of Africa: the great depression and World War II. Neither had African causes; the second was fought only tangentially in tropical Africa. Both, however, brought about fundamental shifts in the world political economy that deeply touched material life and ultimately initiated far-reaching social, political and economic change.

For the colonial regimes the depression was a time of stagnation and retrenchment. The limits imposed by the kind of capitalist development being pursued in Africa became very apparent. If that development was to go further, social and economic investments were necessary. Although this was increasingly obvious to the more forward-thinking colonial administrators by the 1930s, funds for new ends were rarely available.

TABLE 9.2    *The growth in the European settler population*

|  | *1935/6* | *1953* |
|---|---|---|
| Southern Rhodesia | 55 419 | 160 000 |
| Angola | 30 000 | 78 826 ('50) |
| Belgian Congo | 18 680 | 76 764 ('52) |
| French West Africa | 19 061 | 62 236* |
| Northern Rhodesia | 9 913 | 50 000 |
| South-West Africa | 31 049 | 49 612 ('51) |
| Mozambique | 10 000 | 48 813 ('50) |
| Kenya | 17 997 | 42 200 |

\* Includes 'assimilated' Africans.
Source: Lord Hailey, *An African Survey* (Oxford University Press, 1957 edn,) p. 144. (1945 edn, p. 109.)

As world trade gradually recovered, political crises in Europe and Asia quickly unfolded leading towards the giant confrontations of World War II. If the depression had marked an era of retrenchment in Africa, the war was the reverse: a forcing-house of quick change and intense pressure. For war-orientated Fascist Italy, this pressure on the colonies began well back in the 1930s. Eritrea was turned into a forward base for the conquest of Ethiopia. New investments brought in a large Italian settler community and rapid urban growth. After the conquest Ethiopia was set upon by the Italians who proceeded to pour money into infrastructure without precedent. Such pressures became generalised in Africa by 1941. Britain relied heavily on African raw materials. The Belgian government, exiled from its homeland after 1940 but still in command in Leopoldville, and the Free French, who by 1942 effectively took over the sub-Saharan African colonies from Vichy officials, were even more dependent on Africa as a base.

African troops were requisitioned for fighting in Asia and the Mediterranean as in World War I, but now the effect of a total imperial war economy was far more intensive. Forced labour was revived in many spheres of the colonial economy, administrations pushed forward both cash crop and foodstuff production as much as their means allowed while imported goods became scarce or unobtainable. The result, in Kenya and Tanganyika, in northern Nigeria and French West Africa, was massive food shortages and famine conditions.

Africans responded by immigration to the towns, where imposed isolation from Europe was creating new job opportunities. It was the war which witnessed the beginning of a wave of entrants to urban areas that has not ceased even now.[1] In the cities conditions for poor migrants were deplorable. Food was short, housing unavailable and sanitation terrible. While employment chances existed for wage-earners, the worker was met with rocketing inflation that exerted its own radical autonomous pressure on living conditions.

The war dramatically exposed the poverty of Africans to Europe. Dependent colonies with limited infrastructures and populations producing little beyond their barest needs could offer little assistance to the mother countries. In this context, and this was particularly noticeable in British thinking, what once had been the idea of isolated reformers fast became generalised. Africa needed a 'new deal', to begin as quickly as possible, both for its own good and, more importantly, for the good of Europe. Catherine Coquery-Vidrovitch, writing about the depression in French West Africa, and John Lonsdale and Anthony Low writing on British East Africa, have noted independently the significance of this transformation. The last two have referred to the post-war years as those of a 'second colonial occupation'.

Behind the second occupation were some entirely new considerations, such as the encouragement of secondary industry or the corresponding attempts to create a small, relatively well-paid and conservative urban working class. Other aspects though were really an extension and an intensification of earlier forms of capital penetration. Thus development plans continued to lay great stress on transport infrastructure connected to the evacuation of export crops. The railway lines were now supplemented by feeder roads and even tarmac highways on which ran imported lorries and vans. Large sums of money were poured into improving existing routes or artificially constructing new ones. A striking example is the Vridi Canal, which cut across from the open Atlantic to the West African lagoon network, opening up Abidjan as a sea port for the Ivory Coast. It was a major example of the work of FIDES, the French *Fonds des Investissements Economiques et Sociales*, which were intended to co-ordinate development finance.

Cash crops remained an inherent part of economic expansion. After years of war the world was prepared to buy unprecedented amounts of agricultural commodities and to pay unprecedented sums for them. Colonial coffers filled to heights unimagined in the 1930s.

The colonial bureaucracies also swelled, and increasingly their characteristic and most numerous members were technical specialists, particularly in agriculture. Until the 1930s the colonial regimes intervened relatively little in peasant agriculture; they preferred simply to squeeze producers. Now grandiose schemes for irrigation and community development were planned. Agricultural experts trained assistants as a taskforce to coerce peasants into producing according to what were assumed to be superior techniques based on European models. Agricultural ordinances with penal sanctions were passed with alacrity. Effective new inputs into peasant agriculture were limited but not insignificant. Ploughs, tractors and particularly chemical fertilisers played an increasingly significant part in expanding production, while frequently exhausting the soil and marking the intensification of social distinctions within the rural population. Greatest of all post-war agricultural experiments was the Tanganyika Ground-nut Scheme. In the mid-1940s there was a world shortage of edible oils and India, the principal exporter of ground-nuts, was unable to make up for the scheduled needs. So, with the advice of Unilever, the British government embarked on a scheme for turning large sections of Tanganyika into a mechanised ground-nut producer. There was little planning and the local colonial administration was scarcely consulted. As a result virtually every choice regarding soil, machines, labour and land was wrong. Old tanks were unconvincingly transformed into agricultural machinery. At the beginning of the 1950s the Ground-nut Scheme was wound up, a disastrous failure to which the British government had dedicated tens of millions of pounds. Rarely, in fact, were grand mechanised schemes very successful. The real backbone of what increase in productive wealth could be found in agriculture lay in the roads stretching deeper into new country, and the excellent post-war produce prices, both of which stimulated most of the old, and created new, cash-cropping zones.

In effectively isolating Africa from Europe, the war spurred on the first significant wave of industrialisation orientated to local markets, producing either the small range of mass consumption goods such as soap powder, matches, beer and cigarettes, or goods designed for the affluent local bourgeoisies, especially where important populations of European or Asian origin resided. Salisbury and Nairobi, Dakar and Leopoldville, Accra and Lagos, Asmara and Addis Ababa were the main centres of industrial growth.

Much of the new industry was related either to export processing or import substitution and involved the dominant export–import houses. The profile of their interests changed rapidly as the 'second colonial occupation' shifted the import cargoes increasingly from basic industrial consumer goods to machinery and capital goods. The import, marketing and servicing of automobiles became big business. Firms such as the United Africa Company withdrew from produce storage in small market canteen centres to concentrate on establishing retail department stores in the major cities. This shift in business interests dovetailed with colonial policy which sought at once to preserve the prosperity of the oligopolies and the security of the peasant base of society by eliminating or streamlining middlemen operations.

In the post-war era co-operative societies expanded their base widely. The co-operatives received state assistance in recognition for functioning as mediators between the small producer and the European firms. The largest in all Africa, the Victoria Federation of Co-operative Unions, organised the marketing of the booming cotton expansion of northern Tanganyika. It was specifically directed at pressing Asian middlemen buyers out of business and, under the façade of co-operative principles, was effectively dominated by the richest and most ambitious Africans of the area. Wealthy farmer-transporter-moneylenders were just as prominent in the cocoa producing co-operatives of western Nigeria and the Gold Coast. In French Africa a somewhat parallel system, the *Sociétés Indigènes de Prévoyance*, had an earlier origin and were historically tied to both the forced cultivation tradition and the French need to establish collaborative linkages with chiefs and big men in rural areas.

Together with co-operatives the other major new, related institution was the marketing board. The boards were formulated in response to depression conditions and fears of producer antagonism against middlemen, or even the expatriate firms, as manifested in the great cocoa holdup in the pre-war Gold Coast. They set seasonal prices for particular export crops on a territorial basis and controlled the licensing of buying agents with whom producers could deal. Initially justified as a means of stabilising peasant income, in practice they withheld large sums for the benefit of the state. In theory these were to be used for development purposes, but the British particularly made use of them to back their currency by placing the balance in Britain. Marketing boards, like co-operatives, were intended as a means of direct state accumulation from the agricultural production process.

The other side of post-war colonial planning was the new emphasis on social welfare. The war revealed the inadequacies, from the point of view of colonial needs, of an ill-housed, badly-fed, illiterate population. The new stage of economic development towards which colonial regimes were preparing required a more qualified, stable working class. Considerable emphasis began to be laid on medicine, including rural and preventative medicine, which, for the first time, had some effect on the health of the masses in many areas. In most colonies a dramatic growth of primary education and state support for it began after the war. By this time school expansion was widely popular in Africa and a conveniently common ground of state and mass ambitions. The spread of schools, even though not effectively universal anywhere before 1960, was a powerful force in integrating African youth into wider colony-wide political and social networks. A remarkable aspect of this spectrum of reforms was its conception and direction in a political void; it represented a programme by and for bureaucrats. Some major administrative decisions seemed remarkably deluded. The British pressed forward with a problematic model of colonial federation, of which one controversial feature lay in the inclusion of a major new white-settler initiative.

During the war consensus developed in Britain about the overriding need for large, amalgamated economic units that could be the arenas of effective new levels of capital penetration in Africa. Of these the most significant was the proposed federation of British Central Africa – the Rhodesias and Nyasaland. As profits from Northern Rhodesian copper-mining mounted, bringing to the Copperbelt a rapid increase in immigrant South African whites, uniting the Rhodesias became a very attractive proposition both to Rhodesian settler interests and to the copper companies. The growing emphasis on industrial markets and services in Southern Rhodesian capitalism strengthened this trend. When in 1948 Afrikaner Nationalists came to power in the South African general election, the British government at first feared an anti-British orientation in Pretoria and sought to buttress Salisbury as an alternative British imperial base.

The Labour government in England was afraid to be seen openly pressing for settler domination in all Central Africa and pursued an incongruous policy of calling for massive new British immigration to the Rhodesias while claiming to champion African rights in the territories. It was apparently Whitehall insistence that led to the inclusion of impoverished Nyasaland in overall federal planning. After years of negotiation, amalgamation of the Rhodesias was rejected in favour of federation, which preserved the internal administrative systems of each territory intact. The Conservative government which came to power in 1951 pressed ahead and two years later established the Central African Federation, which indeed proceeded to attract both new white settlers and substantial British investment capital. With its spurious propaganda about racial partnership, federation never had better than passive African mass support and was feared and hated by the politically conscious. It was the partnership between the horse and his rider in the phrase of Lord Malvern, Southern Rhodesia's long-time premier. In attempting to foist an administrative fiat, the British were placing their heads in a hornets' nest.

Despite parallel economic thinking on the subject the British East African territories of Kenya, Uganda, Tanganyika and Zanzibar were never federated. Kenya settlers sought federation only on terms that would be highly favourable to their political interests, while the colonial officials of Tanganyika and Uganda actually opposed it. As a result, what emerged were the East African common services which eschewed political unification but created a general venue for regional capital development that was almost as attractive to business as the arrangement in Central Africa. The Kenya highlands and Nairobi prospered as the local metropole for this zone.

In Uganda there was the additional problem of how to amalgamate 'indirectly' ruled Buganda into the wider territory. By the early 1950s Britain was committed to a unitary administration for Uganda and so evoked a political crisis of intensifying dimensions. The other model paragon of indirect rule, northern Nigeria, faced a similar dilemma. During the war economic considerations led to the determination of a federal but unitary development for Nigeria, pitting one interest which had favoured the emirates and other artificially preserved or invented monarchies and the other, now potentially triumphant, representing the central bureaucracy. As in Uganda the fruits would prove bitter.

The question of settler power connected closely to that of Federation in British East and Central Africa. During the war settlers held a particularly strategic position to which metropolitan authorities were indebted. After the war ended their numbers grew fast in much of Africa while economic conditions greatly favoured their prosperity.[2] The 'second colonial occupation', in conjunction with excellent demand for tropical produce, created possibilities for a small bourgeoisie in most territories and European colonists had the education, techniques and connections with officialdom to fill that role. It was in the late 1940s that the 'white highlands' of Kenya finally became the scene of capital-intensive and very lucrative agriculture, while African squatters were increasingly evicted and pushed out to the Kikuyu Reserve. The tobacco boom fuelled a big push in capitalist agriculture in Southern Rhodesia. The white population of the Belgian Congo more than tripled in fifteen years after the war while a doubling of the Portuguese in the decade of the 1940s alone finally appeared to fulfil the vain dreams of earlier eras for Angola and Mozambique. Wherever they settled Europeans served their interests best by a rigid group identity and a racism increasingly shorn of old-fashioned paternalism. Nothing roused and united Africans more than their advances. The settler thrust, as much in its economic as its political manifestations, was another main ingredient in the tensions and transformations of the era.

The new colonialists gave overwhelming emphasis to social and especially economic change. Political change was envisioned only rather gingerly, in step with the most liberal colonial thought of the pre-war era. Within the oppressive, racist ideology characteristic of the old colonial rhetoric a more idealistic old coin had occasionally been polished and brought down from the attic for international inspection. In the case of the British the message was that Africans could eventually, in the remote future, follow in the footsteps of their white brethren in colonies of settlement and obtain self-governing institutions within the Commonwealth. The most one could say for its application before 1939 was the presence of legislative councils in nearly all the colonies. Only the all-white legislature in Southern Rhodesia had any real weight, however. In West Africa these councils contained African members, a few of whom were elected on a limited urban property franchise. The French, in contrast, occasionally professed a belief in assimilation, (ideally) the total economic and political integration of the colonies into France with their inhabitants receiving the normal political and legal rights of other Frenchmen. Here a taste existed in the form of the deputy elected to the French Chamber by the voters of the four communes of Senegal and in the personal achievement by several thousand African individuals of French citizenship rights through a stiff bureaucratic procedure.

The war saw greatly renewed propaganda along both these lines. In fact the new thinking in London and Paris involved reforms that represented concessions to precisely those demands made by élite African organisations before the war. In British West Africa the territorial coverage of the legislative councils was extended to include the entire colonies, while in the Gold Coast the franchise was extended. Reforms were proposed in local government to give a large stake in them to the educated and restless. Economic grievances were attended to by the encouragement of industry, the marketing boards and co-operatives, while the social side received the response of substantially increased state involvement in education. Immediately after the war planning for a university in the Gold Coast, and shortly after, one in Nigeria, appeared to be concessions to reach the acme of the coastal élite's dreams. Within the administration the hiring of Africans for high-level positions and the dismantling of the social colour bar were considered. Outside West Africa reforms were less bold. However, here too there was educational expansion and a beginning of legislative representation. The latter started with the appointment of Eliud Mathu as the first African member of the Kenya Legislative Council in 1944.

French reforms were more dramatic and were more dramatically inaugurated at the Brazzaville Conference in 1942 by General Charles de Gaulle after the adherence of the regime in Equatorial Africa to the cause of anti-Nazi, pro-British Free France. After the war constitutional meetings led to the establishment of a pan-imperial representative French Union and the admission of elected African deputies from all territories to the French Chamber of Deputies. The electoral franchise was limited and a special electoral college was designed to appease the French settlers in Africa. Admission of Africans to the highest echelons of the colonial service, municipal self-government and rapid educational expansion were also planned in the French model while the franchise was extended by stages.

The abolition of forced labour in 1946 was the most solid token of a new stage being reached in French Africa. In contrast, there was no equivalent reform in the Belgian and Portuguese systems during the decade following the war. What characterised both these systems was their different relationship to the 'second colonial occupation'. In the Congo the intensification of capital penetration really went back to the 1920s and had proceeded smoothly without political or administrative concessions to Africans. So why not continue in the same mould? Portugal was too backward to advance on this front until after 1960 when it faced the stark challenge of wars for liberation in the colonies. In the quantitatively more significant cases of France and Britain political reform was closely linked to what were seen as the necessary social bases for the new planned level of capitalist development. Both powers appreciated the importance of some kind of new basis for collaboration with Africans.

## Social Confrontation and Class Struggles

The political reforms of the new colonialism were based, at least initially, on an estimate of the social forces of the pre-war era. They were profoundly behind the times.

The greatly altered international political sphere provided a wider setting of pressures that worked to provoke change. The destruction of

1. *Merchant capital:* hide and skin merchant with his goods, Kano (Nigerian savanna)

2. *Merchant capital:* Ivory caravan on march to the coast (mainland Tanzania)

3. *Pre-capitalist ruling classes:* the Timbo *almamy* and his retinue (Futa Djallon, Guinea)

4. *Pre-capitalist ruling classes:* Haile Selassie's ministers prior to the Italian invasion of 1935 (Ethiopia)

5. *Imperialist conquest: Asante, 1896.* The perspective of a 'master race'

6. *Imperialist conquest: Asante, 1896.* 'A sketch from life' showing the Asantehene, his mother and the Ansah brothers of Kumasi

7. *Colonial agriculture:* white settler cultivation, Delamere estate at Njoro, Kenya Highlands

8. *Colonial agriculture:* cocoa production in a rich peasant household, Gold Coast

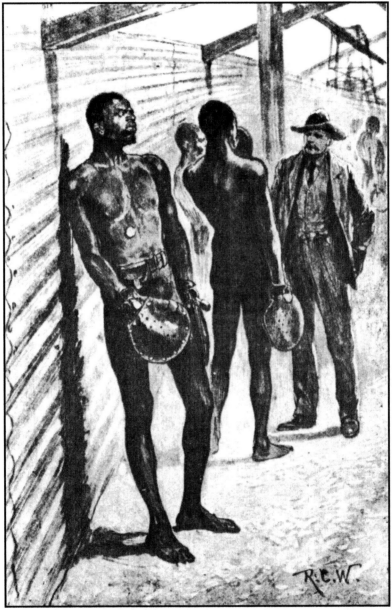

9. *Colonial society:* diamond workers in iron 'mittens' being examined for stolen gems, Kimberley (South Africa)

10. *Colonial society*: Missionaries and staff, Nanzela, Barotseland, Northern Rhodesia

11. *Decolonisation:* The Congo crisis begins, Patrice Lumumba
at a press conference following the intervention of Belgian
paratroopers (1 September 1960)

12. *Decolonisation:* The Congo crisis continues, Tshombe's troops recapture a North Katanga town and American weaponry, February, 1962

liberal political institutions by Fascist regimes in Europe, together with the new prestige and power of the Soviet Union following its decisive role in the defeat of Fascism, left the social groundwork of capitalism in Europe very weak after 1945. Reforms to secure political and social democracy were considered essential in this climate and such considerations were particularly acute in the colonies. The war virtually swept away European colonialism in Asia. There the West faced the stark choice of anti-capitalist regimes, of which a most important one came to power in China in 1950, or compromise with nationalist-minded bourgeoisies, as in India. Perceptions of Africa were necessarily clouded by the far more advanced Asian colonial crisis.

The greatest Western power had almost no stake in maintaining colonial rule. American policy was committed to containing the advance of socialism through establishing ties with nationalists in the colonies who could be won over to the American view of the world. This was a strategy closely related to the desire of American business to establish a stronger position in the trade and material resources of African and other colonies dominated by European industry. American war-time propaganda was often sharply anti-colonial. Later the imperative need for good relations with European allies blunted the thrust, but the general lines of pressure remained constant.

Within Africa the situation differed in 1945 from what it had been a decade earlier. Indeed the economic and social initiatives of the colonial authorities themselves helped to make early political reforms inadequate. Economic pressures had thrown up a rapidly growing wage-labour force and swollen the population of the cities. The boom in commodities that followed led both to rising expectations and to differentiation between the less and more fortunate that fuelled the grievances.

Consequently the 1940s were an era of unprecedented labour organisation and labour insurgency. There were instances of worker action and strikes within the colonial African economy as far back as the late nineteenth century and an important wave of labour unrest struck many African administrations after World War I. The next significant crest followed the return to prosperity in the late 1930s when continuing depression-rate wages brought about several important strikes, notably on the Mombasa docks and the Northern Rhodesian Copperbelt. Britain began to turn to a policy of fostering legal trade unions, permitted also by the French during the Popular Front government of 1936–8. This merely foreshadowed the labour unrest that gathered strength in the last couple of years of the war.

There was virtually no African colony without a major strike phase. The workers who were most able to organise and make their demands stick were those in the public sector, particularly in transport and communications – railway workers, dockers, telegraphists and postal workers. Major and briefly crippling strikes affected the docks of Lourenço Marques in Mozambique and Matadi in the Congo. Those in Lagos (1945) and in Dar es Salaam (1947) successfully spread inland along the lines of rail in Nigeria and Tanganyika to become general strikes. In 1947 the railway workers of French West Africa struck for an unbelievable four months, largely on the issue of racist differentials. Union organisations of indeterminate character and explosive force mushroomed.

The colonial authorities were anxious to prevent labour from turning to overtly political issues that could challenge the basis of exploitation as a whole. They responded to strikes not only with repression (notably severe in the Portuguese colonies and in the wartime Belgian Congo), but with a positive programme of non-political, colonially directed unionism, to which end labour departments were organised. The British government despatched conservative British trade unionists, by agreement with the Trades Union Congress, to spearhead the effort. The result was a formal union structure that came to resemble the economistic Western collective bargaining model. The leadership that emerged from the African unions typically (not always) consisted of outsiders who belonged by training to the clerical stratum or above, organising with the mentality of would-be bureaucrats on the make or petty entrepreneurs. Thus, in Nigeria, union secretaries would often serve several unions at once and were in effect professional self-made go-betweens. Yet this business unionism strategy had only limited success before the middle 1950s. Even the most co-operative union officials could not always effectively control mass action, although they failed to give it revolutionary political leadership. The likelihood of labour unrest dominated colonial fears throughout this period.

Peasant unrest was much less focused and less strategic but it potentially involved much larger numbers. Three not unrelated issues gripped rural Africa: reaction to intensifying cash pressure and differentiation; the apprehensions caused by settler prosperity and expansion; and the resistance to agricultural improvements imposed by force.

All three in conjunction typified British Central and East Africa. Opposition to agricultural ordinances was coupled with a refusal to pay taxes and hostility to the regime of the chiefs. In Tanganyika the most massive rural resistance movement occurred in Lake Province. The peasantry rallied against the attempt to impose what was called 'multi-racial' government, the association of Indians and Europeans, an infinitesimal minority, in the organs of local government. Non-cooperation and sabotage effectively brought provincial administration to a halt. Other social conflicts of the time in Tanganyika show different facets of rural protest: tax resistance among the Pare; anti-chief struggles among the Shambaa; the fight against land alienation to settlers in a land consolidation programme aimed at agricultural efficiency in Meru. These conflicts went back to the war years and intensified to reach a peak in the late 1950s, when the British were hardly able to collect any tax in Tanganyika. During the 1950s anti-chief and anti-agricultural ordinance crises swept the new Central African Federation of the Rhodesias and Nyasaland as well.

In West Africa the classic agriculture-related political issue revolved around the bureaucracy's efforts to stamp out swollen shoot disease among cocoa trees. The government remedy was to destroy all infected shoots and cut down whole areas in order to isolate the disease. Farmers realised this was ineffective and that they could at least get some profit from a poor harvest which was better than none at all. (Indeed, swollen shoot is no longer treated according to the prescriptions of the period.) The resultant conflict was acute and resulted in a deep alienation of cocoa farmers, especially in the Gold Coast, from the colonial state.

Pride of place in any discussion of peasant resistance to colonialism in this era must go to three great armed risings: one in Madagascar in 1947–8; one in central Kenya in 1952–5, usually called 'Mau Mau', and one in Cameroun which began in 1955. All are usually placed in the context of the movement for independence as a form of political nationalism. But more attention should be given to their social context and the material pressures that the African peasantry was feeling. In Kenya and Cameroun the uprisings' links to urban communities and to the labour movement were significant.

In Cameroun the rising took place under the auspices (and, in part, control) of a political party, the *Union des Populations du Cameroun*, with some systematic involvement of radicalised, educated Camerounians. The nationalist politicians and the educated population generally had a far more tangential role in the other two. All three took place in colonies with aggressive and militantly racist settlers. Cameroun's post-war political history had begun with a vicious attack on Africans by the settlers of the port city of Douala. In Madagascar a major geographic focus of rebellion was the plantation sector of the eastern coastal lowlands. In Kenya, Mau Mau sought the recovery of land proclaimed for whites only. Many fighters were evicted squatters who had found a cold welcome in the increasingly cash-orientated, commoditised, crowded Kikuyu Reserve. Mau Mau was in part a fight against the growing intrusion of capitalism into Kenyan agriculture. The guerrillas struck above all at the new class of Kikuyu accumulators. They called themselves the Land Freedom (or Land and Freedom) Army.

Far too little is known still of the actual practice of the guerrilla fighters in all three areas. In Kenya the Land Freedom Army held a secret parliament in the recesses of the remote Aberdare Mountains and called for the emergence of a united African nation in Kenya. Yet a decisive weakness of Mau Mau was its failure to gain much active support among non-Kikuyu. In Madagascar some of the military commanders appear to have been men of considerable political ability; there was a strong element of continuity with peasant movements that had fought in the nineteenth century against the exactions of the autocratic Imerina kingdom. Yet in contrast to Kenya the political leadership was afraid to tamper with the village élites and made compromises with them on a pragmatic basis. In Cameroun several areas (in turn) took up arms, but as in Kenya no national basis for the fighting was found by the UPC. The leadership deliberately restricted their political demands to two minima: formal independence from France and the unification of French with British Cameroun, thus uniting the old German colony. These were two demands which, eventually and ironically, the French were prepared to grant once the UPC was effectively beaten. All three rebellions occurred almost independently of the sympathy of the outside world and this was ultimately a major source of weakness. They never developed the global analysis or linkages which might have brought them more success.

Only with an understanding of this background of urban and rural mass protest and the new colonial context does the post-war expansion of nationalist mass movements – incredible compared with those of earlier times – begin to be explicable. The ideology of nationalism, apart from becoming more insistent, did not change much from that developed by the petty bourgeoisie before the war. Until 1940, however, this class had never succeeded in winning mass support (only rarely had it been sought), nor had it established viable political organisations. After 1945 it could call upon both the need of the colonial regimes for some new sort of association with Africans and the enormous possibilities opened up by proletarianisation, labour struggles and rural discontent. Between these two forces a vacuum had been created.

The classic case in the British colonies was the Gold Coast. The liberalised constitution of 1946 paved the way for the creation of the United

Gold Coast Convention to fight elections. It was led by the old coastal élite based on pre-war alignments who favoured heightened agitation and an eventual development towards independence. The UGCC, however, stood aloof from social issues and continued all too obviously to represent the interests of the most privileged strata. In 1947 the leadership called on the services of a man who had made a name as an organiser for black causes in Britain, the American-educated Kwame Nkrumah.

Nkrumah set the pace for Gold Coast, and indeed African, nationalism. He had a magnificent sense of personal style, spoke powerfully and was a tireless organiser. It was his politics which brought nationalism to the people. He evoked a political imagery and an appeal to the underdog that attracted a nucleus of dedicated militants, frequently from among the unemployed urban school-leavers and ex-servicemen, the new 'urban crowd' of African cities. He made alliances with market women and labour unions. Opposing swollen shoot policy and agitating about cocoa prices he penetrated the countryside. He effectively established a network that covered much of the Gold Coast, cross-cutting language and religious boundaries. When the UGCC, increasingly uncomfortable with his politics, tried to get rid of him, Nkrumah successfully established his own Convention People's Party in 1949.

Nkrumah may be taken as the model radical nationalist. However, the limits to his populist politics need to be considered simultaneously. At the heart of CPP affairs lay an ambitious core of business men and functionaries, less established than the UGCC stalwarts, but with similar aims and ambitions. The CPP is sometimes considered a 'mass' party, but it rested heavily on networks of élite-dominated homeboy associations and the patronage of community notables. It in no way contradicted or compromised the social basis of Gold Coast merchant capital. Nkrumah-style politics could not accommodate a class-based orientation. Instead he emphasised national 'unity', a programme that apparently offered something to all classes but rested heavily on the ambitions of an outside, aspirant bourgeoisie to establish a firmer position in the colonial economy, above all through winning control over the bureaucratic machinery of the colonial state. 'Seek ye first', said Nkrumah, 'the political kingdom'. The other side of the emphasis upon unity was the necessity to balance rival power brokers who based their influence on ethnicity, religion or region and prevent their mutual antagonisms from getting out of control.

Much of Nkrumah's language and emphases had already been polished abroad. By 1945 the number of Africans studying or working in Britain and France had increased significantly. There Pan-Africanism had been born from the element of race consciousness that flowed naturally from the situation of blacks in much of the Americas (classically articulated by Marcus Garvey in the interwar era), offering an ideal that was sufficiently vague to include potential support of bourgeois, workers and peasants. In England many of the major political figures of the nationalist era — Nkrumah, Hastings Banda of Nyasaland and Jomo Kenyatta of Kenya — worked together closely and found support within a small but articulate reforming stratum of metropolitan opinion. A second influence, perhaps as much rhetorical as real, came from the Communist Party whose agitational and organisational skills much impressed Nkrumah and others. Nkrumah may also have taken from Communist influences his relatively early orientation towards state involvement in economic development, especially industrialisation.

After the Gold Coast became independent in 1957 under the name of Ghana (chosen from a favoured antique empire in African nationalist litanies) Nkrumah made it the haven for anti-colonial movements from all over the continent. As the focus of decolonisation shifted southward, a similar role was played by the Tanganyika regime (Tanzania from 1964) of Julius Nyerere, which was granted independence in 1961. Nkrumah and Nyerere were central figures articulating the inspiring rhetoric of radical nationalism. They espoused international non-alignment, African unity and the struggle against dependence and underdevelopment and their influence was everywhere infectious.

Nyerere's Tanganyikan Africa National Union had a similar mix of petty bourgeois ambitions to the CPP, battening upon mass social and economic issues. Co-operative leaders, local notables, urban landlords and traders dominated its cells. Yet most of the African political parties of the late 1940s and the 1950s were even less genuinely mass parties. The framework of ambitious local business men, rich farmers and labour union brokers was much more nakedly obvious and popular involvement largely passive in the Sierra Leone People's Party, the Uganda People's Congress or the National Congress of Nigeria and the Cameroons. They too, however, could occasionally galvanise protest around particular issues and effectively present themselves to the British as potential power brokers.

In Paris the parallel cultural nationalism of Négritude emerged from similar influences. It was particularly associated with the Senegalese poet and teacher, Léopold Sédar Senghor. Yet the political organisations developed after the introduction of elections were largely not nationalist at all; they accepted the broad framework of assimilation proposed in various forms by liberalised French imperialism. Here the radical impulse was at first weak. It gained more strength in a new wave of politicisation in the 1950s, reacting upon the renewed vitality of French capitalism applied to Africa.

## The Political Setting

In 1945 it was hardly the intention of the colonial regimes to get out of Africa in the foreseeable future. However, they were already committed to the new United Nations Organisation system established by the victorious anti-Fascist Allies. The terms of the UNO charter contained an affirmation of the right to popular self-determination which could be applied to the world outside Europe. The very establishment of the UNO already brought certain African questions to the fore. The world organisation had vested rights in the old League of Nations mandates over the ex-German colonies. These continued to be administered by Britain, France, Belgium and South Africa, but the new format refused to allow the amalgamation of smaller territories into the neighbouring colonies and established a commitment to eventual independence, although pressure for speed towards that goal was at first minimal.

Additionally there was the problem of the colonies of defeated Italy: Libya, Somalia and Eritrea. Wranglings over their future continued for many years between the Great Powers. Libya was eventually conceded independence in 1951, the fourth internationally recognised sovereign African state after Ethiopia, Liberia and Egypt.

For the two colonies in the Horn of Africa various solutions were proposed. A British mandate over a unified Somali-speaking territory to include British Somaliland Protectorate and a part of eastern Ethiopia was one possibility. This idea confronted the ambitions of Haile Selassie who sought to end the isolation of Ethiopia from the sea which he felt had been crucial in its seizure by Italy. The strategic value of Ethiopia to the West, due to its proximity to Middle Eastern oil reserves, was substantial and there was a predisposition, especially by the USA, to go some way towards accommodating Ethiopian state claims. As a result the eastern frontier of Ethiopia was left where it had been and Italian Somaliland reverted to Italian control, but with the international guarantee of sovereign independence in ten years. Eritrea was granted autonomy within Ethiopia, which proceeded to receive in return an increasing American military involvement, including the grant of Kagnew air force base in Eritrea. Eritrean autonomy lasted only ten years, from 1952 to 1962. Then the Eritrean assembly, surrounded by troops, was forced at gunpoint to accept integration into Ethiopia as an ordinary province.

A second internationally determined decolonisation decision concerned the Anglo-Egyptian Sudan. The Sudan was to all intents and purposes a British colony, particularly after the White Flag Rebellion of 1923 convinced the British to try and close it to Egyptian nationalist influence. Yet Egypt had residual treaty rights in the Sudan, as well as an enormous cultural influence among the Arabic-speaking intelligentsia of the Nile valley. So long as Egypt was a monarchy the formal, if ineffectual, position of its government was that the Sudan must eventually revert to the kingdom of Egypt. But after the overthrow of Farouk in 1952 the Naguib government (Naguib himself being half-Sudanese in origin) took a far more accommodating stance and established accords with the principal Sudanese political factions. Britain was prepared to proceed with a rapid transition to independence in the Sudan which actually took place in 1956.

This was only a decade after the war ended. Yet within another ten years most of Africa had also become independent. From a distance this seems like a single direct process. Observed more closely, it was a contradictory period marked by distinct if short-lived stages and, at the time, apparently conflicting policies on the part of the colonial powers. Thus it seems best to consider the sequence of developments in Africa by establishing four separate, regionally focused narratives in looking at the decolonisation of British West Africa, British Central and East Africa, the French-run territories and finally, the Belgian Congo where the Belgian withdrawal provoked the most dramatic events in the entire era.

## Independence for British West Africa

For British West Africa the key territory was the Gold Coast, whose decolonisation we have already begun to examine. The reforms of the first post-war constitution in 1946 were meagre, but they initiated unintentionally a timetable whose logic was eagerly seized by nationalists. Once the possibility of self-government within the colonial system had been conceded, pressing the issue towards greater speed and resolution was a viable and extremely attractive tactic.

In the immediate aftermath of the war the Gold Coast at first largely evaded the labour agitation typical of most colonies. Yet social tensions ran high. In 1948 a demonstration of ex-servicemen outside Christianborg Castle, the seat of government in Accra, was fired upon by government troops. This was the signal for days of rioting in which the property of foreign companies, including the principal UAC outlet in Accra, was looted. In the countryside the swollen-shoot agitation turned cocoa farmers against the state. The high point of militancy was the general strike of January 1950. It was initiated neither by Nkrumah nor the CPP, but fell into their laps as the ideal pressure point against the colonial regime, which began to fear that if collaboration with Nkrumah was not established a far more serious threat to capital in the Gold Coast might ultimately emerge. Nkrumah and most of his closest associates were then or soon would be in prison, which gave them the aura of heroes and martyrs, 'Prison Graduates'. By the time of the strike the Coussey Commission had already prepared a condemnation of administrative policies with regard to the 1948 violence, and important concessions were under consideration.

In 1951 a new constitution proposed direct elections for the entire territory and ministerial responsibility to the successful party. The CPP gained a substantial majority of seats and Nkrumah agreed to call off Positive Action and serve as Leader of Government Business. His release from gaol was the archetypal nationalist triumph, a model that politicians elsewhere, with Nkrumah's warm encouragement, sought to emulate.

For six years Nkrumah functioned as a colonial premier, establishing close relations with the British governor, Sir Charles Arden-Clarke. This transitional period was crucial for underpinning the continuity which typified the transition to independence as the state machinery was gradually handed over to Africans. Africans were promoted rapidly in the civil service and began to acquire control over more and more patronage and funds. The CPP government carried out the established colonial development schemes, with a particular emphasis on education which was sure to gain popular approbation.

Not surprisingly the CPP machinery became increasingly closely identified with the state and evoked opposition from strata that had felt left out of Nkrumah's coalition. The CPP had mushroomed so fast that many local power-brokers had simply been left standing in amazement at the beginning of the 1950s. Opposition began to crystallise around regional discontents aligned to Nkrumah's old UGCC opponents. Nkrumah won a second election victory in 1954 impressively but not overwhelmingly. As hostility to him spread in the cocoa-growing Asante region the British obliged him to call a final election in 1956, before proceeding to the grant of independence. Asante was a typical product of the indirect rule system, under which 'traditional' authorities had clustered a nexus of influence and patronage that was being undermined by the ascendancy of centralised initiative implied in the plans for decolonisation. The relatively high level of wealth provided by cocoa gave weight to the local power élite; in equivalently governed areas that had only meagre resources, no such effective opposition movements arose. The anti-Nkrumah forces did succeed in weakening the CPP in Asante tremendously, but their alliance on a national scale was motley and could offer no effective alternative to the vitality of the CPP and its now unshakeable association with a programme for immediate independence. Thus the CPP won some 72 out of 104 seats in the 1956 election and Nkrumah led the Gold Coast to independence as the new state of Ghana in 1957.

Why were the British authorities prepared to work with Nkrumah and concede major constitutional reforms? Privately, colonial officials remained convinced that they alone could render the 'second colonial occupation' effective and profitable. They could presumably have exerted enough force to suppress nationalism in the colony for another generation. Yet there was a sense that the handwriting was on the wall, whatever the economic imperatives. The die was cast by 1951 and decolonisation began to look like a European scramble out of Africa, reversing the rapid conquest of sixty to seventy years earlier.

One of the most significant aspects of the Gold Coast experience was the absence of overt challenge to the interests of Western security or business interests in the transition years after Nkrumah entered the government. The commodity boom was still in full swing and generated optimism that the economic underpinnings of at least the more substantial colonies were firm enough to withstand political readjustment. In the event the lessons established in the Gold Coast were quickly applied elsewhere. In 1951 Sierra Leone held its first colony-wide legislative elections, while regional assemblies on a wide franchise were placed in operation in Nigeria.

Decolonisation in Nigeria displayed fundamental structural similarities to, but also important differences from, the Gold Coast. The broad social issues were very similar. Shortly following the end of hostilities in Europe government workers in Nigeria staged a remarkably effective general strike. The labour movement showed militancy and intensifying politicisation, despite attempts by the state to impose a business union system, and problems posed by its own fragmentation. Labour agitation was coupled with the emergence of a volatile urban crowd, open to radical and nationalist activism. The first major post-war political party, the National Congress of Nigeria and the Cameroons (NCNC), bore a strong resemblance to the CPP. Its leader, Nnamdi Azikiwe, was a journalist who, like Nkrumah, had received much of his education in the USA. He established ties with the labour movement, fed off popular agitation and inherited the mantle of the more populist strand of pre-war Lagos politics as typified by Herbert Macauley.

What made Nigeria different was particularly its incomparably greater size and population, in which the capital, Lagos, carried much less weight than Accra. Nigeria had been a united colony economically, but the administration of different areas, particularly north and south, had been entirely distinct. It contained the most highly developed stratum of bourgeois in Africa, notably merchants and professional men, and they advanced their fortunes very markedly in the post-war years. However, they generally operated local or, at most, regional networks and their relative strength as a class was coupled with intense internal rivalries as they jockeyed for positions in the new national arena created by the process of decolonisation. The problem posed by Asante within the Gold Coast was magnified enormously in Nigeria. Powerful local notables had the means and the will to prevent being upstaged from the centre. This was most markedly true of the north, where the old ruling class and a merchant stratum had profited from the indirect rule system.

The NCNC had radical elements, some of them loosely associated as 'Zikists', but their influence was always tempered by the strength of the Nigerian bourgeoisie. The last major instance of an NCNC appeal to class concerns was its protest campaign after striking demonstrators were murdered by colonial troops at the coal mines of eastern Nigeria in 1949. By 1950 the Zikists were mostly purged from the party largely dominated by business interests.

While Nkrumah came from a small, out-of-the-way corner of the Gold Coast with little political influence, Azikiwe was an Igbo from eastern Nigeria. Tribal boundaries had become particularly politically salient in Nigeria and the Igbo were a 'tribe' which dominated one of the three regions demographically. In the 1920s they had accepted Christianity and schooling on an immense scale, often as tickets out of their impoverished homeland, the most densely populated section of tropical Africa. From the 1920s Igbo artisans and clerks spread throughout Nigeria and by 1945 were increasingly prominent as well among the new generation of university graduates and ambitious businessmen.

The NCNC was never wholly Igbo in composition, but it evoked hostility from others who used ethnic solidarity as a vehicle of political and economic competition. In the west, much of the Yoruba élite rejected the NCNC and established the rival Action Group whose leader, Obafemi Awolowo, advocated decolonisation towards a rather weak federal Nigeria. Other Yoruba continued to function within the NCNC and, as a result, control of the west was hotly contested through the 1950s. The greatest Yoruba town, Ibadan, continued to back the NCNC under the impress of the patronage system established by its 'boss', Adegoke Adelabu. Adelabu was a flamboyant and corrupt politician, fundamentally demogogic in that his vague populism was devoid of any serious social critique. He was the quintessential Nigerian politician whose following was built on a use of bread and circuses for the masses and manipulation of the petty bourgeois aspirations that stemmed from the strength of the vast bazaar network and myriad of small producers.

In the north two major parties developed – the Northern People's Congress and the Northern Elements' Progressive Union. The NPC was the agency of the strong men of the emirates. At its most effective it represented an attempt to modernise the power base of the administrative hierarchies by coalescing rival groups from different emirates, while according some patronage to the commoner merchants on the one hand and the non-emirate and often non-Islamic minority of the Middle Belt and the hill country on the other. Its leader was Ahmadu Bello, a previously unsuccessful aspirant to the sultanate of Sokoto, often known by his Sokoto title of Sardauna.

NEPU was considerably more radical, taking on itself the grievances of younger disaffected northern officials and well-to-do commoners. It had a nationalist outlook and its populism was often cast in classic Islamic terminology. It shared both the NPC's fears of southern domination and its demands for the 'northernisation', rather than the 'Nigerianisation', of the civil service. NEPU's strength was obscured in elections, thanks to the strength of the administrative and commercial networks the NPC could call into play, as well as coercion, in which British officialdom played an important hand.

By 1945, whereas the British in Lagos envisioned a gradual process of devolution in Nigeria that would reconcile elements from the entire territory, their counterparts in the north strengthened and indeed partly created the provincial chauvinism that typified the NPC in particular. There is little evidence to suggest that the British as a whole sought to weaken potential Nigerian unity; for good economic reasons, quite the contrary. However, those in the north were in good part responsible for the increasingly acrimonious, racist and squalid form that Nigerian politics took.

By 1951 it was clear that Britain would grant Nigeria independence in coming years. Thereafter, political life as defined by the parties and the incipient ruling class focused around the quarrel for spoils. In 1954 a constitution was devised which gave substantial financial powers to the three regional governments. This fundamentally entrenched on a regional basis the three political parties, although the Action Group actually lost control of the west for a time. The coming of independence then required some form of agreement between the parties. In 1959 the NPC finally agreed to independence based on a strongly federal constitution. Nigeria's first government in 1960 was a coalition between the NCNC and the NPC with an NPC premier, Sir Abubakar Tafawa Balewa.

In Sierra Leone the most dramatic social conflicts lay in the peasant revolts of the mid-1950s aimed at authoritarian and venal chiefs. These ultimately reasserted themselves under the patronage of the Sierra Leone People's Party led by Milton Margai. Margai and his machine brought Sierra Leone to independence in 1961 while the principal opposition leader, Siaka Stevens, whose party had a strong hold on urban workers, foundered in gaol. The last British colony in West Africa was the Gambia. By the early 1960s Britain was determined to relinquish its administrative position in Africa and the Gambia was granted independence in 1965, however unlikely it was that this mini-state with a population only equal to that of Luxemburg could function as an effective sovereign entity.

## The End of British Rule in East and Central Africa

The British authorities saw the problem of devolution in the major colonies of East and Central Africa rather differently from that in West Africa or the Sudan. With the exception of Uganda, which presented its own special problems as we shall see, the African bourgeoisie was very much less developed and, in colonial terms, very much less fit to administer the infrastructure it would inherit on independence. Devolution of any effective power to Africans was considered to lie a generation off even at the beginning of the 1950s. At the same time the British were anxious to balance concessions to Africans with support for the white settlers who remained the bulk of the local bourgeoisie. In the economic circumstances of the late 1940s settler agriculture began to boom while in-migration of Europeans increased steadily.

Thus the official British goal was to try to establish a balance between black and white in the interests of regionally based capital development. We have already mentioned one aspect of this, the politics of Federation, applied only to a limited extent in East Africa but established as the basis for a potential new dominion in Central Africa in 1953. Another aspect was generally called 'multi-racialism' which established separate, racially defined electorates. The white and Asian minorities were given vastly greater representation within this system than their numbers warranted, but nominated Africans were also now admitted to the assemblies. Only from the late 1950s did any of the plural racial systems set into motion actually allow Africans to vote.

In reality the compromise sought by Whitehall was an impossible one. Settlers were intransigent and unwilling to take any steps that challenged their hegemony in a 'white man's country'. Even where, as in Tanganyika, truculent settlers were not really a serious political force, the state held out for the 'multi-racial' society in a way no class of Africans found acceptable. The timid advances in African representation meant little or nothing to an increasingly radicalised populace.

African nationalism in East and Central Africa had a much sharper radical edge than in West Africa. The weakness of the bourgeois component may explain this in part. The cause, though, lay more in the escalation of post-war capitalist development, felt by peasants and workers with unprecedented force and identified locally not merely with the distant 'government' but with the racially defined minorities: white settlers, Asian business men and, in Zanzibar, 'Arab' planters.

Post-war Kenya experienced a quickening of tension from the end of the war. The labour movement burgeoned out of control, leading to general strikes in Mombasa in 1947 and in Nairobi in 1950. Chege Kibachia organised a politically orientated general workers' union that appeared for a time to herald the birth of class-based politics. Sharpening rural differentiation, especially on the Kikuyu Reserve, led to increasing anger and frustration on the part of the poor who linked up to the urban crowd in Nairobi and the radical wing of the union there. The old agitational politics of the Kenya African Union seemed tame and inadequate in these harsh times. The only one of the established leadership to keep in effective touch with the new radical trend was Jomo Kenyatta, a brilliant orator and organiser who returned to Kenya in 1946 after fifteen years abroad, mainly in Britain, as a worker, student, political agitator and man of many parts.

Many of the young radicals were Kikuyu who had been initiated in the 1940 age set. They were thus known as the '40 Group'. By the end of the 1940s mass oathing had been initiated by those who were determined to see the status quo in Kenya overturned in any way possible. Oathing evoked the loyalties of Kikuyu peasants in what became a largely Kikuyu movement; it may have alienated Africans for whom it was not a traditional practice. Violence erupted with assassinations of those who, both in Nairobi and Kikuyuland, were felt to be the lackeys of the regime and traitors. In 1952 the governor proclaimed a state of emergency while fighters took to the hills, initiating the Mau Mau rising. Mau Mau took essentially three years and some severe measures indeed to control. Large numbers of Kikuyu were herded into detention villages or imprisoned while the Kikuyu population of Nairobi was mostly expelled and replaced by other Kenyans. The radical wing of the labour movement was also squashed. Kenyatta himself was considered by most of officialdom as the master-mind of Mau Mau. This seems unlikely to be the case although he was much too shrewd a politician entirely to disavow sympathy for the struggle, let alone the causes, of the Land Freedom Army.

The British denounced Mau Mau as a psychological aberration, a retreat into 'darkness and death' by savages with their veneer of civilised behaviour removed. Yet Mau Mau caused British policy to shift towards reform. The crucial element was the Swynnerton Plan, a programme of land consolidation which aimed at securing political stability in Kikuyuland through the creation of a capitalist, small farming class. Closely linked to the Plan was the abrogation of the ban on growing coffee by Africans, a ban which had long been enforced in order to preserve a profitable settler monopoly. Under this aegis African coffee production grew rapidly, and a minority of rich peasants began to grow with it. They came to establish links with the very small but also expanding class of professionally educated Africans, few of whom had any sympathy for the form or the radical potential of Mau Mau.

A great weakness of the Land Freedom Army had been its relative failure to provoke sustained support from non-Kikuyu apart from immediately neighbouring groups. The other Africans in fact benefited from the suspicion that fell on all Kikuyu during the 1950s. Politicians from the Luo-speaking people near Lake Victoria and other newly self-conscious 'tribes' began to make themselves heard. A major figure of the new era was Tom Mboya, a Luo who became the leader of the reconstituted

Nairobi labour movement. Mboya managed to retain his nationalist credentials while establishing a new trade union base with strong American affiliations. He was aided by the interest of British and other firms in Nairobi's growing industrial sector in creating a relatively small, better-paid, stabilised labour force. Mboya and others established the Kenya African National Union in 1960, the first political party among Africans to function throughout Kenya.

KANU demanded independence, an end to the white highlands, African majority rule and Kenyatta's release from detention with an eventual commitment to independence. This proved sufficient as a programme to hold its various factions together and overcome the challenge of a rival party that based itself on the jealousies of the smaller 'tribes'. KANU's effectiveness as a machine and the rapidly growing maturity of the African bourgeoisie led to British concessions, with a devolution process initiated in 1961 that brought independence in 1963. The white highlands were made available to Africans by purchase, but part of the independence package enshrined private property in Kenya. The purchase by the state of settler land was guaranteed by a British loan whose repayment ensured capitalist stability as state policy. From the time of his release Kenyatta, despite his long imprisonment and advanced years, quickly assumed effective control of KANU and became Kenya's first president.

Kenya's southern neighbour, Tanganyika, had already attained independence in 1961, the first of this bloc of countries in East Africa. The Tanganyika African National Union (TANU) has been described as a classic example of an African 'mass' political party. Its most notable accomplishment was the effective welding together of the petty bourgeoisie on a territory-wide basis, cutting through religious and language boundaries. Its leader, Julius Nyerere, was remarkable for his modest habits, personal integrity and moralist's social vision. TANU's struggle was fundamentally against the attempt to foist 'multi-racialism' on Tanganyika. It was conducted on strictly reformist lines, but assisted by the long shadow of Mau Mau, the intensity of rural conflicts and the particular strength of the Tanganyika labour union movement which had organised more than forty per cent of wage labourers. The collapse of British authority in Lake Province was a major precipitating factor in the turn-around of 1958, which brought TANU participation in elections, Nyerere's entry into the government and then independence.

Just out to sea from the Tanganyikan mainland lay the British protectorate of Zanzibar. Britain faced no settler question here but tensions escalated in the 1950s between one nationalist movement that represented the Sultan and the landlord interest, generally qualified as Arab, and another which saw itself as African and wanted the end of landlord power. It was not coherently socialist or class-based, though; indeed it took a much less bold attitude towards the British regime than its rival. A third party, with its strength on the sister island of Pemba where the population was more intermingled and small landowners dominant, held the balance of strength. At first ethnic politics covered up the intensity of class conflict on the plantation island.

Ironically it was within the Zanzibar Nationalist Party, the more nationalist but less African party, that a class-conscious Left, with real strength among the important docker community and other wage workers, formed. This group coupled with some elements in the 'African' Afro-Shirazi Party (ASP) to radicalise Zanzibar politics. The Sultan's party took the reins of power in an independent Zanzibar at the end of 1963. In little over a month a violent coup overthrew the new regime and it looked as though a revolutionary government might emerge. At this point Tanganyika intervened. Zanzibar was incorporated into the new united republic known as Tanzania, with local power in the main going to former ASP stalwarts.

The nationalist struggle in Northern Rhodesia and Nyasaland was first and foremost a struggle against the Central African Federation. Antifederal agitation, based on apprehensions about the introduction of the Rhodesian system into the territories further north, was widespread in the late 1940s. However, the British Conservative Party government decided to go through with Federation. At first, opposition melted away surprisingly. Federation meant retaining the extant administrative system in each territory and thus forbade new land alienations to whites in Nyasaland and Northern Rhodesia. The growing labour movement on the Copperbelt received important concessions in 1955 after a successful African strike significantly increased wages although virtually leaving the racial colour bar in mine work intact. In these circumstances the small organisations of the local African élites proved incompetent at carrying through their opposition.

However, after several years the growing sophistication of new protest associations, the intensity of anti-chief, anti-agricultural ordinance agitation and fears of a more effective Rhodesian domination after the constitutional revision of 1960, brought a mounting wave of agitation, culminating in the proclamation of a state of emergency in Nyasaland in 1959. Britain had been anxious to make Federation work as a viable financial unit, but this seemed increasingly unfeasible. To the enormous anger of Federal premier Sir Roy Welensky, Harold Macmillan dropped the issue of movement to Dominion status and organised instead a policy of greater African representation within the Northern legislatures. Hastings Banda, a Nyasaland doctor who had lived in the USA, Britain and then the Gold Coast for more than thirty years before being brought back by the various factions of the Nyasaland African Congress, was now released from gaol and agreed to co-operate with colonial authority. In Nyasaland the right of secession from the Federation was granted in 1962; Northern Rhodesia followed suit a year later. By 1964 they were independent states under the names of Malawi and Zambia. The intensity of social crisis in these lands was as severe as it had been in Kenya, but thus far their historiography during this period is less well developed.

The decolonisation of Uganda presented problems for the British as severe as anywhere although not quite of the same nature. There was no settler question. As elsewhere in East Africa the large Asian immigrant minority had prospered in the post-war era and, in Uganda, it appropriated the lion's share of the opportunities available for a local bourgeoisie. Therefore anti-Asian feeling was more politically significant than elsewhere, as witness the boycott of Indian-owned shops in 1959–60. The British were less committed to the Asian than to a European settler bourgeoisie, however. The real dilemma they faced in Uganda was what to do with the Buganda protectorate. Buganda had been administered separately from the rest of the territory with only tangential representation on the Legislative Council. Its distinctive role might be compared to Asante in the Gold Coast, but Buganda occupied a yet more pivotal place in the wealth, population and position of its educated stratum in Uganda. Uganda without Buganda was unimaginable to British administrators. Yet the Buganda élite were completely hostile to closer relations with the rest of the territory. The peasantry were deeply involved in social and economic agitation but tended to see the future in terms of a restoration of the full rights of a sovereign *kabaka* who could mend the evils of the day.

In 1952 Sir Andrew Cohen, the British Colonial Office's master mind of decolonisation, came to Kampala as governor to press Buganda into an arrangement. Crisis ensued and the *kabaka* was exiled for two years. The solutions later found were quite superficial. Only in 1962 did the Kabaka Yekka party, dominant in Buganda, agree to a patchwork compromise which brought Uganda to independence. By this point Apollo Milton Obote's Uganda People's Congress had achieved majority support elsewhere in the territory. It included what politically conscious radicals there were, but basically was a federation of rural notables. This militated against any challenge to the status quo other than anti-Indian agitation (which could benefit the aspirant African trader or cotton ginner). Thus Obote's new regime rested on especially insecure foundations, despite the presence of the most sophisticated African bourgeoisie in any of these territories and the weakness of political radicalism.

The Kenya independence bargain and the break-up of the Central African Federation were the finale in this second wave of British decolonisation. There remained several minor colonies of which the British were now anxious to dispose. These were the so-called High Commission territories, Basutoland, Swaziland and Bechuanaland, within the sphere of South Africa, all of which were handed independence by 1968, and the Indian Ocean island territories of Mauritius and the Seychelles which became national states as well.

## Decolonisation in French Africa

The French colonial practice stressed the development of assimilation as a policy. Demands for secession or full national independence outside this framework were treated as treasonable and suppressed. It was the demand for independence which made the UPC completely unacceptable in Cameroun. Nevertheless the French constitution of 1946 allowed for the establishment of political parties which affiliated to the parties of the French political spectrum in order to fight elections for the French parliament.

Only in two areas of French West Africa did viable 'mass' parties appear quickly – Senegal and the Ivory Coast. The scene of the most intense social agitation of the late 1940s, they also felt the major brunt of capitalist development in the first post-war years. In Senegal Léopold Sédar Senghor had returned in 1946 to found the *Bloc Démocratique Sénégalais*. He upstaged the older generation of politicians from the four communes through alliances with the *shaykhs* of the Islamic orders.

The Ivory Coast witnessed a more radical upheaval. The league of Africans who represented the most progressive wing of the new politicians in French-speaking Africa, the *Rassemblement Démocratique Africaine*, established an effective branch there, the *Parti Démocratique du Côte d'Ivoire*. The PDCI capitalised on urban and rural discontent but won as well the adherence of a significant group of prosperous, labour-employing cocoa planters. The leader, Félix Houphouet-Boigny, was a particularly successful planter and chief. His class was locked in struggle with French agricultural settlers who through the war years, monopolised access to forced labourers on their estates. Forced labour affected not only the mass of Ivory Coast peasants, but also nascent capitalists on the land. The PDCI rose to strength on the prestige won from the abolition of forced labour in 1946 and the subsequent rise of a prosperous African cocoa-growing sector.

The RDA worked in alliance with the French Communist Party. It did not agitate strongly for independence, but with the onset of the Cold War the administration was determined to root out reds from the colonies. From 1948 the PDCI suffered from an intense administrative persecution, although it retained a remarkable amount of support. In 1951 Houphouet-Boigny came to terms with a visiting cabinet minister, François Mitterrand, then the leader of a small fragment of moderate socialists in the French chamber. He broke with the Communists and affiliated to Mitterrand's faction. Most of the RDA then joined this or other non-Communist blocs in the chamber. The radical element in PDCI politics was dropped and the French administration began to patronise Houphouet-Boigny. Thus the PDCI, like the BDS in Senegal, grew into an effective electoral machine, but hardly a revolutionary force.

The political organisations in other parts of Equatorial and West Africa were weak and narrowly patron-based at this time. However, the situation changed in the 1950s as French capitalism began to enter into a long wave of growth and confidence that swept many new corners of the colonies. It was within the context of renewed French investment in Africa that a new group of mass parties emerged, notably Sawaba (Freedom) in Niger, the *Parti Démocratique du Guinée* in Guinea and the *Union Soudanaise* in the Sudan. Sekou Touré, leader of the PDG, the Guinean section of the RDA, came from the trade union movement, if not from the ranks of the manual workers. In Guinea a sharp PDG-led struggle was directed against the old aristocracy of the impoverished Futa Djallon, where an attenuated form of slavery survived and much of the population depended on migrants' wages for their livelihood. Muslim traders formed a crucial link in the network of associations that held together the Union Soudanaise. Both parties gave unprecedented scope to demands for independence.

French colonialism experienced its most serious reverses not in sub-Saharan Africa but in Indo-China and, later, North Africa. The French Republic reluctantly granted independence to Vietnam, Morocco and Tunisia and became locked into an intensifying struggle over Algeria.

The Algerian war was, in fact, the main cause of the coup that overthrew the Fourth Republic in France in 1958 and established General Charles de Gaulle in power. De Gaulle, reflecting on this, may have wondered at the good sense of the British in organising an orderly retreat from their colonies so well. He was put in power to carry on the French Empire, but reconsiderations began quickly.

A plebiscite was organised to determine the support of the colonies for continued association within the French Union. One major African politician, Sekou Touré, was unwilling to accept the humiliating demand of rejecting the independence option.[3] Guinea alone in Africa voted *non* in 1958 and De Gaulle proceeded to order a spiteful withdrawal not just of French authority but of technical personnel and movable infrastructure. It was expected that Guinea would quickly collapse into chaos. However, it survived and managed to get its services functioning while interesting other powers in its fate. The chorus of *ouis* could not endure a successful Guinea. There was increasing opposition at the UNO to France on its policies in Togo and Cameroun, the two trust territories it controlled. Armed resistance in Cameroun, if much less damaging than in Algeria, was threatening to French prestige. De Gaulle reversed his policies entirely and announced plans for independence to come in all of the black African colonies in 1960.

Thus the two trust territories, Madagascar and the two federations of West and Equatorial Africa were transformed into fifteen nominally sovereign states. It remains to assess the French role in the break-up of West and Equatorial Africa. It appears likely that a strong element of divide and rule attached to the motivations behind the dissolution of the two federations. The decisive development was the *loi-cadre* of 1956 which had created territorial assemblies while virtually universalising the franchise. It was the *loi-cadre* which provided the steam for separate territorial movements to seek nationhood. Houphouet-Boigny, whose influence in Paris had become very great, adamantly opposed any diminution in his powerful position, particularly given the position of the Ivory Coast as the wealthiest French territory, and wanted no federation. In contrast, Senghor favoured some kind of federal union but his solution, the Mali Federation, embraced only the French Sudan and Senegal by the time of independence and tensions between them brought the federation to a quick end, Sudan choosing to retain the name of Mali.

French decolonisation was far less genuinely a retreat from Africa than its British equivalent. In part it was a nominal change of sovereignty that did not much affect basic French interests. On achieving independence the new nations signed agreements with France on foreign aid and defense that reinforced French cultural and economic predominance and left the French army as a guarantor of the new regimes. Close personal ties bound the new African political leadership with top figures from French politics, while annual summits of 'Francophone' countries were used to harmonise views. The Africanisation of the state services took place far more slowly and decorously than in ex-British Africa.

## The Congo Crisis

As De Gaulle mulled through new options an even more dramatic policy turn-around took place in the Belgian Congo. Through the first post-war decade the Congo economy boomed. As the wage-labour force passed the 1 000 000 mark in the mid-1950s it was more than twice the size of any other in black Africa. The high level of capital penetration built on the advanced character of Belgian business involvement going back to the 1920s. A new element in the situation, though, was the dramatic urban growth, rapid even by African standards, that followed from the ever-wider gap between the harsh life of the peasantry and the possibilities that beckoned in the towns.

During the boom years the Belgians never seriously considered political reform. In the mid-1950s, however, their thinking began to alter, perhaps in the wake of influence from more powerful Western countries, perhaps as a reflection of pressures for modernisation within Belgian capitalism as the Congo boom gave way to stagnation. In 1952 the Catholic party, which had almost invariably controlled the colonial ministry and the governor-generalship of the Congo, was for once thrown out of office and this proved to be the first impetus of rather timid reforms that built up in the 1950s. Secular education was introduced and the first Congolese permitted to go to Belgian universities. In 1957 a university was actually established in Leopoldville. The market economy was allowed more scope in rural areas, permitting the growth of a cash-crop peasantry and a class of petty shopkeepers, especially in the Bas-Congo province between Leopoldville and the Atlantic. Political liberalisation led to the foundation of African urban associations and journals. In 1957 municipal elections were held in the biggest cities. Two years earlier Professor van Bilsen, associated with the Institut Solvay, an influential think-tank for Belgian capitalism, had predicted the independence of the Congo within thirty years. Once unthinkable this marked a decisive break in colonial planning.

The municipal elections introduced the first party political groupings among urban Africans. They revealed bitter cleavages on ethnic lines, typically between people from the vicinity of the town and those, often long orientated to migration who had acquired greater skills, from further away. In the Katanga capital of Elisabethville there was tension between the Luba from Kasai Province and local Katanga people, and in Luluabourg between Luba and Lulua. In Leopoldville the Kongo speakers were ranged against people from up-river. Little of this reflected any genuine cultural or even historical differentiation; it was a question of politics along the lines of protective association in the harsh conditions of survival in colonial society, combined with the ambitions of the rising bourgeoisie, whom the Belgians quaintly called *evolués*, trying to establish a clientele. The increasingly charged atmosphere in Leopoldville, where employment opportunities were diminishing in the late 1950s, led to serious riots in January 1959, attacks on property and substantial violence. To the surprise of the world, within a fortnight King Baudouin announced that Belgium would bring the Congo speedily to full independence.

In less than eighteen months independence had indeed come to pass. What explains the rapid shift? A major element, however hidden in official explanation, may lie in Belgian conviction that rapid decolonisation would be meaningless decolonisation, that the transition to increased African participation in directing the system might best happen under the rubric of a nominal independence. However, the Belgians were certainly feeling under pressure due to decolonisation in neighbouring territories such as the Sudan, Uganda and, in 1960, French Equatorial Africa.

The apparently awesome administrative and economic structure of the Congo was characterised by an equally great rigidity and as such proved remarkably vulnerable to pressure from below once a momentum had been established. In 1959–60 Belgian authority, especially in rural areas, began to crumble rapidly and the defensive posture of uncertain bureaucrats led to an intensifying weakness and disorder. Collapse of local authority was often coupled with the crudest form of manipulation. It is likely too that the Belgian élite was itself deeply divided and unable to pursue a coherent policy.

The leap of the Congoloese petty bourgeoisie to the realisation of its dreams was thus an extremely rapid one, especially in the less developed parts of the colony. The immaturity of this class showed itself in two striking tendencies. First, it was slow to create an ideology that could resolve its own ambitions into a general nationalist posture to win wide popular support. Congo politicians tended to be exceptionally supine and reactionary as a whole. A minority, however, were open to a more radical critique of colonialism and the colonial formulae for decolonisation than virtually any equivalent group in sub-Saharan Africa. Secondly, by 1960 the throng of politicians trying to establish themselves in each provincial centre of this vast country were unable to solder together true national political networks.

The situation might be clarified by a look at the developments in the three nodal points of Leopoldville, Elisabethville and Stanleyville. In the capital and its hinterland the dominant party was the Association des Bakongos (ABAKO), led by Joseph Kasavubu. ABAKO reflected the relative sophistication and wealth of the Kongo élite while containing a strong populist element. It looked not much unlike the 'mass' parties of West Africa. However, it contained a parochial outlook focused on Kongo unity with aspirations in the directions of a restoration of the ancient Kongo kingdom, including parts of Angola and the French Congo. Therefore it was potentially secessionist. In Elisabethville the Confédération des Associations Tribales du Katanga (CONAKAT) and its partners fed on the anti-Luba fears of various Katanga groupings who resented the copper centre's most effective migrants. The large resident European population looked askance at the gradual liberalisation of the Congo system and began to dream of a secession that might take in the eastern part of the colony. CONAKAT's leader, the venal and brutal Moïse Tshombe, established a close alliance with them and plotted the potential break-up of the Congo. In sharp contrast, Stanleyville, the third major centre of the country, was a hodgepodge of heterogeneous Africans. The politics of ethnic competition were much less sharp there and the dominant figure to emerge in the late 1950s was Patrice Lumumba, a radical nationalist committed to Congo unity, and his *Mouvement National Congolais*.

As 1960 advanced the MNC gained ground and Lumumba established a range of useful if tenuous alliances, although sustaining little support from either Elisabethville or Leopoldville. The MNC won the largest number of seats in the one election held before independence and Lumumba became prime minister with Kasavubu as president. The various parties, despite their intense rivalry, were able, as in Uganda, to agree sufficiently for the presentation of a common position in the round table which brought independence in July. Lumumba seemed sure to become the dominant national politician. He had no coherent social outlook; indeed occasionally he took an obsequiously pro-colonial line. At other times, however, he expressed a deep awareness of the sufferings of the Congolese under Belgian rule and possessed the quality of unpredictability which made him highly suspicious in Western eyes. He was capable of a sharp quick development in ways inimical to Belgian interests. This was typified by his famous speech on Independence Day. Enraged by the text of the King of the Belgians, which celebrated the colonial past and had the temerity to extol the virtues of Leopold II himself, Lumumba issued an eloquent diatribe on the racism, oppression and exploitation suffered by Africans under the Belgian yoke (while still expressing hopes for Belgian aid!). The king and the Belgian premier, also present, were insulted and Belgian opinion in high places made up its mind that Lumumba was a madman who had to be eliminated soon.

Within a fortnight they found an excuse. The army mutinied, stung by the attitude of its Belgian commanders (General Janssens was justly famous for writing prominently in the main barracks, Before Independence = After Independence) and indifferent to the squabbles of the new parties. Belgium responded by sending in paratroopers without Congolese government request. Shortly thereafter, Tshombe proclaimed the independence of Katanga while an equivalent figure, Albert Kalondji, produced his own secessionist declaration in Kasai. Lumumba disposed of no force to deal with the situation. Instead he appealed to the UNO for assistance. The secretary-general, Dag Hammarskjöld, saw UNO intervention as a means for the organisation to establish itself as an effective world peace-keeping force and dispatched a multinational army. The Western powers made sure, however, that the UNO concerned itself with the establishment of a more 'rational' government in Leopoldville before organising any intervention in Katanga that might negatively affect the mining interests of the UMHK.

In September Lumumba was arrested by Joseph Mobutu, his former press secretary who had been despatched into the service to create the beginnings of a loyal army. Subject to a rather mild detention he began to consider closer links with the Soviet Union and the Soviet bloc, one solution that the West was unprepared to tolerate. A new army mutiny called for his release. It was suppressed but the bickering cliques of politicians in Leopoldville began to fear that Lumumba was becoming the focus of support in mounting popular discontent. The wealth of the Congo ensured that they and their friends were now moving, with a rapidity unprecedented in Africa, into control of substantial fortunes in an atmosphere of unbridled corruption and contempt for the people.

At this juncture Lumumba arranged an escape. It was a failure. Unable to reach his home province of Orientale, still under the administration of his associate Antoine Gizenga, he was returned to Leopoldville. Soon after he was flown secretly to Elisabethville and murdered on Tshombe's orders early in 1961.

The Lumumbists still held Orientale, but Gizenga agreed to negotiate with the politicians and, after long rounds of talks, was eventually imprisoned. The *Binza* clique dominated affairs in the capital while complex intrigues surrounded the lengthy attempts to find a basis for agreement with Tshombe. Only in 1963, after Hammarskjöld too had come to a mysterious end over its airspace, was Katanga finally reintegrated into the Congo. By this time US influence, which sought the integration of Katanga into a reunified 'Katangalised' Congo in which American interests could vie effectively with those of Belgium and Europe generally, was in the ascendant.

The Congo decolonisation exercise was now apparently complete. However, the new ruling class was especially blatant in its ostentation and especially unconvincing in its nationalist pretensions. For the masses the confused events of 1959–61 had brought about a real withdrawal of state authority together with a longing for a genuine 'second independence'. By 1963 cadres associated with the MNC and related groups were already filtering into the countryside to organise independent Africa's first major revolutionary confrontation. The rural rebellions of the mid-1960s, however, belong more properly to the next chapter's discussions.

Decolonisation was as quick a phase in African history as the scramble of the late nineteenth century, and at least as complex an historical process. Its causes lay partly outside Africa also, in the changing force-field of world affairs as well as the structural alterations in the needs of capital which now showed substantially less interest in the initial extractive processes that had characterised the African colonial systems in their heyday.

In part, independence negotiations set the stage, as they were meant to do, for a new alliance between an emergent indigenous ruling class and Western business. This new ruling class was a creature of colonialism but it had its own trajectory of development based on the unleashing of capitalist forces since at least the start of the century. Yet the European retreat, if not whole-hearted and largely strategic, was genuinely a retreat. The immense wave of popular resistance to the state in the 1940s and 1950s had made African colonies potentially ever more difficult to administer. It was this groundswell which transformed the ineffectual little nationalist societies of the pre-war years into dynamic political agencies contending for state power. Caught between the pressures that the West continued to exert in Africa, political and economic, the popular expectations on whose back they had ridden and the need to fulfil their own ambitions, they would have their chance to show their mettle.

## Notes

1. See figures in Table 9.1.
2. See figures in Table 9.2.
3. Bakary Djibo of Sawaba in Niger tried the same but he was effectively eliminated from power with French connivance. Niger voted *oui*.

# 10

# TROPICAL AFRICA, 1960–80: CLASS, STATE AND THE PROBLEM OF DEVELOPMENT

'In our revolution, we believe that we have broken the chain of a consumer economy based on imports, and we are free to decide our destiny. And in order to realize the interests of the Somali people, their achievement of a better life, the full development of their potentialities, and the fulfilment of their aspirations, we solemnly declare Somalia to be a socialist state.'

> Siyaad Barre, 1970 speech cited in Ahmed Samatar, *Socialist Somalia*, Zed Press, p. 1

'United Nations dem come get name for us
Dem go call us underdeveloped nation
We must be underdeveloped
To dey stay ten-ten in one room O'

> Fela Anikulapo-Kuti, 'Original Sufferhead' (in pidgin)

## Neo-colonial Myths and Realities

The attainment of independence inaugurated an uncertain and increasingly crisis-ridden period of transition in Africa. Colonialism largely destroyed the fundamental rhythm of pre-capitalist social and economic life without fully advancing a new, self-sustained process of accumulation. The commoditisation of agriculture had been pivotal to the processes of capitalism in colonial Africa. After 1960 continued growth along these

204

lines faltered while varying in extent from country to country and crop to crop. With the 1970s export-orientated agriculture (and the entire agricultural economy) entered into sharp decline in most countries. While circulation of goods and even productive activity had become dependent on industrial processes, the independent African states lacked finance, infrastructure and skills in order to reproduce an industrial society. Secondary industrial growth occurred quite rapidly, particularly through the 1960s, but from a very low base and with a high reliance on imported capital goods, spare parts, raw materials, know-how and technology. Intended to further the prospects of national economic independence, industrialisation necessarily deepened dependence on international trade.

Kwame Nkrumah, the Ghanaian president who deserves pride of place among African nationalists for his early insistence on the importance of industrial development and economic independence, was responsible more than any other individual for popularising 'neo-colonialism' as the source of independent Africa's troubles and the gap between promise and performance of the new states. The 'neo-colonial' idea is pithily captured in the Swahili phrase, *uhuru wa bendera*, 'flag independence'. The existence of neo-colonialism, which can most simply be defined as the continuation of practices of domination after independence by the old colonial powers, is incontrovertible. The independence bargain invariably contained guarantees for the property rights of Western business enterprise and strategic or military arrangements that ensured continuity for a time at least on the most basic imperial desiderata.

Direct intervention in political affairs through the operations of foreign troops and intelligence agencies was common in the wake of the Congo crisis of the early 1960s. Western involvement in Kwame Nkrumah's overthrow was a response to his increasing alignment with the Soviet Union in the mid-1960s. President Apollo Milton Obote of Uganda's tough line on South Africa and Rhodesia, together with his reluctance to continue allowing Israeli military aid to the southern Sudanese rebels via Uganda helped to bring about his downfall in 1971. In contrast, the long-time president of oil-rich Gabon, Léon Mba, owed his survival from the wrath of his own people to French paratroop intervention in timely fashion. American and Soviet policy made costly use of the nationalist antagonisms of the peoples of the Horn of Africa for strategic advantage in what was seen in both Washington and Moscow as the back-door of the Middle East.

Foreign corporations, especially the transnational giants, continued to seek and obtain advantages in pursuit of their profits, marketing and

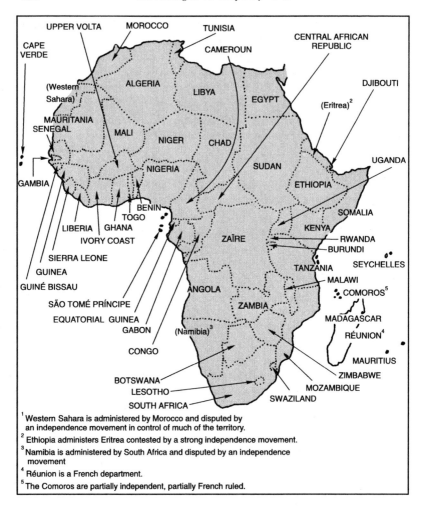

Map 4.   Independent Africa, 1982

supply needs in Africa at the same time. African economic development continued to depend on their technology, trading strategies and expertise. Where nationalisations occurred, like those in the copper mines of Zaïre and Zambia, they were inevitably followed by lucrative management and technology transfer arrangements as well as financially advantageous compensation payments. Where African states became partners in ventures with transnationals, a strategy of product development, sales and labour control could often be worked out whereby 'Africanisation' could suit the transnational firms' interests. None the less this represented a retreat, albeit in a sophisticated form, back to a trading company mode and an older tradition of economic involvement more than a qualitative shift. Trading companies, such as Unilever's United Africa Company, proceeded even before independence to speed up their exit from the produce business and to concentrate on more technologically and industrially sophisticated operations where they could long continue to hold the upper hand.

Nkrumah's panacea for evading the dilemma lay in Pan-Africanism, the establishment of a union government that could pool together the resources of many capital-poor lands. Undoubtedly the autonomous development potential of many of Africa's smaller or less populous states is meagre under any circumstances and co-operation on many issues between neighbour states welcome. Yet political unity guarantees no solutions. If a unified state contained more people, more skills and more capital, it would have correspondingly more tasks to accomplish as well, more infrastructure to create, more poverty to fight. Impoverished territories developed under colonialism along similar lines do not have potentially complementary economies in the short term.

The larger African political units and pan-state entities have concentrated development narrowly and oppressively in one or a small number of centres, intensifying contradictions between town and country. The classic example was the ill-fated East African Community, initially hailed particularly by President Nyerere of Tanzania as the herald of African unity. The common services worked heavily to the advantage of one partner, Kenya, and to the development of the Nairobi area as an industrial and service centre. Ultimately tensions broke up the Community in 1977. At first, the Tanzanian economy did well from the decline and collapse of 'unity', particularly its industrial sector.[1] Worthy an ideal as it may seem at first sight, Pan-African unity cannot itself be the engine of African transformation. In practice, despite the lip service paid to it, Pan-Africanism has had to face the entrenched interests of state apparatuses throughout the continent. In the wake of the Congo crisis the Organisation for African Unity was born in 1963. It has played a useful arbiter's role in certain international conflicts, but in general functions as a kind of trade union for the existing constellation of continental regimes, more a bulwark against change than a force pointing towards effective united action.

In a world of giant trade and finance oligopolies, the weakest capitalist fish fare poorly in the competitive sea. The African bourgeoisie were, and are, little fish indeed. It is hardly surprising, when we appraise ourselves of their weaknesses, to see them ensnared in the plots and plans of European trade ministries, 'aid' planners or the World Bank minions. Simultaneously, however, these very weaknesses inhibit their ability to work efficiently in the interests of international finance and industry. 'Neo-colonial' Africa as it became *cannot* be mistaken for the ideal demanded and striven for by transnational corporations; its utility to them has declined as administrations have become more unstable, arbitrary and corrupt with basic economic services frequently disrupted. This is the reality in large parts of Africa today. To the extent that capital takes the development of Africa seriously, the regime of a thug like Idi Amin Dada in Uganda (1971–9), once the colonial 'pearl' of East Africa, was an economic disaster. If we take 'imperialism' to mean the policies of the Western states and firms in Africa, imperialism is certainly going to oppose the struggles of workers or peasants that threaten capital, and during the Cold War was prepared to threaten states that were friendly with its enemies. However, imperialism does not profit from, and use of the term cannot explain, many crucial aspects of what is usually termed 'underdevelopment' in Africa and other parts of the world.

The serious investigator of such issues has to consider as well the failure of those who manage African states to preside over economic development, *however* this ambiguous phrase is politically and socially defined. Most writing on 'underdevelopment' falls short of resting upon a serious appraisal of class forces. In fact, in the 'right-wing' countries, there appears to be a capitalism without capitalists, especially in the smaller and most dependent cases. In their 'left-wing' counterparts socialist struggles were pursued without a working-class base, either in formal organisational terms or more broadly in terms of popular support. Development without either a strong capitalist class or a politicised and mobilised proletariat presents a fundamental quandary, one that has proved largely beyond the abilities of African states to solve.

Much writing on the left, or by radical African nationalists has tended to assume that Africa is being deliberately 'underdeveloped', that is to say, kept dependent and impoverished. This assumes that capitalism is rather more monolithic and less contradictory than it actually is, reducing it almost to a conspiracy. Were it possible, under politically friendly auspices, 'imperialism' acting as a united force would like nothing better than the rapid development of productive forces in Africa for reasons both of political stability and of profit. Not that it does act so rationally or in unison. To comprehend why Africa's situation is what it is, a consideration of social forces is fundamental and lies at the heart of this chapter.

## The Ruling Class in Contemporary Africa

What is Africa's ruling class? A satisfactory answer to this question has eluded most analyses. The commonest is to describe it as a petty bourgeoisie, a phrase which has been used in these pages. This is, however, a somewhat vacuous and negative definition. The term has been used for a heterogeneous group who control and consume surplus that they do not labour to produce, without actually participating in industrial management or commanding huge financial resources. It is very generally agreed that the dominant class in tropical Africa cannot be big capital, because it is not really represented internally.

In most countries the ruling class also exhibits relatively little continuity with the old pre-colonial ruling elements. In contrast to Asia or Latin America, landowning has not been a major aspect of economic and political dominance. During the colonial period in many areas monarchical governments were preserved and utilised. As we have seen, the classes that profited from these systems had generally collected tribute and slaves rather than possessing the land in hereditary ownership. Nor did they effectively crystallise into a landowning class during the colonial period; their authority did not allow for it and the profits were probably not especially encouraging. Particularly where the nationalist movements were more radical, the chiefs and the other instruments of indirect rule were a magnet for mass antagonisms. In such countries as Guinea, Mali and Tanzania the chiefdoms were abolished on the assumption of independence. Conflicts involving surviving pre-colonial forms ran deep and shaped political forces.

Barotseland's pre-independence conflict with the United National Independence Party in Northern Rhodesia was characteristic. Under the indirect rule system the *litunga* was the nexus of clientship networks under the patronage of the British and Barotseland served as a mines labour reservoir, particularly for South Africa. UNIP's anti-South African, anti-Rhodesian perspective was, in this context, an economic threat and bitterly opposed by the hierarchy. Barotseland appeared ready at one point to secede and make common cause with Tshombe's Katanga and

Rhodesia. However, the *litunga* himself lacked full influence over educated Lozi who repudiated him and opted for UNIP and Zambian independence. In independent Zambia Barotseland lost its separate autonomous status entirely. The parallel situation in Uganda provoked a far deeper crisis. Whereas Barotseland was a relatively remote and backward region holding less than one-tenth of the population of Zambia, Buganda held the capital, the richest parts of the country and one-fifth of Uganda's people. No national party succeeded in gaining a real purchase on Buganda and Apollo Milton Obote, leader of the Uganda People's Congress, had to accept a coalition with the Kabaka Yekka party, pledged to the maintenance of Buganda sovereignty, to lead Uganda to independence. The *kabaka* became President of Uganda. This compromise proved very fragile. In 1966 the breakdown in relations between the Ugandan state and Buganda culminated in violence, the storming of the *kabaka*'s palace and his exile from the country.

Elsewhere in East Africa independence brought about the collapse of traditional ruling classes both in Rwanda and in Zanzibar. In both cases the colonial era had lent to the character of class rule a strong racist odour; as a result, popular vengeance and racial massacres seized both countries. The only surviving ex-colonial monarchies in 1980 were those in Swaziland and Lesotho (where the king's power is nominal). In Botswana, the first president and dominant political figure, Seretse Khama (died 1980), was also the paramount chief of the most important section of the Tswana. It is hardly coincidental that all of these survivals occurred under the shadow of the Republic of South Africa and its Bantustan system. The most weighty indirect rule system of all, that in northern Nigeria, has not experienced revolution. Yet the power of the emirs of the north has markedly declined with every major twist in the fortunes of the state.

The African ruling class are thus neither aristocrats nor planters. Even when they obtain revenues from commercial farming, as notably in Kenya or the Ivory Coast, they are attached by an umbilical cord to the state bureaucracy. Indeed it is not unreasonable to suggest that the new ruling class comprises first and foremost those who took over from, or Africanised, the colonial state hierarchy. Following popular usage in Tanzania, the German radical scholar on development, Michaela von Freyhold, has referred to them simply as 'nizers'. Others have attempted working definitions to encompass all the activities of the 'nizers' – auxiliary bourgeoisie, bureaucratic bourgeoisie – none of them entirely satisfactory. None, at least, successfully conveys the relationship of this class with others in society as well as its internal ambiguities.

Perhaps the most straightforward way of looking at African state officials is as the agents of Western capital, in power to execute its demands much as colonial officialdom once was. Evidence for this type of function is particularly satisfying for the least changed countries in Africa, where decolonisation was unproblematic and largely manipulated from Europe. However, in most nations there is strong evidence as well to suggest that state agencies are used by Africans to obtain advantages for their own class interests. General Olusegun Obasanjo, military head of state in Nigeria from 1976 to 1979, referred in a memorable phrase to 'gate-keepers', the class of Nigerians who in effect hold state office for the sake of charging a toll on foreign enterprise seeking to do business in Nigeria. The gatekeepers function as *rentiers* – essentially parasitic – battening themselves on the thrust of Western finance capital like barnacles to a whale.

Yet the parasitism has a tendency to turn itself into a more 'conventional' form of capitalist accumulation. Under conditions less hectic than those in oil-boom Nigeria the state has also been manipulated, it is argued, in the interests of a burgeoning local bourgeoisie no more parasitic or discreditable than its colleagues elsewhere in the world. African capitalists, precisely because of their competitive weaknesses, necessarily lean heavily on state connections and power to establish their place in the sun in the shadow of the giant foreign corporations. In a substantial debate in the late 1970s such writers as Nicola Swainson and Colin Leys have furthered Kenya as the ideal example for spotlighting the trend. After independence Kenya did not entirely turn its back on the colonial heritage of white settlerdom. Capitalist private land tenure was pressed ahead while the old white highlands became non-racial, agro-business highlands. This was the fruition of 'land consolidation'. African accumulators therefore held a solid base in capitalist agriculture and could move under the effective political umbrella of the Kenya African National Union, the nationalist political party which pressed forth with African capitalism while retaining substantial popular backing in the country. Defenders of this thesis see the Kenyan bourgeoisie advancing in strength through the increasingly efficient use of state power.

Should this picture be accepted as the basic pattern, it would have important consequences theoretically. It would suggest that countries such as Kenya ought to be seen primarily as developing capitalist states with the indigenous ruling class, its foreign allies notwithstanding, in fundamental contradiction to the masses rather than an undifferentiated 'neo-colonialism' or 'imperialism' represented locally merely by a thin stratum of agents or stooges.

It can be objected that the continuing backwardness and dependence of the African bourgeoisie is obscured by such a portrait. African capitalists undoubtedly command little of the finance, technology or industrial base that presses forward accumulation within the capitalist world at large. The policies of the Nigerian state since 1960, the home of probably the wealthiest and most sophisticated class of African entrepreneurs, have done everything to advantage those entrepreneurs with favourable treatment in contract awards, financial assistance, tariff legislation and 'Nigerianisation' legislation designed to place the hands of local capitalists on the driving wheel of the economy. Yet Nigerian business remains dominated by money-lending, contracting, rack-renting, importing and the establishment of 'gatekeeper' relationships with foreign enterprise, building on compradore traditions that go back to the slave trade. Only a small amount of Nigerian capital is concentrated in industry; Nigerian company directors and shareholders are often sleeping partners in enterprises operated with a logic beyond their effective control.

The Ivory Coast has sometimes been depicted as the French-speaking Kenya. Yet studies that focus on it have tended to stress the colonial continuities and the extreme nature of Ivory Coast dependency.[2] Through the 1960s and even much of the 1970s the Ivory Coast economy boomed, largely through rising volumes of cash crops produced by both African cultivators and European-managed (largely corporate) plantations. As dirt roads cut swathes through the forest to establish new tree farms and fields, the virgin timber was hauled off for export. Economic growth was closely linked to continued French influence – special trade arrangements offering the Ivory Coast a secure market in return for consuming over-priced French exports and acceptance of the CFA franc as currency totally convertible with the French franc. In twenty years of independence the European population of the Ivory Coast tripled, from 20 000 to 60 000. This seems to present the *portrait non-pareil* of dependence and the 'development of underdevelopment' in Africa.

Paradigm of dependence though it may be, however, the Ivory Coast regime is financially associated with most significant foreign investment and production ventures and the state has endowed a small wealthy class of Ivorian entrepreneurs. The heart of the Ivory Coast phenomenon is the high level of collaboration obtained between the local and international (largely French) bourgeoisie. To a large extent the oppressed in Ivorian society are migrants from other ex-French territories who form a majority of the wage-employed population. Ivorians are, at all social levels, as prosperous as any tropical Africans and productive forces have developed there more than elsewhere in West Africa. The system appears to be as self-sustaining as that of its neighbours. Dependence cannot thus be said to have brought about instability or impoverishment particularly in the Ivory Coast when compared with equivalent states.

Whatever their specific relationship to foreign enterprise African accumulators in every bureaucracy have used their offices, connections and qualifications to further their personal advancement and feather their own nests. At the same time the state service contains a significant technocratic element, reproducing itself through education and envisioning itself as a permanent salariat. For this stratum anti-colonial nationalism has developed into an ideology of patriotism that sometimes supports and sometimes struggles with the private sector 'national' bourgeoisie. The technocrats are not would-be capitalists, but nor are they simply selfless servants of the people. They have acceded to a standard of living enormously more affluent than that of the mass of the population, measured both in terms of private consumption and socialised benefits and entitlements. Within the general African sea of poverty lie considerable islands of welfareism, in which access to subsidised housing, free health care, schooling and other amenities is apportioned according to civil service rank. In defence of the island, technocrat and compradore, gatekeeper and national bourgeois unite. Technocrats are then potentially also in a position of confrontation with workers and peasants. There are sharp parallels between their situation (even in the unabashedly capitalist states) and those of the 'new ruling class', the *apparatchiki* of the Soviet Union, Poland, China and other Communist states.

## Class, Party and State

The relationship of those who wield state power in Africa to the West and other foreign forces has perhaps been given more attention by scholars than their crucial relationship to the mass of Africans. In the 1960s the political parties which had apparently brought Africa to independence were the main focus of such analysis as existed. Most of these parties are no longer in power or in existence. Even where they have continued to survive they have become imbricated within the machinery of the state. Party militants of the late colonial period tended everywhere to be local businessmen, chiefs and civil servants who on independence sought to transform their activism into commercially advantageous linkages, often with success. The 'mass' party of populist mythology was largely an illusion outside rallies and demonstrations called from the top.

A common feature of the African political party was its all-purpose appeal. The party invariably claimed to represent the 'Africans', but never admitted to speaking for the interests of specific classes. A vaguely articulated 'African socialism' rejected the possibility of a class analysis of African society and tried speciously to reconcile the aspirations of the ambitious few with the needs of the majority. A socialist or communist party actually building upon the movement of the oppressed in society emerged almost nowhere.

Once in power the ruling parties anxiously moved towards the creation of the one-party state, often expressed as the logical outcome of the African political genius, coupled with a more or less ruthless attempt to destroy autonomous organisations. Working-class organisations suffered here particularly and notably in the 'left-wing' countries such as Ghana and Tanzania. In Nkrumah's Ghana, where the unions had played such a vital role in the assumption of power by the Convention Peoples' Party, independence brought about confrontation, the takeover of the union leadership by Pan-Africanist party men notorious for their corruption and a general strike of the workers in 1961. The strike was broken, but it cost Nkrumah the support of the working class. In Nyerere's Tanzania a parallel conflict marked the relationship between the Tanganyika African National Union and the Tanganyika Federation of Labour, abolished in 1964 and replaced by a federation totally dependent on state patronage. In Tanzania the state was quick to insist that truculent workers were privileged 'aristocrats of labour', whose seemingly low earnings none the less represented an exploitation of peasant production and the even poorer rural population.

Yet the legitimacy of the state required its continued presentation in populist form. Both in Ghana and in Tanzania (as in such relatively 'right-wing' states as Nigeria and Kenya) attempts to smash or to subordinate the unions were initially coupled with a genuine rise in the workers' real wage. The state sought to make itself the workers' patron: in return for obedience the populace was to be rewarded with increased and improved amenities, particularly in the spheres of health and education. The CPP regime in Ghana made unprecedented efforts by West African standards to put state resources into public welfare. During the 1950s conditions in world trade were sufficiently favourable as to allow for massive expenditures on health and particularly educational facilities. It was as provider of amenities, above all, that the independence regimes sought legitimacy from their own populations.

Among the former British colonies Tanzania took this the furthest. Social improvement was coupled with economic development as national goals under state auspices. This was the brunt of President Nyerere's eloquent Arusha Declaration of 1967 which introduced what were then considered to be sweeping nationalisation measures (always with generous compensation to foreign owners), coupled in 1971 with the Leadership, or *Mwongozo* Code, prescribing good conduct for the bureaucracy. In Tanzania the regime has talked in terms of African socialism or, more recently, the Tanzanian road to socialism, but the Tanzanian case reveals an outlook that is essentially populist. At least one writer has systematically explored the striking parallels between utopian Tanzanian ideology and nineteenth-century populist thought, the socialism of wishful thinking, exactly in reaction against which Marx and Engels evolved their 'scientific', class-based analysis of socialism.[3] The language and practice of Tanzanian 'socialism' has been sufficiently ambiguous, however, to allow for the flourishing of a radical political consciousness able to exert pressure on the state. It has been imitated during the Obote period in Uganda, in Kenneth Kaunda's Zambia and elsewhere.

A striking feature of ruling bureaucracies in tropical Africa lies in the extent to which recruitment is based largely on educational qualifications. Only the military in grabbing power bypass the formalised hierarchy which still adheres closely to late colonial norms enshrined in the secondary schools or universities of the continent. The heart of the African educational system, itself in good part still dependent upon European aid and models, is, as much as before independence, the mastery of English or French. This has a functional character; bureaucratic structures built around English or French language usage do hold the national entities together, but the emphasis on European language study reinforces the imitativeness and cultural dependence of the African intelligentsia and its institutions.

Education also serves the purpose of building a myth of social mobility. The poor cultivator, worker or craftsman is encouraged to press his children at all costs into a giant lottery from which a few, with ability and luck, will eventually draw 'deserved' success. The state, in its technocratic aspect, also intends that mass education will bring about the acquisition of patriotic values, state loyalty and useful habits. However, this is only fitfully why the African masses have pressed forward with frenzied enthusiasm for more schools.

Generally only secondarily involved in production, the African state managers engage to place themselves where they have the best strategic access to the most cash and goods in circulation. Thus they can be the ultimate patrons in a patrimonial society network on a national scale. If the state intrudes as a gatekeeper for the multinationals, it does so as well for the mass of Africans in the humbler pursuit of basic goods and services. A study of life in Lisala, a town in provincial Zaïre, graphically illustrates the point. From beer to salaries, schooling to foodstuffs, access to the individual in the state apparatus who has the power to permit the circuit of goods to proceed to the next stage is vital.[4] In such an economy mass consciousness tends to be geared towards admiration for the big man, however grudgingly, at least so long as there is some payoff for the client within the patrimonial relationship. Some of the most convincing studies of popular culture demonstrate a continuing admiration for the holders of wealth and power together with the intense significance of the cash nexus.[5]

Patronage, populism, relations with Western political and economic managers, these are the hallmarks and the strengths of the African ruling strata. In accounting for their weaknesses, we must start with the severe problems of disunity that has made the establishment of any national cohesion in several states problematic. Internal divisions and weaknesses within the ruling elements have been striking. It is the more fortunate states, such as the Ivory Coast or Tanzania, which have experienced little difficulty in sustaining territorial unity. Several countries faced, or continue to face, secessions or break-up.

The most well-known example is the most populous African country, Nigeria. The federal structure of independent Nigeria in 1960 reflected the economic and political development of the country under colonial rule. Rival élites, based in each of three regions, were unable to establish working alliances within a national framework and the political institutions of the First Republic quickly broke down. From the farcical General Election of 1964 little remained of parliamentary democracy or stability as crisis intensified. A general strike in 1964 unified the urban working class temporarily but failed to give rise to a coherent political movement that could cut through the impasse. Early in 1966 a military conspiracy brought about the assassination of the federal prime minister and the premiers of the northern and western regions. The army chief of staff,

General Ironsi, was able to assert control for a while. Attempts under Ironsi to destroy federalism were feared by the regionally based élites who saw the new unitary regime as an agent of eastern, or Igbo, domination, particularly in the north. At different times the élites of each region appeared to contemplate secession seriously. In the end it was the eastern region, in the wake of the murder of Ironsi in a counter-coup and the massacres of easterners in northern cities, which actually broke away and proclaimed itself the Republic of Biafra. Biafra eventually got support from a motley collection of allies – Tanzania and Zambia, much of the Catholic Church, France and the Ivory Coast, South Africa and Portugal. It took three years of heavy fighting, from 1967 to 1970, until Biafra was effectively besieged by the Nigerian army and the last representative of its government surrendered after terrible losses.

Geographically the largest African country, Sudan has equally experienced civil war conditions for most of its existence as an independent state. An army mutiny on the eve of independence in 1955 began a cycle of violence in the southern part of the country, where the British had long excluded northern Arab influence and deeply anti-Islamic missionary attitudes prevailed. The budding élite of the south (which has something over one-quarter of the Sudanese population) saw no future for itself in a broader national circuit that looked north and east to the Arab world and had little interest in, or time for, its problems. Only in 1972 did General Nimeiri succeed in negotiating an agreement with the south to end the fighting, abandoning the purely forceful methods of previous Sudanese regimes, a solution which Nimeiri himself revoked after a decade, leading to renewed violent conflict in the early 1980s.

A third and wide-ranging civil war long engulfed the huge territory of Chad which lies between Sudan and Nigeria. As in other instances, no clearcut ideology marked the protagonists apart from their international affiliations. The extremely weak local (and regionally divided) ruling strata have never succeeded since independence in establishing a unified national authority.

The problems of African regimes have not only been regional or secessionist. In many states the weak hold of the politicians very early gave way to military coups that swept them from power. Coups were particularly frequent during the middle and late 1960s. If broadly speaking, they can be explained in terms of the weakness of class and state, part of a crisis in the establishment of state legitimacy, the particular factors bringing them about have varied so notably as to defy common assessment. Some, like that led by Idi Amin in Uganda, have been under the aegis of the head of the armed forces. Others, like that which toppled the Margai regime in Sierra Leone (1967), were led by non-commissioned officers. The Ghana coup that overthrew Kwame Nkrumah in 1966 was notoriously hatched by right-wing, naively pro-Western policemen and army officers. That in nearby Dahomey (1972) reflected a populist, anti-corruption, rather left-wing bent.

The soldiers' rule presented no real solution to the problems of state legitimacy and authority in Africa. Soldiers may be able to seize power fairly easily, but how can they hold it without transforming themselves into something like what they replace? In time many of the soldiers in office, such as Matthieu Kérékou in Dahomey (renamed the Popular Republic of Benin), his neighbour Etienne Eyadema in Togo or Mobutu Sese Soko in Zaïre, became in effect non-elected politicians, sometimes with patrimonial party machines organised to certify their entrenchment in office. Wherever politics of the nationalist era ended in army takeovers the power of the non-elected civil service intensified and became stronger. It was the bureaucracy which fared the best out of military rule.

In the late 1970s coups became rather less frequent; the search for stabler political bases in Africa continued. The examples of Tanzania and Kenya, whose one-party states allowed individuals to contest legislative elections vigorously (although not to question fundamental state policies or to form organised tendencies within the parties) were much admired. Ghana tried to restore civilian rule in 1969–72 and again in 1979–81. After thirteen years of military rule, civilian politicians took power in Nigeria in 1979 on the basis of a complex constitution that owed much to the US model of checks and balances with allowances made for strong centres of regional power in nineteen states. In Senegal Léopold Sédar Senghor retired to his French villa in 1980 and a liberalisation allowed for the legalisation of opposition parties.

Not surprisingly these states contained perhaps the most sophisticated bourgeoisies in Africa from the point of view of their historical antiquity, their scope of economic interests or their cultural self-confidence; all were eager to legitimate class society in West Africa through political means. From the perspective of the early 1980s, military rule seemed most characteristic of the smaller francophone territories. The most brutal and lawless military regime, that of Amin in Uganda, was overthrown by a Tanzanian military expedition in 1979 after Amin annexed a corner of Tanzania. Shortly afterwards his equally murderous colleagues, Jean

Bédel Bokassa (Emperor Bokassa I) in the Central African Republic and Macias Nguema in Equatorial Guinea, the tiny ex-Spanish colony, were also eliminated, with the respective connivance of French and Spanish agents. At first sight it might seem that a certain stabilisation of regimes was becoming more characteristic of Africa. Right-wing mercenaries from the era of Tshombe and the first Congo crisis were increasingly stopped in their tracks and disappeared from the scene, the OAU established an international presence with some credibility, Africans generally began to assume more and more effective control over the state machinery as the Africanisation schemes in each country gained ground. In reality, however, the growing class confidence of the African state hierarchy began to be undermined through intensified challenge from below in the context of a changing political economy.

## Notes

1. The international blockade of Rhodesia during the Ian Smith era caused parallel benefits, as well as hardships, in Zambia.
2. This is no longer the case. See Y.-A. Fauré and J.-F. Médard, *Etat et bourgeoisie en Côte d'Ivoire* (Editions Karthala, 1982).
3. Suzanne Mueller, 'The Historical Origins of Tanzania's Ruling Class', *CJAS*, XV (1981) and other articles.
4. Michael Schatzberg, *Politics and Class in Zaïre* (Africana 1980).
5. G. S. Darah, 'Ig'ho Sh'ema Sua: A Note on Capitalist Ideology in Urhobo Oral Literature', *Theory and Practice*, 2, 1977, Ibadan, and studies of popular literature in Yoruba by Karin Barber.

# 11

## SOUTHERN AFRICA IN CRISIS

'I won't be a member of the Communist Party that seeks to use the
apartheid colonial state, that seeks to use the latter's institutions, as an
alternative to organs of people's power.'

> Theo Molapa, 'Letter of resignation', *The African Communist* (135) 1993,
> p. 19

'I am also often used as an accessible target by angry blacks and women
staff and students, who vent their anger at me. I accept this role with all
its pain because it is a bridge to a better future.'

> Mamphela Ramphele, vice-chancellor, University of Cape Town,
> *Mamphela Rampele: A Life* (David Philip, 1995), p. 223

### The Nationalist Party Victory and its Implications

World War II was a time of social and economic pressures in South Africa
just as it was further north. It spurred an intensified industrial growth that
gave to secondary industry an unprecedented importance in national life.
The proportion of Africans increased greatly among factory workers and
the flood of new migrants to the cities, responding to job opportunities,
swamped the existing locations allocated for Africans. As Chapter 8
suggested this gave to African workers a new bargaining power that took
the form of strikes and squatter movements, particularly in the Johannesburg area.

The response of the state was equivocal. Within the Smuts government there was an important liberal wing that favoured social, economic and even political reforms that would incorporate the industrialised African into capitalist South African society. Eloquent spokesmen for this point of view, notably Jan Hofmeyr, Smuts' lieutenant, did not tire of pointing out that, whatever its charms, segregation could no longer regulate economic growth. The reserves' economic viability had declined enormously and large developmental expenditures would have been required to recreate conditions whereby Africans would voluntarily want to reproduce a workforce there. Conservatives, however, cleaved to segregation. Yet the force that captured the imagination of more whites lay in the opposition.

When Hertzog abandoned the Pact and formed the United Party with Smuts in 1933, most of his Cape following, led by Malan, seceded and regrouped after the next election as the Purified Nationalists. A particular strength of the Cape Nationalists was their association with an ambitious class of entrepreneurs who stood behind the emerging Sanlam-Saambou building society/insurance complex and needed state patronage to expand. The Broederbond, a small Nationalist organisation of great importance in the 1930s and 1940s, had a particularly strong business orientation and spearheaded the movement towards Afrikaner economic 'self-help'. Hertzog's own son Albert was the central figure in a parallel drive to turn the unionised workers into Afrikaner nationalists, especially on the mining belt around the Rand.

At first Malan suffered from having to meet the competition of rival groups which were directly under the influence of European fascism and more orientated to the notion of an authoritarian, corporatist state and a generalised white race identity. These groups gained impetus when Smuts brought South Africa into World War II on the British side and Hertzog resigned from the cabinet. Only when the defeat of Germany became imminent and Fascist and semi-Fascist groups failed to achieve any effective unity was Malan's triumph against them assured.

The Nationalists won the 1948 election in the Transvaal, where they reversed Smuts' long-time dominance in the countryside and secured an important base in working-class constitutencies in the outer Rand. Transvaal farmers had been hard hit by the growth of industry which threatened their ability to control cheap black agricultural labour as well as the low support prices of the Smuts government on maize. The urban workers reacted against the weakness and corruption of the old British leadership of the mine-workers' union and the decay of the Labour Party. A third and equally important element was popular reaction to the waverings of the

Smuts regime on segregation; the Nationalists appeared to stand firm on the need to repair the dikes that had been damaged by the economic and social strains of the war years. The massive 1946 black mine-workers' strike, despite its brutal suppression, characteristically frightened whites, particularly the least skilled.

The Malan government did not offer a fundamentally different policy on race than had been developed previously under Smuts or Hertzog. *Apartheid*, the new key word, was closely related to segregation. As Dunbar Moodie has noted, it was in fact first applied in Afrikaans to separation from white English speakers, not from Africans. The most original aspect of Nationalist ideology was its use of the state to advance the place of Afrikaners in the South African capital accumulation process through ethnic solidarity and, in so doing, to replace class cleavages with an outlook of ethnic cohesion. The ideology of Afrikanerdom, however, strongly encouraged as well the intensification of a racially defined social order as a logical extension of its world view.

As such the Nationalists were very successful. Under state patronage Afrikaners rose in the ranks of an expanding bureaucracy while the Afrikaans medium universities grew rapidly and trained the youth. Useful connections helped Afrikaner capitalists such as Anton Rupert of Rembrandt Tobacco to find their place in the sun. The general prosperity of South African capitalism, coupled with the maintenance of segregation, built up loyalty to the party. The 1948 electoral victory depended on the constitutional overloading of seats to benefit farmers, but thereafter the nationalists moved from strength to strength in subsequent elections, reaching majority support among whites nationwide by the end of the 1950s.

This was the principal systemic and intended result of *apartheid*. Of perhaps greater significance in the long term was the rejection by the new regime of the initiatives that it appeared might be in the offing under Smuts to accommodate the South African system to the needs of expanded industrialisation. Plans that had been under discussion to give the vote to Indians, to install a national health system and to procure more secure tenure for Africans in the cities were shelved. Henceforth South African economic growth would have to accommodate an ever-more rigidly defined segregation mechanism. It must be emphasised that this did not, as some of the liberals of the 1940s feared, hobble the economy; harsh labour controls and poor wages made for high profits in many sectors. This required increasing state intervention which meant as well to stifle political opposition to the system. There was no sinister master plan of control, however. Nationalist legislation, including that aimed at the suppression of the state's opponents, developed in a piecemeal manner particularly before 1960.

Nationalist politics of the 1950s had two main objects. One was to strengthen re-election prospects. To this category belongs the admission to the Senate of representatives from South-West Africa and the successful fight to eliminate from the Cape franchise coloured people, as had once been done to Africans. The second, more important object consisted of legislation to intensify the segregation system, to close its loopholes and in general to make it more inflexible. Intermarriage and indeed, sexual intercourse between whites and 'non-whites' was made illegal by the Immorality Act while all South Africans were forced to carry (or possess in the case of whites) identification labelling them according to race. Arguably the most significant piece of Nationalist legislation was the Group Areas Act of 1950 (consolidated in 1957) which led to the ever-more formalised segregation of racial groups in urban areas and formed part of a process that involved moving around Africans, coloureds and Indians on a big scale over the next twenty years. The Act and related policies served many interests; it was indirectly a great boon to property speculators and, in striking at Indian merchants, seemed to assist white shopkeepers handsomely.

Vast new black townships were organised so that they could be patrolled and, if necessary, cut off in the case of insurrection. The limited rights of black urban property owners were attacked as well as the right to live in the 'white' cities at all. Through the destruction of shanty towns and massive construction of new housing, urban segregation policy hit at the squatters' movement and attempted to draw a line on black migrations from the farms and reserves to the city. The biggest new urban centre for Africans was the South Western Township of Johannesburg – Soweto.

The state also intensified the pass system, incorporated into the larger framework of influx control. All Africans had to carry a police-endorsed pass showing that they were employed or in transit at all times in 'white' areas. Before the war legal pressure on Africans had mostly consisted of poll tax administration; now Africans were gaoled and harassed primarily as pass offenders. This marked the end of pressures to induce labour to the cities with the new emphasis instead on penning as many Africans as possible into the reserves. By making it hard for Africans to live perma-nently in the towns the state benefited white farmers who needed a tied labour force. Government aid to agriculture spearheaded the development of a prosperous agro-business sector and enabled capitalist farmers to eliminate the last pockets of rural squatting by Africans.

Hendrik Frensch Verwoerd, appointed Minister of Native Affairs in 1950, was the most consistent and ruthlessly coherent architect of the renewed 'positive' segregation, generally called separate development, and his influence increased when Malan retired in 1954 and the Transvaal wing of the party came to the fore with Johannes Strijdom as the new premier. All future development for the 'Bantu' as the state began to refer to the natives, was to be focused in the reserves and on thoroughly segregated institutions. The powers of chiefs were increased as government agents. It was an ironic sign of the times that the Zulu paramountcy, once so feared by whites and deliberately smashed by British imperialism, was restored in 1952. The Bantu Education Act provided for a completely separate and pedagogically distinct educational system for Africans, leading logically in 1959 to the establishment of separate institutions of higher education in the homelands, as the reserves were now called. The state also sponsored research into the possible economic development of the homelands as a means of underpinning separate development politics (Tomlinson Commission, 1956). Whereas once it had been crucial for capital to undermine their viability and to press African labour out to the mines and cities, now the political stability of the system required some economic reconstitution just so that these areas could continue to function as props in a cheap migrant labour structure.

Conditions for Africans in the Union were abysmal in the 1950s. Industrial growth was slower and more uneven than during the previous decade, while material possibilities in the homelands for anything beyond a resting space between jobs diminished. Under Nationalist auspices life in the cities was insecure and degrading. The vast new housing schemes were badly overcrowded, poorly provided with amenities and linked to a demoralising bureaucratic surveillance. Alcoholism and other facets of social despair were especially rife. Violent crime associated with *tsotsi*, delinquent youth, developed on a scale spectacular by any international comparison.

It might be expected that African resistance could capitalise on the prevalence of such harsh conditions of life. This was true only to a limited extent, however. In 1949, for instance, Zulu workers took out their frustrations on the Indian population in Durban race riots that cost dozens of lives while the police intervened only at a late stage. Hundreds of thousands of Africans turned to the consolation of independent churches, often as followers of one or another prophet, in what was almost invariably a rejection of political conceptualisation of their lives. Political organisations failed to come up with programmes and, more crucially, association and action that could counter the pressures felt by black South Africans. The major African organisation during the 1950s was the revitalised African National Congress (ANC). In 1949, under the influence of the Youth League Africanists, the ANC adopted the Programme of Action, which appeared to promise militant resistance to state oppression. The ANC moved as well towards alliances that extended its scope. After the Durban riots the pact with the Indian National Congresses of the Transvaal and Natal was reaffirmed and links were also forged with coloured leaders who before 1948 had been partly exempt from aspects of the segregation system.

The Communist Party, which had enjoyed a revival from the time of the war and succeeded in electing 'non-European' representatives to Parliament and the Cape Assembly, was outlawed in 1950. Having dissolved itself shortly before, the CP now sought to find common ground with Congress and its African members became prominent within Congress. The Congress alliance system led ultimately to the Congress of the People, held in 1955 at Kliptown, which adopted the Freedom Charter as a defiant alternative to the Union constitution. The Charter committed the ANC and other constitutent parts to a somewhat vague socialist formulation, advocating nationalisation of some leading sectors of the economy, redistribution of land and democratic representation. The alliance form of the Congress, representing as it did discrete 'peoples' racially defined (except for the primarily white Congress of Democrats), showed the extent to which the ideology of segregation had come to permeate even the strongest opposition to the system that existed at this time. Part of the Youth League, in fact, was deeply hostile to the participation of non-Africans in ANC affairs and even the rather general commitment of the Charter to social democracy. Decrying Communist influence and egged on by virulently anti-Communist white liberals, they moved towards a more overtly oppositionist stance within Congress.

This 'Africanist' tendency reflected as well a discontent with the political practice and élite leadership of the ANC. During the early 1950s the ANC devoted its efforts to the Defiance Campaign, a passive resistance drive influenced by the Gandhian model of civil disobedience. It participated in pass burnings and defied signs marking off racially exclusive amenities in public facilities. Passive resistance had its greatest success in the eastern Cape and among Natal Indians. Thousands of defiers were arrested but the campaign eventually petered out without result. The Kliptown Congress was also followed by many arrests and treason trials that lasted for five years. The courts, applying formal legal criteria, did not sustain state charges of treason but they forced the ANC and its allies to devote energy and time to courtroom activity that further debilitated the movement. Yet an intensification of militancy was on the agenda in the late 1950s. Influx control, imposition of unpopular chiefs, regulations and removals of Africans from 'white' areas led to serious rural unrest in a number of areas, most dramatically Pondoland in the eastern Cape. Early in 1959 violence broke out in Pretoria and in Cato Manor, Durban. The Africanists were anxious to capitalise on this unrest and, late in 1958, they had broken away from Congress to form the Pan-African Congress (PAC). Committed to action, the PAC had no actual new strategy to hand. When the ANC declared a renewed pass-burning campaign the PAC countered with one aimed at an earlier date in March 1960. In two places, Sharpeville outside Vereeniging in the Transvaal and Langa, a Cape Town township, police-inspired violence broke out. Sixty-nine Africans died when the police fired into an unarmed, fleeing crowd at Sharpeville, an event publicised throughout the world which revealed the hard core of the South African system, while suggesting its potential fragility.

In the wake of Sharpeville the grip of the state appeared to loosen. Pass inspections were suspended, a stay-at-home brought cities, especially Cape Town, to a halt, riots broke out in a number of places and an African demonstration took 30 000 black marchers through the streets of the centre of Cape Town. International financial confidence in South Africa suddenly plummeted, hitting the regime where it most hurt and threatening the basis of South African consumer society as stock and property values fell and investment funds were withdrawn. It appeared that the day of reckoning was at hand.

However, neither the ANC nor the PAC was capable of taking up the initiative. Instead the government, led since 1958 by Verwoerd following the death of Strydom, succeeded in gaining the upper hand so effectively that the pundits who had expected the imminent collapse of the South African system after Sharpeville, with equally limited prophetic talent, would speak of it lasting forever a decade later. It is, however, essential to examine those elements of policy carried through by Verwoerd and his successor, B. J. Vorster, which brought about what their friends considered a new lease of life and their enemies an unprecedented period of silence and oppression.

A major element of Verwoerd's strategy was sheer repression. The ANC and PAC were banned in 1960 and obliged to go underground, a step for which they had laid few plans. They both opted for a policy of armed struggle based on sabotage that would lead ultimately to guerrilla warfare. This failed to bring about, as hoped, an effective wave of popular risings. In 1964 much of the internal leadership of the ANC and Congress movement was surprised and arrested at a farmhouse in Rivonia, not far from Johannesburg. Most were found guilty and sentenced to long gaol terms. Nelson Mandela, the most important active underground ANC leader, had been arrested earlier and was linked to the Rivonia defendants. His opposite number in the PAC, Robert Mangaliso Sobukwe, was also interned. The Rivonia trials brought effective ANC and PAC activity to an end while the ANC-linked South African Congress of Trade Unions was also virtually stifled.

The state had fared poorly in securing convictions from the Treason Trials. Now legislation itself was altered to give the police a freer hand. Ninety-day detentions without legal process were instituted and made renewable. Reports of torture and suspicious deaths of prisoners spread. Within the townships a strong network of informers served intelligence purposes.

The liberation movements found it difficult to operate effectively from exile. The PAC proved especially vulnerable to splits and internal dissensions. Its onetime anti-Communism gave way to a nominal Maoism. The Congress Alliance held up far better but remained an uneasy conglomeration of petty bourgeois nationalists and Soviet-linked Communists. Neither could seriously challenge Pretoria in the middle and late 1960s.

Verwoerd determined to extend his separate development orientation to a level never previously envisioned, establishing homeland governments, encouraging their autonomous development, introducing elections and ultimately leading them to independence and separate citizenship. This, at least, was the picture to be planted abroad: South Africa too was prepared to 'decolonise'. By 1963 elections were prepared in the Transkei. On the strength of the large number of state 'nominated' seats, Kaiser Matanzima, who championed separate development, became the first prime minister of a Bantustan.

South African retention of effective power through its officials in the Bantustans, its overwhelming economic influence and security arrangements gave to this initiative elements of a farce. However, unlikely candidates as were the Bantustans for any meaningful independent existence, their expanding bureaucracies provided jobs for new strata of educated Africans tied to the system in a new way and a basis of accumulation for a small number of Africans with access to loans and political influence.

Repression, too, could be indigenised through developing homeland police and army personnel. On the fringe of the Bantustans, border industry growth centres were planned as a means of freeing capital from some of the restraints that influx control imposed on industrial expansion elsewhere and to take advantage of virtually captive and particularly cheap labour. Within the homelands economic development was more a matter of advertising brochures than actual practical activity, although some officials in South Africa understood the needs from their own perspective for some kind of revitalisation of the homelands to prevent their economies from collapsing even further. Figures from the 1960s begin to show the proportion of Africans there able to feed themselves through agriculture down to as low as ten per cent.

In the cities politicians proclaimed that the day when the tide would turn and the population would start to become proportionately more white and less African was around the corner. Influx control was applied with new rigour, often to the discomfiture of business. The police hounded Africans to prove their right to live in town. From the late 1960s special relocation centres began to be created in the homelands for 'redundant' Africans – poorly planned dumping grounds in inhospitable spots that were meant to intensify the dependence of African labour even further and to cut the links of community in urban areas. While Soweto and other townships experienced massive overcrowding, the state (and municipal bodies) imitated the mining companies by expanding the construction of single men's (and some women's) hostels.

The intensification of *apartheid* accompanied a period of highly profitable industrial expansion in the cities of South Africa. Crucial to recovery from the crisis of 1960 were loans from foreign banks and sympathetic assistance from foreign industrialists, particularly mining finance houses. American capital was perhaps decisive although Britain was and remained overwhelmingly the main foreign investor in South Africa. A striking feature of the South African economy was the mergers and the remarkable rise of one particular corporation, Anglo-American, which by the 1960s was an international giant. Anglos expanded from South African gold mining into every facet of the South African industrial economy, at the same time investing in mining and other interests elsewhere in Africa and beyond.

Apart from certain specialised areas such as coal-to-oil technology, energetically pursued by the state for security reasons, and mining machinery, South African industry remained somewhat backward compared with the greatest industrial centres and required inputs of foreign investment to expand and modernise. British, American, European and

Japanese industrial investors led the '60s boom, sinking more funds into South African industry and the Johannesburg stock exchange than the rest of the continent put together. As imports of manufactures declined and capital goods imports rose, South Africa had become a mature import-substitution economy. It continued, however, to depend heavily on exporting primary goods – minerals and food products. Manufactured goods found a market mainly in South Africa's weak neighbours, Botswana, Lesotho and Swaziland, in the Central African Federation and Mozambique. From 1957 in fact, this African trade tended proportionately to decline in significance.

The realities of the boom forced the Nationalist regime to consider itself increasingly as the agency for capital in South Africa rather than merely as promoters of a sectional Afrikaner interest. In 1960 Verwoerd organised a referendum for white voters only which, by a small margin, emboldened him to proclaim South Africa a Republic. Shortly afterwards he withdrew the South African application for retention of membership in the Commonwealth. For the first time English-speakers were introduced into the cabinet (1961) and the Nationalists began to abandon notions of Afrikaner *apartheid* for a generalised identity of white supremacy through 'separate development'. The maturity of Afrikaner capitalism was celebrated in 1964 by the establishment of a major Afrikaner mining finance house, Federale Mynbou, with Anglos' blessing. The long boom fathered an economy of affluence among the whites, allowing even the working-class children of former poor whites to enjoy a modest standard of comfort at home and to identify with the international American-derived culture of consumerism which tended to efface all older values.

With each election the fortunes of the United Party fell lower. It never succeeded in presenting a coherent alternative to the Nationalists once it ceased being the party of government. Within the UP the split between those who wanted a liberalisation of *apartheid* and those who stood merely for the ethnic British interest (opposing, for instance, the Bantustan policy as a potential security risk offering blacks too big a concession) grew. A small Liberal Party broke off after the 1953 elections. It had considerable influence among African nationalists, but little vote appeal to whites. The following election in 1958 so demoralised UP liberals that eleven of their MPs resigned to form the Progressive Party. Only one, Helen Suzman, was successful in the next and subsequent elections through the 1960s. With African and then coloured representation removed entirely from Parliament, she alone questioned aspects of government policy and pinpointed contradictory and inhumane aspects of separate development.

The Progressives survived in good part through the backing of Anglos' head, Harry Oppenheimer, whose companies owned much of the English-language press, which was used to propagandise the need for change, for adjustment to developments elsewhere in Africa, for flexibility and liberalisation in state policies. However, the limits to Progressive liberalism in the 1960s must also be stressed: they opposed black trade unions and universal suffrage and, unlike the Liberals, did not object to legislation that forbade them to have black members. Were it not for the Anglos' connection and the sympathy of liberals abroad, the Progressives would have been insignificant.

### The Armed Struggle in Southern Africa

The real challenge to South Africa in the 1960s appeared to come not from any internal source, but from an increasingly unfavourable external situation. Sharpeville came as a jolt as much to Western business and political circles as to those in South Africa. The military, economic, intelligence and political links between South Africa and the West were strong, but for the first time it became transparent that South Africa could be a liability in genuine Cold War strategies. Both the Macmillan government in Britain and the new Kennedy administration that took office in Washington tended to regard a suitably anti-Communist African nationalism as the best possible bet in the changing circumstances in Africa towards 1960. Failure by Pretoria to accommodate the South African system with political reform was worrisome. Harold Macmillan, who had found white settlerdom tiresome and retrograde even when a Colonial Office official before the war, pointedly chose Parliament in Cape Town, rather than Nairobi or even Salisbury, to make his 'winds of change' speech in 1960.

By then, the winds had begun to waft towards the South African periphery. Britain agreed to dismantle the Central African Federation and to promote the two non-settler units, the future republics of Malawi and Zambia, towards independence. The High Commission territories, which as late as the 1950s Pretoria still dreamt of annexing, were destined for a similar fate. Basutoland and Bechuanaland were granted independence as Lesotho and Botswana in 1965 to be followed by Swaziland in 1968. Small and impoverished, they posed no challenge to South African power. Malawi, which like the ex-High Commission territories had been developed essentially as a labour reserve, even moved to establish closer ties with South Africa. However, their existence placed the legitimacy of African nationalism on the political agenda while they were able to use widening trade and aid links with Europe and America to expand their ability to function autonomously.

Far more serious as a threat to Pretoria was the spread of insurgency under the aegis of national liberation movements stretching across the length of southern Africa. South Africa became deeply involved in trying to prop up regimes far weaker than her own while staving off armed opposition from her borders.

The first territory in southern Africa to face an open insurgency was Angola. The Portuguese state, by virtue of its economic weakness and political rigidity, was completely unable to forge the compromises with African nationalism that its peers in Europe were doing during the 1950s. With independence, former Portuguese colonies would undoubtedly break most links with metropolitan trade and industry. Thus Portuguese colonial policy in the 1950s went directly against the wider current. Portugal pressed forward with intensified emigration from Europe, including settlement schemes with attendant land alienation. The position of the mulattos and *assimilados* deteriorated while the colour bar became more blatant. Opposition groups that emerged, notably in Angola, were ruthlessly suppressed to nip rebellion in the bud. Yet Angolans were naturally aware of events north of their frontier in the Congo and elsewhere. They began to consider a resort to arms against the Salazar regime.

Few local observers were surprised when a three-fold insurrection broke out in 1961. The first phase, Maria's War, took the form of a popular rising in the northern district of Uige. Resistance to the collection of cotton and the chiliastic teaching of local prophetic movements make descriptions remniscent of the days of Maji Maji in Tanganyika. The second phase came in the capital, Luanda, where raids were mounted on police stations and government installations, kamikaze actions that were doomed to failure and invited ugly mob action from white crowds. The third and most serious rising took place in the far north-west among Kongo-speaking Angolans who were experiencing a big rural settler influx coupled with deteriorating prices for their coffee. The Kongo rising was essentially an uncontrolled peasant rebellion of wide and terrible force. Some two hundred Portuguese civilians were killed as well as mulattos, *assimilados*, contract plantation workers from the south and even militants from rival organisations to the *Uniaõ das Populações de Angola* (UPA) which had gained support in this area. However, the UPA had little control over what was going on. Although the Portuguese were forced to beat a retreat from a wide zone, no revolutionary organisation or activity emerged in the midst of this chaos. After some months the Portuguese army returned to sweep up most of the area amidst scenes of extraordinary vengeful violence, while a huge proportion of the population fled to the now independent Congo.

Thereafter, for thirteen years, the Portuguese army was obliged to fight a shooting war in Angola. The anti-Portuguese movement, however, was badly divided. Two dominant tendencies emerged. The UPA, later known as the *Frente Nacional de Libertaçaõ de Angola* (FNLA), after absorbing smaller groupings was led by Holden Roberto, a Kongo who had grown up in Belgian territory and emerged from the rival faction quarrels in Kongo politics. Hostile to those he did not consider 'African' and firmly in the Western camp (he was on the payroll of the US Central Intelligence Agency from 1961), he depended on a small cohort of Kongo followers and, increasingly, on the support of a succession of Kinshasa (Leopoldville) governments, particularly that of Mobutu after 1965, into whose family he married. The FNLA counted on the support of the large Angolan Kongo community in Kinshasa, could mount raids across the frontier and maintained an armed maquis that neither noticeably expanded nor contracted over the years in the hilly country north of Luanda.

Roberto always rejected unified action with the *Movimento Popular de Libertaçaõ de Angola* (MPLA), which included some of the most educated black Angolans and had its following in Luanda and its hinterland and other urban communities. The MPLA had strong fraternal links with the anti-Fascist Left within Portugal and accepted a markedly socialist orientation. It appears likely that a small Angolan Communist Party born in the 1950s was a constituent element. Portuguese Communists were crucial to the dramatic prison escape in 1962 of the poet Agostinho Neto. On arrival in Africa Neto became head of the MPLA. Far from its natural urban social base and surrounded by the debilitating atmosphere of Kinshasa, the MPLA deteriorated in morale, entered into opportunist alliances with a bevy of local exiles and appeared on its way to extinction when the Massamba-Débat regime came to power in Brazzaville in 1964, allowing it to resurface in a more sympathetic environment. MPLA militants had been murdered by Roberto's people during the rising of 1960, were prevented by force from entering Angola that way, and consequently felt bitterly towards the FNLA and its Western backers.

The MPLA had a chance to engage in armed struggle against the Portuguese after Zambia achieved independence in 1964. In 1966 guerrilla warfare began in eastern Angola and had considerable success in this thinly peopled region remote from centres of wealth and human density. From 1970, however, friction grew between elements among the fighters and the leadership in exile. A major breakaway under Daniel Chipenda virtually grounded MPLA guerrilla activity beyond the fringe of the Zambian frontier by the beginning of 1974. FNLA efforts to open up a new front in the east also culminated in a breakaway movement under the direction of Jonas Savimbi, *Uniaõ Nacional para a Independencia Total de Angola* (UNITA). On the whole guerrilla successes were then quite limited and did not approach threatening the major economic activities and political bases of Portuguese power. However, the struggle forced the Portuguese to spend vast sums of money militarising Angola and made the stakes of their commitment high.

Across the sub-continent Portuguese Fascism faced a more formidable foe in the *Frente de Libertaçaõ de Moçambique* (FRELIMO), the Mozambique liberation movement. FRELIMO may instructively be compared with the armed groups in Angola. It enjoyed in Tanzania a rear base infinitely less debilitating and manipulative than Zaïre-Congo. Although the Makonde people played a somewhat equivalent frontier role to the Kongo they had much less influence in Tanzania than the Kongo in Zaïre, and they could not shape the course of events in FRELIMO. South of the border, where FRELIMO initiated guerrilla activity in 1964, was a thickly settled zone of peasant agriculture, in contrast to the almost empty savanna of eastern, and the refugee-denuded forests of northern, Angola. Here FRELIMO could form an effective base and initiate programmes of production and social services sufficiently developed to allow them to export small quantities of cash crops and to construct the skeleton of a future national society. The FRELIMO leader, Eduardo Mondlane, was remarkably effective at retaining the support of ideologically diverse elements and thus reducing rival groups outside FRELIMO to the status of non-entities.

Nevertheless, chauvinist and opportunist elements as well as Portuguese infiltrators did emerge into greater prominence. They, operating in collusion with the Portuguese, have been blamed for the assassination in 1969 of Mondlane in Dar es Salaam. This provoked an open crisis in FRE-LIMO, but the FRELIMO Left, among whom Samora Machel emerged as principal spokesman, was triumphant. Their opponents discredited themselves through negotiations with Portugal and the fighters remained faithful to an effectively purged movement.

FRELIMO had little success in assaulting towns, the remaining centres of Portuguese strength in the north, but they were able to expand their zone of operations continuously. In 1968, they succeeded in establishing a new front in Tete Province in the north-west. Within a couple of years they had effectively crossed the Zambesi and began to render inoperable the Beira railway which was vital to Rhodesia. They also raised tremendously the cost of constructing the giant Cabora Bassa dam on the Zambesi. Cabora Bassa, financed by European and South African capital, was meant to feed the Rand with electricity. It was only a new and powerful symbol of the intense symbiosis of Mozambique with South Africa (and Rhodesia). Mozambique supplied labour on a huge scale for the gold mines of the Rand and handled much of South Africa's international trade; these were in fact the dominant features of its colonial economy. The FRELIMO guerrilla movement, gradually expanding southwards, threatened not only the Portuguese treasury but Portuguese political power and with it, South Africa.

The other Portuguese mainland colony lay on the Guinea coast of West Africa, but it deserves mention here because it too was the scene of a major guerrilla struggle. By the end of the 1960s the *Partido Africano da Independencia da Guiné e Cabo Verde* (PAIGC) controlled a large part of the territory and people of Portuguese Guinea (now Guiné-Bissau) and held down a sizeable army. The exceptionally gifted PAIGC leader, Amilcar Cabral (assassinated by Portuguese bomb in 1972) co-ordinated his activities with FRELIMO and MPLA.

Some Portuguese officials understood the need for reform. Thus *assimilado* status was formally abolished and steps taken to reduce the element of force in the labour system. Much of the reform programme, though, was cosmetic or half-hearted; it could not make profound changes that undercut the basis of colonial exploitation. Perhaps the most noteworthy shift was the opening of Angola in particular to much freer investment opportunities by non-Portuguese. The West as a whole was given a bigger stake in a Portuguese victory. This helped to create some prosperity in the colonial economy but, ironically, at the same time it strengthened those elements in Portugal who sought to re-orient Portuguese capitalism from a colonial to a European and Common Market direction. As the few dominant Portuguese monopolies became more competitive, their commitment to Africa lessened.

A third zone of fighting in southern Africa opened up in Rhodesia. With the collapse of the Central African Federation the Rhodesian whites rejected those managers of settler domination whose reform plans since the 1940s had closely paralleled the Smuts liberals of the South African scene. The newly triumphant Rhodesian Front Party was as determined as the Nationalist Party in South Africa to stop the rot and to draw a line on concessions that threatened their power base. Under Confederation the Front had already rallied support around the idea of a Rhodesian declaration of independence. The Unilateral Declaration was proclaimed in 1965 with Ian Smith as independent Rhodesia's first and only prime minister, once it was clear that the British government under Harold Wilson of the Labour Party had absolutely no intention of stopping the move by force. Britain instead opted for a policy of sanctions, a policy that could achieve little without the co-operation of Portugal and South Africa. Indeed, it was sanctions in particular that brought South Africa together with her neighbours to attempt jointly to put out the brushfires of revolt.

Smith held no mandate for a Rhodesian equivalent to the Bantustan line propounded south of the Limpopo. Instead, his 1969 constitution was an amalgam of the old Confederation 'multi-racialism', features borrowed piecemeal from South Africa and customary segregation practices. Africans were handed fifteen seats in the sixty-five-man legislature, although they formed some ninety-four or ninety-five per cent of the total population. Even these seats were largely in the hands of state-appointed chiefs. Smith had in his favour a measure of prosperity brought about through the rapid development of industry, unbeset by foreign competition, and a significant flow of South African investment. Rhodesia attracted a stream of Western immigrants and adventurers. Weakness and disunity on the part of Rhodesia Africans was, however, the strongest card in his hand for a long time.

In 1963 the nationalist movement, dominated by Joshua Nkomo's Zimbabwe African People's Union (ZAPU), split. Organisationally inept it had lacked any clear strategic or ideological orientation. It never had come to grips with the special problem posed by white settlers in Rhodesia, relying entirely on a decolonisation formula that would 'transfer' power to blacks from on high in Britain. The new group, called Zimbabwe African National Union (ZANU), was led by Revd. Ndabaningi Sithole. Sithole and Nkomo were soon under arrest and both parties banned. ZANU was fortunate in the calibre of its exiled leader, Robert Mugabe, who came under the influence of Mondlane and Nyerere and helped to formulate a more militant kind of politics. Both ZANU and ZAPU felt forced to turn to armed struggle and from 1966 chronic raids were conducted across the Zambesi to engage Rhodesian security forces. The UDI regime could manage the Zambesi front. Rhodesia's real problems began when FRELIMO moved into Tete Province in 1968 and then proceeded to cross the Zambesi and to politicise the Shona peasantry in Mozambique.

FRELIMO offered ZANU an excellent base of operations and fighting in eastern Rhodesia began in earnest. As ZANU activities became more effective they took on the character of a peasant insurrection. A final insurgency had by then begun in South-West Africa. The South West African Peoples' Organisation (SWAPO), with a strong base in the northern part of the country, committed itself to guerrilla activity in 1966. The fighting was often sporadic but SWAPO had an unshakeable base among the Ovambo, who constituted half the population and a majority of the working class of South-West Africa. This was, moreover, an insurgency in a territory where South Africa claimed direct control and it required an ever-mounting military involvement by the South African state. South Africa sent as well materiel, troops and police to fight in Rhodesia and it co-operated closely with the Portuguese. Yet all these wars could not be won by an unholy southern alliance; the cost of holding the ring grew constantly and not least was the fear of international isolation.

In the 1950s it was South Africa that had spurned any diplomatic contact with the African nationalist movements elsewhere on the continent while fretfully advising the colonial powers against decolonisation. Only well after Sharpeville was it realised that this had been a serious miscalculation. Condemnation of *apartheid* became a pillar of the foreign policy of all African states, even if honoured more rhetorically than practically. The assistance of independent African states was helpful to the rising guerrilla movements of the south.

South Africa tried to counter this with an outward policy of 'dialogue', beginning with the most dependent labour-exporting states, Malawi and Lesotho. In the late 1960s Pretoria began to court a whole phalanx of right-wing African countries – Mauritius, Madagascar (Malagasy Republic), Gabon, the Ivory Coast, Zaïre, Liberia, Ghana, the Central African Republic. Reactionary African regimes had little stomach for a confrontation with the South. Western advice lay in the direction of compromise while the South African state seemed internally invulnerable. Vorster realised that the Rhodesian situation was intractable so long as the Smith regime rode high and corresponded secretly with President Kaunda of Zambia in the hopes of finding some formula of compromise that could bring to power in Salisbury a docile black government.

Thus the internal strengths of the South African regime, which appeared so manifest in the late 1960s, coincided with an increasingly complicated and far less favourable situation in southern Africa as a whole. The 1970s saw the complacency of Pretoria disappear as blows to its hegemony began to reach their target.

## The Challenges of the 1970s and 1980s

By the early 1970s South Africa had passed through a cycle of remarkable industrial growth which had made the operation of its political system paradoxically both easier and more difficult. Although it became tougher for Africans to gain residence rights in town, jobs were more available and wage levels tended to creep up after remaining extremely low from the late 1940s onward. Economic development required and engendered the expansion of skills, education and jobs in the bureaucracy for Africans, and, with it, the numbers of young people with higher expectations. To the majority of observers the state appeared to be in remarkable control of the situation. In reality, the boom paved the way for a new wave of struggle in the 1970s that coalesced with the problems South Africa confronted along the northern frontiers.

In the spring of 1969 a community of workers with a long history of militancy, the dock workers of Durban, went out on strike. The workforce was expelled from Durban and summarily replaced by a completely new body of men from the impoverished homelands. Despite its failure, the strike kindled a modest spark of labour revival that would develop further. The real turning of the tide occurred in late 1971 when virtually the entire labour force of South-West Africa came out, returning to Ovamboland, and demanded the end to the entire degrading migrant contract system. After weeks of pressure, the state was forced to intervene and offer some compromises to the workers. Through 1972 and 1973 strikes spread, notably in Natal and the Transvaal. The bitterness of workers coincided with a significant downturn in the South African economy; the long boom was over and prospects for economic growth evaporated. From the strikes emerged a new, unaffiliated labour movement which threatened to take openly political forms.

The expansion of Bantu Education had evoked the growth of an enlarged student body that began to challenge the university authorities and state hegemony. Breaking with the predominantly white liberal National Union of South African Students (NUSAS), African university students attempted to build a new unity of the oppressed in adopting the word 'black' for themselves and thus forging links with Indian and coloured comrades. 'African' implies the assumption of a nationality with pre-colonial roots; 'black' is an identity based on resistance to oppression within industrial South Africa that crosses cultural barriers. From the student movement grew a larger Black Consciousness movement that established outreach programmes through urban black communities.

At first the emphasis on blackness allowed for a measure of government tolerance in accordance with separate development philosophy. From 1973, however, Black Consciousness leaders and organisations began to be repressed as they challenged state hegemony. They had struck roots, more informal and vague than organisational, in the black townships and particularly among black schoolboys and girls. In 1976 Soweto exploded with demonstrations that began with the government attempt to impose Afrikaans on a par with English for African secondary school students. The state responded with all the firepower at its command, but despite the deaths of hundreds the marches and demonstrations continued for months and spread to all parts of the country, involving coloured as well as African crowds on a large scale, a virtually unprecedented phenomenon in South Africa.

The 1976 insurgency clearly had another indirect and external cause. It was inspired by the collapse of Portuguese power in Africa. In the early 1970s Portugal was strained to its limits. Inflation, labour migration to France, draft evasion and mounting military budgets led to a coup in April 1974 that finally finished off the *Estado Novo*. While other European countries had solved their colonial issues satisfactorily from the political point of view, through various forms of decolonisation procedures, in Portugal the African wars led to the collapse of the state itself and thus threatened the foundation of Portuguese capitalism. After a short period the Armed Forces Movement, itself influenced by the ideas of the African liberation organisations, seized power and put in office men sympathetic to independence for the colonies. Thus in 1975 FRELIMO triumphed in Mozambique and began the difficult struggle to reorientate colonial economic, political and cultural life.

The situation in Angola was more complex. The West was determined to prevent the MPLA from enjoying a similar accession to power, despite its success in re-establishing strong bases of support in urban Angola. Savimbi's UNITA and Roberto's FNLA formed an alliance, drew on undercover American aid and forged ties with South Africa, which in turn was very eager to put paid to Angola-based SWAPO guerrilla activities. As Portuguese power waned in 1975, the South African army marched north in force with UNITA while FNLA proceeded from the other direction to the capital. By November the South Africans were hardly one hundred miles from Luanda while FNLA guns bombarded the northern suburbs. The MPLA, which had by then proclaimed independence, was largely saved through the intervention of a contingent of Cuban troops. Gradually the MPLA and its Cuban friends drove the rival right-wing nationalist groups beyond the borders. Well before this Pretoria had ordered its troops to retreat in good order.

The results for the South Africans were bad. All possibilities of dialogue with African states were at an end. Instead of hoped-for credit at helping to install Savimbi and Roberto in power, South Africa had now to face the victory of an uncompromised MPLA enjoying the friendliest relations with Cuba and the Soviet Union.

Mozambican independence allowed ZANU to expand its activities in Rhodesia. Despite Rhodesia carrying the war into Mozambique on a big, damaging scale, the days of UDI were numbered. In 1978 Ian Smith was obliged to set up an internal settlement and to allow Bishop Abel Muzorewa to take office as prime minister of 'Zimbabwe-Rhodesia'. Muzorewa had become a national political figure by standing up and denouncing the Smith regime before the British sponsored Pearce Commission in 1972 but he did not pursue any real efforts to break settler power and he continued the war. In the following year the situation for Rhodesia was so poor that Muzorewa and Smith accepted British-run negotiations for a referendum, in which South Africa, hoping for a Muzorewa victory, acquiesced. ZANU and ZAPU had by then, under intense pressure from the 'Frontline States' – Zambia, Mozambique, Angola, Tanzania and Botswana – agreed to a formal alliance. The Patriotic Front, as it was called, was initially reluctant to participate in a referendum under an unpurged Rhodesian administration. However, they could not get support for a refusal to co-operate with Western plans. The more conservative Frontliners feared a growing radicalisation of the Zimbabwe struggle. Zambia and Mozambique particularly suffered the consequences of the fighting so severely that they exerted pressure to get the consent of the Patriotic Front to the referendum. In the event, ZANU won a strong victory and Mugabe became prime minister of an independent Zimbabwe in April 1980. This was the end of South Africa's last really dependable ally in Africa.

The combined result of labour militancy (which, with ups and downs, developed qualitatively and quantitatively), the dramatic Soweto rising which forever ended the myth of the African masses' acquiescence in Pretoria's policies and the collapse first of Portugal and then of Rhodesia, placed the South African regime in a state of mounting disarray. Nor was the economy as buoyant as in the past. It became more difficult to get foreign loans and investment to meet the restructuring needs of the 1970s. Even the good gold prices that typified much of the decade could not easily be translated into jobs and production expansion. The independence of Mozambique in particular affected South Africa's dependence on ultra-cheap foreign labour. The gold mines felt obliged to raise wages very substantially in order to attract South African black workers. Labour militancy also forced wages to rise in industry and, unlike the gold mines, industrial firms could not avoid the squeeze on profits through favourable world prices.

Superficially the government enjoyed an unprecedented parliamentary majority with the collapse and dissolution of the old United Party. However, the leadership was torn by feuds and afraid of change that would threaten its political base. The Nationalists (and indeed even the Broederbond) were divided between *verkramp* and *verlig*, conservative and reforming factions, and the direction of change, seen as essential after Soweto, was equally under dispute. In this atmosphere Vorster fell from office in 1978, to be replaced by the Cape *verlig*, P. W. Botha, with some of Botha's major rivals driven from office in the Muldergate scandal.

Some of the direction of reform pointed back to the United Party commissions of the early 1940s. African trade unions were allowed to register for the first time in South African history in 1979. Urban Africans received for the first time in a generation the right to hold houses on long leases. In the middle 1980s, the pass laws controlling the movement of Africans within South Africa were scrapped and the Immorality and Mixed Marriages Act abolished. The state moved towards encouraging black homeownership and business rights in townships. The tightly regulated *apartheid* system was being modified and riddled with increasingly obvious contradictions.

By this time also, from 1983, a new Constitution was created which assembled Houses of Parliament for coloureds and Indians and would bring them into the South African cabinet. But the state was not prepared to accept entirely the logic of incorporating the entire citizenry into the South African polity. Increasing favours were showered on to the Bantustans and their leaders while a series of farms to the east of Pretoria was patched together as a Ndebele homeland that was allegedly seeking sovereign independence. On the one hand, the reforms were intended to create a stable, capitalist consumer society. On the other, National Party politicians were not prepared to preside over their own exit from power; they also feared that democratisation would initiate a social and economic revolution.

In exile, the ANC revived under an increasingly revolutionary ethos with the SACP and the guerrilla movement, Umkhonto we Sizwe, the focus of organisation and propaganda. Against this the state launched the so-called 'total onslaught'. In particular, those neighbouring states who harboured guerrillas and ANC activity were targeted for destruction.

Intense occupation of northern South-West Africa, into which white conscripts were sent in large numbers drove SWAPO activists largely into exile. South Africans took a widening role in Jonas Savimbi's UNITA movement and participated actively in the Angolan civil war. When the Samora Machel government in Mozambique gave facilities and encouragement to the ANC, the South Africans took over an insurgent exile movement, that had been financed by the Rhodesians, called RENAMO.

FRELIMO had come to power with an extraordinary amount of good will and enthusiasm for constructing a new society in Mozambique. However, revolutionary fervour on the part of urban-based bureaucrats and militants did not necessarily win over the massive peasantry scattered over the vast national territory. Dreams of a rapid transition to an urbanised, industrialised modern society were matched by few realities on the ground beyond an impressive new infrastructure of social services. Government projects and settler farms were nationalised and run by the state without the expertise or equipment for efficient management; the surrounding peasantry resented being turned into proletarians rather than having a land reform divide up fertile land amongst themselves. In many areas, ethnic and cultural resentments were fuelled by the dismissal of chiefs as colonial stooges, and by campaigns against polygamy and African medicine. As a result, RENAMO raids found local support while deeds of terror were carried out in areas loyal to FRELIMO. The South Africans found fertile ground for their activities. After 1980 conditions in Mozambique deteriorated dramatically and rapidly; the economy and social services collapsed and FRELIMO lost control of large areas of the countryside. When COMECON, the Communist equivalent of the Common Market, refused to accept Mozambique as a full member, the writing was on the wall: the East was not prepared to go far enough to save socialist Mozambique from her enemies.

By 1984, Mozambique was prepared to sign the Nkomati Accord with South Africa. With this important turning point, the ANC was unceremoniously turned out of Mozambique. However, the South Africans kept up the pressure. The war continued and evidence suggests continuing and substantial South African aid to RENAMO. In 1986, Samora Machel was killed in a mysterious plane crash just over the South African frontier. By this time, one door had been shut to the ANC. Elsewhere too, the South Africans were active in neutralising or shutting down their operations. In Angola, a stalemate was reached. South African intervention peaked at the siege/battle of Cuito Canavale (1987–8). Committed Cuban intervention, coupled with the declining capacity of South African aircraft and a loss of nerve in being prepared to sacrifice the lives of conscripts, led to South African withdrawal. The potential for further 'total onslaught' seemed lost. This, together with the far more internationally dramatic decline of the Soviet Union and its capacity, brought together the possibility of negotiations over the fate of South-West Africa.

In some respects, the South Africans saw these negotiations as a dress rehearsal for their own domestic drama. In return for Soviet and Cuban withdrawal from Angola, from which the ANC pulled out (as it did from Zambia as a military force), the South Africans agreed to allow the UNO to preside over a free election for an independent Namibia which duly came about in 1990. Sam Nujoma's SWAPO formed the government but quickly shed any revolutionary or socialist pretensions. Namibia accepted a constitution negotiated with minority parties and agreed to a framework to which the Western powers and South Africa could hardly object. As a small, thinly peopled republic dependent on mineral exports and very much within a South African economic orbit, the new Namibia resembled its pacific neighbour, Botswana. To a very large extent, South Africa's total strategy policy had been a success.

The real challenge to South Africa, however, came not from military invasion but from within. Within a year of the proclamation of the tricameral constitution, the townships were again aflame. The township risings of the middle 1980s occurred on a much wider scale than anything previously known. Whereas the forces of order had been able before to counter youth action by rallying covertly workers afraid of losing jobs and uncommitted to urban life, now a rapidly growing and demonstrably more disciplined trade union movement was being mobilized against the state. Civic organisations, sometimes under the control of the unions, sometimes taken over by quasi-terrorist youth groups, sometimes neither, were able virtually to oust state control in the townships. State efforts at reform through commercialising township social and economic relations (growing differentiation, economic rents and service charges, growing power to black authorities willing to co-operate with the state) backfired dramatically and created a groundswell of support, and perhaps more importantly, a belief in the possibility of a different future, by the majority of once dispirited township dwellers. As the economy stagnated, the state found it had only limited capacity to purchase approval. Waves of revolt spread to previously untouched corners of the country although they still remained predominantly urban.

The Botha government turned to repression and it is in the 1980s that state-inspired assassination and terror like that in Latin American dictatorships became a significant feature of South African political life. However, the government was unwilling and unable to abandon reform. Botha appeared at times to favour a Napoleonic regime, placing himself above parties on a platform that would allow him to 'cross the Rubicon'. But, despite the revenues and power at his disposal, he was reluctant to do more than get his toes wet. A first tentative series of moves leading to significant political negotiation began in the middle 1980s when it was clear that tricameralism had failed. A committee of Commonwealth politicians – the Eminent Persons Group – was drawn in as potential power-brokers, although a crucial part of the political establishment could not face the music at this point and torpedoed negotiations with a series of cross-border raids.

There was really no retreat from this path for long, however. On the one hand, the ANC, both in the form of its top exile leadership and in the increasingly significant imprisoned leader Nelson Mandela, moved towards a negotiations model that would fall far short of dismantling South African capitalism or even its social institutions. On the other, many links began to build up, both between the external and internal opposition (the loosely organised United Democratic Front and the Congress of South African Trade Unions, which had largely evaded repression) and with such forces as the powerful businessmen and key cultural figures who met with the ANC in Lusaka and elsewhere. In the end, it was not P. W. Botha, but F. W. de Klerk, who succeeded him as state president in 1989, who was prepared to take the unprecedented step of unbanning the ANC and the SACP, freeing key political prisoners and undertaking the abolition of all the laws that had signalled the foundation of *apartheid*.

### The End of Apartheid

Mandela was released early in February 1990 and thereafter embarked on four years of negotiation in an interim political period whose late phases were marked by political co-responsibility. Assessing this period is not easy. During the early phases both parties seemed equally inflexible and prone to internal crises. De Klerk had no clear strategy and relied too much on the support of African allies or at least fellow enemies of the ANC, notably Chief Mangosuthu Buthelezi, the one leader of a homeland whose patrimonial system enjoyed wide public support in rural Kwa Zulu. Tensions and manoeuvres on both sides (the notorious 'Third Force' which emerged with state backing was a major part of this) brought about unprecedented levels of violence. De Klerk failed to realise that there was no road back; the West would not allow him to abandon the ANC, which in turn limited the muscle power of the security state to intervene.

In any case, the strength of the ANC lay not in its arms nor its guerrilla efforts, which had largely failed, but in its acceptance by virtually all Africans (apart from the Natal Zulu constitutency of Buthelezi and his Inkatha Freedom Party) as their champions. The ANC was unable to force the situation into a revolutionary one. It was obliged to accept that change would come according to the pace of the law and, in effect, that they would at most be able to preside over a capitalist South Africa where civil society would, at least at first, be much as it had always been. However, it was able to win the major concession of something approaching straightforward majority rule.[1] In return, the ANC agreed to the four provinces being replaced by nine with considerably enhanced powers and the creation of all kinds of representative mechanisms, which seemed to assure some representation (and patronage) for all those with any kind of constituency who were prepared to co-operate. The context was one of deteriorating economic conditions and an overhanging threat of renewed, accelerated violence.

To the surprise of international opinion, in circumstances where the range of choice had seemed to narrow for countries all over the world, this stalemate proved to be the foundation of a compromise which led to quite peaceful elections in 1994. A key stumbling block was removed with the easy overthrow of the most truculent of Bantustan leaders, Lucas Mangope of Bophuthatswana, and the pitiful failure of efforts to rescue him on the part of the white far Right. Both these menaces to a pacific solution suddenly eviscerated. In the election, characterised by very high turnouts, the ANC won well over sixty per cent of the vote. However, this in turn depended on their overwhelming support amongst African voters outside of Kwa Zulu Natal, as the province was now known. White, Indian and coloured voters all turned to the National Party as their principal bulwark while Kwa Zulu Natal gave just over fifty per cent of the vote to the IFP, according to disputed results.

The 'new South Africa' was presided over by Mandela, a man of great charm and stature who made an impressive advertisement for the political transformation that had taken place. South Africa, freed of sanctions and international opprobrium, began to experience moderate but real economic growth and also was able to develop relations with the rest of Africa on a new basis. However, the problematic character of transition has to be underlined. It became obvious that the great problem that lay ahead was to find some way of reconciling the differences, cultural, social and economic, between a core population used to living according to the ways of wealthy nations formed by European settlers and their descendants and a much larger periphery, whose poverty was conditioned by the decay of the institutions of the past and massive levels of unemployment. The core was less and less white but that did not necessarily solve the problem. Social forces tended to lead towards the decay of middle-class institutions and prerogatives (although not necessarily those of the rich) to the at best slight advantage of the far more numerous poor. As a result, the ANC did not endear itself to the middle class, beset by very high crime rates and swingeing taxes while its constituency of the poor protested against the absence of 'delivery' on promises.

Civic activists had particularly promised that the new regime would bring massive housing projects on a far bigger scale than any known under *apartheid*, and no longer on a racial basis. In the early years of the new government, the minuscule rate of housing construction actually fell even further. In reality, a vigorous home construction policy in the midst of such massive unemployment could only be a dream. The work of transforming schools, hospitals, local governments, arts councils, integrating the Bantustans, was clearly going to take many years. To move beyond this required something other than the conservative management strategies of the Government of National Unity – retained in 1996 even when the National Party decided to go into opposition – with their ambitions of balanced budgets and high real interest rates. The ANC favoured a strategy of corporatism of a type which seemed harmonious and effective in European countries. However, the deep antagonism between business, far more autonomous and self-confident than is normal in Third World countries, and labour, so instrumental in the ANC's rise to power, did not really dissipate. If the government accepted in principle business advice to 'privatise' state corporations, it was equally reluctant to turn against its SACP and COSATU election allies, from whom came so much of its sense of moral rectitude and historic significance.

The context of the transition had meant that an inward-looking South Africa had less of an influence on the African continent than expected. The compromise that underlay the South African deal allowed conservative regimes in the region (for instance, Swaziland, where the king and Mandela were related by marriage) to survive. Mozambique began to revive economically on the strength of renewed South African investment and other economic links in large part but there was little or no influence to pull it back in a more left-wing direction. The process through which South Africa becomes more and more part of the continent as a whole has begun but has not yet developed very far.

Afraid of being ensnared in economic and political problems beyond its comprehension or ability to solve, South Africa dealt gingerly with her neighbours. It is true that trade and investment figures showed rapid increases, especially dramatic with countries further afield, but they followed a pattern long-set with investment in fields such as mining, tourism and breweries and successful competition in winning infrastructural contracts. The balance of trade was drastically in South Africa's favour (by contrast with South African trade elsewhere in the world). South Africa at first showed little aptitude at forging relationships that would allow some kind of mutually advantageous regional or continental system of relationships to emerge. Thus, as the twentieth century approached its end, the 'rainbow nation', while now integrated once again into the family of nations on a normal basis, remained a distinct and somewhat awkward part of the African continent, unclear as to how its destiny would bring it, if at all, in closer tandem with its geographic context.

## Notes

1. The exceptions being the willingness to enter a Government of National Unity with any party obtaining more than ten per cent of the vote and making the head of any party with twenty per cent of the vote a deputy president and the arrangements for amalgamating local government districts on a parity rather than one-person one-vote basis.

# 12

# THE AGE OF STRUCTURAL
# ADJUSTMENT

'People talk about capitalism as one mode of development and communism or socialism as another mode, but at least they're both on the
move, using different paths. They have something in common, namely
a certain level of social integrity, a certain national character, a demand
for accountability. All of which is missing in most of the third world. But
without it, your capitalism or your socialism, or whatever it is, isn't
going to work.'

Flight-Lieutenant Jerry Rawlings of Ghana, as quoted in interview,
*The Guardian* (New York), April 28 1982

### Intensifying Contradictions in the 1970s

There are two principal, closely interconnected ingredients in what can be
considered a developing crisis in African states: the problematic relationship between the state and the mass of people and the deteriorating
condition of the economy in the large majority of African countries.

For the mass of Africans the oppressors have been identified again and
again in the course of demonstrations, riots and revolts, as the agents of
the state. For worker and cultivator they constitute an ambitious class of
private accumulators eager to subject the population to collective state
appropriation. The bureaucracy is so corrupt, so committed to procedural
and managerial practices of limited productive value despite its ideology of
development, that its incessant growth can only be felt as a hated burden

by the peasantry in particular, whose commodity sales sustain the state in many cases. During the late colonial period such state devices as the marketing boards and the *sociétés de prévoyances* proved indirect, but effective means of collecting heavy imposts from the peasantry. As these funds began to be turned over to the authority of the politicians they became all the more precious. The growth of the state depended on this form of expropriation, the only way funds could be gathered on an extensive scale from cultivators. Some of the money was returned in the form of improved social services, but these did not in fact compensate for the losses the peasantry suffered through poor producer prices paid by the statutory agencies. This formed the economic core to social and cultural grievances.

In the rhetoric of radical anti-colonialism that informed the African regimes of the left, little attention was given to this basic contradiction between state and society. If Nkrumah's Ghana is taken as an example it demonstrates with particular clarity that contradiction and the alienation of the masses from the regime. Nkrumah himself was full of majestic dreams of a new Africa which took incoherent, but sometimes visually impressive, shape in the industrial harbour and factory centre of Tema, the great Akosombo dam bridging the Volta and an impressive expansion of social services. All this rested on the cocoa economy, which the state milked despite increasing strain as the world price for the commodity collapsed in the early 1960s.

There was no real political or social basis for revolution within the populist Convention People's Party whose cadres, once tasting power, sought only the good life through their new positions. When they encountered opposition, including that of the working class, they crushed it, creating a mockery of a personality cult around Nkrumah, dubbed the *Osagyefo* or Redeemer. The social relations at the heart of the production of cocoa, foodstuffs and petty commodities in Ghana could not be transformed by administrative fiat into functioning within state farms as Nkrumah desired. When producer prices fell even the expanded services and new industries the state offered decayed. No attempt was made, or could be made in the context of the politics and practices of an Nkrumah, ever more removed from Ghanaian realities, to assess the class forces of Ghana in a revolutionary way. His turn left from 1961 onwards occurred in a social and political vacuum. Few coups were so welcome to the ordinary people in Africa as the reactionary one that toppled the Pan-Africanist dreamer in 1966. Nkrumah's closest contemporaries, Sékou Touré of Guinea, Modibo Keita of Mali (also overthrown in a coup of 1968) and on the other side of Africa, Nyerere, Obote and Kaunda, ran into similar difficulties even if their regimes did not all go as rotten as that of the CPP. It is not through this radical variant of African populist nationalism that post-colonial popular movements can best be observed in Africa, but vice versa.

After independence peasant resistance first emerged on a spectacular scale in the Congo, overwhelmed by risings that swept more than half of its immense territory between 1964 and 1968. Demands for a 'second', real independence were expressed with most clarity in the Kwilu region of the western Congo, where Pierre Mulele, an articulate leader who had absorbed Maoist ideas of a peoples' rising along with radical nationalism, was the foremost spokesman. Mulelism as a formal ideology used an often mechanical Marxist language, but it contained the crucial advance of speaking in class terms to African peasants. In the east and north the *simba*, teenage soldiers fighting in the hopes that magic medicine could fend off the effects of bullets, evoked memories of Maji Maji half a century earlier. All the harsh efforts at control, the brutality of Belgian rule as well as the disillusionment of independence under the nouveaux riches whose rise rapidly followed upon the elimination of Patrice Lumumba, now found its cultural antithesis. Only at length and with the use of European mercenaries did the new regime of Mobutu, once Lumumba's press secretary and now the USA's main man in Kinshasa, regain control of the situation. This kind of peasant rising, in its scale, violence and dependence on pre-colonial ritual and symbol, however out of context, has had no direct successors.

At the same time across the River Congo one of the most blatantly dependent and reactionary of the ex-French regimes, that of the defrocked *abbé*, Fulbert Youlou, in the Brazzaville Congo, was overthrown after a combination of strikes, student demonstrations and urban struggle. This brought a notably more radical regime to power. The Brazzaville revolution of 1964, if less spectacular than the great risings in the Leopoldville Congo beginning in that year also, formed a model for later mass revolts in Africa. Popular forces threw out Youlou but found no real political outlet. Radical army men stepped in to create a relatively left-wing regime that none the less failed to come to grips with the fundamental issues that had alienated people from the state. Events in the Congo were repeated in Sudan in 1968, where the trade union-based Communist Party (the only significant CP in tropical Africa) played a particularly active role until its destruction by Nimeiri, and in 1972 in the Malagasy Republic.

During the late 1970s populist urban risings built up renewed momentum in West Africa – the coup associated with Flight Lieutenant Jerry Rawlings in Ghana in 1979 which overthrew the military regime of

Colonel Acheampong, the bloody end of a century of True Whig Party rule and America-Liberian oligarchy in Liberia shortly thereafter and a revolution in Gambia in 1981 only suppressed through the intervention of Senegalese forces. This sweep of events indicated the disgust of large sectors of the people, including the most organised among the workers and the least co-opted among the educated, for the putrefying condition of the state apparatus, inept at devising any strategy to relieve popular miseries. Yet they all relied on no clear ideological trend or party organisation; they were great cries of anguish to which elements from the military most sympathetic to the sufferings of the population responded by seizing power. Men such as Nigeria's Brigadier Murtala Muhammad (head of state from 1975 until his death in an unsuccessful coup attempt in 1976) offered honesty, a high moral code and ruthless purges as understandable but insufficient answers to mounting structural problems.[1]

The most awesome political convulsion of the 1970s was the Ethiopian Revolution of 1974, which put paid both to the half-century political career of Haile Selassie and the imperial monarchy. In his last years Haile Selassie had presided over feudal and capitalist elements uncomfortably juxtaposed. The abolition of feudal dues in 1973 removed an important pillar of support for the monarchy. While the emperor relied increasingly on educated courtiers, the great feudal aristocracy lost power and influence. They could no longer present a bulwark against social currents reacting to the spread of capitalism. In the countryside estate-based export agriculture was beginning to throw peasants off the land in parts of the cash crop-producing south. In the cities secondary industry and a proletariat were at last developing. The educated bureaucrats created by the regime only felt frustrated and alienated by the corrupt feudal crust. They were not ready to back the state.

In 1973 drought convulsed much of Ethiopia while the inept imperial regime simply pretended it did not exist. Starvation and misery stalked the land while grain was sold abroad to pay for oil, industrial and luxury imports. A February army mutiny over stinking food in an isolated desert outpost was the first blow in the 'creeping coup' that led by September to the deposition of the emperor and the proclamation of sweeping changes, notably comprehensive land reform. Social forces long hidden in Ethiopia were now at liberty to develop: trade unions, the radical students' movement, ethnic and religious minorities. Over this presided a heterogeneous amalgam from the military, the Dergue.

The Dergue is an excellent example of the remarkable strategic position and political ineptitude of the military and bureaucratic Left in Africa.

Originally its slogan was the bland and inoffensive 'Ethiopia First'. It effectively accepted peasant land takeovers and the elimination of feudal and royalist elements from the Ethiopian state system, but it had nothing to offer on the increasingly burning 'national question'. Revolution had heartened the various ethnic, regional and religious entities that had gained consciousness as the victims of state oppression. Part of the Dergue was prepared to consider a negotiated settlement especially with the nationalists of Eritrea, but in the end the dominant Dergue faction under Lt.-Col. Mengistu Haile Mariam stood by Greater Ethiopia and Amhara cultural dominance as a basis for the state and the fighting went on. In 1976 Mengistu led the brutal suppression of the insurgent students and workers belonging to the Ethiopian Peoples' Revolutionary Party which had begun an ill-conceived armed campaign. He then turned against their fellows in the Meison movement who had until then always collaborated with the military.

In 1977 Mengistu found his armies being pushed inland by Somali insurgents in the east while the radicalised Eritrean Peoples' Liberation Front (EPLF), increasingly the strongest element within the Eritrean movement, succeeded for a time in seizing virtually every Eritrean town, confining the Ethiopians to a couple of big cities. Only the support of Soviet and Cuban armies enabled him to survive and carry on what increasingly looked like an imperial war. The radical social character of many of the insurgencies in Ethiopia – Eritrean, Somali, Tigre, Oromo – exposed the hollowness of the regime's leftism. Mengistu was unable to consolidate a political movement outside the army or to develop an economic strategy. The old regime in Ethiopia was effectively dead, but no force in Addis Ababa had emerged to canalise, rather than to suppress, revolutionary energies.

Central to the onset of the Ethiopian upheaval was the great drought, the crisis in Ethiopian agriculture and the drastic decline in trade due to the rapid rise in the price of imported oil. Therefore the fall of the Ethiopian regime was just one tremor in a continent-wide earthquake. From 1973 economic conditions in most of tropical Africa deteriorated markedly as demand for exports to the industrialised states fell while the price of imports, especially of oil, rocketed disastrously. African industrialisation and infrastructure has been built up, quite as much as American and European, on cheap oil and the change induced by the price rise was catastrophic. Stagnation in the world economy put the squeeze on backward, weak African productive systems.

As governments pressed peasantries to produce they met unprecedented resistance and the virtual collapse in many countries of the cash-crop export structure. Peasants, short of a great inchoate upheaval as the Congo had known in the 1960s, were unlikely to crystallise an effective political protest but they were able to 'strike' with devastating effect by ceasing to produce the desired commodities and to concentrate instead on food crop production which fetched better prices in the towns and was less effectively subject to state control. This in turn brought home the crisis that had generally caught up with African agriculture – its failure to compete on the world market or even to produce sufficient surplus to feed the continually growing towns. From the end of colonial rule on, African agricultural production grew more slowly than the overall population.

The 1973 drought struck the entire sub-desert belt of West Africa. Herds and populations had grown in part thanks to new wells which now ran dry. Moving southwards pastoralists antagonised cultivators and were forced to sell herds. Large refugee populations built up in the main administrative centres such as the capital of Mauritania, Nouakchott and the capital of Niger, Niamey, where food relief was given out. Military coups swept out the regimes in Mauritania and Niger.

In Senegal the drought led the peasantry to refuse to grow ground-nuts. They were openly supported by the Murid *shaykhs*. Nor did conditions change with the improved weather. By 1980 Senegalese ground-nut exports had fallen to pre-World War II levels and could no longer keep pace with the bills for imported oil alone. The roster of African countries increasingly unable to feed themselves – oil-rich Nigeria, 'socialist' Tanzania, 'revolutionary' Angola, 'neo-colonial' Zaïre are just a few – long and depressing.

Where possible African states (and by implication, Western businesses) turned to minerals for export earnings. Most countries in the western and more mineralised half of the continent had come to depend on minerals by the late 1970s for most of their export income. Nigeria was the greatest success story here as Africa's premier oil exporter. Oil exports allowed the Nigerian economy and state revenues to expand spectacularly in an apparently costless way, without qualitative social change. Production is extremely capital-intensive and requires few workers while the state derives an enormous rent for allowing the trans-national oil oligopolies to extract Nigerian natural resources. This largesse can then be distributed along well-established lines of patronage and used to reinforce the existing social order. This apparently perfect success formula for the Nigerian surplus-absorbing class, however, brought its problems – severe inflation, the extension of unproductive services in an imbalanced way, the collapse of agriculture unable to compete with food imports and the consequent proletarianisation of peasants by the hundred thousand. Within the cities all clambered to get their little share of the available goods. In the words of the novelist Iyayi, 'everywhere life was one heated and confused argument, leading nowhere'.[2] State expenditures began to skyrocket to absorb revenues. There were many less spectacular mineral exporters who none the less were also busily avoiding social change through selling goods produced by only a tiny fraction of workers: Guinea, the world's largest holder of bauxite reserves, phosphate-selling Togo, oil-and manganese-exporting Gabon, uranium-rich Niger, to name but a few.

## Crisis after 1980

In the 1970s, the state of African economies was decidedly mixed. Many countries were suffering from a decline in the value of the agricultural commodities that they sold to the world while many of the post-colonial elected governments had given way to military regimes or degenerated into corrupt dictatorial systems. However, for those countries, most notably Nigeria but also Angola, the Congo Republic and Gabon and later Cameroun, the dramatic hike in oil prices after 1973 provided windfall incomes. Moreover, the price of some mineral products such as phosphates and uranium continued to hold good. The Niger Sahara yielded uranium deposits for the French nuclear industry while unprecedented diamond discoveries on the edge of the Kalahari in Botswana became DeBeers' main money-spinner; both states, which had seemed hopelessly poor at independence, profited considerably. Aid conditions were not unfavourable. Talk of a new international order in trade relationships found prominent and respectable support.

From the end of the decade, however, the situation deteriorated very substantially. The 1980s were marked by a decline in production and income per capita in most African countries, a declining share in world trade participation and an impending sense of crisis. At the material heart of this lay the rising African debt. Before 1980, few African states were significantly in debt.

However, recycled petrodollars had begun to flow into the wealthiest and most bankable of them such as Zaïre and the Ivory Coast. After 1980, changes in the financial regimes in America and Europe suddenly saw these debts mount, measured in hard currency, as Western banks sought greater liquidity. The prices of virtually all of Africa's export commodities deteriorated quite sharply in comparison to imported manufactured and capital goods. Once it had looked relatively plausible to evaluate international commercial relationships in terms of national exploitation: rich countries sought cheap raw materials for their industries and working populations in return for little. Now it increasingly appears that the poor countries of Africa are simply left out of the picture, forced to accept less and less for commodities that the world can manage without.

Aid that came with strings gave way to loans on harder terms. Africa had learnt to gain something from the competition for favours between different donors and from Western fears of 'losing' another chunk of territory to communism. In the 1980s, the West increasingly ceased to bother with this kind of competition, while a crisis-laden Soviet Union dropped out of the race and a booming but inward-looking People's Republic of China lost interest. Aid consolidated. At the start of the 1980s, the Bretton Woods institutions – the World Bank and International Monetary Fund – increasingly took charge of the whole aid game barring humanitarian relief, not so much in sourcing aid but in giving the go-ahead to aid projects and certifying the worth of recipient countries. Squeezed to the limit, every African country was forced to proceed through what were generally termed 'structural adjustment programmes' (SAPs), engineered by the Bank.

The World Bank itself had undergone a dramatic transformation. It had already shifted its international interests to developing countries and was employing a growing army of relevant experts. While the Bank had previously supported industrialisation efforts and assumed the leading role of the state in developing nations, it now returned to precepts that had marked orthodox economic policy in the days before the great depression. For the bankers, the villains in Africa were the governments of the continent. These were now defined as fundamentally parasitic, 'rent-seeking', corrupt, wasteful and living beyond their means. Thus, even the welfare functions they had undertaken were unaffordable if worthy endeavours. The Bank went rural; it was committed to agrarian reform and development as the key to further progress in Africa. The African states were said to be subject to 'urban bias'; they squeezed rural producers to advantage unproductive urban dwellers who were ballooning in numbers as well as in their ability to cause political trouble.

The Bretton Woods institutions now insisted that Africans must learn the lesson that intensifying economic links with the world economy was an unmitigated blessing, as though the dependency school had never existed.

If this meant abandoning support for unviable secondary industry and attempts to construct national economies in favour of re-establishing sectors of the economy where they held a comparative advantage in terms of trade, i.e. in the sale of primary agricultural and extractive products, so much the better. Even where more generous counsels prevailed this kind of wisdom was ensconced. Thus the Lomé Convention of 1975 – renewed at intervals thereafter – guaranteeing entry to Europe of African agricultural products (which did not compete with homegrown ones) offered little incentive to structural change in Africa. Alternative sources of aid, such as the Scandinavian countries, were no longer prepared to support African efforts to find a different road to development. If these precepts were pressed on Africa sincerely and were little different than the new economic wisdom being taught to everyone, even in Western countries, it was just possible to detect an element of sly satisfaction and revenge against the spirit of charged African nationalism lurking under these cool prescriptions. The Lagos Plan of Action, adopted by the Organisation of African Unity (OAU) just before the World Bank released its report, *Accelerated Development in Sub-Saharan Africa* in 1981, reiterated once again what African intellectuals themselves thought important: the imperative of industrialisation; the need for countries on the continent to co-operate closely and develop in tandem; the requirement for Western participation in some kind of new order that would open windows of opportunity to African producers. This line of argument was simply swept aside.

In the context of the debt crisis where African countries such as Ghana, Mozambique or Tanzania were starved of foreign goods, the necessity to adopt this development approach as the only possible means of restarting the economy became apparent sooner or later. This was an even more striking development perhaps in those countries such as the Ivory Coast, Kenya or Malawi which had been the darlings of the Right, had experienced significant economic growth through following the precepts of an earlier orthodoxy, and which were now the more precipitately plunged into crisis, precisely because they had been entrusted with generous loans and had prospered on the basis of promoting cash-crop production whose international purchasing power was fading. Where the equivalent SAP programmes instituted painful shock medicine in countries such as England or Malaysia, in Africa they became indefinite, renewed in phases as the need for credits and loan from overseas piled up.

The heart of the theory behind structural adjustment was financial, summarised in breezy catchphrases of the age such as 'getting prices right' or 'market clearing prices'. Inconvertible African currencies that could buy little and were illicitly traded for small sums on street corners were to be replaced with readily available convertible money at whatever exchange rate the market could bear and import controls were to be removed. Beyond this, governments were pressured to reduce spending of all sorts, to *privatise* or sell state assets, especially those with monopoly control over economic activities, to cut the numbers of civil servants and aim at balancing the budget. State farms, state commercial monopolies and other such activities were to be disbanded. Unproductive industries were to be denied support. Of particular importance was insistence on the removal of market controls over African farming; marketing boards were, if not disbanded, deprived of their monopoly authority to purchase particular crops. On the assumption that the prices which had been offered producers were consistently low and exploitative, this, it was hoped, would lead to a new resurgence in African agriculture. If colonial planning had placed considerable emphasis in its day on food security in the countryside, this was now to be abandoned or minimised in favour of letting market prices alone regulate production and distribution.

## Structural Adjustment in Ghana and Uganda

Could structural adjustment work in practice? Perhaps the best places to test this hypothesis are Ghana and Uganda. Ghana after 1981 and Uganda after 1986 were the scene of popular new governments that came to power by force and seemed to represent a new brush sweeping the scene. In both cases, by contrast with most of Africa, economic growth rates were high, approximately five per cent or more in Ghana through the decade of the 1980s and even higher in Uganda by the middle 1990s. Paradoxically, the central figures of these regimes, Jerry Rawlings and Yoweri Museveni, were at first identified as heroes of the radical left.[3] The first was the gallant air force officer unprepared to sit aside and tolerate the continued decay of Ghana whilst Museveni, a youthful intellectual unwilling to accept the results of the post-Amin election in 1980, took to the countryside and eventually marched into Kampala after years of popular insurrection in the Luwero Triangle of northern Buganda. The president, Obote, was overweening and corrupt and proved unable to bring the predatory state of Idi Amin under control; indeed, it is often argued that the post-Amin Obote years were worse than those under Amin in terms of abuses against human rights. Both could be identified particularly with hostility to the residue of indirect rule, the governance of chiefs and so-called traditional authorities upholding ethnic claims in the countryside. Both were astute strategists who seemed to bear comparison in stature not unfavourably with their predecessors, Nkrumah and Nyerere, in the previous generation. Both championed and based themselves on new institutions of apparently direct democracy in the countryside and supported the cause of poor producers. Both, however, after short stints in power, decided to accept the logic of the SAPs and became energetic champions of measures designed to promote them as thoroughly as possible.

Evaluating the two governments requires taking a number of issues into consideration. There were certainly real benefits in the financial reforms instituted. If currencies such as the Ghanaian cedi and the Ugandan shilling were now worth very little, at least they were completely and conveniently convertible. The goods flowed back into shops and what people earned was now worth something. Higher salaries chasing non-existing goods had at any event become valueless.

Most observers also find a genuine shift in returns to agricultural producers. In Ghana, while cocoa producers had been earning as little as a quarter of the value of their crop, their returns rose to approximately half. In Uganda, while the coffee marketing board continued to have a significant role in processing, it no longer controlled buying and this advantaged many growers. Both Ghana and Uganda found areas in the economy to privatise. The most profitable gold mine in Ghana, Ashanti Gold Fields, was sold to foreign interests and refurbished, becoming once again a major source of foreign exchange. In Uganda, the Asians expelled under Idi Amin had their property restituted and their numbers started to increase again significantly in the 1990s. The Madhvanis, for instance, rehabilitated the sugar estates around Jinja and sugar again became a prosperous concern in Uganda. In Uganda, particularly, the good public image created by adherence to the SAP itself not only attracted continuous flows of aid but also began to have an effect on tourism, while international organisations moved their operations from Nairobi, beset by crime and physical dangers, to Kampala, rendered safe by Museveni's demilitarisation of Ugandan society. At least some aspects of physical infrastructure were renewed or reconstructed.

The limits to SAP success need to be signalled as well, however. First, the meaner, leaner state demanded by aid donors has meant that the welfare provisions on which the state's legitimacy historically depended have not only not been restored but in some respects have fallen back further. Privatised education, social welfare and health care are not only extremely inequitable and unlikely to create adequate coverage, they also place key decisions about policy in the hands of foreign donors, the so-called non-governmental organisations or NGOs, and their local partners. Uganda is probably the African country most seriously affected by the AIDS epidemic but it has no capacity to establish and finance even a basic national health policy.

Second, important elements of the economy are not really restored by means of SAPs. Secondary industry, for instance, cannot really be revived according to the precepts of the SAP. It might be more instructive to turn here momentarily to Zimbabwe, because of the relatively important weight of industry in the Zimbabwean economy. When Zimbabwe adopted the ESAP, its own version of structural adjustment, after 1990, it turned with amazing abandon to opening its gates wide to foreign industrial competition. Zimbabwean industry was completely unable to adapt and in the middle 1990s, major companies were closing down and a significant de-industrialisation of the economy forecast. The end of international sanctions against South Africa, opening the floodgates to South African imports, proved to be an unfortunate coincidence for Zimbabwean industrialists.

Third, both Ghana and Uganda were countries whose economies had regressed very substantially in the post-colonial period. The gains that were achieved under SAPs were impressive but they started from very low points on the graph. Thus in Ghana, production figures achieved in the middle 1990s were only on a level or somewhat higher than those of twenty years earlier. This was quite a different proposition from one that could assert a whole new trajectory of growth. If Uganda became a favourite of aid donors, it is important to signal that the state budget continued to depend heavily on aid, despite an aura of self-reliance that was not unlike Nyerere's.

Finally, even when they were most successful, it was a success that at best tended to restore the colonial structures of the economy. Dreams of pan-African co-operation, industrialisation that could sustain the rapid growth of African cities and even the most basic of development desiderata – increased productivity and skill levels – were set aside in this mindframe. Africa has massive needs for social and physical infrastructure which can only hope to benefit investors indirectly and in the long term, however judiciously constructed. There is little scope for such investment on a hard money basis. Given the strength of feeling of the class that had come to power within the African state, de-nationalisation of state enterprise and renewed entry of foreign owners and investors represented a dramatic historic reversal. Yet only a limited range of conventional investments interested foreigners (for instance, almost nothing in Ghana outside the mining sector). Even the warmest defenders of structural adjustment cannot claim to find much sign of new investment flowing into these model countries. The World Bank began to have a strong stake in continuing their viability so liquid resources continued to be made available to them but they cannot be said to be paying back the accumulated debts that initiated the crisis in the first place.

However, if we turn from Ghana and Uganda elsewhere, the record of the SAPs in promoting African development is more consistently unsuccessful. Zambia was an early test case for them, associated with the electoral defeat of Kenneth Kaunda in 1991 and his replacement by Frederick Chiluba in a fair multi-party election. In Zambia, the basis of the colonial and post-colonial economy was copper. While problems of mismanagement in the nationalised copper mines were significant, they were not as crucial as the drastically reduced price of world copper. As elsewhere, currency reform did allow for goods to flow into Zambia again but at prices that few could pay. There was no fundamental basis in production that could power the restoration of the Zambian economy.

Privatisation operates in a very different context in Africa from the European model that its ideological sponsors have in mind. In Africa, 'rent-seeking bureaucrats' were hardly just a fantasy and reform aimed at weeding them out made sense, but to a large extent it was just these individuals who were able to arrange reform to suit themselves. Thus, in the once radical epigone state of Guiné-Bissau, Rosemary Galli and Jocelyn Jones consider that this class were able to use new ideological currents to stake out for themselves profitable areas for their activities effectively on a monopoly basis. For Galli and Jones, the economic history of radically different stages in the terms of development is effectively always a history of renegotiated relations between the domestic class of officials and the international donor bureaucracy. Galli has pointed particularly to the activities of the *ponteiros*, 'merchants and concessionaires who have direct ties to the state class' and who have been the principal beneficiaries of the liberalisation of the economy. In the evocatively named *Tropical Gangsters*, Robert Klitgaard paints a similar picture from the perspective of a reforming World Bank-linked advisor in Equatorial Guinea. The growing importance of Western NGOs required local partners and it was this class which fulfilled this need the best. The hunger for

Western currency pressed educated Africans into the service of whatever activities were negotiable in this sense.


## Decay of the State; Drive for Democracy

Even the World Bank came to question after 1990 the initial relish with which the new ideologues pressed the need to push back the powers of the African state. However, the nature of change, even beyond the specific prescriptions of structural adjustment, served to weaken the state, especially insofar as it might have served as a bulwark against simple ratification of the interests of foreign investors and bankers. The decay of the state and its consequences has been a major theme of concern to contemporary commentators on African affairs.

Certainly the positive side of the coin lay in the retreat that was suffered by one-party states and regimes that tolerated no opposition. At bottom, such political systems had failed to deliver the goods. In certain countries, for instance, the poor Sahelian republic of Mali, the popular rising which overturned the entrenched military dictatorship of Moussa Traore at the cost of many human lives, was arguably more important in the forging of some kind of national consciousness than the independence bargain a generation earlier.

Certain dramatic events seemed to contain within them the seeds for the creation of a new state that would resolve the crisis of the old. After Uganda, perhaps most important as an internal political change exerted by violent means was the overthrow of the revolutionary government in Addis Ababa in 1991. Although opposition to the Mengistu regime was complex, the key element was the armed struggle in Tigre, the northern province which had become somewhat marginalised in Ethiopian political life since the nineteenth century. While Mengistu had presided over the demise of Ethiopian feudalism, he had insisted on a system of state farms and blocked outright peasant ownership of land. This and the continued toll of drought made the success of a peasant insurrection possible. The new government, once in power, called for a new constitution of Ethiopian statehood based on ethnic self-determination and specifically rejecting the Amhara character that had remained strong in the central government even after the fall of the monarchy. Eritrea, after thirty years of fighting, was permitted to go its own way. The EPLF insurgents occupied the territory and presided over an election that established a legal basis for an independent Eritrea. Both Eritrean and Ethiopian revolutionaries had no choice but to reject the Maoist and other Third Worldist revolutionary doctrines of their youth (the Tigreans had begun as admirers of Hoxha's Albania). In securing international sympathy, the EPLF had in any event long shifted towards pragmatism while appealing internally to a diverse ethnic and religious mix of people. In these countries, more hopefully than virtually anywhere in the Africa of the 1990s, a kind of new order was slowly being constructed on an indigenous base of some strength.

Some observers would also find impressive the insurgent regime that took power in Rwanda in 1994. Again, a post-colonial system, unable to deliver much and beset by the declining purchasing power of cash cropping, lost its support base. The Hutu revolution overthrew the Tutsi aristocracy cum ethnic group as it had coalesced before and during colonialism but it was never able to incorporate Tutsi refugees or to create a society free of cliques and patronage. A president willing to negotiate a solution in the context of growing pressure from the main international supporter, France, for democratisation, was assassinated by fanatics in an environment of rapidly mounting tension. An army consisting largely of such refugees who had been actively involved fighting at Museveni's side in Uganda, and long operative on the frontier, was able to break through military lines and overthrow the government. By this time, however, the most horrendous genocidal murders of Tutsi and those Hutu seen as their friends within the country, had been instigated. The new government had to deal with the legacy of genocide in which much of the population could be accused of complicity, the presence of a huge new Hutu refugee population in Zaïre under the sway of the overthrown regime's minions, and the need to win over the large Hutu majority to a new understanding of national unity if any kind of new stability was to be attained. Moreover, across the border in Burundi, where a Tutsi dominated regime had never been overthrown, these events were like an unlanced boil, provoking terror and the threat of terror, on the part of both Hutu and Tutsi.

However, it would be naive not to point out that the pressure for democratisation, especially a democratisation rather dogmatically defined in terms of a multi-party electoral system with perhaps a free press, did not in good part come from the West along with the SAPs. The discourse of development, which had tended to favour strong and effective government, even military rule, in the 1970s, was swinging towards an insistence on 'good governance' recognisable in these terms; only democracy could enforce the hard conditions of the SAP plausibly. Movement towards democratisation was made a condition of further aid. When

French President François Mitterrand made it clear to the francophone states in 1990 in a speech at La Baule, that this would be a key element in the policy, it clearly undermined the previous political logic. In francophone countries, the institution of a national conference (Conférence des forces vives) in Benin that established an electoral process which unseated Mathieu Kérékou, the once Marxist military dictator, in 1991, was a key catalyst. The institution of civilian rule, opposition parties and a lively press was particularly marked in such countries as Mali, Niger and Madagascar with their very limited experiences of formal democracy. In Rwanda, too, aid-linked pressure for democracy and negotiations was a factor in the spectacular and bloody events of the middle 1990s.

A spectacular example of democratisation was Mozambique. The violent RENAMO insurgency, often in an environment of terror and destruction, and backed by the old South African government, gave way to a reasonably fair electoral contestation following an internationally monitored ceasefire. FRELIMO, no longer harbouring any socialist pretensions under the leadership of a president interested in economic deals with South African business and Eastern spiritualists, won a relatively narrow victory and was able to resume power peacefully. Mozambique had never held a contested election or experienced much that could be called democratic previously.

Nevertheless, many of the stronger African regimes were able to survive this kind of pressure with growing efficacy. General Mobutu, despite a very poor Western press, remained able to secure enough revenues to sustain security forces and prevent the opposition forces in such a large and complex country as Zaïre from coalescing. The Benin-style national conference was unable to find a basis for unseating him. Paul Biya in Cameroun and Daniel arap Moi in Kenya survived multi-party elections, despite accusations of fraud in the former case and because of a deeply divided opposition in the latter. Such astute politicians as Biya and Moi, even in the wake of the economic decay of two of Africa's initially most prosperous countries, were well able to structure rural patronage networks so as to withstand the storms blowing over them. If the American embassy in Nairobi had become the linchpin in the drive for democratisation in Kenya, its willingness to endorse the re-election of Moi in 1992 marked the end of the drive. In the most important of all the ex-French colonies, the Ivory Coast, the death of Félix Houphouet-Boigny in 1993 was eventually followed by an election which retained the PDCI machine in power very effectively. Although still alive, the even older president of Malawi, Hastings Banda, lost his grip and was forced to abrogate power shortly afterwards. But as in Kenya, elections revolved around a three-way contest with each side having command of a regional basis. In this case, Banda's people were ousted for the time being. Mahmood Mamdani argues that so long as democratisation drives are dominated by urban lawyers and churchmen and do not engage with the rural patrimonial structures that remain intact, they are unlikely to alter the political basis of the African state significantly.

Elections also failed to transform Nigerian politics. The 'Second Republic' had been overthrown by a renewed military coup in 1984. The apparent 1993 success at the polls of millionaire businessman-newspaper magnate Chief Moshood Abiola, who himself had been implicated in earlier military governments, seemed unacceptable to those in the military who counted on permanent access to the resources of the Nigerian state. SAP advocate Ibrahim Babangida gave way to Sani Abacha who retained an unprecedentedly tight hold on the reins of power in Nigeria while claiming to preside, once again, over a slow return to an electoral system. Cynics who wondered how fast or far this process of return would be allowed to proceed can be forgiven. Despite the diminution in oil revenues as Nigerians acquired the appetite to absorb the flow of money, and as oil prices fell, Nigeria still had such a valuable resource that it remained in the unusual position of being able to thumb its nose at the world and a threatened boycott.

The success of Babangida and Abacha in blocking democratic change in Nigeria, and the parallel success of Mobutu in Zaïre, still able to command a modicum of resources to support army and police units, were probably signal in bringing the movement towards democratisation to a halt. However, the link between democratisation and structural adjustment also became more frayed with time. The 1992 elections that brought Jerry Rawlings to civilian power in Ghana were not given the stamp of approval by many observers. Jeffrey Herbst suggests shrewdly that Rawlings operated in a curious vacuum of power. If he found a political base, it would most likely be amongst sections of the rural population who had gained from the revival of the economy. Some businessmen and workers have also gained but there is a sense in which Rawlings' success has come from his standing above any local interests. His belief in a revived Ghanaian capitalism cannot really be matched by a constitutency amongst emergent Ghanaian capitalists. It has been argued that this independence from any single sector of civil society is itself apt to lead to authoritarian practices. Rawlings is clearly most uncomfortable with the idea of any coherent structured opposition group and his success in preventing the emergence of such is probably central to understanding political power and how it has operated in late twentieth-century Ghana.

Uganda shows some interesting parallels. Museveni's strong support basis lay in the rural Revolutionary Councils that his supporters tended to control. He, similarly, was hostile to organised opposition, however democratic, and particularly to any adhesion to the old politics, much of which revolved around ethnic or religious loyalties. He presided over a constitutional assembly process and Uganda finally held national elections in 1996 but, to some Western dismay, Museveni, who won a large victory, did not permit political parties to reassemble.

It is difficult to gainsay the advantages for Africans in the increased freedom of expression that does exist in many countries or in the considerably greater autonomy for so-called civil society to develop independent of state orders. However, the fundamental nature of the SAPs, in limiting the effective capacity of the state, makes one wonder how stable a basis for democracy has in fact been established when the state is able to deliver so little.

In some places, the decay of the state has been remarkable and really disastrous. Apart from Ethiopia, the other government of the Horn with military antecedents and revolutionary pretensions was that in Somalia where the Siyaad Barre government had claimed to have introduced 'scientific socialism' into a land where the pastoralist majority had never easily been absorbed by any state. With declining economic conditions, Somalis got less and less benefit from the regime in Mogadishu. However, many were able to benefit from the wealth of the nearby Arab peninsula, where livestock could be sold and jobs found. The narcotic *qat* could be grown extremely profitably in the marginally agricultural highlands of northern Somalia where previously little farming had taken place. These circumstances fed into the decline and then defeat of the Barre regime, followed by the fragmentation of authority in the country. The northern, formerly British, part effectively resumed its separate existence albeit without any international recognition while different 'warlords' exerted differing levels of authority elsewhere, often with no noticeable decline in delivery of public services. However, during phases of intense conflict, such strong men were successful in manipulating food supplies and controlling access to aid workers in such a way as to create famine in an attempt to control maximum numbers of people under their authority.

In two of the smallest West African countries, Sierra Leone and (especially) Liberia, warring factions destroyed any remnant of central state authority. State decay undermined the corrupt regime of Samuel Doe in Liberia, who met a televised brutal end; none of the rival groups contesting for power with different ethnic, clan or military affiliations have successfully replaced him. ECOWAS, the association of West African states, made available a military peacekeeping force which created a limited focus of order in Liberia but so far has failed to regulate a new situation.

Somalia and Liberia are spectacular examples of the collapse of African states. In other cases, remote and border regions have been able to sponsor popular insurgencies such as the Casamance in southern Senegal and the arid north of Mali and Niger where, as in Somalia, the capacity of a weak state to establish systematic control over nomadic people has lessened measurably. In Uganda, the remarkable revival of peaceful order in the south has been matched by violence in the north, probably assisted from over the frontier and associated with religious prophecy movements. Perhaps as much to the point, Museveni's Uganda no longer offers resources to poor men from the north who previously served as soldiers and policemen and used the state as a means of replenishing themselves. More mundane and typical is the commonplace decay in state authority and capacity to deliver, beyond extracting certain symbolic and material signs of tribute. One of the most poignant if banal evocations of this decay can be found in a description by a militant supporter of the once red-hot revolutionary process in Guiné-Bissau which will always be associated with Amilcar Cabral. A look at Kandjadja, a provincial settlement near the frontier, over decades shows that in recent years the presence of the state has virtually disappeared. There is no capacity to deliver health or schooling and the teacher is of little interest to the community which prefers the traditional Islamic learning that remains available. Patrimonial or 'tribal' authorities who can deliver something count for more than state officials in practice. Money is made by taking advantage of trans-frontier smuggling and competitive supply routes. 'Seen from a local viewpoint, this political set-up is new, post-colonial or "modern" in a partial or partially superficial sense.'[4] The presence of the 'modern' in terms of amenities depends heavily on charitable work from foreigners in NGOs. NGOs, however essential for the moment, laudable and, despite a seductive 'small is beautiful' philosophy, can never substitute for the regulatory capacity of an indigenous state, capable of working out a national or regional policy or for strategies devised internally by people in tune with the local power structure.

Similarly, the growing reliance in development discourse on the 'informal sector', the economy unregulated by the state and able to absorb an apparently unlimited amount of human labour, is problematic. It often seems to make a virtue of necessity, the breakdown of the formal wage-granting part of the economy forces people to survive through small-scale production, commerce and activities not sanctioned by the state. It is true that there are windows of opportunity in this sector. In much of Africa, it is only here that women, no longer able to function within the mechanisms of the large patriarchal family, and far less likely than men to find waged labour, are able to survive. None the less, 'survive' is all most denizens of the informal sector can do. Only a few accumulate within this sector successfully and then according to networks which are understudied and not well understood. Certainly it is likely that those with state connections, past or present, are still apt to be the best-placed, whether in dealing with actual economic structures functioning autonomously of the purview of the state or in terms of advantageous arrangements with foreigners. In Zaïre, where the 'second economy' is so powerful and obvious, the state often seems to observers like a parasite that lives off a burgeoning, highly commercialised and unregulated world. The decline of the state, which structural adjustment has nudged along rather than caused, promotes this development as much or more than the prototypical mean, lean capitalist state that delivers the goods.

## A New Africa Struggles into Being

This book began with a critique of 'essentialist Africa', with any assumption that the real Africa is about people with a certain stereotyped physical appearance, who live in villages under chiefs, who have a limited relationship to the market economy, and whose lives are structured around kinship groups and extended families in an ancient world of ritual and tribally determined art. Colonialism brought substantial change to the lives of men and women which were at least in some ways part of such a picture. But the post-colonial decades are distending the picture to breaking point in ways that make the distinctive capture of cultural change harder and harder for those who wish to observe and generalise. One pioneering anthropologist who is trying to do that is T. Abdou Maliqalim Simone. In an article with Edgar Pieterse on how some Africans are trying to make sense of the fragmented world around them, he claims with some exaggeration that Dakar is in some senses a sixth borough of New York City. 'Religious fundamentalists coincide with communists coincide with fashion models and gangsters.'[5] His working-class Dakarois combine elements of ritual and belief that are ancient with new ideas from the changing world of Islam and from the dominant consumerist patterns of the West. They may intensify or even rigidify ethnic loyalties while establishing linkages with kin and friends and picking up new consumer habits in Paris and New York. No nation-building project holds such people together very easily.

There is a kind of material gap that is yawning wider and wider between this reality and the continued low productivity of African agriculture and industry. In the end, the challenge to create industrial and service activities that are flexible and functional in the modern world, not simply transplants purchased elsewhere, and to allow for growing productivity on the land in a way that does not strangle the varied, remarkable but often fragile African ecosystems, is one that Africans will have to find ways, perhaps painfully and slowly, of meeting. Otherwise no nation-building project can hold together a rapidly growing, increasingly fragmented population.

However, one cannot understand Africa today only in these rather sombre productionist strictures. The increasing complexity of civilisation in Africa is also creative. There is a growing recognition that Africa is producing a far more hybrid and reflexive art today that cannot simply be dismissed as no longer 'authentic' because it is post-tribal. African music, as witness the remarkable work of people like Salif Keita, Baba Maal or Cesaria Evora, reflects such hybrid influences and has achieved far more influence and attention internationally as a result.

Contemporary change in religious and spiritual life parallels such patterns in the arts. In some African countries, for instance the Sudan, 'fundamentalist' Islam has become a powerful discourse in which people seek meaning for their lives. However, a study of 'born again' pentecostalism in southern Nigeria, aimed at reforming social manners and economic life, shows parallel trends although thus far failing to engage with national politics in the same way. African intellectuals are becoming more diverse and sophisticated, despite and perhaps because of the hard conditions under which many of them labour; that so many live much of the time outside Africa does not make them un-African. African sportsmen and women are often world-beaters. The development failures of recent decades tempt one to dismiss Africa, in the jejune and superficial words of some specialists as a collection of 'basket cases'. In fact, out of hard times, creativity and originality are also being born and Africa's integration with, and influence on, our contemporary world deepens.

## Notes

1. There is something deeper at stake in the political ferment in Ghana following the second Jerry Rawlings coup which ended civilian rule in 1981.
2. F. Iyayi, *Violence* (Longman, 1979), p. 65.
3. By contrast, a third figure, superficially equivalent, was the young soldier Thomas Sankara, who became prime minister of Upper Volta in a military regime in 1983 and, after struggles that led to his imprisonment, was freed and proclaimed president shortly thereafter. He was a classic example of the radical egalitarian nationalist with strong emotional affinities to liberation movements in Africa and elsewhere, a distaste for the perquisites and measured life of the African bureaucracy, and a romantic longing to stand outside existing social forces. By contrast with either Museveni or Rawlings, however, he compromised less and less with the forces of international order and was assassinated by a close associate in 1987. His stature in francophone Africa can be equated with that of Cabral, Nkrumah or Nyerere. He was the last major figure cast in this mould to date.
4. Lars Rudebeck, 'The Effects of Structural Adjustment in Kandjadja, Guiné-Bissau', *Review of African Political Economy*, 49, 1990, 43.
5. Abdou Maliqalim Simone & Edgar Pieterse, 'Civil Societies in an Internationalized Africa', *Social Dynamics*, XIX, 2, 1993, 46.

# ANNOTATED BIBLIOGRAPHY

## 1  Africanist History and the History of Africa

For the standard British Africanist analysis, see Roland Oliver and John Fage, *A Short History of Africa* (Penguin, 1st edn., 1962, 5th edn., 1975); John Fage, *History of Africa* (Hutchinson, 1978) and the multi-volume *Cambridge History of Africa*, edited by Oliver and Fage. A more recent contribution is John Iliffe, *Africans; The History of a Continent* (Cambridge University Press, 1995). The American style is epitomised in Curtin, Feierman, Thompson and Vansina, *African History* (Longman, 1978), although the last two authors are originally from South Africa and Belgium respectively. Africans are largely responsible for the *UNESCO History of Africa* (Unesco, Paris, 1985–) Paul Tiyambe Zeleza, *A Modern Economic History of Africa*, v. 1 (CODESRIA, 1993) is useful and due to be continued.

Pre-Africanist views that may be noted with profit are W. E. B. DuBois, *The World and Africa* (International Publishers, 1965), reflecting a specific Afro-American tradition and Samuel Johnson's *History of the Yorubas* (Routledge & Kegan Paul, 1966 reprint), a typical but distinguished example of the kind of written histories Africans were producing during the colonial period.

Consensus and criticism within the field can be better understood by a progressive examination of Vansina, Mauny and Thomas, Ranger and Fyfe, the three collections discussed in the text and cited in the notes. On method and oral tradition, see its foremost champion, Jan Vansina, *Oral Tradition* (Routledge & Kegan Paul, 1965) as well as the nuanced and thoughtful *Oral Tradition as History* (James Currey 1984). On the perspective of an African collector and analyst of traditions, see Mamadou Daiwara, 'Les recherches en historie orale menées par un authochtone', *CEA*, 97 (1985). A collection presenting a critical view of anthropology is Talal Asad, ed., *Anthropology and the Colonial Encounter* (Ithaca Press, 1973). A brilliant portrait of one of the most influential anthropologists of the colonial era has been penned by Richard Brown: 'Passages in the

Life of a White Anthropologist: Max Gluckman in Northern Rhodesia', *JAH*, XX (1979). Some of the earliest criticisms of Africanist history by Wrigley, Saul and Ochieng are cited in the text. The underdevelopmentalist hypothesis is raised in E. A. Alpers, 'Rethinking African Economic History' *KHR*, I (1973) and Samir Amin, 'Underdevelopment and Dependence in Black Africa – Origin and Contemporary Forms', *JMAS*, X (1972). See also Walter Rodney, *How Europe Underdeveloped Africa* (Bogle-L'Ouverture, 1972). For a survey see Bogumil Jewsiewicki and David Newbury, ed., *African Historiographies* (Sage, 1986). Arguably the finest work in the South African liberal tradition is C. W. DeKiewiet, *A History of South Africa: Social and Economic* (Oxford University Press, 1940). The tradition was extended under Africanist influence with Leonard Thompson and Monica Wilson, eds, *Oxford History of South Africa* (Oxford University Press, 1969–71). See Leonard Thompson, *A History of South Africa*, (Yale University Press, 1990) for a more current book. Among the landmarks of the new historiography of southern Africa are: Charles van Onselen, *Chibaro* (Pluto Press, 1976) and *The Seed is Mine*, (Hill & Wang, 1996) and Shula Marks and Anthony Atmore, eds, *Economy and Society in Pre-industrial South Africa* (Longman, 1980). Drawing on underdevelopmentalist and Marxist thought is the major collection by Neil Parsons and Robin Palmer, *The Roots of Rural Poverty in Central and Southern Africa* (Heinemann, 1977).

A notion of the critical ideas of some of the established African historians emerges from J. F. A. Ajayi's essay in the Ranger collection cited earlier, E. A. Ayandele, 'How Truly Nigerian is Nigerian History?' in his *Nigerian Historical Studies* (Frank Cass, 1979) and Bethwell A. Ogot, 'Towards a History of Kenya', *KHR*, IV (1976). An interesting synthesis that has moved fairly far from the Africanist paradigm is Catherine Coquery-Vidrovitch and Henri Mouniot, *L'Afrique noire de 1800 à nos jours* (Presses Universitaires de France, 1974). Ailsa Auchnie, 'African Historical Research in the Paris Region', *AA*, LXXX (1981) usefully surveys the situation of African historiographic work in contemporary France. For a critical look at African studies in France see Jean Copans, *La longue marche de la modernité africaine*, (Karthala, 1990).

The writings cited in the notes by Said, Swai and Bernstein and Depelchin have particularly influenced the writing of this chapter. For an expanded version of Swai's hypothesis, see A. J. Temu and B. Swai, *Historians and Africanist History: a Critique* (Zed Press, 1981).

For examples of ways in which post-modern thinking has been introduced into African studies, see Atieno Odhiambo and David Cohen, *Burying SM; Tne Politics of Knowledge and the Sociology of Power*, (Heinemann, 1992), Achille Mbembe, 'Domaines de la nuit et autorité onorique dans les maquis du sud-Cameroun 1955–58', *JAH*, XXXI (1991), James Ferguson, 'Mobile Workers, Modernist Narratives', *JSAS*, XVI (1990) and Kirk Hoppe, 'Whose Life is it Anyway? Issues of Representation in Life Narrative Texts of African Women', *IJAHS*, XXVI (1993).

## 2  Material and Cultural Development in Africa before the Nineteenth Century

Marx's scattered writings on pre-capitalist society have been collected in a number of editions, including one with a distinguished introduction by Maurice Godelier in French. A convenient English version was edited by Eric Hobsbawm, *Pre-capitalist Economic Formations* (International Publishers, 1964). The one Marxist classic on related material is Friedrich Engels' *The Origin of the Family, Private Property and the State* (Pathfinder Press, 1972). The serious student should also consult Lawrence Krader's edition of *Marx's Ethnological Notebooks* (Van Gorcum, 1974).

The modes of production debate was inaugurated in France in the 1960s. Many of the early articles are collected in *Sur le 'mode de production' asiatique*, introduced by Jean Suret-Canale (Éditions Sociales, 1974). Catherine Coquery-Vidrovitch's seminal article, 'Research on an African Mode of Production' is translated in Martin Klein and G. Wesley Johnson, eds, *Perspectives on the African Past* (Little, Brown, 1972). Many relevant articles have been published in the London journal *Critiques of Anthropology*. Others are available in three important collections, M. Bloch, ed., *Marxist Analysis and Social Anthropology* (Random House, 1975), David Seddon, ed., *Relations of Production* (Frank Cass, 1978) and Harold Wolpe, ed., *The Articulation of Modes of Production* (Routledge & Kegan Paul, 1980). Claude Meillassoux has provided a provocative exposition of his concept of lineage society in *Maidens, Meal and Money* (Cambridge University Press, 1980). Studies specifically inspired by these issues include Marc Augé, *Pouvoirs de vie, pouvoirs de mort* (Flammarion, 1977); J. P. Olivier de Sardan, *Le Système de relations économiques et sociales chez les Wogo*, (Musée de l'Homme, 1969); Pierre-Philippe Rey, *Colonialisme, néo-colonialisme et la transition au capitalisme* (Maspéro, 1971) and Eric Pollet and Grace Winter, 'L'organisation sociale du travail agricole des Soninke', *CEA*, VIII (1968). American considerations of the debate with some interesting case studies are edited by Donald Crummey and Charles Stewart, *Modes of Production in Africa* (Sage, 1981).

On agrarian systems in Africa, Thomas Bassett and Donald Crummey, eds, *Land in African Agrarian Systems*, (University of Wisconsin Press, 1993) is a very useful recent collection. It can be supplemented with Andrew Smith, *Pastoralism in Africa*, (Hurst, 1992) or John Galaty and Pierre Bonté, eds, *Herders, Warriors and Traders; Pastoralism in Africa*, (Westview, 1991).

Meillassoux has also edited a wide-ranging and major collection on slavery in Africa, *L'esclavage en Afrique précoloniale*, (Maspéro, 1975). See his *The Anthropology of Slavery; The Womb of Iron and Gold*, (Athlone Press, 1991). This and other work is critically surveyed by Frederick Cooper, 'The Problem of Slavery in African Studies', *JAH*, XIX (1979). On forms of slavery in Africa see also Paul Lovejoy, *Transformations in Slavery*, (Cambridge University Press, 1983), Claire Robertson and Martin Klein, eds, *Women and Slavery in Africa*, (University of Wisconsin Press, 1983) and Marion Johnson, 'The Slaves of Salaga', *JAH*, XXVII (1987). For a related form of structured dependency relations, F. Adeniyi Orogo, "Iwofa": An Historical Survey of the Yoruba Institution of Indenture,' *AEH*, 14 (1985).

These pages cannot embrace the vast literature of specialist interest on pre-colonial Africa. This selection is based on those works that cover major areas or have some wider import. For more detailed references, the multi-volume *Cambridge History of Africa* is a good starting point. The *Cambridge Encyclopaedia of Archaeology* (Cambridge University Press, 1980) provides a convenient, brief overview of recent provenance. J. E. G. Sutton, 'The Aquatic Age in Africa', *JAH*, XV (1974) is a provocative discussion of one facet of the transition to agriculture in Africa. See also J. D. Fage and Roland Oliver, eds, *Papers in African Prehistory* (Cambridge University Press, 1970); J. R. Harlan *et al.*, eds, *Origins of African Plant Domestication* (University of Chicago Press, 1976); L. Krzyzaniak, 'New Light on Early Food Production in the Central Sudan', *JAH*, XIX (1978). Hunting and gathering communities in Africa are the subject of J. Woodburn, *Hunters and Gatherers: Material Culture of the Nomadic Hadza* (The British Museum Trustees, 1970) and Richard Lee, *The !Kung San; Men, Women and Work in a Foraging Society* (Cambridge University Press, 1979) which addresses issues from a materialist perspective. A critique of how anthropologists have treated such societies is the foundation of Edwin Wilmsen, *Land Filled with Flies* (University of Chicago Press, 1989.)

The West African past is surveyed in the compendium, J. F. Ade Ajayi and Michael Crowder, *History of West Africa* (Columbia University Press, 1976). Some of the most interesting thinking on the ancient states of the upper Niger Basin has been done by East Europeans. These include Marian Malowist, 'Social and Economic Stability of the Western Sudan', *Past and Present*, XXXIII (1966, with a rejoinder by A. G. Hopkins, XXXVII, 1967); Michel Tymowski, 'Société sans état et sociétés à organisation étatique en Afrique noire', *Africana Bulletin* (Warsaw) 40 (1992) and 'Les domaines des princes du Songhay', *Annales*, XXV (1970) and L. E. Kubbel, *Songhaiskaya Derzhava* (Nauk, Moscow, 1974). On the Saharan world 1000 years ago, E. Ann McDougall, 'The View from Awdaghast: War, Trade and Social Change in the South Western Sahara from the Eighth to the Sixteenth Centuries', *JAH*, XXVI (1985) is interesting and, for a slightly later period, Richard Roberts, *Warriors, Merchants and Slaves; The State and the Economy in the Middle Niger Valley 1700–1914*, (Stanford University Press, 1987).

A survey of territories further to the west is found in Boubacar Barry, *Le Sénégambie de Xe au XIXe siècles*, (Harmattan, 1988) and the economy of early Senegambia surveyed in Philip Curtin, *Economic Change in Pre-colonial Africa* (University of Wisconsin Press, 1975). James Searing, 'Aristocrats, Slaves and Peasants: Power and Dependency in the Wolof States 1700–1850', *IJAHS*, XXI (1988) is very useful. On the Mossi-Volta section of the savanna (Upper Volta-Ghana), see Nehemiah Levtzion, *Muslims and Chiefs in West Africa* (Clarendon Press, 1968) and Michel Izard, *Introduction à l'histoire du royaume mossi* (Centre National des Recherches Scientifiques, 2 vols, 1970). On the central savanna, H. F. C. Smith, 'The Beginnings of Hausa Society' in Jan Vansina, Raymond Mauny and L. V.

Thomas, eds, *The Historian in Tropical Africa* (Oxford University Press, 1964) is still thought-provoking. So is Nicole Echard, *L'Experience du passé; ethno-histoire de l'Ader haoussa* (Paris, 1972). The best introduction to the most famous *jihad* state is Murray Last, *The Sokoto Caliphate* (Longman, 1967). See also his 'Administration and Dissent in Hausaland', *Africa*, XL (1970); Marilyn Waldman, 'The Fulani jihad: a Reassessment', *JAH*, VI (1965); M. G. Smith, *Government in Zazzau, 1800–1950* (Oxford University Press, 1960); Michael Mason, 'Captive and Client Labour and the Economy of Bida Emirate, 1857–1901', *JAH*, XIV (1973).

On post-*jihad* society in western West Africa, there are several stimulating articles: Youssouf Guèye, 'Essai sur les causes et les conséquences de la micropropriété au Fouta Toro', *Bulletin de l'Institut Français de l'Afrique Noire*, série B, XIX (1957); Walter Rodney, 'Jihad and Social Revolution in Eighteenth Century Futa Djallon', *JHSN*, IV (1968); Roger Botte, 'Révolte, pouvoir, réligion; les Hubbu du Futa Djallon', *JAH*, XXIX (1988); Marion Johnson, 'The Economic Foundations of an Islamic Theocracy – the Case of Masina', *JAH*, XVII (1976) and Richard Roberts, 'Production and Reproduction of Warrior States: Segu Bambara and Segu Tukolor', *IJAHS*, XIII (1980).

Standard treatments of major states in the forest and adjacent West African forest include Ivor Wilks, *Asante in the Nineteenth Century* (Cambridge University Press, 1975) and Robin Law, *The Oyo Empire, c. 1600–1836* (Clarendon Press, 1977). See also Kwame Arhin, 'Trade, Accumulation and the State in Asante in the Nineteenth Century', *Africa*, LX (1990) and Simi Afonja, 'Changing Modes of Production and the Sexual Divisions of Labour among the Yoruba', *Signs*, VII (1981). On Yoruba culture see Frank Willett, *Ife in the History of West African Art* (McGraw-Hill, 1967). Raymond Dumett, 'Precolonial Mining and the State in the Akan Region' considers the Terray thesis empirically in George Dalton, ed., *Research in Economic Anthropology* (2), 1979. Terray's *magnum opus* is now available: *Une histoire de royaume abron de Gyaman* (Karthala, 1995). On a similar theme for an area to the west, B. Marie Perinbam, 'Political Organization of Traditional Gold Mining: The Western Loby c. 1850–c. 1910, *JAH*, XXIX (1988) is a convincing study. On West African states generally there is an interesting if technicist hypothesis in Jack Goody, *Technology, Tradition and the State* (Oxford University Press, 1971).

The most vigorous debate about forest societies has centred on the state of Dahomey. Much of the discussion focuses on a period when the Atlantic slave trade was already of great significance, yet it is relevant to this chapter. See Melville Herskovits, *Dahomey* (J. J. Augustin, 1938); Karl Polanyi, *Dahomey and the Slave Trade* (University of Washington Press, 1966); I. Akinjogbin, *Dahomey and its Neighbours* (Cambridge University Press, 1967); Georg Elwert, *Wirtschaft und Herrschaft von 'Daxome' (Dahomey) in 18. jahrhundert*, (Renner, Munich, 1973); Robin Law, 'Royal Monopoly and Private Enterprise in the Atlantic Trade: the Case of Dahomey', *JAH*, XVI (1975) and *The Slave Coast of West Africa 1550–1750* (Clarendon Press, 1990); K. Moseley, 'The Political Economy of Dahomey' in George Dalton, ed., *Research in Economic Anthropology* (2), 1979. The same can be said of

Robin Horton, 'From Fishing-Village to City-State: A Social History of New Calabar' in Mary Douglas and Phyllis Kaberry, eds, *Man in Africa* (Tavistock, 1969). The main lines of early Ethiopian history are traced in Taddesse Tamrat, *Church and State in Ethiopia 1270–1527* (Clarendon Press, 1972) and, for an earlier period yet, Yurii Kobishchanov, *Axum* (Pennsylvania State University Press, 1979). A very useful assessment of much relevant literature is available in Donald Crummey, 'Society, State and Nationality in the Recent Historiography of Ethiopia', *JAH*, XXXI (1990). A feel for class society in Ethiopia emerges from Richard Caulk, 'Armies as Predators: Soldiers and Peasants in Ethiopia, *c. 1850–1935*', *IJAHS*, XI (1978). Allen Hoben, *Land Tenure among the Amhara of Ethiopia* (University of Chicago Press, 1973), is a useful contemporary study of economic and social relations in the Ethiopian highlands. James McCann is planning a more comprehensive agrarian history of Ethiopia. On the region of the modern Sudan, R. S. O'Fahey and J. L. Spaulding, *Kingdoms of the Sudan* (Methuen, 1974) on Sennar and Dar Fur; Anders Bjorkelo, *A Prelude to the Mahdiyya; Peasants and Traders in the Shendi Region 1821–88*, (Cambridge University Press, 1988) and Lidwein Kapteins, 'The Historiography of the Northern Sudan from 1500 to the Establishment of British Colonial Rule; A Critical Overview', *IJAHS*, XXII (1989) are all important.

A large swathe of African history is surveyed in the two-volume *History of Central Africa*, edited by David Birmingham and Phyllis Martin (Longman, 1983–) which begins with material relevant to this chapter. Jan Vansina, *Kingdoms of the Savanna* (University of Wisconsin Press, 1966), and *Paths in the Rainforest* (University of Wisconsin Press, 1990) are introductions to the southern savanna and forest regions respectively. The most useful monographs on the history of this area include: Georges Balandier, *Daily Life in the Kingdom of the Kongo* (George Allen & Unwin, 1968); W. G. L. Randles, *L'ancien royaume du Congo dès origines à la fin du XIXe siècle* (Mouton, 1968); Joseph Miller, *Kings and Kinsmen* (Clarendon Press, 1976); Andrew Roberts, *History of the Bemba* (Longman, 1973); Mutumba Mainga, *Bulozi under the Luyana Kings* (Longman, 1973) and Thomas Reefe, *The Rainbow and the Kings; a History of the Luba Empire to 1891* (University of California Press, 1981). More concerned with social structure are John Thornton, *The Kingdom of the Kongo; Civil War and Transition 1641–1718*, (University of Wisconsin Press, 1983) and W. G. Clarence-Smith, 'Slaves, Commoners and Landlords in Bulozi, 1875–1906', *JAH*, XX (1979). For the states south of the Zambesi, the reader turns to D. N. Beach, *The Shona and Zimbabwe, 900–1850* (Africana, 1980).

The first essays in Shula Marks and Anthony Atmore, eds, *Economy and Society in Pre-Industrial South Africa* (Longman, 1980) consider pre-conquest South Africa. The standard history of the *Mfecane*, now badly in need of reinterpretation, is J. Omer-Cooper, *The Zulu Aftermath* (Longman, 1965). For one *Mfecane* state, see J. Cobbing, 'Evolution of the Ndebele amabutho', *JAH*, XV (1974). One contributor to Marks and Atmore, Jeff Guy, has also considered Zulu society in a full-length book, *The Destruction of the Zulu Kingdom* (Longman, 1979). For foraging and especially pastoral communities, Richard Elphick, *Kraal and Castle* (Yale University Press, 1977) is valuable. Guy's 'Analysing Pre-capitalist Societies in Southern Africa', *JSAS*, XIV (1987) is most useful.

An early attempt to synthesise pre-colonial East African history is made in Gervase Matthew and Roland Oliver, eds, *History of East Africa*, I (Clarendon Press, 1963). Two continually cited studies of inter-lacustrine states are Semakula Kiwanuka, *A History of Buganda* (Longman, 1971) and S. R. Karugire, *History of Nkore in Western Uganda to 1891* (Clarendon, 1971). Other treatments of East African states are Steven Feierman, *The Shambaa Kingdom* (University of Wisconsin Press, 1974) and R. G. Willis, *A State in the Making* (Indiana University Press, 1980). Rwanda has been assessed by many writers; some of the most interesting pages on it are to be found in a special issue of the *CEA* XIV (1974). This includes the class analysis of Claudine Vidal, 'Economie de la société féodale rwandaise'. Some of the more successful attempts to recreate the history of peoples without state institutions have been made in East Africa. These include B. A. Ogot's path-breaking *History of the Southern Luo* (East African Publishing House, henceforth EAPH, 1967); Godfrey Muriuki, *History of the Kikuyu 1500-1900* (Oxford University Press, 1974) and John Lamphear, *Traditional History of the Jie* (Oxford University Press, 1976). Descriptions of early trade within eastern, southern and south-central Africa are to be found in Richard Gray and David Birmingham, eds, *Precolonial African Trade* (Macmillan, 1970). For Madagascar, see Gerald Berg, 'Riziculture and the Founding of the Monarchy in Imerina', *JAH*, XXII (1981) and Gwyn Campbell, 'Slavery and Fanompoana: The Structure of Forced Labour in Imerina 1790-1861', *JAH*, XXIX (1988).

## 3 The European Intrusion in the Era of Merchant Capital

The slave trade has inspired a large literature, much of it concerned with quantitative analysis only. Basil Davidson, *Black Mother* (Little, Brown, 1961) is a moving introduction; a more recent survey is M. Craton, *Sinews of Empire* (Doubleday Anchor Books, 1974). Philip Curtin has drawn an effective, short picture based on the history of the sugar industry in his chapter in Ajayi and Crowder, *History of West Africa*, 1, already cited; Walter Rodney provided a strong, brief summary in a pamphlet published by the Historical Association of Tanzania in 1967 entitled *West Africa and the Atlantic Slave Trade*. Curtin's slave-counting exercise, *The Atlantic Slave Trade: A Census* (University of Wisconsin Press, 1969) is most valuable for its demonstration of the ebb and flow of the trade and the relative importance in it of different parts of Africa. More recent research is collected in Henry Gemery and Jan Hogendorn, eds, *The Uncommon Market*, (Academic Press, 1979) and J. E. Inikori, ed., *Forced Migration*, (Hutchinson, 1981).

On chartered slave trade companies, see Abdoulaye Ly, *La compagnie du Sénégal* (Présence Africaine, 1958) and K. G. Davies, *The Royal African Company* (Longman,

1957). Other aspects of the trade are discussed in Walter Rodney, 'Gold and Slaves on the Gold Coast', *Transactions of the Historical Society of Ghana*, X (1969) and Marion Johnson, 'The Ounce in Eighteenth Century West African Trade', *JAH*, VI (1966). The new American crops introduced during this period are surveyed in William O. Jones, *Manioc in Africa* (Stanford University Press, 1959) and Marvin Miracle, *Maize in Tropical Africa* (University of Wisconsin Press, 1966). Michael Mason, 'Population Density and "Slave Raiding" – the Case of the Middle Belt', *JAH*, X (1969) and Jean-Pierre Warnier, 'Traite sans raids au Cameroun', *CEA*, 113 (1989) are striking and surprising accounts of the local impacts of slaving on important source areas.

A large and important literature on the slave trade, slavery and the rise of industrial capitalism was born with Eric Williams' classic, *Capitalism and Slavery*; this does not really belong to the sphere of African history, however. On the general impact of slaving in Africa see J. D. Fage, 'Slavery and the Slave Trade in the Context of West African History', *JAH*, X (1969), the important rejoinder by C. C. Wrigley, 'Historicism in Africa: Slavery and Slave Formation', *AA*, LXX (1971) and Walter Rodney, 'African Slavery and other Forms of Social Oppression on the Upper Guinea Coast in the Context of the Atlantic Slave Trade', *JAH*, VII (1966). A recent anti-dependency polemic is contributed by John Thornton, 'Precolonial African Industry and the Atlantic Trade 1500–1800', *AEH*, 16 (1987).

Standard histories of French involvement in the Senegambia are André Delcourt, *La France et les établissements français au Sénégal entre 1713 et 1763* (Institut Français de l'Afrique Noire, Mémoire 17, 1952) and Léonce Jore, 'Les établissements français sur la côte occidentale d'Afrique 1758 à 1803', *Revue française d'histoire d'outre-mer*, LI (1964). The impact on African society receives attention in Philip Curtin, *Economic Change in Pre-colonial Africa*, Boubacar Barry, *Le royaume de Waalo*, (Maspero, 1972) and Abdoulaye Bathily, 'La traite atlantique des esclaves et ses effets sociaux et économiques en Afrique: le cas de Galam au XIXe siècle', *JAH*, XXVII (1986). The region between the Gambia and present-day Liberia is the subject of Walter Rodney, *A History of the Upper Guinea Coast, 1545–1800* (Clarendon Press, 1970). For the Gold Coast, there is John Vogt, *Portuguese Rule on the Gold Coast* (University of Georgia Press, 1979), Kwame Daaku, *Trade and Politics on the Gold Coast, 1600–1720* (Clarendon Press, 1970) and Ray Kea, *Settlements, Trade and Politics in the Seventeenth-century Gold Coast* (John Hopkins Press, 1982).

Most of the books cited in the last chapter on the forest states of West Africa treat the slave trade. See as well: A. F. C. Ryder, *Benin and the Europeans, 1485–1897* (Longman 1969); James Graham, 'Slave Trade, Depopulation and Human Sacrifice in Benin History', *CEA*, V (1965); P. Morton-Williams, 'The Oyo Yoruba and the Atlantic Trade,' *JHSN*, III (1964); Toyin Falola, 'Power Relations and Social Interactions among Ibadan Slaves 1850–1900', *AEH*, 16 (1987); Kwame Arhin, 'The Financing of Ashanti Expansion, 1700–1820', *Africa*, XXXVII (1967) and Pierre Verger, *Trade Relations Between the Bight of Benin and Bahia 17th–19th Centuries*, (Ibadan University Press, 1976). On the impact of the slave trade in the Niger delta, the most important work is contained in E. J. Alagoa, 'Long Distance Trade and States in the Niger Delta', *JAH*, XI (1970); David Northrup, 'The Growth of Trade among the Igbo Before 1800', *JAH*, XIII (1972) and A. J. H. Latham, *Old Calabar, 1600–1891* (Clarendon Press, 1971).

For Angola, there is now a massive study in the form of Joseph Miller, *The Way of Death; Merchant Capitalism and the Angolan Slave Trade 1730–1830* (James Currey, 1988). See as well David Birmingham, *Trade and Conflict in Angola* (Clarendon Press, 1966) and Joseph Miller, 'Lineages, Ideology and the History of Slavery in Western Central Africa' in Paul Lovejoy, ed., *Ideologies of Slavery in Africa* (Sage, 1982) Standard histories of Kongo cited previously are by Georges Balandier and W. G. L. Randles. The work of revision and reinvestigation has begun with John Thornton, 'Demography and History in the Kingdom of Kongo, 1550–1750', *JAH*, XVIII (1977). For the region north of the River Zaïre, see Phyllis Martin, *The External Trade of the Loango Coast, 1576–1870*, (Clarendon Press, 1972).

For the Zambesi and the region to the north of it, the most important studies are: M. D. D. Newitt, *Portuguese Settlement on the Zambesi* (Longman, 1973); Allen Isaacman, *Mozambique; the Africanization of a European Institution* (University of Wisconsin Press, 1972) and Edward Alpers, *Ivory and Slaves in East Central Africa* (Heinemann, 1975).

On South Africa under the Dutch, Richard Elphick and Hermann Giliomee, eds, *The Shaping of South African Society, 1652–1840* (Maskew Miller Longman, 1989) and Nigel Worden, *Slavery in Dutch South Africa* (Cambridge University Press, 1985) are major sources.

## 4  The Era of Legitimate Commerce, 1800–70

A general overview of the issues discussed in this chapter can be found in Martin Klein, 'Slavery, the Slave Trade and Legitimate Commerce in Late Nineteenth-Century Africa', *Études d'histoire africaine* 11 (1971). On the abolition of slavery and the slave trade the reader can still profit by consulting Eric Williams, *Capitalism and Slavery* (Capricorn, 1944), but empiricist critiques require consideration, notably Roger Anstey, *The Atlantic Slave Trade and British Abolition, 1760–1810* (Humanities Press, 1975) and Seymour Drescher, *Econocide* (University of Pittsburgh Press, 1977). A major reinterpretation of the link between political conflict and abolition is the thrust of Robin Blackburn, *The Overthrow of Colonial Slavery 1776–1848* (Verso, 1988).

Nineteenth-century West Africa is covered by numerous economic historians but, as with other areas, few works are limited exclusively to this period of history. One with its strongest pages on the nineteenth century is A. G. Hopkins, *Economic History of West Africa* (Longman, 1973). A very informative economic study is David Eltis and Lawrence Jennings, 'Trade Between Western Africa and the Atlantic

World in the Pre-colonial Era', *American Historical Review*, XCIII (1988). Of note are the relevant articles in Claude Meillassoux, ed., *The Development of Indigenous Trade and Markets in West Africa* (Oxford University Press, 1971) and the economic studies of Colin Newbury such as 'Trade and Authority in West Africa from 1850 to 1880' in Lewis Gann and Peter Duignan, eds, *Colonialism in Africa*, I (Cambridge University Press, 1969).

For this epoch in Senegambia, the reader should consult the relevant pages in Barry and Curtin's studies cited earlier. Aspects of the impact of ground-nut exports are discussed in Ken Swindell, 'Serawoolies, Tillibunkas and Strange Farmers: Development of Migrant Groundnut Farming along the Gambia River, 1848–95', *JAH*, XXI (1980) and George Brooks, 'Peanuts and Colonialism: Consequences of the Commercialization of Peanuts in West Africa, 1830–70', *JAH*, XVI (1975). For another commodity see James Webb, 'The Trade in Gum Arabic', *JAH*, XXVI (1985).

On Sierra Leone there is Leo Spitzer, *The Creoles of Sierra Leone* (University of Wisconsin Press, 1974) and Allen Howard and David Skinner, 'Network Building and Political Power in North-west Sierra Leone 1800–65', *Africa*, LIV (1985). Magdalene Davis, 'The Love of Liberty Brought Us Here', *Review of African Political Economy*, 31 (1984) provides an analytical introduction to Liberia. For the Gold Coast in this period see Edward Reynolds, *Trade and Economic Change on the Gold Coast, 1807–74* (Longman, 1974). Freda Wolfson, 'A Price Agreement on the Gold Coast Krobo Oil Boycott, 1858–65', *Economic History Review*, VI (1953) is worth a look.

The Saros in Yoruba-speaking lands are the subject of Jean Herskovits Kopytoff, *A Preface to Modern Nigeria* (University of Wisconsin Press, 1965). The strengths and limitations of their position in Abeokuta, the greatest Saro centre inland from the coast, is central to Agneta Pallinder-Law, 'Aborted Modernization in West Africa? The Case of Abeokuta', *JAH*, XV (1974).

On other political and economic aspects of nineteenth-century Yorubaland, the more significant titles would include: S. A. Akintoye, *Revolution and Power Politics in Yorubaland, 1840–83* (Longman, 1971); Bolanle Awe, 'Militarism and Economic Development in Nineteenth-Century Yoruba Country–the Ibadan Example', *JAH*, XIV (1973); Babatunde Agiri, 'Slavery in Yoruba Society in the Nineteenth Century' in Paul Lovejoy, ed., *The Ideology of Slavery in Africa* (Sage, 1981); E. A. Ayandele, *The Missionary Impact on Modern Nigeria, 1842–1914* (Longman, 1966) and T. G. O. Gbadamosi, *The Growth of Islam among the Yoruba, 1841–1908* (Longman, 1978).

The Niger delta region is examined in K. O. Dike, *Trade and Politics in the Niger Delta, 1830–85* (Clarendon Press, 1956); G. I. Jones, *Trading States of the Oil Rivers* (Oxford University Press, 1963); Obaro Ikime, *Merchant Prince of the Niger Delta* (Heinemann, 1968). More recent and analytically the most valuable are A. J. H. Latham, *Old Calabar 1600–1891* (Clarendon Press, 1973) and David Northrup, *Trade Without Rulers* (Clarendon Press, 1978). A. E. Afigbo, *Ropes of Sand; Studies in Igbo History and Culture*, (University of Nigeria Press, 1981) also takes the story further.

A number of family and individual studies of the coastal compradore class exist. They include Raymond Dumett, 'John Sarbah the Elder and African Merchant Entrepreneurship in the Gold Coast in the Late Nineteenth Century', *JAH*, XIV (1973); A. G. Hopkins, 'Richard Beale Blaize, 1854–1904', *Tarikh*, I (1966); David Ross, 'The Career of Domingo Martinez in the Bight of Benin, 1853–64', *JAH*, VI (1965); and Margaret Priestley, *West African Trade and Coast Society* (Oxford University Press, 1969). A class perspective is suggested in Edward Reynolds, 'Rise and Fall of an African Merchant Class on the Gold Coast, 1830–70', *CEA*, X (1974) and developed in Susan Kaplow, 'The Mudfish and the Crocodile', *Science and Society*, XLI (1977).

The *jihad* movements, covered in the last chapter's bibliography, dominate the historiography of the savanna region of West Africa for the nineteenth century. This rubric does not, however, really fit the empire-builder Samori, whose career is studied in three volumes by Yves Person, *Samori, une révolution dyoula* (Institut Fondamentale de l'Afrique Noire, 1968–75). A summary of French colonial intentions during this era, exclusive of Senegal, is contained in Bernard Schnapper, *La politique et le commerce français dans le golfe de Guinée de 1838 à 1871* (Mouton, 1961).

For East and Central Africa, this chapter relies on books covered in other chapter bibliographies, including work by Iliffe, Andrew Roberts, D. A. Low, W. G. Clarence-Smith and J. Forbes Munro. The nineteenth century looms large in Richard Grey and David Birmingham, eds, *Pre-colonial African Trade*, already cited. Zanzibari history is surveyed in Abdul Sheriff, *Slaves, Spices and Ivory in Zanzibar*, (James Currey, Ohio University Press, Heinemann & Tanzania Publishing House, 1987). There is an excellent study of the slave plantations on the Kenya coast and the island of Zanzibar by Frederick Cooper, *Plantation Slavery in Kenya and Zanzibar* (Yale University Press, 1977) and an interesting piece on the dislocations in East African women's lives: Marcia Wright, 'Women in Peril', *African Social Research*, XX (1975). The immediate interior away from the Indian Ocean coast is the subject of Thomas Herlihy's 'Ties that Bind; Palm Wine and Blood Brotherhood at the Kenya Coast during the Nineteenth Century', *IJAHS*, XVII (1984). On the Lake Malawi region, see Harry Langworthy, 'Central Malawi in the Nineteenth Century' in R. J. Macdonald, *From Nyasaland to Malawi* (EAPH, 1975) and Leroy Vail, 'Suggestions Towards a Reinterpreted Tumbuka History' in B. Pachai, *The Early History of Malawi* (Longman, 1972). Tippu Tip's memoirs are available in Swahili and English: *Maisha ya Hamed bin Muhammad yaani Tippu Tip* (reprint of Edward Arnold edn, Nairobi, 1966). On the Zambesi valley in the nineteenth century, sources cited elsewhere – Newitt, Isaacman, Vail and White, are the most helpful. For Angola there is in particular Clarence-Smith's *Slaves, Peasants and Capitalists in Southern Angola* (Cambridge University Press, 1979) and David Birmingham, 'The Coffee Barons of Cazengo', *JAH*, XIX (1978).

Davenport's general history is a passable detailed introduction to nineteenth-century South African events and provides a useful bibliography. Among older works still of interest, C.W. de Kiewiet, *The Imperial Factor in South Africa* (Cambridge

University Press, 1937) and J. S. Galbraith, *Reluctant Empire* (University of California Press, 1963) are prominent. David Welsh, *The Roots of Segregation: Native Policy in Colonial Natal, 1845–1910* (Oxford University Press, 1970) can still be consulted. Patrick Harries, 'Plantations, Passes and Proletarians: Labour and the Colonial State in Nineteenth Century Natal', *JSAS* XIII (1987) is an important supplement. There is a major revisionist interpretation of the imperial factor: Anthony Atmore and Shula Marks, 'The Imperial Factor in South Africa in the Nineteenth Century: Towards a Reassessment', *Journal of Imperial and Commonwealth History*, III (1974). The most influential and exciting research of the 1970s is collected in a book edited by the same pair, *Economy and Society in Pre-industrial South Africa* (Longman, 1980). Two of the contributors have produced relevant books, Jeff Guy writing on the Zulu, cited elsewhere and Colin Bundy, *Rise and Fall of the South African Peasantry* (University of California Press, 1979). An important corrective to Bundy is Jack Lewis, 'The Rise and Fall of the South African Peasantry: A Critique and a Reassessment,' *JSAS*, XI (1984) while Timothy Keegan demonstrates the limits of the peasant prosperity thesis in 'Trade, Accumulation and Impoverishment: Mercantile Capital and the Economic Transformation of Lesotho and the Conquered Territory.' *JSAS*, XII (1986). Another aspect is traced by Charles Ballard, 'Repercussions of Rinderpest: Cattle Plague and Peasant Decline in Colonial Natal', *IJAHS*, XIX (1986). An earlier disaster is the subject of J. B. Peires' eloquent *The Dead Will Arise; Nongqawuse and the Great Xhosa Cattle-Killing Movement of 1856–57* (Ravan Press, Indiana University Press & James Currey, 1989). For an original look at the confrontation of white settlement and black interest in the new economy see Keletso Atkins, *The Moon is Dead; Give Us Our Money!* (Heinemann & James Currey, 1994). Of a number of articles on the emergent African entrepreneurial class, Norman Etherington, 'Mission Station Melting Pots as a Factor in the Rise of South African Black Nationalism', *International Journal of African Historical Studies*, IX (1976) is an interesting example. The post-emancipation fate of the western Cape is discussed in Nigel Worden and Clifford Crais, eds, *Breaking the Chains; Slavery and Its Legacy in the Nineteenth Century Cape Colony*, (Witwatersrand University Press, 1994) and Hermann Giliomee, 'Western Cape Farmers and the Beginnings of Afrikaner Nationalism 1870–1915', *JSAS*, XIV (1987). For the transition at Kimberley towards more revolutionary changes in South African society, there are two excellent monographs to consult: Robert Turrell, *Capital and Labour on the Kimberley Diamond Fields 1871–90* (Cambridge University Press, 1987) and William Worger, *South Africa's City of Diamonds; Mine Workers and Monopoly Capitalism in Kimberley 1867–95* (Yale University Press, 1987).

Another region with a fairly well-developed historiography for the nineteenth century is the Ethiopian plateau; it is, however, largely political and dynastic in character. This is the case with Sven Rubenson, *The Survival of Ethiopian Independence* (Heinemann, 1976); R. H. Kofi Darkwah, *Shewa, Menilek and the Ethiopian Empire, 1813–89* (Heinemann, 1975) and Zewde Gebre-Selassie, *Yohannis IV of Ethiopia* (Clarendon Press, 1975). Social and economic considerations have some purchase on Mordechai Abir, *Ethiopia: the Era of the Princes* (Longman, 1968); Donald Crummey, 'Initiatives and Objectives in Ethio-European Relations, 1827–62', *JAH*, XV (1974) and 'Tewodros as Reformer and Modernizer', *JAH*, X (1969). On the Horn of Africa in the legitimate trade era, Edward Alpers, 'Muqdisho in the Nineteenth Century', *JAH*, XXIV (1983) and Lee Casanelli, *The Shaping of Somali Society*, (University of Pennsylvania Press, 1982) make a good beginning. The standard work on Egyptian rule along the middle Nile is Richard Hill, *Egypt in the Sudan, 1820–81* (Oxford University Press, 1959). For Madagascar, the political and economic side are usefully examined in the published articles of Gwyn Campbell, notably 'Madagascar and the Slave Trade 1810–95', *JAH*, XXII (1981); 'Missionaries, Fanompoana and the Menalamba Revolt in Late Nineteenth Century Madagascar', *JSAS*, XIV (1987) and 'An Industrial Experiment in Pre-colonial Africa: The Case of Imperial Madagascar', *JSAS*, XVII (1991). However, the whole cultural context of Christianisation and political change is also the subject of the magisterial work of Françoise Raison-Jourde, *Le Bible et le pouvoir à Madagascar au XIXe siècle*, (Karthala, 1991). She has also written the important essays in *Les souverains de Madagascar*, (Karthala, 1983).

## 5   The Conquest of Africa

For a general view of imperialism by a Marxist contemporary, V. I. Lenin, *Imperialism: the Highest Stage of Capitalism* (International Publishers edn., 1939) remains compelling. On very similar lines, see Nikolai Bukharin, *Imperialism and World Economy* (Merlin Press edn., 1971). John Hobson, *Imperialism: A Study* repays examination. This is also true of the work of other contemporary thinkers, such as Rosa Luxemburg. For recent critical assessments, the most significant used here are the excellent edited collection by Bob Sutcliffe and Roger Owen, *Studies in the Theory of Imperialism* (Longman, 1972); V. G. Kiernan, *Marxism and Imperialism*, (St Martin's Press, 1975); Anthony Brewer, *Marxist Theories of Imperialism* (Routledge & Kegan Paul, 1980) and Bill Warren, *Imperialism: Pioneer of Capitalism* (New Left Books, 1981).

Important examples of the anti-economic (and anti-Marxist) school of imperialist historians are Ronald Robinson and John Gallagher, with Alice Denny, *Africa and the Victorians* (St Martin's Press, 1961) and David Fieldhouse, *Economics and Empire 1830–1914* (Weidenfeld & Nicolson, 1973). Weighty collections generally following this line of thought are to be found in Prosser Gifford and William Roger Louis, eds, *Britain and France in Africa* and *Britain and Germany in Africa* (both Yale University Press, 1967 and 1971) and Lewis Gann and Peter Duignan, eds, *Colonialism in Africa*, already cited, Vol. I. There is a more balanced interpretation in George Sanderson, 'The European Partition of Africa: Coincidence or Conjuncture', in E. F. Penrose, ed., *European Imperialism and the Partition of Africa* (Cass, 1975) and a novel and important analysis in A. G. Hopkins, *An Economic History of West Africa*, already cited. For a French equivalent to the anti-Marxist British school, see Henri Brunschwig, *French Colonialism 1871–1914: Myths and Realities* (Pall Mall, 1961). The diplomatic history of the scramble is surveyed in a broader context of European power politics in W. L. Langer, *European Alliances and Alignments, 1871– 90 and The Diplomacy of Imperialism, 1890–1902* (Alfred A. Knopf, 2nd edns., 1950 and 1951)

For the material foundation of British imperialism, see Eric J. Hobsbawm, *Industry and Empire* (Weidenfeld & Nicolson, 1968) and P. J. Cain and A. G. Hopkins, 'The Political Economy of British Expansion Overseas, 1750–1914', *EHR*, XXXIII, N.S. (1980). These two authors have also recently produced a new general interpretation to try and combine the economic and non-economic schools in a new synthesis: *British Imperialism, Innovation and Expansion 1688–1914* and *Crisis and Deconstruction 1914–90*, (Longman, 1993). The social context is explored in Bernard Semmel, *Imperialism and Social Reform* (Harvard University Press, 1960) and Richard Price, *An Imperial War and the British Working Class* (Routledge & Kegan Paul, 1972). A different side of imperialism is approached in John MacKenzie, *Imperialism and the Natural World*, (Manchester University Press, 1990).

On France see C. M. Andrew and A. S. Kanya-Forstner, 'The French Colonial Party: Its Composition, Aims and Influence', *HJ*, XIV (1971) and John Laffey, 'The Roots of French Imperialism in the Nineteenth Century: The Case of Lyon', *French Historical Studies*, VI (1969/70). Colin Newbury has written several pieces on the impact of French protectionism such as 'The Protectionist Revival in French Colonial Trade: The Case of Senegal', *EHR*, N.S. XXI (1968) For a provocative and important reinterpretation, see Jacques Marseille, *Empire colonial et capitalisme français; histoire d'un divorce*, (Albin Michel, 1984).

There is a large literature on the imperialism of the Second Reich. Major works include Fritz Ferdinand Müller, *Deutschland–Ostafrika–Zanzibar* (Rutten und Loening, East Berlin, 1959); Manfred Nussbaum, *Vom 'Kolonialenthusiasmus' zur Kolonialpolitik der Monopole* (Akadamieverlag, East Berlin, 1962) and Hans-Ulrich Wehler, *Bismarck und der Imperialismus* (Kiepenheuer und Witsch, 1969). Wehler's ideas are summarised in the Owen and Sutcliffe collection and criticised in Gifford and Louis by Henry Turner.

Neal Ascherson, *The King Incorporated* (George Allen & Unwin, 1963) tells well the story of Leopold II; there is no general adequate history of his machinations. For the narrative of Portuguese expansion, see Eric Axelson, *Portugal and the Scramble for Africa* (Witwatersrand University Press, 1967) and R. J. Hammond, *Portugal and Africa, 1815–1910* (Stanford University Press, 1966), but also the significant revision, W. G. Clarence-Smith, 'The Myth of Uneconomic Imperialism: The Portuguese in Angola', *JSAS*, V, 1979.

Issues relating to medicine and ideology are handled in Philip Curtin, *The Image of Africa* (University of Wisconsin Press, 1964) and the technological aspect of expansionism in Daniel Headrick, *The Tools of Empire* (Oxford University Press,

1981). There are rather flattering biographies of a number of the major African conquistadores such as Margery Perham, *Lugard* (Collins, 2 vols, 1956–60); J. E. Flint, *Sir George Goldie and the Making of Nigeria* (Clarendon Press, 1960) and Roland Oliver, *Sir Henry Johnston and the Scramble for Africa* (Chatto & Windus, 1964). On a major business figure within British imperialism, see John S. Galbraith, *Mackinnon and East Africa, 1878–95* (Cambridge University Press, 1972).

The conquest of West Africa is considered generally in John D. Hargreaves, *Prelude to the Partition of Africa* (Macmillan, 1963) and *West Africa Partitioned: The Loaded Pause* (University of Wisconsin Press, 1974); Obaro Ikime, *The Fall of Nigeria* (Heinemann, 1977) and Michael Crowder, ed., *West African Resistance* (Hutchinson, 1971). There is a valuable set of volumes collecting primary source material in C. W. Newbury, *British Policy Towards West Africa: Select Documents* (Clarendon, 1965–71). The context of conquest in southern Nigeria is considered in: S. A. Akintoye, *Revolution and Power Politics in Yorubaland, 1840–1893*, cited previously; Bolanle Awe, 'The End of an Experiment: The Collapse of the Ibadan Empire 1877–93', *JHSN*, III (1965); Walter Ofonagoro, *Trade and Imperialism in Southern Nigeria, 1881–1929* (Nok, 1979); S. J. S. Cookey, *King JaJa of the Niger Delta* (Nok, 1974) and A. E. Afigbo, 'Patterns of Igbo Resistance to British Conquest', *Tarikh*, IV (1973). A. G. Hopkins, 'Economic Imperialism in West Africa: Lagos 1880–92', *EHR*, N.S., XXI (1968) is of seminal importance. The lands to the west of Lagos, including Dahomey, are the subject of C. W. Newbury, *The Western Slave Coast and its Rulers* (Clarendon Press, 1961). A Beninois historian, Luc Garcia, has written *Le royaume Dahomé face à la pénétration coloniale* (Karthala, 1988). For northern Nigeria the main study of the conquest is Roland Adeleye, *Power and Diplomacy in Northern Nigeria, 1804–1906* (Longman, 1971).

For the conquest of contemporary Ghana see Adu Boahen, 'Politics in Ghana, 1800–74' in Ajayi and Crowder, *History of West Africa*, II, cited already and Thomas Lewin, *Asante Before the British; the Prempean Years, 1875–1900* (Regents Press of Kansas, 1978). Some of the economic context emerges from Kwame Arhin, 'Ashanti Rubber Trade in the 1890s', *Africa*, XLII (1972) and Raymond Dumett, 'The Rubber Trade of the Gold Coast and Asante in the Nineteenth Century', *JAH*, XII (1971).

Considerations of the French intrusion in West Africa are in A. S. Kanya-Forstner, *The Conquest of the Western Sudan* (Cambridge University Press, 1969); Martin Klein, *Islam and Imperialism in Senegal* (Stanford University Press, 1968), Mamadou Diouf, *Le Kayoor au XIXe siècle; pouvoir ceddo et conquête coloniale*, (Karthala, 1990); Jeanne-Marie Kambou-Ferrand, *Peuples voltaïques et conquête coloniale 1885–1915* (Harmattan, 1993) and Yehoshuah Rash, *Les premières années françaises du Damergou; des colonisateurs sans enthousiasme* (P. Geuthner, Paris, 1973). Klein, Diouf and Kambou-Ferrand focus on the African experience as does Timothy Weiskel, *French Colonial Rule and the Baule Peoples* (Clarendon Press, 1980).

The study of imperialism in East Africa is less well developed. David Arnold, 'External Factors in the Partition of East Africa' read with A. J. Temu, 'Tanzanian

Societies and Colonial Invasion, 1875–1907' in Martin Kaniki, ed., *Tanzania under Colonial Rule* (Longman, 1980) makes a serviceable introduction. The special circumstances of Buganda are discussed in D. A. Low, *Buganda in Modern History* (University of California Press, 1971); C. C. Wrigley, 'The Christian Revolution in Buganda', *Comparative Studies in Society and History*, II (1959) and John Rowe, 'The Purge of Christians at Mwanga's Court', *JAH*, V (1964). There is a survey of British involvement in Nyasaland in A. J. Hanna, *The Beginnings of Nyasaland and Northern Rhodesia 1858–95* (Clarendon Press, 1956).

For north-east Africa, the struggle over Ethiopia is treated in Harold Marcus, *The Life and Times of Menelik II: Ethiopia, 1844–1913* (Clarendon Press, 1975) and Sven Rubenson, 'Adwa: The Resounding Protest' in Robert Rotberg and Ali Mazrui, eds, *Protest and Power in Black Africa* (Oxford University Press, New York, 1970). For the Islamic revolution in the Sudan, see P. M. Holt, *The Mahdist State in the Sudan 1881–1898* (Clarendon Press, 1958). The race to the Nile is covered in G. Sanderson, *England, Europe and the Upper Nile, 1882–1899* (Edinburgh University Press, 1965) and Marc Michel, *La mission Marchand* (Mouton, 1972). For the English-speaking reader, a clear introduction to the conquest of Madagascar is Phares Mutibwa, *The Malagasy and the Europeans; Madagascar's Foreign Relations, 1861–1895* (Longman, 1974). See also Steven Ellis, *The Rising of the Red Shawls* (Cambridge University Press, 1985), which can be read parallel to the next paragraph references.

On resistance to the European conquest of East Africa, studies include G. H. Mungeam, 'Masai and Kikuyu Responses to the Establishment of British Administration in the East Africa Protectorate', *JAH*, XI (1970); J. M. Lonsdale, 'The Politics of Conquest: The British in Kenya, 1894–1908', *HJ*, XX (1977), Edward Steinhart, *Conflict and Collaboration: Kingdoms of Western Uganda, 1890–1907* (Princeton University Press, 1977) and Jonathon Glassman, *Feasts and Riot* (Heinemann, 1995), on the Abushiri rising in coastal German East Africa.

There is a large and controversial literature on various aspects of the conquest of South Africa. It is surveyed and assessed in Atmore and Marks, cited for the previous chapter and included in the E. Penrose collection on European imperialism. This analysis is extended in Marks and Stanley Trapido, 'Lord Milner and the South African State', *HWJ*, 8 (1979). Some of the process of revision is encapsulated in a series of writings on the Jameson Raid: G. A. Blainey, 'Lost Causes of the Jameson Raid', *EHR*, N.S. XVIII (1965); R. V. Kubicek, 'The Randlords in 1895: A Reassessment', *JBS*, II (1972) and R. Mendelsohn, 'Blainey and the Jameson Raid: The Debate Renewed', *JSAS*, VI (1980).

The growing force of Afrikaner nationalism is discussed in Floris van Jaarsveld, *The Awakening of Afrikaner Nationalism* (Human & Rousseau, 1961). A classic study of the politics of confrontation between Britain and the South African Republic is J. S. Marais, *The Fall of Kruger's Republic* (Clarendon Press, 1961). Transvaal society is re-interpreted in Stanley Trapido's contribution to the Atmore & Marks book cited earlier, 'Reflections on Land, Office and Wealth in the South African Republic 1850–1900'. Norman Etherington has written a very important consideration of Confederation, 'Labour Supply and the Genesis of South African Confederation in the 1870s', *JAH*, XX (1979). On the Boer War itself, Peter Warwick, ed., *The South African War* (Longman, 1980) is the most useful first resource to date. The perspective of dominated populations is explored in Bill Nasson, *Abraham Esau's War* (Cambridge University Press, 1991).

The intrusion of Rhodes' chartered company north of the Limpopo and the consequent conflict with Lobengula and the Ndebele state has often been recounted, for example in Philip Mason, *The Birth of a Dilemma* (Oxford University Press, 1958) and Stanlake Samkange, *The Origins of Rhodesia* (Heinemann, 1968). A recent analysis more widely set is David Beach, *War and Politics in Zimbabwe 1840–1900* (Mambo Press, 1986) see also J. Cobbing, 'Lobengula, Jameson and the Occupation of Mashonaland', *RH*, IV (1973) and Ian Phimister, 'Rhodes, Rhodesia and the Rand', *JSAS*, 1 (1974). The situation in what was to become South-West Africa is analysed by Brigitte Láu, 'Conflict and Power in Nineteenth Century Namibia', *JAH*, XXVII (1986).

# 6  The Material Basis of Colonial Society, 1900–40

A compendium of essays on colonial Africa in four volumes, most of which reflect the apologist viewpoint of the editors is Lewis Gann and Peter Duignan, eds, *Colonialism in Africa* (Cambridge University Press, 1968–1975). The fifth volume contains an important bibliography. Among regional and national studies some of the best come from the French tradition. Jean Suret-Canale, *French Colonialism in Africa, 1900–1945* (C. Hurst, 1971), is stronger on economic than social history. Catherine Coquery-Vidrovitch, *Le Congo au temps des grandes compagnies concessionaires, 1898–1930* (Mouton, 1972) is on French Equatorial Africa. An outstanding synthesis was achieved by Michel Merlier, *Le Congo de la colonisation belge à l'indépendance* (Maspéro, 1962). A number of authors have expanded on Merlier's vision in general articles, notably Jean-Philippe Peemans, 'Capital Accumulation in the Congo under Colonialism: The Role of the State' in the Gann and Duignan collection. By contrast the best single national history in English is strongest on social and cultural developments: John Iliffe, *A Modern History of Tanganyika* (Cambridge University Press, 1979). A pathbreaking reinterpretation is made by Anne Phillips, *The Enigma of Colonialism; British Policy in West Africa* (James Currey, 1989).

There is a solid historical literature in German, particularly on economic factors, dealing with the old German colonies. Of particular significance are: Helmuth Stoecker ed., *Kamerun unter Deutscher Herrschaft* (Deutscher Verlag der Wissenschaften VEB, 1960–8); Rainer Tetzlaff, *Koloniale Entwicklung und Ausbeutung* (Duncker und

Humboldt, 1970); Karin Hausen, *Deutsche Kolonialherrschaft in Afrika; Wirtschaftsinter-*
*essen und Kolonialverwaltung in Kamerun vor 1914* (Atlantis Verlag, 1970); Albert Wirz,
*Von Sklavenhandel zum Kolonialhandel* (Atlantis Verlag, 1972) and Helmut Bley, *South
West Africa under German Rule, 1894–1914* (Northwestern University Press, 1971).
Bley is a liberal who views imperialism as a prefiguration of fascism; Stoecker and
Tetzlaff were Marxist analyses from the German Democratic Republic. More
recent contributions include Peter Geschiere, 'European Planters, African Peasants
and the Colonial State: Alternatives in the *Mise en Valeur* in Makaland, South East
Cameroun in the Antebellum Period, *AEH*, XII (1983) and Wolfgang Werner, 'A
Brief History of Land Dispossession in Namibia', *JSAS*, XIX (1993).
     For an overview of British East Africa the best compendium remains Vincent
Harlow and Elizabeth Chilver, *History of East Africa*, II (Clarendon Press, 1965). For
Kenya, there is a serviceable descriptive introduction in Carl Rosberg and John
Nottingham, *The Myth of 'Mau Mau'; Nationalism in Kenya* (Stanford University Press,
1966). Studies of the political economy are Richard Wolff, *The Economics of Coloni-*
*alism*, (Yale University Press, 1974) and on the whole region, Edward Brett,
*Colonialism and Underdevelopment in East Africa; The Politics of Economic Change 1919–*
*1939* (Heinemann, 1973). Bruce Berman, *Control and Crisis in Colonial Kenya; The
Dialectic of Domination* (James Currey, Ohio University Press & Heinemann, 1990)
and the essays in Berman and John Lonsdale, *Unhappy Valley* (James Currey, Ohio
University Press & Heinemann, 1992–94, 2 volumes) are important further inter-
pretations. On particular regions, J. Forbes Munro, *Colonial Rule and the Kamba*,
(Clarendon Press, 1975) and Charles Ambler, *Kenyan Communities in an Age of
Imperialism*, (Yale University Press, 1988) are good. On Uganda see Mahmood
Mamdani, *Politics and Class Formation in Uganda*, (Onyx Press, 1980) and Jan Jelmert
Jorgensen, *Uganda, A Modern History*, (St Martin's Press, 1981).
     On British Central Africa two liberal standards are Philip Mason, *The Birth of a
Dilemma*, already cited and Richard Gray, *The Two Nations*, (Oxford University
Press, 1960). D. J. Murray, *The Governmental System in Southern Rhodesia* (Clarendon
Press, 1980) is a solid Weberian study of interest groups and the state. Of
pioneering importance is Giovanni Arrighi, *The Political Economy of Rhodesia*, (Mou-
ton, 1967). An excellent synthesis has been written by Ian Phimister, *An Economic
and Social History of Zimbabwe 1890–1948* (Longmans, 1988). The relevant pages in
Andrew Roberts, *A History of Zambia*, make an introduction to colonial Northern
Rhodesia. For Malawi see B. S. Krishnamurthy, 'Economic Policy, Land and
Labour in Nyasaland, 1890–1914' in Pachai's already cited *The Early History of
Malawi* and the Roderick Macdonald collection, *From Nyasaland to Malawi*.
     Reference has already been made to the Belgian Congo. However, a number of
works on the period of the Congo Free State should be noted: Neal Ascherson's
biography, W. R. Louis and Jean Stengers, eds., E. D. Morel's *History of the Congo
Reform Movement* (Clarendon Press, 1968).; Robert Harms, 'The End of Red
Rubber: A Reassessment', *JAH*, XVI (1975); Roger Anstey, 'The Congo Rubber
Atrocities', *AHS*, IV (1971); Mutwale-Muyimbwe, 'Les sources publiques de

financement de l'Etat Indépendant du Congo, 1885–1907', *Cahiers du CEDAF,* V (1973). For Ruanda-Urundi, two works are Catherine Newbury, *The Cohesion of Oppression; Clientship and Ethnicity in Rwanda 1860–1960,* (Columbia University Press, 1988), a local study, and Joseph Gahama, *Le Burundi sous l'administration belge,* (Harmattan, 1983). On the contemporary slave trade scandal in Angola see James Duffy, *A Question of Slavery* (Harvard University Press, 1967).

On the political economy of Portuguese Africa see Gervase Clarence-Smith, *The Third Portuguese Empire,* (Manchester University Press, 1985); Michel Cahen, 'Corporatisme et colonialisme au Mozambique', *CEA,* 92/93 (1984); James Duffy, *Portuguese Africa* (Harvard University Press, 1958) and Malyn Newitt, *Portugal in Africa, the Last Hundred Years* (C. Hurst, 1981), with a good bibliography. A good case study is Otto Roesch, 'Migrant Labour and Forced Rice Production in Southern Mozambique: The Colonial Peasantry of the Lower Limpopo Valley', *JSAS,* XVII, (1991). In Portuguese there is Armando Castro, *O Sistema Colonial Português em Africa* (ed. Caminho, 1978).

Overviews of the French mainland colonies have already been noted. See also Sheldon Gellar, *Structural Changes and Political Dependency: Senegal 1885–1945* (Sage, 1976) and on a special topic, Abdoulaye Ly, *Les mercenaires noires* (Présence Africaine, 1957) and Myron Echenberg, 'Les migrations militaires en Afrique Occidentale Française 1900–40', *CJAS,* XIV (1980). Two extraordinary colonial travel volumes are Geoffrey Gorer, *Africa Dances* (Faber & Faber, 1935) and André Gide, *Voyage au Congo,* (Gallimard, 1927).

There is a useful general history of West Africa in Michael Crowder, *West Africa under Colonial Rule* (Hutchinson, 1968). An overview on Nigeria by Gavin Williams in his edited book, *Nigeria: Economy and Society* (Rex Collings, 1976) may be supplemented by Robert Shenton, *The Development of Capitalism in Northern Nigeria* (James Currey, 1986). On Ghana, Rhoda Howard has attempted an underdevelopmentalist overview, *Colonialism and Underdevelopment in Ghana* (Croom Helm, 1978). See also Geoffrey Kay's book of readings, *The Political Economy of Colonialism in Ghana* (Cambridge University Press, 1972).

On colonial north-eastern Africa, works to consult are: I. M. Lewis, *The Modern History of Somaliland* (Weidenfeld & Nicolson, 1965); Abdi Ismail Samatar, *The State and Rural Transformation in Northern Somalia 1884–1986,* (University of Wisconsin Press, 1986); Peter Woodward, *Sudan 1898–1989,* (Lester Crook, 1990); Irma Taddia, *L'Eritrea-Colonia 1890–1952; paesaggi, strutture, uomini del colonialismo,* (Franco Angeli, 1986) and Alberto Sbacchi, *Ethiopia under Mussolini; Fascism and the Colonial Experience* (Zed Press, 1985).

The economic and social themes at the core of this chapter were advanced enormously by a seminal collection that bears on all aspects of agriculture, Robin Palmer and Neil Parsons, eds, *The Roots of Rural Poverty in Southern and Central Africa* (Heinemann, 1977). Martin Klein, *Peasants in Africa,* (Sage, 1980) is a very useful collection as well as the more general volumes on agriculture and pastoralism cited for Chapter 2. V. M. Ivanov, *Agrarian Reforms and Hired Labour in Africa* (Progress

Publishers, 1979) is an interesting Russian assessment. Judith Heyer *et al.*, *Rural Development in Africa* (St Martin's Press, 1981) considers colonial economic history. A major study of the impact of the decline and abolition of slavery is Frederick Cooper, *From Slaves to Squatters* (Yale University Press, 1980), which deals with Zanzibar and the Kenya coast. Also on this theme are Denise Bouche, *Les villages de liberté en Afrique Occidentale Française, 1887–1910* (Mouton, 1968); Tim Weiskel, 'Labour in the Emergent Periphery: From Slavery to Migrant Labour among the Baule Peoples 1880–1925' in W. L. Goldfrank, ed., *The World System of Capitalism; Past and Present* (Sage, 1979) and Philip Igbafe, 'Slavery and Emancipation in Benin 1897–1945', *JAH*, XVI (1975). There is also a good collection, Suzanne Miers and Richard Roberts, eds, *The End of Slavery in Africa*, (University of Wisconsin Press, 1988).

A pioneering study of colonial labour in Africa by a South African Communist in Moscow from the beginning of the 1930s has been reissued: Albert Nzula, *Forced Labour in Africa* (Zed Press, 1979). I have written a short general modern survey, *The African Worker*, (Cambridge University Press, 1988). Aspects of labour history are taken up for Kenya in Anthony Clayton and Donald Savage, *Government and Labour in Kenya, 1895–1963* (Frank Cass, 1974); Sharon Stichter, *Migrant Labour in Kenya* (Longman, 1982); K. K. Janmohamed, 'African Labourers in Mombasa 1895–1940', in Bethwell Ogot, ed., *Hadith* (2), 1972, and Roger van Zwanenberg, *Colonial Capital and Labour in Kenya 1919–1939* (East African Literature Bureau, 1975). On Zimbabwe, Tsuneo Yoshikuni, 'Strike Action and Self-Help Associations: Zimbabwean Worker Protest and Culture after World War I,' *JSAS*, XV (1989) is significant. For an apparently prosaic but omnipresent part of colonial and post-colonial labour in Africa see a case study by Karen Hansen, 'Domestic Labour in Zambia', *JSAS*, XIII (1986).

The scattered history of labour in West Africa would include, in a developing literature, A. G. Hopkins, 'The Lagos Strike of 1897: an Exploration in Nigerian Labour History', *Past and Present*, XXXV (1968); Roger Thomas, 'Forced Labour in West Africa; the Case of the Northern Territories of the Gold Coast 1906–27', *JAH*, XIV (1973); Michael Mason, 'Working on the Railway: Forced Labour in Northern Nigeria, 1907–12' and Arnold Hughes and Robin Cohen, 'An Emerging Nigerian Working Class: The Lagos Experience 1897–1939', both in Robin Cohen, Jean Copans and Peter Gutkind, eds, *African Labor History* (Sage, 1978); Gilles Sautter, 'Le chemin de fer Congo-Océan', *CEA*, VII (1967) and Ibrahim Abdullah, 'Liberty or Death; Working-Class Agitation and the Labour Question in Colonial Freetown 1938–39', *International Review of Social History*, 40 (1995). A general study of forced labour in French West Africa is achieved in Babacar Fall, *Le travail forcé en AOF*, (Karthala, 1993). The relationship to colonial views of African population is explored in Dennis Cordell and Joel Gregory, 'Labour Reservoirs and Population: French Colonial Strategies in Koudougou, Upper Volta', *JAH*, XXIII (1982).

On labour migration, see Samir Amin, ed., *Modern Migrations in West Africa* (Oxford University Press, 1974), and Sharon Stichter, *Migrant Labourers*, (Cambridge University Press, 1988). Some case studies are: W. M. Freund, 'Labour Migration to the Northern Nigerian Tin Mines 1903–45', *JAH*, XXII (1981); Marvin Harris, 'Labour Migration among the Mozambique Thonga', *Africa*, XXIX (1959); J. P. Chrétien, 'Des sedentaires devenus migrants: motifs des départs des burundais et des rwandais vers l'Uganda', *Cultures et développement*, X (1978); F. E. Sanderson, 'Development of Labour Migration from Nyasaland 1891–1914', *JAH*, II (1961) and Segun Osoba, 'The Phenomenon of Labour Migration in the Era of British Colonial Rule', *JHSN*, IV (1969). A key controversy over proletarianisation is marked by the interchange between James Ferguson, 'Mobile Workers, Modernist Narratives,' *JSAS*, XVI (1990) cited for Chapter 1 and a response by Hugh Mamillan in *JSAS*, XIX (1993).

Quite unlike anything else are the finely observed and fiercely empiricist books of Polly Hill: *Migrant Cocoa Farmers of Southern Ghana* (1962); *Studies in the Rural Capitalism of West Africa* (1970); *Rural Hausa; a Village and a Setting* (1972) *and Population, Prosperity and Poverty in Kano 1900 and 1970* (1977), all published by Cambridge University Press. An environmental aspect is critical to Paul Richards, *Indigeous African Revolution*, (Hutchinson, 1985). An excellent contrast to Hill's approach and area may be found in Jean-Marc Gastellu, *Riches paysans de Côte d'Ivoire*, (Harmattan, 1989). Ken Swindell, *Farm Labour* (Cambridge University Press, 1985) repays much re-reading.

In the scholarship produced during the late colonial period, the Makerere school of writers on Ugandan agriculture had a special importance and remains valuable despite the now transparently heavy celebration of the cash crop. A classic is C. C. Wrigley, *Crops and Wealth in Uganda* (Kampala, 1959). Two late works deriving from this school are H. W. West, ed., *The Transformation of Land Tenure in Buganda since 1896* (Afrika Studiecentrum, Leiden & Cambridge University Press, 1971) and Audrey Richards *et al.*, *Subsistence to Commercial Farming in Present-Day Buganda* (Cambridge University Press, 1973).

Among a list of works of analytic merit on cash cropping in various parts of tropical Africa, the best should include: Sara Berry, *Custom, Cocoa and Socioeconomic Change* (Clarendon Press, 1975); Yves Mersadier, 'La crise de L'arachide sénégalaise au début des années trente', *BIFAN, série B* (28), 1966; Jan-Yves Marchal, 'L'office du Niger: îlot de prospérité paysanne ou pôle de production agricole?', *CJAS*, VIII (1974); Herman Pössinger, 'Interrelations between Social and Economic Change in Rural Africa: the Case of the Ovimbundu of Angola' in Franz-Wilhelm Heimer, ed., *Social Change in Angola* (Weltforum Verlag, 1973); Leslie Bessant and Elvis Muringai, 'Peasants, Businessmen and Moral Economy in the Chiwesha Reserve 1930–68', *JSAS*, XIX (1993); Tony Barnett, 'Production of Cotton and the Reproduction of Underdevelopment' in Ivar Oxaal, ed., *Beyond the Sociology of Development* (Routledge & Kegan Paul, 1975); John Tosh, 'Lango Agriculture during the Early Colonial Period: Land and Labour in a Cash-Crop Economy', *JAH*, XIX (1978) and E. S. Atieno-Odhiambo, 'The Rise and Decline of the Kenya Peasant' in P. Gutkind and P. Waterman, eds, *African Social Studies: A Radical Reader* (Heinemann,

1977). For a pastoral equivalent, see Abdi Samatar, 'Merchant Capital, International Livestock Trade and Pastoral Development in Somalia', *CJAS*, XXI (1987) and Douglas Johnson, 'Political Economy in the Upper Nile; The Twentieth Century Expansion of the Pastoral Common Economy', *JAH*, XXX (1989). On white settlers, a standard work is M. P. K. Sorrenson, *Origins of White Settlement in Kenya* (Oxford University Press, 1968). Isaac Mazonde, 'Vorsters and Clarks; Alternative Models of European Farmer in the Tuli Block of Botswana', *JSAS*, XVII (1991) is perceptive. For the view from below there is Frank Furedi, 'Kikuyu Squatters in the Rift Valley 1918–29' in Bethwell Ogot, ed., *Hadith*, V (1972) and Robin Palmer, 'Working Conditions and Worker Response on Nyasaland Tea Estates 1930–53', *JAH*, XXVII (1986). The settler land problem is the focus of Palmer's *Land and Racial Domination in Rhodesia* (Heinemann, 1977). There is an excellent survey of the economy of settlerdom in the Congo: Bogumil Jewsiewicki, 'Le colonat agricole européen au Congo beige 1910–60', *JAH*, XX (1979). On a large plantation system, Leroy Vail and Landeg White, *Capitalism and Colonialism in Mozambique* (Heinemann, 1980) is outstanding. For early 'development' planning, Dickson Eyoh, 'National Policy vs. Local Power: The Lafia Project in Nigeria 1916–34', *CJAS*, XXIV (1990) is instructive.

The ecological aspect of colonial agriculture has been opened up by the work of Heige Kjekshus: *Ecology Control and Economic Development in East Africa* (Heinemann, 1977). See also Leroy Vail, 'Ecology and Society: the Example of Eastern Zambia', *JSAS*, III (1977), Terence Ranger, 'Whose Heritage? The Case of the Matobo National Park', *JSAS*, XV, (1989), Fiona Mackenzie, 'Political Economy of the Environment: Gender and Resistance under Colonialism, Murang'a District, Kenya', *CJAS*, XXV (1991) and Kate Showers, 'Soil Erosion in the Kingdom of Lesotho: Origins and Colonial Response', *JSAS*, XV (1989). On colonialism and conservation, David Anderson & Richard Grove, eds., *Conservation in Africa*, Cambridge University Press, 1987 and Stephen Ellis, 'Of Elephants and Men: Politics and Nature Conservation in Africa', *JSAS*, XX (1994) provide a critical gaze.

Late twentieth-century concerns have been the obvious inspiration for more and more research into poverty and deprivation in Africa, especially rural Africa. Some provocative studies are John Iliffe, *The African Poor; A History* (Cambridge University Press, 1987) and *Famine in Zimbabwe 1890–1960* (Mambo Press, 1990); Michael Watts, *Silent Violence; Food, Famine and Peasantry in Northern Nigeria*, (University of California Press, 1983), James McCann, *From Poverty to Famine in North-east Ethiopia 1900–35*, (University of Pennsylvania Press, 1987), Megan Vaughan and Henrietta Moore, *Cutting Down Trees*, (James Currey & Heinemann, 1995), Diana Wylie, 'The Changing Face of Hunger in Southern African History 1890–1980', *Past and Present*, 122 (1989) and Gregory Maddox, 'Mtunya; Famine in Central Tanzania 1917–20', *JAH*, XXXI (1990).

Colonial mining is much less well-served than agriculture in the literature. Charles van Onselen made a major breakthrough in placing the mines in the context of African labour and social history in *Chibaro: African Mines Labour in*

*Southern Rhodesia*, (Pluto Press, 1976). See also Agwu Akpala, 'Background of the Enugu Colliery Shooting Incident of 1949', *JHSN*, III (1965); John Higginson, *A Working Class in the Making: Belgian Colonial Labour Policy, Private Enterprise and the African Mineworker*, (University of Wisconsin Press, 1989); Charles Perrings, *Black Mineworkers in Central Africa* (Heinemann, 1979); Bill Freund, *Capital and Labour in the Nigerian Tin Mines* (Longman, 1981.)

The history of colonial capitalist enterprise in Africa is far better developed in French than in English as note the work of Suret-Canale and Coquery-Vidrovitch, although see A. G. Hopkins, 'Big Business in African Studies', *JAH*, XXVIII (1987). Business receives detailed attention in the special edition of the *Revue française d'histoire d'outremer*, LXIII (1976), edited by Coquery-Vidrovitch, entitled 'L'Afrique et la crise de 1930'. She has also written the important article: 'L'impact des intérêts coloniaux: SCOA et CFAO dans l'Ouest africain 1910–65', *JAH*, XVI (1975). Her two-volume edited collection, *Entreprises et entrepreneurs en Afrique Noire XIX–XX siècles*, (Harmattan, 1983) continues into the post-colonial era. A standard source for Belgian Africa is P. Joye and R. Lewin, *Les trusts au Congo* (Brussels, 1961). On narrower aspects of capitalism in Central Africa there is S. E. Katzenellenbogen, *Railways and the Copper Mines of Katanga* (Clarendon Press, 1973); Lewis Gann, 'The Northern Rhodesian Copper Industry and the World of Copper', *RLJ*, XVIII (1955) and Peter Slinn, 'Commercial Concessions and Politics During the Colonial Period: The Role of the British South Africa Company in Northern Rhodesia 1890–1964', *AA*, LXX (1971).

Different aspects of how the trading minorities of colonial Africa live and work can be studied in Dharam Ghai, ed., *Portrait of a Minority: Asians in East Africa* (Oxford University Press, 1970); John Zarwan, 'The Social and Economic Network of an Indian Family Business in Kenya 1920–70', *Kroniek van Afrika*, N.S. VI (1975); Vishnu Padayachee and Robert Morrell, 'Indian Merchants and Dukawallahs in the Natal Economy c. 1875–1914', *JSAS*, XVII (1991); Toyin Falola, 'Lebanese Traders in Southwestern Nigeria', *AA*, 89 (1990); Said Bumedouha, 'Adjustments to West African Realities: The Lebanese in Senegal', *Africa*, LX, (1990) and David Himbara, *Kenyan Capitalists, the State and Development* (Lynne Rienner, 1994), which carries the story to the present. On African merchant strata, Mahir Saul, 'Development of the Grain Market and Grain Merchants in Burkina Faso', *JMAS*, XXIV (1986), Jean-Loup Amselle, *Les négociants de la savane*, (Ed. Anthropos, 1977) and Jean-Pierre Warnier, *L'esprit d'entreprise au Cameroun*, (Karthala, 1994) are samples of a growing literature.

Michael Crowder emphasised the importance of indirect rule as a mechanism of British domination in colonial Africa, notably in the edited collection, Crowder and Obaro Ikime, eds, *West African Chiefs* (University of Ife Press, 1970). His views have been criticised in M. Semakula Kiwanuka, 'Colonial Policies and Administrations: the Myth of Contrasts', *AHS*, III (1970). For other assessments see Hubert Deschamps, 'Et maintenant, Lord Lugard', *Africa*, XXXIII (1963) and I. F. Nicolson, *The Administration of Nigeria* (Clarendon Press, 1969). A powerful contemporary assessment of the long shadow of this kind of political structure has been made by Mahmood Mamdani, *Citizen and Subject*, (Princeton University Press & James Currey, 1996).

There are numerous, generally narrowly administrative, case studies, especially for Nigeria. The best-known include J. A. Atanda, *The New Oyo Empire* (Longman, 1973); Philip Igbafe, *Benin under British Administration* (Longman, 1979); Adamu Fika, *The Kano Civil War and British Overrule, 1882–1940* (Oxford University Press, 1978); A. I. Asiwaju, *Western Yorubaland under European Rule* (Longman, 1976) and, on the Gold Coast, William Tordoff, *Ashanti under the Prempehs, 1888–1935* (Oxford University Press, 1965). The most penetrating are A. E. Afigbo, *The Warrant Chiefs* (Longman, 1972) and J. D. Y. Peel's dense and informative *Ijeshas and Nigerians c1890s–1970s*, (Cambridge University Press, 1983) Other areas are examined in Michael Twaddle, 'The Bakungu Chiefs of Buganda under British Colonial Rule, 1900–30', *JAH*, X (1969) and Gerald Caplan, *The Elites of Barotseland* (C. Hurst, 1970). A very sympathetic portrait of a colonial chief is drawn by Francis Deng, *The Man called Deng Majok*, (Yale University Press, 1986).

# 7 Culture, Class and Social Change in Colonial Africa, 1900–40

Two novels on the same part of Nigeria that evoke the meaning of conquest from the point of view of the two sexes are Chinua Achebe, *Things Fall Apart* (Heinemann, 1966) and Buchi Emecheta, *The Joys of Motherhood* (Allison & Busby, 1979). There is a perspective on art and African history suggested by the special issue of the *CJAS*, XXII (1988).

Views of social change in twentieth-century Africa unlike this chapter can be found in Peter Lloyd, *Africa in Social Change* (Penguin, 1967) and Claudine Vidal, *Sociologie des passions* (Karthala, 1991). A feature of the more recent literature on Africa has been the Annales school-like emergence of local and regional studies covering long time periods with much to say on both material and social life, a technique which has particular power and authority when applied to rural contexts. Some examples are David Cohen and E. S. Atieno Odhiambo, *Siaya; The Historical Anthropology of an African Landscape* (James Currey, Heinemann & Ohio University Press, 1989); Landeg White, *Magomero; Portrait of an African Village* (Cambridge University Press, 1987); Elias Mandala, *Work and Control in a Peasant Economy; A History of the Lower Tchiri Valley in Malawi 1859–1960*, (University of Wisconsin Press, 1990) and Steven Feiermann, *Peasant Intellectuals; Anthropology and History*, (University of Wisconsin Press, 1990). Class analysis is central to Gavin Kitching's complex *Class and Economic Change in Kenya* (Yale University Press, 1980) and K. W. Post's 'Peasantization in Western Africa' in Gutkind and Waterman, cited previously. The makings of a new bourgeoisie are the subject of Joan Vincent,

'Colonial Chiefs and the Making of a Class', *Africa*, XLVII (1977) on Uganda and Martin Chanock, 'The New Men Revisited' in R. Macdonald, ed., *From Nyasaland to Malawi*, cited previously.

The literature specifically on African women and their modern history is now highly developed, especially in the USA but increasingly including African authors. Ester Boserup presented a debatable paradigm in *Women's Role in Development* (George Allen & Unwin, 1970). Amongst collections, see Nancy Hafkin and Edna Bay, eds, *Women in Africa* (Stanford University Press, 1976); the special issue on women of *CEA* XVII (1977); M. J. Hay and Marcia Wright, *African Women and the Law: Historical Perspectives* (Boston University Press, 1982); Sharon Stichter and Jane Parpart, eds, *Patriarchy and Class; African Women at Home and in the Workforce* (Westview Press, 1988) and Cherryl Walker, ed., *Women and Gender in Southern Africa*, (James Currey & David Philip, 1990). Elizabeth Schmidt, *Peasants, Traders and Wives; Shona Women in the History of Zimbabwe 1890–1939* (Heinemann, 1992) touches the bases of this literature effectively. Monographs that have bristled with ideas are Claire Robertson, *Sharing the Same Bowl; A Socioeconomic History of Women and Class in Accra, Ghana*, (Indiana University Press, 1984) and Luise White, *The Comforts of Home; Prostitution in Colonial Nairobi* (University of Chicago Press, 1990). Other readings to be recommended are Mona Etienne, 'Women and Men, Cloth and Cultivation: Transformation of Production and Distribution Relations Among the Baule', *CEA*, XVII (1977); Jane Guyer, 'Food, Cocoa and Division of Labour by Sex in Two West African Societies', *CSSH*, XXII (1980); Achola Pala Okeyo, 'Daughters of the Lakes and Rivers' in Mona Etienne and Eleanor Leacock, eds, *Women and Colonization* (Praeger, 1980); Jane Parpart, 'The Household and the Mineshaft', *JSAS*, XIII (1986), Megan Vaughan, 'Household Units and Historical Process in Southern Malawi', *Review of African Political Economy* 34 (1985); Jean Davison, 'Tenacious Women: Clinging to Banja Household Production in the Face of Changing Gender Relations in Malawi, *JSAS*, XIX (1993); Abdou Maliqalim Simone, 'From Reproduction to Reinvention: Women's Roles in African Cities', *African Insight*, XXV (1995, with a contemporary focus); Catherine Coles and Beverly Mack, *Hausa Women in the Twentieth Century*, (University of Wisconsin Press, 1991) Chantal Rondeau, *Les paysannes de Mali*, (Karthala, 1994) and Christine Obbo, *African Women* (Zed Press, 1980). These readings tend to be those which take an historical perspective and which consider gender relations, beyond the question of women's history *per se*. Far less has been written on childhood but especially with reference to labour see Beverly Grier, 'Invisible Hand; The Political Economy of Child Labour in Colonial Zimbabwe', *JSAS*, XX (1994) and Karen Hansen, 'Labor Migration and Urban Child Labor during the Colonial Period in Zambia' in Bruce Fetter, ed., *Demography from Scanty Evidence; Central Africa in the Colonial Era*, (Lynne Rienner, 1990).

Two collections that reveal the dominant trends in writing on religion in colonial Africa are T. O. Ranger and I. Kimambo, *The Historical Study of African Religion* (Heinemann, 1972) and Ranger and John Weller, eds, *Themes in the Christian History of Central Africa* (Heinemann, 1975), a more parochial volume. Of theoretical insight

is W. van Binsbergen, *Religious Change in Zambia* (Kegan Paul International, 1981).
The close relations of church and state in the Belgian colonies are discussed in
Marvin Markowitz, *The Cross and the Sword: The Political Role of the Missions in the
Congo, 1908–60*, (Stanford University Press, 1973) and Ian Linden, *Church and
Revolution in Rwanda* (Manchester University Press, 1977). On the mission mind,
Andrew Ross, 'The Blantyre Mission and Problems of Land and Labour, 1891–
1915' in R. Macdonald, ed., *From Nyasaland to Malawi*, cited above and T. O.
Beidelman, 'Social Theory and the Study of Christian Missions in Africa', *Africa*,
XLIV (1974) are suggestive. On the relationship between capitalism and mission
Christianity, see J. Bertin Webster, 'The Bible and the Plough' and Sara S. Berry,
'Christianity and the Rise of Cocoa-Farming in Ibadan and Ondo', *JHSN*, II
(1963) and IV (1968) respectively, and J. McCracken, *Politics and Christianity in
Malawi* (Cambridge University Press, 1977).

Studies of non-Christian African religious movements include Audrey Wipper,
*Rural Rebels*, (Oxford University Press, 1977) and Elizabeth Hopkins, 'The Nya-
bingi Cult of Southwestern Uganda' in Robert Rotberg and Ali Mazrui, eds, *Protest
and Power in Black Africa*, previously cited. The independent churches and their
relationship to the colonial order have fascinated many writers on Africa. Some of
the most interesting studies are Karen Fields, *Revival and Rebellion in Colonial Central
Africa* (Princeton University Press, 1985); Matthew Schoffeleers, 'Ritual Healing
and Political Acquiescence; The Case of the Zionist Churches in Southern Africa',
*Africa*, LXI, (1991); Norman Long, *Social Change and the Individual* (Manchester
University Press, 1968); Wyatt MacGaffey, *Modern Kongo Prophets; Religion in a Plural
Society*, (Indiana University Press, 1983); Damaso Feci, 'La vie cachée et vie publique
de Simon Kimbangu selon la littérature coloniale et missionaire belge', *Cahiers du
CEDAF*, 9/10, 1972; Thomas Turner and Kasongo Wembolua, 'Le Vandisme
(Sankuru-Zaïre) et sa signification politique', *Cahiers du CEDAF* (1978) and J. D. Y.
Peel, *Aladura: a Religious Movement Among the Yoruba* (Oxford University Press, 1968).
Some understanding of the forces within the Islamic community during the colonial
period can be derived from Donal Cruise O'Brien, *The Mourides of Senegal* (Clar-
endon Press, 1971), John Paden, *Religion and Political Culture in Kano* (University of
California Press, 1973) and Jean Copans, *Les marabouts de l'arachide* (Le Sycomore,
1980). There is a *Journal of Religion in Africa* published in the Netherlands.

The social context of disease and colonial perspectives on health has become a
subject of considerable academic enquiry in the African historical literature after
1980. Two interesting studies are Megan Vaughan, *Curing their Ills; Colonial Power
and African Illness*, (Polity Press, 1992) and Randall Packard, 'Maize, Cotton and
Mosquitoes: The Political Economy of Malaria Epidemics in Colonial Swaziland',
*JAH*, XXV (1984) A useful overview can be obtained from Steven Feierman and
John Janzen, eds, *The Social Basis of Health and Healing in Africa*, (University of
California Press, 1992).

A good assessment of formal education in Africa exists in Kenneth Blakemore
and Brian Cooksey, *Sociology of Education for Africa* (George Allen & Unwin, 1981).

An early critical assessment is D. B. Abernethy, *The Political Dilemma of Popular Education in Southern Nigeria* (Stanford University Press, 1969). Other writings with a critical edge include Denise Bouche, 'Les écoles françaises au Soudan à l'époque de la conquête, 1884–1900', *CEA*, VI (1966) and 'Autrefois, notre pays s'appelait le Gaule', *CEA*, VIII (1968), Brendan Carmody, 'Conversion and School at Chikumi', *Africa*, LVIII (1988); Carol Summers, 'Educational Controversies: African Activism and Educational Strategies in Southern Rhodesia 1920–34', *JSAS*, XX (1994) and T. O. Ranger, 'African Attempts to Control Education in East and Central Africa', *Past and Present*, XXXII (1965).

For analyses of legal systems in colonial Africa, there is an excellent set of readings in Kristin Mann and Richard Roberts, eds, *Law in Colonial Africa*, (Heinemann & James Currey, 1991). Other topics are considered in Francis Snyder, *Capitalism and Legal Change; An African Transformation* (Academic Press, 1981); Sally Falk Moore, *Social Facts and Fabrications* (Cambridge University Press, 1986); Issa Shivji, *Law, State and the Working Class in Tanzania* (James Currey, Heinemann & Tanzania Publishing House, 1986); Omoniyi Adewoye, *The Judicial System in Southern Nigeria, 1854–1954* (Longman, 1977) and Douglas Johnson, 'Judicial Regulation and Administrative Control: Customary Law and the Nuer 1898–1954', *JAH*, XXVII (1986). On a related subject, John McCracken, 'Coercion and Control in Nyasaland: Aspects of the History of a Colonial Police Force', *JAH*, XXVI (1986) was a pioneering contribution.

African societies and organisations of a 'modern' type generally get a bland or ahistorical treatment, but an interested reader could begin by consulting T. O. Ranger, *Dance and Society in Eastern Africa, 1890–1940* (Heinemann, 1975), Wolfgang Werner, 'Playing Soldiers': The Truppenspieler Movement among the Herero of Namibia 1915–c. 1945', *JSAS*, XVI (1990) and Bruce Fetter, 'African Associations in Elisabethville, 1910–35', *Études d'histoire africaine*, VI (1974). For ethnicity and tribalism in colonial society, some useful readings could include Richard Waller and Thomas Spear, eds, *Becoming Maasai*, (James Currey, 1993); Abner Cohen, *Custom and Politics in Urban Africa* (University of California Press, 1969); Obaro Ikime, *Niger Delta Rivalry: Itsekiri-Urhobo Relations and the European Presence, 1884–1936* (Longman, 1969); M. J. Hay, 'Local Trade and Ethnicity in Western Kenya', *AEHR*, III (1975); John Lonsdale, 'When did the Gusii (or Any Other Group) Become a Tribe?', *KHR*, V (1977); Aidan Southall, 'From Segmentary Lineage to Ethnic Association' in M. Owusu, ed., *Colonialism and Change* (Mouton, 1975) and the special issue on 'l'archipel peul', *CEA*, 133–35, (1993). Major collections reflecting a fashionable interest in ethnicity in the 1980s are Leroy Vail, ed., *The Creation of Tribalism in Southern Africa* (University of California Press & James Currey, 1989) and Jean-Pierre Chrétien & Gérard Prunier, eds, *Les ethnies ont une histoire* (Karthala, 1989) An original aspect is proposed by Jeff Guy and Motlatsi Thabane in 'Technology, Ethnicity and Ideology: Basotho and Shaft Sinking on the South African Gold Mines', *JSAS*, XIV (1988). On the related subject of language use, Johannes Fabian, *Language and Colonial Power*, (Cambridge University

Press, 1986) and William Samarin, 'The Colonial Heritage of the Central African Republic: A Linguistic Perspective', *IJAHS*, XXII (1989) are stimulating.

Some essays in writing urban history in Africa (a much stronger French than English tradition with urban studies that look from the colonial into the post-colonial period) include: Catherine Coquery-Vidrovitch's collection, *Processus d'ur-banisation en Afrique*, (Harmattan, 1988, 2 volumes). Other select titles might be Marc le Pape, 'De l'espace et des races à Abidjan entre 1903 et 1934'; Odile Goerg, 'Conakry, une modèle de ville coloniale?' both in *CEA*, 99 (1985); Marc Pain, *Kinshasa; le ville et la cité*, (Editions de l'ORSTOM, 1984); Guy Maïnet, *Douala: Croissances et servitudes*, (Harmattan, 1985), Claude Meillassoux, *Urbanization of an African Community* (University of Washington Press, 1968); Bruce Fetter, *The Creation of Elisabethville, 1910–40* (Stanford University Press, 1976); David Birmingham, 'Carnival at Luanda', *JAH*, XXIX (1988) and Bogumil Jewsiewicki, 'Histoire économique d'une ville coloniale: Kisangani', *Cahiers du CEDAF* (1978).

There is a considerable literature on the economic and political life of the West African bourgeoisie during the colonial period. See especially: J. Ayo Langley, *Pan-Africanism and Nationalism in West Africa, 1900–45* (Clarendon Press, 1975); J. K. Obatala, 'An African Case Study in the Bourgeois Origins of Cultural National-ism', *Science and Society*, XXXVI (1972); Patrick Cole, *Modern and Traditional Elites in the Politics of Lagos* (Cambridge University Press, 1975); Kristin Mann, *Marrying Well; Marriage, Status and Social Change among the Educated Elite in Colonial Lagos* (Cambridge University Press, 1985); A. G. Hopkins, 'Economic Aspects of Political Movements in Nigeria and the Gold Coast, 1918–39', *JAH*, IX (1968); Felicia Ekejuiba, 'Omu Okwei, the Merchant Queen of Ossomari', *JHSN*, III (1967); G. Wesley Johnson, *The Emergence of Black Politics in Senegal* (Stanford University Press, 1971) and Samir Amin, 'La politique coloniale française à l'egard de la bourgeoisie commerçante sénégalaise' in Claude Meillassoux, ed., *Development of Indigenous Trade and Markets in West Africa*, already cited. Looking beyond the elite at the problem of class and political economy is Sam Rhodie, 'The Gold Coast Cocoa Hold-Up of 1930–31', *Transactions of the Historical Society of Ghana*, IX (1968). A more recent assessment is Gareth Austin, 'Capitalists and Chiefs in the Cocoa Hold-Ups in Southern Asante 1927–38', *IJAHS*, XXI (1988).

Writing on African 'resistance' in eastern and south-central Africa has created something of a school and has focused primarily on post-conquest revolts. The classic studies are by Terence Ranger: *Revolt in Southern Rhodesia, 1896–7* (Heine-mann, 1967) and 'Connections Between Primary Resistance Movements and Modern Mass Nationalism in East and Central Africa', *JAH*, IX (1968). Ranger is subjected to an important critique by Julian Cobbing, 'The Absent Priesthood', *JAH*, XVIII (1977). Other studies following from Ranger's analysis are numerous; among the most highly considered is John Iliffe, 'Origins of the Maji Maji Rebellion', *JAH*, VIII (1967). Women's activities are central in Audrey Wipper, 'Kikuyu Women and the Harry Thuku Disturbances: Some Uniformities of Female Militancy', *Africa*, LIX, (1989). The Chilembwe rising is the subject of

George Shepperson and T. Price, *Independent African* (Edinburgh University Press, 1958), a landmark in the historiography of Africa. Also important are George Mwase, *Strike a Blow and Die* (Harvard University Press, 1967) and Shepperson's reconsideration, 'The Place of John Chilembwe in Malawi Historiography', in B. Pachai, ed., *The Early History of Malawi* (Longman, 1972). For other revolts, see Paul Lovejoy and Jan Hogendorn, 'Mahdism and Resistance to Colonial Rule in the Sokoto Caliphate 1905–6', *JAH*, XXXI (1990), J. A. Ballard, 'The Porto Novo Incident of 1923', *Odu*, N.S. 11 (1965); Sikitele Gize, 'Racines de la révolte pende de 1931', *Etudes d'histoire africaine*, V (1973) and J. P. Chrétien, 'Une révolte au Burundi en 1934', *Annales*, XXV (1970).

## 8 Industrialisation and South African Society, 1900–40

The best currently available detailed survey of modern South African history is T. R. H. Davenport, *South Africa: a Modern History* (Macmillan, 2nd edn., 1978) by a liberal scholar who at least refers to a wider range of perspectives. William Beinart, *Twentieth-Century South Africa*, (Oxford University Press, 1994) is an interesting interpretation giving much emphasis to social and rural themes. The second volume of Monica Wilson and Leonard Thompson, eds, *Oxford History of South Africa* (Oxford University Press, 1969–1971) remains interesting in parts.

For a general introduction to the fundamental features of South African development, Alf Stadler, *The Political Economy of Modern South Africa*, (Croom Helm & David Philip, 1987) is good. A classic liberal analysis of the political economy can be found in Sheila van der Horst, *Native Labour in South Africa* (Frank Cass, 1971 edn.). See also Herbert Blumer, 'Industrialisation and Race Relations' in Guy Hunter, ed., *Industrialisation and Race Relations* (Oxford University Press, 1965). A number of the classic radical studies attempting to link the racial system in South Africa to industrial capitalism as a whole – by Wolpe, Legassick, Johnstone and others – can be found in Harold Wolpe, ed. *The Articulation of Modes of Production*, (RKP, 1980) and William Beinart and Saul Dubow, eds, *Segregation and Apartheid in Twentieth-Century South Africa*, (Routledge, 1995).

The work of a second generation of South African Marxists can be found as well in the *Review of African Political Economy*, 7, (1977) and subsequent debate. See too, Robert Davies, *Capital, State and White Labour in South Africa, 1900–60* (Harvester Press, 1979). Merle Lipton, *Capitalism and Apartheid*, (Wildwood House, 1985) partially accepts and partially critiques the 'revisionist' writers on the relationship of capitalism to apartheid. Terence Moll, 'Did the Apartheid Economy Fail?', *JSAS* XVII (1991) reflects much current thinking on the state of this debate. A third phase of writers tend to be bunched together as the 'social' historians. Their concerns begin to emerge with Shula Marks and Stanley Trapido, eds, *The Politics of Race, Class and Nationalism in Twentieth Century South Africa* (Longman, 1987). One of the best collections of their work is Belinda Bozzoli, ed., *Class, Community and Conflict; South African Perspectives*, (Ravan Press, 1987). Another, taking the story somewhat further than the material in this chapter, is Philip Bonner *et al.*, *Apartheid's Genesis 1935–62*, (Ravan Press, 1993). A very useful collection on economic development that exists in four volumes is D. Hobart Houghton and Jennifer Dagut, *Source Material on the South African Economy* (Oxford University Press, Cape Town, 1972–3). The second volume of Z. A. Konczacki, Jane Parpart and Tim Shaw, *Studies in the Economic History of South Africa*, (Cass, 1991) is also worth investigating.

There is a large sociological and anthropological literature on African society in South Africa. Deserving special attention are the books of Bengt Sundkler on separatist churches, *Bantu Prophets in South Africa* (Oxford University Press, 1961 revised edn.) and *Zulu Zion and Some Swazi Zionists* (Gleerups, 1976) and those of Philip Mayer, *Townsmen or Tribesmen* (Oxford University Press, 1961) and his edited collection, *Black Villagers in an Industrial Society* (Oxford University Press, 1981). A look at new cultural forms emerging can be found in Veit Erlmann, *African Stars: Studies in Black South African Performance*, (University of Chicago Press, 1991). On education, a stand-out in the literature is Jon Hyslop, 'State Education Policy and the Social Reproduction of the Urban African Working Class: The Case of the Southern Transvaal', *JSAS*, XIV (1988) which looks ahead to the material in Chapter 11 as well. The life of one part of the urban working class is captured for a later generation (but with earlier relevance no doubt too) by Jacklyn Cock in *Maids and Madams* (Ravan Press, 1981). Outstanding accounts of community life in South Africa include Monica Wilson and Archie Mafeje, *Langa* (Oxford University Press, 1963); Pierre van den Berghe, *Caneville* (Wesleyan University Press, 1964); J. B. Loudon, *White Farmers, Black Labourers* (Afrikastudiecentrum, Leiden and Africa Studies Centre, Cambridge, 1970) and Rob Gordon, *Mines, Migrants and Masters* (Ravan Press, 1977). On social change in the reserves, William Beinart, 'Joyini Inkomo': The Origins of Migrancy from Pondoland', *JSAS*, V (1979) is impressive. Colin Murray, *Families Divided* (Cambridge University Press, 1981) is a major study of labour migration.

On the residual rural areas left for blacks, valuable accounts are found in William Beinart, 'Soil Erosion, Conservationism and Ideas about Development: A Southern African Exploration 1900–60', *JSAS*, XI (1984); Pat McAllister, 'Resistance to "Betterment" in the Transkei: A Case Study from the Willowvale District', *JSAS*, XV (1989) and Fred Hendricks, 'Loose Planning and Rapid Resettlement; The Politics of Conservation and Control in Transkei 1950–70', *JSAS*, XV (1989). A complex, long-term regional study has been produced by the anthropologist Colin Murray: *Black Mountain: Land, Class and Power in the Eastern Orange Free State 1880s–1980s* (Witwatersrand University Press, 1986). Murray's terrain includes 'white' farm country. For more on what has been termed agrarian history, see the important collection, edited by Beinart, Delivs and Trapido *Putting a Plough to the Ground; Accumulation and Dispossession in Rural South Africa 1850–1930*, (Ravan Press, 1986) and William Beinart and Colin Bundy, *Hidden Struggles in Rural*

*South Africa; Politics and Popular Movements in the Transkei and Eastern Cape 1890–1930*, (Ravan Press, 1987).

The political history of struggle is described by three moving if unbalanced accounts: Edward Roux, *Time Longer than Rope* (University of Wisconsin Press, 1964); H. J. and R. Simons, *Class and Colour in South Africa* (Penguin, 1969) and 'A. Lerumo', *Fifty Fighting Years* (Inkululeko, 1971). There is a competent narrative history of the early ANC in Peter Walshe's *The Rise of African Nationalism in South Africa, 1912–52* (University of California Press, 1970). Gwendolen Carter and Thomas Karis, *From Protest to Challenge: A Documentary History of African Politics in South Africa, 1882–1964* (Hoover Institution Press, 1972–7), is an invaluable documentary collection in four volumes.

Marion Lacey, *Working for Boroko: The Origins of a Coercive Labour System in South Africa* (Ravan Press, 1981) covers the years of this chapter specifically. A very different perspective informed by the social history phase and also post-modernism is Patrick Harries, *Work Culture and Identity; Migrant Labourers in Mozambique and South Africa c. 1869–1910*, (Heinemann & Witwatersrand University Press, 1994). See also Alan Booth, 'Homestead, State and Migrant Labour', *AEH*, 14 (1985). A large study of the migrant labour regimes over time is Jonathan Crush, Alan Jeeves and David Yudelman, *South Africa's Labor Empire; A History of Black Migrancy to the Gold Mines*, (Westview Press, 1991). An attractive overview using a rich weave of sources is Luli Callinicos, *Working Life 1886–1940*, (Ravan, 1987).

On the war and reconstruction, a recent article by Shula Marks and Stanley Trapido, 'Lord Milner and the South African State', *HWJ*, 8 (1979) is itself of great importance and also refers extensively to a large controversial literature on the period. Among the most important are also Donald Denoon, *A Grand Illusion* (Longman, 1973) and Tim Keegan, 'Restructuring of Agrarian Class Relations in a Colonial Economy: the Orange River Colony 1902–10', *JSAS*, V (1979). The political history of unification was skilfully assessed in Leonard Thompson, *The Unification of South Africa* (Clarendon Press, 1960). Shula Marks has written a history of the Bambatha Rebellion, *Reluctant Rebellion* (Clarendon Press, 1970).

For the post-First World War period, the Rand Revolt serves as the central focus of a major analysis, Frederick Johnstone, *Class, Race and Gold* (Routledge & Kegan Paul, 1976). Francis Wilson, *Labour in the South African Gold Mines* (Cambridge University Press, 1972) is a detailed liberal assessment of gold-mining labour. Apart from Crush *et al.*, Randall Packard, *White Plague, Black Labour*, (Witwatersrand University Press, 1990) and Elaine Katz, *The White Death* (Witwatersrand University Press, 1995) on tuberculosis and miners' phthisis add an important dimension. On the ICU, P. L. Wickins, *The Industrial and Commercial Workers' Union of Africa* (Oxford University Press, 1978) can now be supplemented by Helen Bradford, *A Taste of Freedom*, (Yale University Press, 1987) on the rural activities of this popular movement cum trade union. There is also Kadalie's own account, *My Life and the ICU* (Frank Cass, 1970). There is little equivalent material about other African politicians of this period, but see D. D. T. Jabavu, *The*

*Black Question in South Africa* (Negro Universities Press, reprint 1969) and the documents in Carter and Karris. Perhaps the most interesting assessment of early African politics is to be found in Shula Marks, *The Ambiguities of Dependence in South Africa*, (Johns Hopkins Press, 1986).

Davenport, among others, can be used as a guide to the vagaries of 'white' politics and the large literature on the subject. Saul Dubow, *Racial Segregation and the Origins of Apartheid in South Africa 1919–36* (Macmillan, 1989) looks at its intersection with the state and the way the modern South African system was debated and fought over. The imperial historian Keith Hancock wrote an authorised two-volume biography of *Smuts* (Cambridge University Press, 1965–8) while the novelist Alan Paton produced an engaging and attractively written biography of his chief lieutenant, *Hofmeyr* (Oxford University Press, 1964). A classic statement of the liberal capitalist outlook is contained in R. F. A. Hoernlé, *South African Native Policy and the Liberal Spirit* (Negro Universities Press, reprint, 1969). His career has been explored by Martin Legassick, 'Race, Industrialization and Social Change: The Case of R. F. Hoernlé, *AA*, LXXV (1976). On capitalist ideology in South Africa more generally, there is an important study: Belinda Bozzoli, *The Political Ideology of a Ruling Class* (Routledge & Kegan Paul, 1981).

A number of essays try to capture the turbulent 1940s when much social contestation moved to the labour and urban spheres, notably David Hemson, 'Dock Workers, Labour Circulation and Class Struggles in Durban 1940–59', *JSAS*, IV (1977); Alf Stadler, 'Birds in the Cornfield: Squatter Movements in Johannesburg, 1944–7', *JSAS*, VI (1979); Dan O'Meara, 'The 1946 Miners' Strike and the Political Economy of South Africa', *Journal of Commonwealth & Comparative Politics*, XIII, (1975); Dunbar Moodie, 'The South African State and Industrial Conflict in the 1940s', *IJAHS*, XXI (1988) and 'The Moral Economy of the Black Miners' Strike of 1946', *JSAS*, XIII (1986). On the early labour movement, Baruch Hirson, *Yours for the Union; Class and Community Struggles in South Africa*, (Zed Press & Witwatersrand University Press, 1989) pioneered new approaches. Luli Callinicos captures the period for one key section of the country in *A Place in the Sun; The Rand on the Eve of Apartheid*, (Ravan Press, 1993). One cannot but mention on the subject of Rand history the two-volume urban history, taken back to the nineteenth century, however, by Charles van Onselen, *New Babylon, New Nineveh*, (Longman, 2 volumes, 1982).

## 9  The Decolonisation of Africa, 1940–60

Only recently has this period been treated as a historical one, deserving analytical discussion. There is a lot of material from the 1960s but it has dated badly and now looks mainly like journalism of varying quality. A number of surveys present the main facts, such as Rudolf von Albertini, *Decolonisation: The Administration and Future of the Colonies* (Doubleday, 1971). John Hargreaves, *The End of Colonial Rule in West Africa* (Macmillan, 1979) and J. E. Flint, 'Planned Decolonization and its Failure in British Africa' *AA*, 82 (1983) are suggestive and serious. Thomas Hodgkin, *Nationalism in Colonial Africa* (New York University Press, 1956) is a classic that set the tone for later assessments and still bears re-reading. Jack Woddis, *Africa: The Lion Awakes* (Lawrence & Wishart, 1961), is journalistic but very useful as a survey of the labour insurgency of the post-war era that liberal and nationalist writers have often conveniently forgotten. There are several relevant sections on the already cited collection of Gutkind, Cohen and Copans, *African Labour History* (Sage, 1978), that touch on this period.

For an introduction to the great Malagasy rising of 1947–8, Jacques Tronchon, *L'Insurrection Malgache de 1947* (Maspéro, 1974) is stimulating. On the UCP rebellion in Cameroun the standard work is Richard Joseph, *Radical Nationalism in Cameroun* (Oxford University Press, 1977). There is a large bibliography on Mau Mau. Two major introductions can be found in Rosberg and Nottingham, *The Myth of Mau Mau*, cited earlier, and Robert Buitenhuys, *Mau Mau Twenty Years After* (Mouton, 1973) while Berman and Lonsdale, cited for Chapter 6, is important. Several primary accounts by participants are available: Waruhiu Itote, *Mau Mau General* (EAPH, 1971); J. M. Kariuki, *Mau Mau Detainee* (Oxford University Press, 1963) and Donald Barnett and Karari Njama, *Mau Mau From Within* (Monthly Review Press, 1966). Mau Mau was the subject of a special issue of the *Kenya Historical Review*, V(2) (1977) and the important articles of Frank Furedi, 'The African Crowd in Nairobi', *JAH*, XIV (1973) and 'The Social Composition of the Mau Mau Movement in the White Highlands', *Journal of Peasant Studies*, 1 (1974). See also Tabitha Kanogo, *Squatters and the Roots of Mau Mau*, (James Currey, Ohio University Press & Heinemann, 1987), Sharon Stichter, 'Workers, Trade Unions and the Mau Mau Rebellion', *CJAS*, IX (1975), Luise White, 'Separating the Men from the Boys: Construction of Gender, Sexuality and Terrorism in Central Kenya', *IJAHS*, XXIII (1990) and Furedi's *The Mau Mau War in Perspective*, (James Currey, Heinemann & Ohio University Press, 1989).

On particular countries, the reader should look at previous lists of general histories cited earlier. For British West Africa, two particular studies carry special weight: Martin Kilson, *Political Change in a West African State* (Harvard University Press, 1966), which highlights the peasant struggles in rural Sierra Leone and K. Post and G. Vickers, *The Price of Liberty* (Cambridge University Press, 1973), a biography of Adegoke Adelabu that powerfully conveys the realities of nationalist politics in Nigeria.

The standard sources on Nigeria are informative and so far still to be replaced: James Coleman, *Nigeria: Background to Nationalism* (University of California Press, 1958); Richard Sklar, *Nigerian Political Parties* (Princeton University Press, 1963); C. S. Whitaker, *The Politics of Tradition: Continuity and Change in Northern Nigeria* (Princeton University Press, 1970, best of the lot); B. J. Dudley, *Parties and Politics in Northern*

*Nigeria* (Cass, 1968), and on the economic background, Gerald Helleiner, *Peasant Agriculture, Government and Economic Growth in Nigeria* (Richard Irwin, 1966). A brief corrective is Segun Osoba, 'The Nigerian Power Élite, 1952–65' in the Gutkind and Waterman reader cited previously.

The equivalent liberal standards for the Gold Coast are: David Apter, *The Gold Coast* (Ghana in later editions) *in Transition* (Princeton University Press, 1955) and Dennis Austin, *Politics in Ghana, 1946–60* (Oxford University Press, 1964). Most of the work on Nkrumah stresses the independence period. An illuminating exception is Richard Rathbone, 'Businessmen in Politics: Party Struggle in Ghana 1949–57', *JDS*, IX (1973). John Cartwright, *Politics in Sierra Leone, 1947–67* (University of Toronto Press, 1970) is the standard work for its subject.

British East Africa is treated in the third volume of the *History of East Africa* edited by D. A. Low and Alison Smith (Clarendon Press, 1976). Apart from Mau Mau, other aspects of Kenya are discussed in M. P. K. Sorrenson, *Land Reform in the Kikuyu Country* (Oxford University Press, 1967); David Anderson and David Throup, 'Africans and Agricultural Production in Colonial Kenya: The Myth of the War as a Watershed', *JAH*, XXVI (1985); John Spencer, *The KAU* (KPI, 1985); E. S. Atieno-Odhiambo, 'Seek Ye First the Economic Kingdom: A History of the Luo Thrift and Trading Corporation', *Hadith*, V (B. Ogot, ed. 1975) and Clayton and Savage's labour history already cited. On Tanganyika, there is Cranford Pratt, *The Critical Phase in Tanzania, 1945–68* (Cambridge University Press, 1976); G. A. Maguire, *Towards 'Uhuru' in Tanganyika* (Cambridge University Press, 1969); Lionel Cliffe, 'Nationalism and the Reaction to Enforced Agricultural Improvement in Tanganyika During the Colonial Period', in the collection, Lionel Cliffe and John Saul, *Socialism in Tanzania* (Tanzania Publishing House, 1973) and, on labour, W. H. Friedland, 'Co-operation, Conflict and Conscription: TANU–TFL Relations, 1895–64', in J. Butler and A. A. Castagno, eds, *Boston University Papers on Africa*, I (1967). For Uganda, Gardner Thompson, 'Colonialism in Crisis: The Uganda Disturbances of 1945', *AA*, 91 (1992) is a recent re-examination.

On British Central Africa, Federation inspired a myriad of rather interchangeable liberal assessments of 'race relations' for British consumption. One of the better is Patrick Keatley, *The Politics of Partnership* (Penguin, 1963). Change on the Copperbelt is studied in an anthropology classic, A. L. Epstein, *Politics in an Urban African Community* (Manchester University Press, 1958); Robert Bates, *Unions, Parties and Political Development* (Yale University Press, 1971); Elena Berger, *Labour, Race and Colonial Rule* (Clarendon Press, 1974) and J. R. Hooker, 'Role of the Labour Department in the Birth of African Trade Unionism in Northern Rhodesia', *IRSH*, X (1965). Among works already cited the reader should turn to Roberts' general history and Caplan on Barotseland for Zambia. Other works on Zambia include David Mulford, *Zambia: The Politics of Independence, 1957–64* (Oxford University Press, 1967); Ian Henderson, 'The Economic Origins of Decolonisation in Zambia, 1940–5', *Rhodesian History*, V (1974); Thomas Rasmussen, 'The Popular Basis of Anti-Colonial Protest' in William Tordoff, ed., *Politics in Zambia* (Manchester University Press, 1974); Mwelwa Musambachime, 'Rural Political Protest: The 1953 Disturbances in Mweru-Luapula', *IJAHS*, XX (1987) and Mac Dixon-Fyle, 'Agricultural Improvement and Political Protest on the Tonga Plateau, Northern Rhodesia', *JAH*, XVIII (1977). For an interesting essay on Malawi in the Roderick Macdonald collection already cited see Roger Tangri, 'From the Politics of Unionism to Mass Nationalism'. Tony Woods covers a subject usually associated with more industrialised colonies in 'Bread with Freedom and Peace; Rail Workers in Malawi', *JSAS*, XVIII (1992). Rhodesia is considered primarily in Chapter 11, but note also James Barber, *Rhodesia: The Road to Rebellion* (Oxford University Press, 1967) and Peter Harris, 'Industrial Workers in Rhodesia, 1946–72', *JSAS*, I (1975).

Ruth Schachter Morgenthau, *Political Parties in French West Africa* (Clarendon Press, 1964) has long been the introduction to her subject for English language readers. It is, in reality, much stronger on French than on African politics and has little to say on social and economic history. Jean Suret-Canale, *Afrique Noire: de la colonisation à l'indépendance, 1945–60* (Editions Sociales, 1972) is less successful than the preceding volume on the colonial era. A pathbreaking article by Fred Cooper, 'The Senegalese General Strike of 1946 and the Labour Question in Post-War French Africa', *CJAS*, XXIV (1990) will hopefully open the road to other studies. There is some inspired journalism in Georges Chaffard, *Les carnets secrets de la décolonisation* (Calmann-Levy, 1967). For a survey on Equatorial Africa, see Elikia M'Bokolo, 'Forces sociales et idéologies dans la décolonisation de l'AEF', *JAH*, XXII (1981).

On the Belgian Congo, Crawford Young, *Politics in the Congo* (Princeton University Press, 1965) is a mine of information. There is an eloquent brief assessment in Gerard Althabe, *Les fleurs du Congo* (Maspéro, 1972). Thomas Kanza, *Crisis in the Congo* (Penguin, 1972) is an interesting account from the moderate Left. Also on the crisis of 1960 and its aftermath are: Catherine Hoskyns, *The Congo Since Independence* (Oxford University Press, 1965); the impassioned journalism of Jules Chomé, notably *La crise congolaise* (Editions des remarques congolaises, Brussels, 1960); Jules Gérard-Libois, *Katanga Secession* (University of Wisconsin Press, 1966) and Conor Cruise O'Brien, *To Katanga and Back* (Simon & Schuster, 1962). The American role is revealed in Steve Weissman, *American Foreign Policy in the Congo 1960–1964* (Cornell University Press, 1974).

More specialised study can be guided by the numerous volumes of annotated primary source material on the Congo and also Ruanda-Urundi published by the Brussels research centre, CRISP. Among monographs, Herbert Weiss, *Political Protest in the Congo* (Princeton University Press, 1967), a regional study, is especially interesting. Finally, for the first part of the period covered in this chapter, note B. Jewsiewicki, Kiloma Lema and Jean-Jacques Vellut. 'Documents pour servir à l'histoire du Zaïre: grèves dans le Bas Congo en 1945', *Études d'histoire africaine*, V (1973) and Maurice Lovens, 'La révolte de Masisi-Lubutu (Congo belge, janvier–mai 1944)', *Cahiers du CEDAF* 3/4, 1974.

On the ferment of the 1940s in Eritrea see G. K. N. Trevaskis, *Eritrea, A Colony in Transition* (Oxford University Press, 1960) and Lloyd Ellingson, 'Emergence of

Political Parties in Eritrea, 1941–50', *JAH*, XVIII (1977). Compare with Gebru Tareke, 'Peasant Resistance in Ethiopia: The Case of Weyane', *JAH*, XXV (1984). For the nationalist era in the Sudan the best sources at present are Gabriel Warburg, *Islam, Nationalism and Communism in a Traditional Society: The Case of the Sudan* (Frank Cass, 1978) and Peter Woodward, *Condominium and Sudanese Nationalism* (Collings, 1979).

Many African politicians of the decolonisation era have produced memoirs or political manifestos. A sampling includes: (Kenya) Jomo Kenyatta, *Facing Mount Kenya* (Secker & Warburg, 1953); Bildad Kaggia, *The Roots of Freedom* (EAPH, 1975); Tom Mboya, *Freedom and After* (Little, Brown, 1963); Oginga Odinga, *Not Yet Uhuru* (Heinemann, 1967); (Zaïre) Anicet Kashamura, *De Lumumba aux colonels* (Buchet-Castel, 1966); Ludo Martens, *Abo; une femme de Congo*, (Harmattan, 1994); (Senegal) Mamadou Dia, *Mémoires d'un militant du Tiers-Monde* (Publisud, 1985); (Malawi) M. W. K. Chiume, *Kwacha* (EAPH, 1975); (Nigeria) Nnamdi Azikiwe, *Zik: A Selection from the Speeches* (Cambridge University Press, 1961), and Sir Ahmadu Bello, *My Life* (Cambridge University Press, 1962). There is a published collection of *Speeches and Writings of Patrice Lumumba* (Little, Brown, 1972). Apart from Post and Jenkins the best biographies of African politicians are Jeremy Murray-Brown, *Kenyatta* (George Allen & Unwin, 1972) and Philip Short, *Banda* (Routledge & Kegan Paul, 1974). Janet Vaillant, *Black, French and African* (Harvard University Press 1990) is a useful biography of Senghor.

African writers of fiction convey the feeling of the period well in certain novels. These include, in a short selection, James Ngugi (Ngugi wa Thiongo), *A Grain of Wheat* (Heinemann, 1967) and *Weep Not, Child*, (Heinemann, 1964) which power-fully evokes Mau Mau; Sembene Ousmane's epic of the great railway workers' strike in French West Africa, *God's Bits of Wood* (Doubleday, English translation, 1962) and the tragicomic fiction of Chinua Achebe, *No Longer at Ease* (Obolensky, 1961) and *A Man of the People* (Heinemann, 1966).

## 10    Tropical Africa 1960–80: Class, State and the Problem of Development

For the material in Chapters 10 and 12, where articles as opposed to books must play a major part as sources of more information, two important journals are the British-based *Review of African Economy* and the French *Politique Africaine*. A number of scholarly journals on contemporary Africa are also important, containing a host of articles varying both in outlook and quality. A short list must include *African Affairs*, the *Journal of Modern African Studies*, the *African Studies Review* (USA) and the *Revue française de politique africaine*. For some years, the American Social Science Research Council (SSRC) sponsored so-called 'state of the art' review articles on many aspects of African society which are extremely useful and appeared in the

*African Studies Review.* A number of important collections are orientated towards the issues stressed in this chapter: Peter Gutkind and Peter Waterman, eds, *African Social Studies: A Radical Reader* (Heinemann, 1977); Gutkind and Immanuel Wallerstein, eds, *The Political Economy of Contemporary Africa* (Sage, 1976); Richard Sandbrook and Robin Cohen, eds, *Development of an African Working Class* (Longman, 1975) and Henry Bernstein and Bonnie Campbell, eds, *Contradictions of Accumulation in Africa* (Sage, 1985).

The underdevelopment paradigm has been developed most effectively for Africa by the Egyptian economist Samir Amin whose many works on tropical Africa include *Neo-Colonialism in West Africa* (Penguin, 1973); *Développement du capitalisme en Côte d'Ivoire* (Editions du Minuit, 1967); 'Underdevelopment and Dependence in Black Africa: Origins and Contemporary Forms', *Journal of Modern African Studies* X (1972). Other influential writing in similar vein includes Reg Green and Ann Seidman, *Unity or Poverty? Economics of Panafricanism* (Penguin, 1969) and Tamas Szentes, *The Political Economy of Underdevelopment* (Akademiai Kiadoi, 1976).

On African politics in general, Immanuel Wallerstein, *Africa: The Politics of Unity* (Random House, 1967) covers the factual developments in the early years of interstate relations. There are useful assessments in Crawford Young, *Ideology and Development in Africa*, (Yale University Press, 1982) and Nelson Kasfir, ed., *State and Class in Africa*. (Frank Cass, 1984).

At the local level so much more rarely considered, Dele Olowu, 'Local Institutes and Development: The African Experience', *CJAS*, XXIII (1989) provides a different dimension. On the relationship of the African state to the economy Robert Bates' influential *Markets and States in Africa*, (University of California Press, 1981) is provocative. A very helpful general assessment and description of military and state power is Ruth First's *The Barrel of a Gun* (Allen Lane, 1970). An excellent article on militarism in Africa can be found in Robin Luckham, 'The Military, Militarization and Democratization in Africa: A Survey of the Literature and Issues', *African Studies Review*, XXXVII (1994). Yves Benot, *Idéologies d'indépendances africaines* (Maspéro, 1969) is a penetrating assessment of the outlook of the African ruling class; a useful collection along these lines in English is William Friedland and Carl Rosberg, eds, *African Socialism* (Stanford University Press, 1964). Among the better studies of the myth of educational opportunity in Africa are Pierre van den Bergh, *Power and Privilege at an African University* (Routledge & Kegan Paul, 1973) and Benoît Verhaegen, *L'enseignement universitaire au Zaire* (CEDAF, 1978). See also Abernethy on Nigeria, cited earlier.

Apart from the Sandbrook and Cohen collection, a number of important studies have looked at the history and sociology of the emergent African industrial proletariat, including Sandbrook's *Proletarians and African Capitalism: The Kenyan Case 1960–72* (Cambridge University Press, 1975); Cohen's *Labour and Politics in Nigeria* (Heinemann, 1974); Richard Jeffries, *Class, Ideology and Power in Africa: The Railwaymen of Sekondi* (Cambridge University Press, 1978); Adrian Peace, *Choice, Class and Conflict* (Harvester, 1979); Bruce Kapferer, *Strategy and Transaction in an*

*African Factory* (Manchester University Press, 1972); Michael Burawoy, 'The Colour of Class in the Copper Mines', *Zambian Papers*, 7 (1972) and R. D. Grillo, *Race, Class and Militancy* (Chandler, 1974), dealing respectively with Ghana, Nigeria, Zambia in two cases and Uganda (for those books without the relevant country in their title). For an alternative approach see Carola Lentz and Veit Erlmann, 'A Working Class in Formation? Economic Crisis and Strategies of Survival among Dagara Mine Workers in Ghana', *CEA*, 113 (1989) as well as James Ferguson's piece mentioned in Chapter 1. Both reflect the perspective of a slightly later period.

On specific regions and countries, the literature is more substantial than for any historic period and what follows is only selective and perhaps arbitrary, excluding numerous standard sources in favour of interesting interpretations. The collections and journals mentioned above are taken as read; selections from them are not included below with few exceptions.

For West Africa in general, a useful if uneven collection is John Dunn, ed., *West African States: Failure and Promise* (Cambridge University Press, 1978). On Nigeria, the analytical quality of the literature is generally rather poor. An interesting sketchy book of essays is Gavin Williams, ed., *State and Society in Nigeria* (Afrografika, Idanre, Nigeria, 1981). The wisdom of mainstream Western scholarship focusing on the military, ethnicity, etc. is collected in Robert Melson and Howard Wolpe, eds, *Nigeria: Modernization and the Politics of Communalism* (Michigan State University Press, 1972). The best account of the civil war is John de St Jorre, *The Brothers' War* (Houghton Mifflin, 1972). On the army and army rule, see Robin Luckham, *The Nigerian Military* (Cambridge University Press, 1972) and S. K. Panter-Brick, ed., *Nigerian Politics and Military Rule* (Athlone Press, 1970). The rising tide of peasant agitation and organisation in Western Nigeria during the 1970s is the subject of C. F. Beer, *Politics of Peasant Groups in Western Nigeria* (Ibadan University Press, 1976). A feel for local politics comes forward from Sandra Barnes, *Patrons and Power; Creating a Political Community in Metropolitan Lagos*, (Indiana University Press, 1986).

Not surprisingly, Ghana under Nkrumah has attracted much higher quality work in general just as it attracted many interesting scholars during that period. Nkrumah's view of his own life is expressed in his autobiography, *Ghana, an Autobiography* (Nelson, 1957) and his downfall in *Dark Days in Ghana* (International Publishers, 1969). An apologetic biography prepared after his death in exile is Basil Davidson, *Black Star* (Allen Lane, 1973). The most coherent defence of his economic policies is Roger Genoud, *Nationalism and Economic Development in Ghana* (Praeger, 1969). The fall of Nkrumah brought about a serious reconsideration of his significance and the beginning of a materialist analysis of contemporary Africa, landmarks in which have been: Bob Fitch and Mary Oppenheimer, *Ghana: End of an Illusion*, (Monthly Review Press, 1967); Jitendra Mohan, 'Nkrumah and Nkrumahism', *Socialist Register* (1967) and Roger Murray, 'Second Thoughts on Ghana', *New Left Review*, 42 (1967) and particularly Bjorn Beckman's outstanding *Organizing the Farmers* (Scandinavian Institute of African Studies, 1976). Another excellent work on Ghana by a Scandinavian is Jette Bukh, *The Village Woman in Ghana*

(Nordiska Afrikainstitut, 1979) which, among other subjects, considers the decline of the cocoa economy. A good monograph on aspects of post-independence Sierra Leone is David Fashole Luke, *Labour and Parastatal Politics in Sierra Leone*, (University Press of America, 1984).

Nkrumah's contemporary Modibo Keita presided over a similarly contradictory 'socialist' regime in Mali. Among several assessments of significance are Claude Meillassoux, 'Class Analysis of the Bureaucratic Process in Mali', *Journal of Development Studies*, VI (1970); W. I. Jones, 'The Mise and Demise of Socialist Institutions in Rural Mali', *Genève-Afrique*, XI (1972) and Guy Martin, 'Socialism, Economic Development and Planning in Mali 1960–68', *CJAS*, X (1976). See also Claus Ernst, *Tradition and Progress in an African Village* (C. Hurst, 1976).

The Republic of Guinea was fairly closed to research under Sékou Touré's regime and has inspired a particularly polemical literature (or a bland one, in some cases). Among available studies are B. Ameillon, *Guinée, bilan d'une indépendence* (Maspéro, 1964) and Ladipo Ademolekun, *Sékou Touré's Guinea* (Methuen, 1976). William Derman, *Serfs, Peasants and Socialists* (University of California Press, 1973) is an important study of rural social relationships. Touré himself had his speeches and writings published over many years in a multi-volume series from Conakry.

The richest literature on francophone West Africa (especially in translation) deals with Senegal. Donal Cruise O'Brien, *Saints and Politicians* (Cambridge University Press, 1975) contains several stimulating essays. Left scholarship in English on the republic is collected by Rita Cruise O'Brien, ed., *The Political Economy of Development: Dependence in Senegal* (Sage, 1979). Robert Fatton, *The Making of a Liberal Democracy; Senegal's Passive Revolution* (Lynne Rienner, 1985), Monar Couba Diop et Mamadou Diouf, *Le Sénégal sous Abdou Diouf*, (Karthala, 1990) and Catherine Boone, 'Making of a Rentier Class: Wealth, Accumulation and Political Control in Senegal', *Journal of Development Studies*, XXVI (1990) bring the story to the post-Senghor era. There is an excellent study of the authoritarian political system of Cameroun in Jean-François Bayart, *L'Etat au Cameroun* (Presses de la fondation nationale des sciences politiques, 1979) while Roger Charlton and Roy May, 'Warlords and Militarism in Chad', *Review of African Political Economy*, 45/46 (1990) is an introduction to part of the former French Equatorial Africa. On the Ivory Coast, a recent collection is Y.-A. Fauré and J.-F. Médard, *Etat et bourgeoisie en Côte d'Ivoire* (Editions Karthala, 1982).

For some radical francophone regimes, see Hugues Bertrand, *Le Congo: formation sociale et mode de développement economique* (Maspéro, 1975) and Maureen Covell, *Madagascar: Politics, Economy and Society*, (Frances Pinter, 1987). The French relationship with Africa has recently been reviewed in a special issue of *Politique africaine* commemorating the end of the Mitterrand presidency (58, 1995). For special facets see Guy Martin, 'Uranium: A Case Study in Franco-African Relations', *JMAS*, XXVII (1989) and Nicholas van der Walle, 'The Decline of the Franc Zone; Monetary Politics in Francophone Africa', *AA*, 90 (1991).

Our major source on the peasant risings of the 1960s in the Leopoldville Congo republic is Benoît Verhaegen, *Rebellions au Congo* (CRISP, Brussels, 2 vols, 1966–9) with a rich selection of documents. Renee Fox, Willy de Craemer and Jean-Marie Ribeaucourt, 'The Second Independence: A Case Study of the Kwilu Rebellion of the Congo', *Comparative Studies in Society and History*, VIII (1965) is also important. The emerging system was captured by Jean-Claude Willame, *Patrimonialism and Political Change in the Congo*, (Stanford University Press, 1972) and Jean-Philippe Peemans, 'The Social and Economic Development of Zaïre since Independence', *AA*, LXXIV (1975). On Zaïre and its fundamental problems since rebaptism under General Mobutu, readings include Crawford Young and Thomas Turner, *The Rise and Decline of the Zaïrian State*, (University of Wisconsin Press, 1985), Jean-Claude Willame, *L'automne d'un despotisme*, (Karthala, 1992); Michael Schatzberg, *Politics and Class in Zaire* (Africana, 1981) and Emizet Kisangani, 'Implementation of Stabilization Policies in an Authoritarian Setting: Zaïre 1970–80', *CJAS*, XXI (1987) as well as the special issue of *CJAS* edited by Bogumil Jewsiewicki, XVIII (1984).

There is an excellent one-volume study of independent Kenya: Colin Leys, *Underdevelopment in Kenya* (Heinemann, 1975) which the author corrected in favour of a greater emphasis on internal class formation in 'Capital Accumulation, Class Formation and Dependency – the Significance of the Kenyan Case', *Socialist Register* (1978). Other important contributions on class, state and dependency in books on Kenya include: Alice Amsden, *International Firms and Labour in Kenya 1945–70* (Frank Cass, 1971); Nairobi Christian Council of Churches, *Who Controls Industry in Kenya?* (EAPH, Nairobi, 1968), Nicola Swainson, *Development of Corporate Capitalism in Kenya* (Heinemann, 1980) and Raphael Kaplinsky, ed., *Readings on the Multinational Corporations in Kenya* (Oxford University Press, 1978). Himbara's book, referred to with reference to Chapter 6, is a recent contribution. Power and local politics are the subject of Geoff Lamb, *Peasant Politics* (Friedmann, 1974) and David Parkin, *Palms, Wine and Witnesses* (Chandler, 1972), while Gary Wasserman, *The Politics of Decolonization* (Cambridge University Press, 1976), Christopher Leo, *Land and Class in Kenya*, (University of Toronto Press, 1984) and Angelique Haugerud, 'Land Tenure and Agrarian Change in Kenya' *Africa*, LIX (1989) have explored the 'Africanization' of the once white highlands.

On the Zanzibar revolution see Michael Lofchie, *Zanzibar: Background to Revolution* (Princeton University Press, 1965) and Anthony Clayton, *The Zanzibar Revolution and its Aftermath* (C. Hurst, 1981). No African state is so well-studied as unified Tanzania on which a rich literature developed during the 1970s, particularly on social change in rural society, Tanzania remaining a very rural country then. Several Dar es Salaam-based journals played a role in this, notably *African Review*, *Utafiti* (in English despite the title) and *Maji Maji*, the organ of the university branch of the party youth league. All published many important articles. Julius Nyerere has been a very eloquent defender of his own concept of socialism, put forth in several collections, *Freedom and Unity* (Oxford University Press, 1967); *Freedom and Socialism* (Oxford University Press, 1968) and *Freedom and Development* (Oxford University Press, 1973). For a critical view by a former cabinet minister and politician of the Left, A. M. Babu, *African Socialism or Socialist Africa?* (Zed Press, 1981) is a corrective from the Left. The best writing from the late 1960s into the new decade was collected in John Saul and Lionel Cliffe, eds, *Socialism in Tanzania* (Tanzania Publishing House, 2 vols, 1973). Saul's important analyses may also be found in his volume with Giovanni Arrighi, *Essays on the Political Economy of Africa* (Monthly Review Press, 1973) and *State and Revolution in Eastern Africa* (Monthly Review Press, 1980). Cliffe edited a somewhat later collection that continues the themes of Saul and Cliffe, *Rural Co-operation in Tanzania* (Tanzania Publishing House, 1975). A deeply critical and more coherently Marxist analysis with its roots in the Tanzanian student movement was Issa Shivji, *Class Struggles in Tanzania* (Heinemann and Tanzania Publishing House, 1976). It is a sort of signal post for two more recent collections, Andrew Coulson, ed., *African Socialism in Practice* (Spokesman Books, 1979) and Bismarck Mwansasu and Cranford Pratt, eds, *Towards Socialism in Tanzania* (Tanzania Publishing House and University of Toronto Press, 1979). As the titles imply, the first is on the whole critical and the second defensive towards the state. Other major works published in Dar es Salaam are the 'Studies in Political Science' pamphlet series, the long list of papers produced by the Economic Research Bureau and Henry Mapolu, ed., *Workers and Management* (Tanzania Publishing House, 1976). More recent analyses of the state and rural development of particular merit are Michaela von Freyhold, *Ujamaa Villages in Tanzania* (Heinemann, 1979) and the searching articles of Suzanne Mueller, notably 'Retarded Capitalism in Tanzania', *Socialist Register* (1980). I once attempted a synthesis with more citations in 'Class Conflict, Political Economy and the Struggles for Socialism in Tanzania', *AA*, LXXXI (1981). Dianne Bolton considers the sisal industry in *Nationalisation: A Road to Socialism*, (Zed Press, 1985).

On Zambia, perhaps the most distinctive contributions have been those that have considered the nationlisation of the copper industry: Antony Martin, *Minding their Own Business: Zambia's Struggle Against Western Control* (Hutchinson, 1972); M. Bostock and C. Harvey, eds, *Economic Independence and Zambian Copper* (Praeger, 1972) and Richard Sklar, *Corporate Power in an African State* (University of California Press, 1975). For useful introductions to Zambian politics and economy, see William Tordoff, ed., *Politics in Zambia* (Manchester University Press, 1974) and Tim Shaw 'Zambia: Dependence and Underdevelopment', *CJAS*, X (1976). An interesting case study can be found in Jotham Momba, 'The State, Rural Class Formation and Peasant Participation in Zambia: The Case of the Southern Province', *AA*, 88 (1989). Some important work on the former High Commission Territories clustered within and around South Africa are Hugh Macmillan, 'Swaziland: Decolonisation and the Triumph of Tradition', *JMAS*, XXIII (1985), Pauline Peters, 'Struggles over Meaning and Struggles over Power: Cattle, Water and the State in Botswana, *Africa*, LIV (1984), Jack Parson, *Botswana; Liberal Democracy and the Labor Reserve System in Southern Africa*, (Westview & Gower, 1984), and James Ferguson on Lesotho, *The Anti-Politics Machine*, (Cambridge University Press, 1990).

Events in the Horn were dominated by the Ethiopian Revolution which has been the subject of a number of studies. These include Marina and David Ottaway, *Ethiopia: Empire in Revolution* (Africana, 1978) and Fred Halliday and Maxine Molyneux, *The Ethiopian Revolution* (New Left Books, 1981), Christopher Clapham, *Transformation and Continuity in Revolutionary Ethiopia*, (Cambridge University Press, 1988) and Dessalegn Rahmato, *Agrarian Reform in Ethiopia* (Scandinavian African Studies Institute, 1984). See also John Markakis, 'Garrison Socialism: The Case of Ethiopia', Middle East Research and Information Project (MERIP) Report IX (1979); Addis Hiwet, 'Analysing the Ethiopian Revolution', *Review of African Political Economy* 30, (1984) and Michael Stahl, 'Capturing the Peasants through Cooperatives: The Case of Ethiopia', *Review of African Political Economy*, 44 (1989). For background the best sources on pre-revolutionary Ethiopia are John Markakis, *Ethiopia: Anatomy of a Traditional Polity* (Clarendon Press, 1974) and John Cohen and Dov Weintraub, *Land and Peasants in Imperial Ethiopia* (Van Gorcum, 1975). For the parallel revolutionary regime see David Laitin and Said Samatar, *Somalia: Nation in Search of a State*, (Westview and Gower, 1987) and Ahmed Samatar, *Socialist Somalia*, (Zed Press, 1988). Norman O'Neill and Jay O'Brien, eds, *Economy and Class in the Sudan* (Avebury, 1988) provides material on that country. I. M. Lewis, *Nationalism and Self-Determination in the Horn of Africa*, (Ithaca Press, 1983) is a useful regional book.

Fiction is often a powerful force for comprehending social conditions. Ayi Kwei Armah's symbolic portrayal of the Nkrumah years in Ghana, *The Beautyful Ones are Not Yet Born*, Ngugi wa Thiongo's *Petals of Blood* on Kenya and Ben Okri, *Dangerous Love*, are testimony to a political and social sensibility with striking common features.


## 11   Southern Africa in Crisis


There is clearly going to be far more written on the late twentieth-century struggles over the fate of southern Africa, although in some areas good analyses and powerful books do exist. None the less, the student will still have to turn to articles and even more journalistic material. South African journals that followed the changing pattern of events and contained analytical pieces include *Work in Progress*, *Africa Perspective*, the *South African Labour Bulletin*, *Agenda* and *Transformation*, the latter three still in existence. There is still (mid-1996) very little considered analysis available on post-apartheid South Africa. For the struggle years in South Africa, perhaps the best analyses of their day have been John Saul and Stephen Gelb, 'Crisis in South Africa: Class Defense, Class Revolution', *Monthly Review*, XXXIII (1981), also issued as a book by the review press and Robert Price, *The Apartheid State in Crisis; Political Transformation in South Africa*, (Oxford University Press, 1991).

On the development of the apartheid system, Martin Legassick, 'Legislation, Ideology and Economy in Post-1948 South Africa', *JSAS*, 1 (1974) is still very valuable, but see also Doug Hindson, *Pass Controls and the Urban African Proletariat*, (Ravan Press, 1987), Deborah Posel, *The Making of Apartheid 1948–61; Conflict and Compromise* (Clarendon Press, 1991) and Alan Mabin, 'Comprehensive Segregation:

The Origins of the Group Areas Act and its Planning Apparatuses', *JSAS*, XVIII (1992). Some of the readings on South African society suggested for Chapter 8 are relevant here too.

For Afrikaner nationalism, see Patrick Furlong, *Between Crown and Swastika*, (Witwatersrand University Press, 1991), T. Dunbar Moodie, *The Rise of Afrikanerdom* (University of California Press, 1975); Heribert Adam and Hermann Giliomee, *Ethnic Power Mobilized* (Yale University Press, 1977) and Dan O'Meara, *Forty Lost Years* (Ravan Press, 1996). The last two have much to say about the changing state. This was also true of Heribert Adam, *Modernizing Racial Domination*, (University of California Press, 1971). There is some historical discussion in Albie Sachs' *Justice in South Africa* (University of California Press, 1973). On the architect of separate development, Alex Hepple, *Verwoerd* (Penguin Books, 1967) is interesting.

On the Bantustans see Gwendolen Carter *et al.*, *South Africa's Transkei* (Northwestern University Press, 1967). More recent descriptions include Jeffrey Butler, Robert Rotberg and John Adams, *The Black Homelands of South Africa* (University of California Press, 1977), Barry Streek and Richard Wicksteed, *Render unto Kaiser; A Transkei Dossier*, (Ravan Press, 1982) and D. C. Hindson, 'Orderly Urbanization and Influx Control; From Territorial Apartheid to Regional Spatial Order in South Africa', *CEA*, 99 (1985).

For the ANC, consult the autobiography of Chief Albert Luthuli, *Let My People Go* (Collins, 1962) and the collected speeches of his successor as president, Nelson Mandela, *No Easy Walk to Freedom* (Heinemann, 1965). Mandela's *Long Walk to Freedom* (Macdonald Purnell, 1995) is a remarkable testimony in some respects. For the turn to armed struggle Basil Davidson, Joe Slovo and A. R. Wilkinson, *Southern Africa: The New Politics of Revolution* (Penguin, 1976) is instructive. The best assessments of the movement are Stephen Davis, *Apartheid's Rebels*, (Yale University Press, 1987) and Stephen Ellis and Tsepo Sechaba, *Comrades Agaionst Apartheid; the ANC and SACP in Exile* (James Currey & Indiana University Press, 1992).

Tom Lodge, *Black Politics in South Africa since 1945* (Longmans 1983) is still useful. Gail Gerhart sympathetically chronicles the rise of the Africanist tendency in *Black Nationalism in South Africa* (University of California Press, 1978). On particular facets, see also Govan Mbeki, *South Africa: The Peasants' Revolt* (Penguin, 1964) on the Pondoland risings. Cosmas Desmond, *The Discarded People* (Penguin, 1971), while Laurine Platzky and Cherryl Walker, eds, *The Surplus People; Forced Removals in South Africa* (Ravan Press, 1985) describe the dumping of Africans into the homelands.

Events in the 1970s started to cause considerable re-examination of the underpinnings of the South African system. Accounts that considered the significance of Soweto are Alex Callinicos and John Rogers, *Southern Africa After Soweto* (Pluto Press, 1977); Baruch Hirson, *Year of Fire, Year of Ash* (Zed Press, 1979) and J. Kane-Berman, *South Africa: The Method in the Madness* (Pluto Press, 1979). R. W. Johnson, *How Long Will South Africa Survive?* (Macmillan, 1977) has some original and stimulating ideas. The public writings and courtroom evidence of Steve Biko are collected in *The Testimony of Steve Biko* (M. Temple Smith, 1979).

For the 1980s, William Cobbett & Robin Cohen, eds., *Popular Struggles in South Africa*, (ROAPE & James Currey, 1988) and Colin Bundy, 'Street Sociology and Pavement Politics', *JSAS*, XIII (1987) are useful. For some detailed studies, Charles Carter, 'We are the Progressives: Alexandra Youth Congress Activists and the Freedom Charter 1983–85', *JSAS*, XVII (1991), Ineke van Kessel, 'From Confusion to Lusaka;'; The Youth Revolt in Sekhukhuneland', *JSAS*, XIX, (1993) and Nkosikathi Gwala, 'Political Violence and the Struggle for Control in Pietermaritzburg', *JSAS*, XV (1989) are all stimulating. On the labour movement there is more available. See Steven Friedman, *Building Tomorrow Today* (Ravan Press, 1987) and Jeremy Baskin, *Striking Back; A History of COSATU*, (Ravan Press, 1991).

On different aspects of social change in recent years in South Africa some interesting studies are Michael de Klerk, 'Seasons that Will Never Return', *JSAS*, XI (1984) on labour and the grain economy of the Highveld; Andries du Toit, 'The Micro-Politics of Paternalism: The Discourses of Management and Resistance on South African Fruit and Wine Farms', *JSAS*, XIX (1993) and Mamphela Ramphele, *A Bed Called Home; Life in the Migrant Labour Hostels of Cape Town*, (David Philip, Ohio University Press & Edinburgh University Press, 1993). Elsa Joubert's *Poppie* (Hodder & Stoughton, 1980) powerfully expressed the impact of labour control/ Bantustan policy on the lives of black working-class women in particular. Joseph Lelyveld's *Move Your Shadow*, (Michael Joseph, 1986) and Rian Malan's *My Traitor's Heart* (Vintage Books, 1991) represented for many the most impressive journalist witnesses of their time.

On conflicts elsewhere in southern Africa there is also a large but uneven literature. Two long if far from authoritative studies of Angola are John Marcum, *The Angolan Revolution* (MIT Press, 1969–78) and René Pelissier, *La guerre du minotaure* (Orgeval, France, 1978). Basil Davidson wrote an attractive account of the MPLA in the field during their strongest phase, *In The Eye of the Storm* (Longman, 1972). For a critical survey of Angola since the MPLA victory see W. G. Clarence-Smith, 'Class Structure and Class Struggle in Angola in the 1970s', *JSAS*, VII (1980) and the contribution of Michel Cahen to *Bourgs et villes en Afrique lusophone* (Harmattan, 1989). For the aligned revolution, outside this region of course, in Guinea-Bissau and its consequences, see Rosemary Galli and Jocelyn Jones, *Guinea-Bissau: Politics, Economics and Society* (Frances Pinter, 1987).

Eduardo Mondlane's account of the Mozambican revolution covers up conflicts but is valuable: *The Struggle for Mozambique* (Penguin Books, 1969). See also John Saul, 'FRELIMO and the Mozambique Revolution' in Saul and Arrighi, *Essays in the Political Economy of Africa*, cited earlier. Mozambique's many intellectual supporters did not provide as effective or convincing an engaged literature as was found in Tanzania. For a sample, however, see John Saul, ed., *A Difficult Road; The Transition to Socialism in Mozambique*, (Monthly Review Press, 1985). For the mortal struggle between FRELIMO and RENAMO, see Alex Vines, *RENAMO; Terrorism in Mozambique* (James Currey & Indiana University Press, 1991) and a remarkable monograph by an anthropologist on one region, Christian Geffray, *La cause des armes au Mozambi-*

*que; anthropologie d'une guerre,* (Karthala, 1990). Bertil Egero provides a thoughtful assessment in *A Dream Undone; The Political Economy of Democracy 1975–84,* (Nordiska Afrikainstitutet, 1987). Some essays emphasizing particular aspects of the Mozambican experience are Signe Arnfred, 'Women in Mozambique; Gender Struggle and Gender Politics', *Review of African Political Economy,* 41 (1988); Merle Bowen, 'Peasant Agriculture in Mozambique', *CJAS,* XXIII (1989) and Otto Roesch, 'Rural Mozambique since the FRELIMO 4th Party Congress: The Situation in the Baixo Limpopo', *Review of African Political Economy,* 41 (1984) and 'RENAMO and the Peasantry in Southern Mozambique', *CJAS,* XXVI (1992). Joseph Hanlon surveys the postrevolutionary scene of the 1990s in *Mozambique: Who Calls the Shots?* (James Currey & Indiana University Press, 1991) which also comments on the weight of the so-called Non-Governmental Organisations (NGOs) such as to have a much wider relevance.

On the Rhodesian war the best accounts are Kees Maxey, *The Fight for Zimbabwe* (Rex Collings, 1975) and David Martin and Phyllis Johnson's book 'authorised' by ZANU, *The Struggle for Zimbabwe* (Monthly Review Press, 1981). On the social context and impact, see Terence Ranger, *Peasant Consciousness and Guerrilla War in Zimbabwe* (James Currey, 1985); Irene Staunton, *Mothers of the Revolution* (Baobab Books, 1990); Norma Kriger, *Zimbabwe's Guerrilla War; Peasant Voices,* (Cambridge University Press, 1992) and David Maxwell, 'Local Politics and the War of Liberation in North-eastern Zimbabwe', *JSAS,* XIX (1993). For the UDI regime see Larry Bowman, *Politics in Rhodesia* (Harvard University Press, 1973) and Martin Loney, *Rhodesia: White Racism and Imperial Response* (Penguin, 1975). There is a sensitive feeling for African politics in the future minister Nathan Shamuyarira's *Crisis in Rhodesia* (André Deutsch, 1965). The new regime was evaluated in Colin Stoneman and Lionel Cliffe, *Zimbabwe: Politics, Economics and Society,* (Frances Pinter, 1989) and Jeffrey Herbst, *Politics in Zimbabwe,* (University Press of Zimbabwe, 1990.) Some supplementary material of particular value would be Jocelyn Alexander, 'State, Peasantry and Resettlement in Zimbabwe', *Review of African Political Economy,* 61 (1994); Ben Cousins *et al.,* 'Social Differentiation in Communal Lands in Zimbabwe', *Review of African Political Economy,* 53 (1992) and Dan Wiener et al, 'Land Use and Productivity in Zimbabwe', *JMAS,* XXIII (1985).

For Namibia the literature has been less interesting. Ruth First, *South West Africa* (Penguin, 1963) gave a good background description. See also Reg Green, Marja-Liisa and Kimmo Kiljunen, eds, *Namibia: The Last Colony* (Longman, 1982). On the liberation war, a recent study greatly strengthens our knowledge, Colin Leys and John Saul, *Namibia's Liberation Struggle; The Two-Edged Sword,* (James Currey & Ohio University Press, 1995).

# 12   The Age of Structural Adjustment

In trying to understand current African politics and the debate about democratisation, I have been especially influenced by Mahmood Mamdani, *Citizen and Subject,* cited above; by Basil Davidson, *The Black Man's Burden: Africa and the Curse of the Nation-State*, (James Currey, 1992) which blames the colonial experience for foisting a particular kind of state-form on Africa; and, although only partially concerned with Africa, Michel Cahen's *Ethnicité politique*, (Harmattan, 1994), a polemic against the attempt to erase ethnicity from the political map of the world. Then there is Jean-François Bayart, *The State in Africa; The Politics of the Belly* (Longman 1983), learned and provocative in its attempt to force the reader to re-think African politics from within. This theme is fascinatingly explored as well in Bayart, ed., *Le politique par le bas en Afrique noire*, (Karthala, 1992). E. Terray, ed., *L'état contemporain en Afrique*, (Harmattan, 1987) is a good collection.

For an introduction to the current political context in Africa, Peter Gibbon, Y. Bangura and A. Ofstad, *Adjustment, Authoritarianism and Democracy: The Politics of Economic Liberalisation in Africa*, (Scandinavian Institute of African Studies, 1992) follows well from the radical literature of the 1970s. On the degeneration of the Nigerian state and its context, Michael Watts, ed., *State, Oil and Agriculture in Nigeria*, (Institute of International Affairs, Berkeley, 1987) and Toyin Falola and Julius Ihonvbere, *The Rise and Fall of Nigeria's Second Republic 1979–84* (Zed Books, 1985) are useful. Kenyan democratisation, with special reference to the role of religion, is explored in detail in Hervé Maupeu, 'Une opposition en régime autoritaire: l'exemple du Reveil est-africain au Kenya', *CJAS*, XXV (1991). A major example of political democratisation has been the Republic of Benin: Chris Allen, 'Restructuring and the Authoritarian State: "Democratic Renewal" in Benin', *Review of African Political Economy*, 54 (1992). On some of Africa's most serious crisis areas where the post-colonial state has apparently collapsed: Hussein Adam, 'Somalia: Militarism, Warlordism or Democracy?' *Review of African Political Economy*, 54 (1992); A. B. Zack-Williams, 'Sierra Leone: Crisis and Despair', *Review of African Political Economy*, 49 (1990); Rene Lemarchand, 'L'ecole franco-burundaise', *CJAS*, XXIV (1990) *et seq.*; Filip Reyntjens, *L'Afrique des Grands Lacs au Crise*, (Karthala 1994) and Mahmood Mamdani, 'From Conquest to Consent as the Basis of State Formation; Reflections on Rwanda', *New Left Review*, 216 (1996) can all be recommended.

A useful set of collections whose readings expose the African crisis and the meaning of structural adjustment are: Peter Lawrence, ed., *World Recession and the Food Crisis in Africa* (ROAPE & James Currey, 1986); John Ravenhill, ed., *Africa in Economic Crisis*, (Macmillan, 1986) and John Ravenhill & Thomas Callaghy, eds, *Hemmed In; Responses to Africa's Economic Decline*, (Columbia University Press, 1993). There have been many African ripostes to structural adjustment. One of the best is Bade Onimode, *A Future for Africa; Beyond the Politics of Adjustment*, (Earthscan, 1992). A French interpretation is found in G. Duruflé, *L'ajustement structurel en Afrique*, (Karthala, 1988). This chapter has emphasised two countries in particular. For Ghana, some readings on the structural adjustment period are George Dei, 'The Renewal of a Ghanaian Rural Economy', *CJAS*, XXVI (1992); Jeffrey Haynes, 'Railway Workers and the PNDC Government in Ghana 1982–90', *JMAS*, XXIX, (1991); John Loxley, 'Structural Adjustment Programmes in Africa: Reflections on

Ghana and Zambia', *Review of African Political Economy*, 47 (1990); Jeffrey Herbst, *The Politics of Reform in Ghana 1982–91*, (University of California Press, 1993) and E. Gyimah-Boadi, ed., *Ghana under PNDC Rule*, (CODESRIA, 1993). For Uganda, companion pieces might be Holger Bernt Hansen & Michael Twaddle, *Uganda Now*, (Heinemann, Ohio University Press & James Currey, 1988); Emmanuel Nabuguzi, 'Peasant Responses to Crisis in Uganda: Rice Farmers in Busoga', *Review of African Political Economy*, 56 (1993); Mahmood Mamdani, 'Uganda: Contradictions of the IMF Programme and Perspective', *Development and Change*, XXI (1990) and E. A. Brett, 'Rebuilding Organizational Capacity in Uganda under the National Resistance Movement', *JMAS*, XXXII (1994). Perhaps the next best studied example is Zambia. Apart from the Loxley article cited just above, Carolyn Baylies and Morris Szeftel, 'The Fall and Rise of Multi-party politics in Zambia', *Review of African Political Economy*, 54 (1992); Hans-Otto Savo, 'The International Monetary Fund and Zambia: The Contradictions of Exchange Rate Auctioning and the Desubsidisation of Agriculture', *AA*, 87 (1988) and Jürgen Wolf, 'Zambia under the IMF Regime', *AA*, 88 (1989) are particularly useful. Pieces on less studied countries are Myriam Gervais, 'Structural Adjustment in Niger; Implementations, Effects and Determining Political Factors', *Review of African Political Economy*, 63 (1994); Lars Rudebeck, 'The Effects of Structural Adjustment on Kandjadja, Guinea-Bissau', *Review of African Political Economy*, 49 (1990); Horace Campbell, 'Tanzania and the World Bank's Urban Shelter Project; Ideology and International Finance', *Review of African Political Economy*, 41 (1988);

Some of the most important current studies of the African situation in the structural adjustment era have focused on agriculture. See especially Peter Lawrence's collection, already cited, Philip Raikes, *Modernizing Hunger; Famine, Food Surplus and Farm Policy in the EEC and Africa*, (James Currey & Heinemann, 1988); Peter Gibbon, Kjell Havnevik & Kenneth Hermele, *A Blighted Harvest; The World Bank and African Agriculture in the 1980s*, (James Currey, 1993) and Hamid Ait Amara and Bernard Founou-Tchuigoua, eds, *African Agriculture; The Critical Choices*, (Zed Press and United Nations University, 1990). But what is actually happening in African agriculture? Some perceptive answers can be found in Sara Berry, *No Condition is Permanent; The Social Dynamics of Agrarian Change in Sub-saharan Africa*, (University of Wisconsin Press, 1993); Dominique Desjeux, *Stratégies paysannes en Afrique noire*, (Harmattan, 1987); Christian Santoir, 'Décadence et résistance de pastoralisme; les peuls de la vallée du fleuve Senegal', *CEA*, 133 (1993); Fiona Mackenzie, 'Local Initiative and National Policy: Gender and Agricultural Change in Muranga's District, Kenya', *CJAS*, XX (1986); Maureen Mackintosh, *Gender, Class and Rural Transition; Agribusiness and the Food Crisis in Senegal*, (Zed Press, 1989) and Martha Starr, 'Risk, Environmental Variability and Drought-Induced Impoverishment: The Pastoral Economy of Central Niger', *Africa*, LVII (1987). On one key aspect that continues to expand: Barbara Dinham and Colin Hines, *Agribusiness in Africa* (Earth Resources Research, 1983). The radical green perspective is portrayed by Lloyd Timberlake, *Africa in Crisis: The Causes, the Cures of Environmental*

*Bankruptcy*, (Earthscan, 1985) While the developmental literature remains largely focused on agriculture, useful surveys are found in Faysal Yachir, *Mining in Africa Today; Strategies and Prospects*, (United Nations University and Zed Press, 1988) and Roger Riddell, ed., *Manufacturing Africa*, (ODI & James Currey, 1990). Some scathing attacks on the structure of aid have been written in recent years. Ferguson's *Anti-Politics Machine* is perhaps the most remarkable. On large projects and their implications, see Gunilla Andrae and Bjorn Beckman, *The Wheat Trap* (Zed Press, 1985) and Adrian Adams, *La terre et les gens du fleuve*, (Harmattan, 1985). In the previous chapter, Hanlon's critique of NGOs in Mozambique was highlighted. Others in at the kill are Richard Hogg, 'Development in Kenya; Drought, Desertification and Food Scarcity', *AA*, 86 (1987), William Adams and David Anderson, 'Irrigation Before Development: Indigenous and Induced Change in Agricultural and Water Management in East Africa', *AA*, 87 (1988) and Doug Porter *et al.*, *Development in Practice; Paved with Good Intentions* (Routledge, 1991).

How do Africans cope? On the economic plane, creative perspectives required to penetrate beyond conventional analyses can be found in Janet MacGaffey, *The Real Economy in Zaire*, (James Currey & University of Pennsylvania Press, 1991); Johan Pottier, *Migrants No More; Settlement and Survival in Mambwe Villages*, (Manchester University Press, 1988); Nicholas van Hear, ' "By-Day Boys" and Dariga Men', *Review of African Political Economy*, 31 (1984); Lars Rudebeck, 'Kandjadja, Guinea-Bissau: 1976–86: Observations on the Political Economy of an African Family', *Review of African Political Economy*, 41 (1988) and T. L. Maliyamkomo and M. S. D. Bagachwa, *The Second Economy in Tanzania*, (Heinemann, James Currey & Ohio University Press, 1990.) On the urban side, one may note Emmanuel Ndione, *Dakar; une société en grappe*, (Karthala, 1993); Abdou Touré, *Les petits métiers à Abidjan; l'imagination au secours de la conjoncture* (Karthala, 1985); Ph. Antoine *et al.*, *Abidjan, 'côté cours'*, (Karthala, 1987) and Aili Tripp, 'Women and the Changing Urban Household Economy in Tanzania', *JMAS*, XXVII (1989). Politically, there are already several references above to collapsed central states. At the micro-level, it is also useful to explore work such as Suzanne Heald, 'Mafias in Africa: The Rise of Drinking Companies and Vigilante Groups in Bugisu, Uganda', *Africa*, LVI (1986) and Ray Abrahams, 'Sungusungu: Village Vigilante Groups in Tanzania', *AA*, 86 (1987).

A few writers are also trying to explore the development of new cultural forms: Karin Barber, *I Could Speak Until Tomorrow; Oriki, Women and the Past in a Yoruba Town* (Edinburgh University Press, 1991); Otwin Marenin, 'The Anini Saga: Armed Robbery and the Reproduction of Ideology in Nigeria', *JMAS*, XXV (1987) and Abdou Maliqalim Simone and Edgar Pieterse, 'Civil Societies in an Internationalised Africa', *Social Dynamics* (Cape Town), XIX (1993). Simone also has a fascinating study of changing Sudanese Islam, *In Whose Image? Political Islam and Urban Practice in Sudan*, (University of Chicago Press, 1994). For a Christian parallel see Ruth Marshall, 'Power in the Name of Jesus', *Review of African Political Economy*, 52 (1991).

# INDEX

Abacha, General Sani, 263
Abaluhyia, 134
Abdurrahman, A., 155
Aberdare Mountains, 180
Abidjan, 168,170
Abiola, Chief Moshood, 263
abolition, 51–5, 64; Cape, 67, 109–11,
  127
Aborigines' Rights Protection Society,
  142
Abyssinia, *see* Ethiopia
Accra, 56, 168, 171, 185, 187
Acheampong, Col., 250
Achebe, Chinua, 31, 147
Achimota College, 143
Action Group, 188–9
Addis Ababa, 168, 171
Adelabu, Adegoke, 188
Adwa, 87
Afghanistan, 94
Afonso, Dom (Mbemba-a-Nzinga),
  ruler of Kongo, 39
African Americans, 3, 8, 10; *see also*
  United States of America
African Mineworkers' Union, 165
African mode of production, 22
African National Congress (South
  Africa), 154, 157, 161, 165, 225–7,
  241–2, 243–5
African Political Organisation (South
  Africa), 155
*African Studies since 1945*, 9
Afrikaners, 2, 48, 88–9, 90, 92,
  93, 152–3, 156, 158–62, 165,
  229
Afro-Shirazi Party, 193
age sets, 21,29

agriculture, 17–19, 20, 25, 28, 254–7,
  264; in the Congo, 102, 104;
  in crisis, 205–6, 248, 251–3,
  257; corporate, 109; and East
  African states, 28, 60; peasant,
  111–18, 126–8; post-war, 170–2;
  settler, 106–9; and slave trade,
  39; and slavery, 47; South African,
  48, 67–9, 89, 151–2, 161, 164,
  221, 223–4, 228
aid, foreign, 253–5, 257–8, 261, 264
AIDS, 258
Akan, 27
Akosombo Dam, 248
Albania, 261
alcohol, 44; alcoholism, 224;
  monopoly, 89; revenue, 115;
  and trade, 48,54
Alexandria, 83
Algeria, xii, 9, 65, 81, 196–7
All-African Convention, 162
Althusser, Louis, 10
*amaro*, 57
American Colonization Society, 58
Ambler, Charles, 59
Amharic, Amharinya, 25, 95, 251
Amin, Idi, 208, 218, 256
Amin, Samir, 10
ancestor worship, 19
Andrianampoinimerina, 62
Anglicisation, 152
Anglo-American, 160, 165, 228–30
Anglo-Boer War, 2, 75, 90, 93, 96ff,
  150–2, 158
Anglo-Oriental, 105
Angola, 20, 29, 40, 41, 42–5, 46, 50,
  56, 70, 102, 104, 122, 123, 169,

Angola (*contd*)
174, 200, 231–3, 238–9, 241, 252, 253
anthropology, 2, 5, 8, 19, 23, 120; Marxist, 11
Antilles, Lesser, 41
apartheid, 10, 221–3, 228–9, 236, 243, 245
Aquatic Age, 17
Arabia, 24, 55, 60, 264
Arabian Sea, 30
Arabic, Arabs, 25, 30, 55, 60, 109, 140, 190, 193, 217
archaeology, 17, 25
Arden-Clarke, Sir Charles, 185
Arguin, 42
*Armée noire*, 143
Aro Society, 46
Arusha Declaration, 215
Asante, 19, 27, 45, 55, 63, 79–80, 85, 92, 93, 94, 100, 121, 127–8, 185–6, 194
Ashanti, *see* Asante
Ashanti Gold Fields, 257
Asia, 11, 14, 18, 24, 30, 36, 37, 47–8, 49, 94, 116, 169, 177, 209; *see also* India, China, etc.
Asian mode of production, 30
Asmara, 171
assimilation policy, 122, 175, 231, 234
Assinie, 65
*Association des Bakongos* (ABAKO), 200
Atlantic Ocean, 18, 29, 41, 43
Attahiru, 94
automobiles, 101, 172
Awolowo, Obafemi, 188
Axum, 24–5
Azikiwe, Nnamdi, 187

Babangida, Ibrahim, 263
backwardness, historic, 15
Bagamoyo, 60
Bahia, 57–8
Baikie expedition, 64
Balewa, Sir Abubakar, 189, 216
Bamako, 81
Bamba, Ahmadu, 140, 143
Bambatha rebellion, 95, 141–2, 152–3

bananas, 18, 123–4
Banda, Hastings Kamuzu, 182, 194, 262
Bank of British West Africa, 114
banks, 130, 131, 253–4
Bannerman, James, 56
Bantu Education Act, 224, 237; Bantu languages, 27–8, 134; South African usage, 224
Bantustans, 227–8, 229, 235, 240, 243–5
Baran, Paul, 10
Barotseland, 121, 209–10; *see* Bulozi
Barre, Siyaad, 264
Bas-Congo, 198
Basel Mission Trading Company, 115
Basutoland, 121; *see* Lesotho
Bathurst (Banjul), 64
Baudouin, King of the Belgians, 199, 201
bauxite, 253
Baya rebellion, 142
Bechuanaland, *see* Botswana
beeswax, 53
Beira, 234
Beit, Sir Alfred, 90
Belgium in Africa, 3, 82, 101–5, 112, 121, 137, 169, 176, 183, 184, 198–202, 249
Bello, Sir Ahmadu, Sardauna of Sokoto, 188, 216
Benadir coast, 60
*beni* dancing, 133
Benin (kingdom), 24, 27, 44–5, 63, 93, 121
Benin Republic (*see also* Dahomey), 218, 262
Benue river, 65
Berlin conference, 84, 101
Beti, Mongo, 130
Beyers, C. F., 158
Biafra, 217
Biafra, Bight of, 53
bicycles, 101
Binza group, 202
Bioko, 115
Bismarck, Otto von, 84, 102
Biya, Paul, 262

Black Consciousness Movement, 237,
    238
*Bloc Démocratique Sénégalais*, 195
Bloemfontein, 90
Blood River, 68
blood tax, 100
Boer War, *see* Anglo-Boer War
Boers, *see* Afrikaners
Bokassa, Jean Bédel, 218–19
Bondelswarts, 159
Booth, Joseph, 146
Bophuthatswana, 244
Bordeaux, 56, 143
Borno, 26
Boston University, 4
Botha, Louis, 89, 153, 155
Botha, P. W., 240, 242–3
Botswana, 88, 90, 164, 195, 210, 229,
    230, 239, 242, 253
bourgeoisie, African, 4, 130–2; and
    nationalism, 180; South African,
    151; and world capitalism, 187,
    189–90, 207–9
brass, 44
Brazil, 35, 41, 51, 54, 57–8
Brazza, Savorgnan de, 82
Brazzaville, 82; Conference I, 176
Bretton Woods, 254
bridewealth, 70, 112
Brière de l'Isle, 80
Britain in Africa, 4, 7, 35, 41, 51–4,
    56, 57, 60, 61, 63–5, 66–7, 77–8,
    79, 80, 82–90, 92–4, 103–5,
    109–10, 112, 115, 116, 120–1,
    135–6, 140, 143–4, 152, 154,
    155, 161, 164, 169–70, 171,
    173–6, 177–9, 180, 182,
    184–95, 197, 198, 217, 228–9,
    230, 239
British South Africa Company, 86, 89,
    103, 105, 109, 141
*Broederbond*, 221, 240
Buganda, 28, 59, 60, 62, 85–6, 92, 100,
    110, 116, 121, 128, 136, 174, 194,
    210, 256
Bukharin, N. I., 76
Bulhoek, 159
Bulozi, 29, 63, 121

Bunyoro, 92, 100
Burmi, 94
Burundi, 261
Buthelezi, Chief Mangosuthu, 243–4
*bywoners*, 93

Cabora Bassa, 234
Cabral, Amilcar, 234, 265
Cairo, 61
Calabar, 47
Cameroun, 28, 84, 102, 106, 112, 117,
    123–4, 130, 179–80, 195, 197,
    253, 262
Canada, 57
canals in Bulozi, 29
Cape of Good Hope, 36, 47–50, 65–9,
    88, 89–90, 171, 221, 225, 226;
    Cape liberalism, 68–9, 173–5;
    African vote, 161
Cape Town, 48, 88, 146, 157,
    226, 230
Cape Verde islands, 40
Cape Vert, 65
capital, finance and settlers, 108–9;
    monopoly, 74–9; merchant
    capital and capitalism, 34–5, 40,
    41–2, 49–50, 61, 71, 113–14,
    137, 181; investment in Central
    African Federation, 173;
    capitalism, and the African state,
    210–11; 'black', 142; and
    Christianity, 137–8; and
    apartheid, 222, 228–9; and the
    colonial state, 119; Ghanaian,
    263; industrial, 49; and
    imperialism, 74–9; in the Ivory
    Coast, 212–13; in Kenya,
    211–12; and labour migration,
    117; and mining, 103–6;
    peripheral; xii; and race, 14; and
    the slave trade, 42; slavery, 52;
    in South Africa, 49; in the
    West, 147
Carnarvon, Lord, 87–8
Carnegie Foundation, 4
Carr, Henry, 131–2
Cary, Joyce, 130
cassava (manioc), 39, 43, 115

Catholics, 39, 58, 85, 102, 104, 137,
    138, 198, 217
Cato Manor, 226
cattle, 48, 59, 108, 117; killing, 70
Cayor, 80–1
Cazengo, 70
Central Africa, 7, 28–9, 84, 89,
    103–6, 133, 135, 173, 178–9,
    193–4, 197
Central African Federation, 173–4,
    193–4, 197, 229, 234
Central African Republic, 141, 219,
    236
Central Intelligence Agency (USA), 232
Cetewayo, 88
Chad, 100, 217
Chad, Lake, 26, 81, 86
Chagga, 117
Chamberlain, Joseph, 90
Changamire dynasty, 38
chartered companies, 100, 101–3, 119
chiefs, 23–4, 112, 119–22, 128, 130,
    132, 136, 154, 178, 209, 257
Chilembwe, John, 145–7
Chiluba, Frederick, 259
Chimurenga, 95, 136, 141
China, 15, 46, 94, 151, 177, 213, 254
Chipenda, Daniel, 233
Chokwe, 20, 70
Christianity, 24–5, 27, 36, 39, 46, 56–8,
    70, 85–6, 92, 95, 136–9, 147, 153,
    162, 187, 224–5, 267
Christianborg Castle, 185
Church of England, 92
circumcision, female, 138
civic organisations, 242, 245
class, xi, 9, 11–12; in the Congo,
    198–9; in contemporary Africa,
    209–14, 215, 259; and
    colonialism, 97–9, 109–11,
    125–32; and culture, 133;
    struggles and decolonisation,
    176–83, 202–3; and imperialism,
    91–3; and 'legitimate commerce',
    69–71; in pre-colonial Africa, 15,
    22, 24–6; and mode of production,
    31–2; and race, 150–1, 162; and
    resistance, 141, 146–7; and slave

trade, 47, 49–50; working, 128–9,
    172–3, 214
clerks, 129, 131–2, 187
clientage, 54, 60, 209, 216, 265
cloth trade, 27, 39, 40–1, 42, 44–5, 54
cloves, 60, 109
cocoa, 114–15, 117, 123, 127–8, 131,
    179, 181, 185, 186, 195–6, 212,
    257; hold-up, 144, 172
coconuts, 60
coffee, 62, 70, 108, 115, 117, 191, 212,
    231
Cohen, Abner, 134
Cohen, Sir Andrew, 194
Cokers, 46
collaboration and resistance, 91–6, 100,
    140–7
colonialism, and capitalism, 97–9; and
    class, 125–32; and colonial society,
    132–47; impact, 204–5;
    Portuguese, 231; post-World War
    II 168–76, 180
colonos, 38, 55
colour bar, 131–2, 152, 160, 162–3,
    175–6, 231
coloureds (South Africa), 155, 165, 223,
    225, 229, 237, 240, 244
COMECON, 241
comey, 47
commerce, see trade
Communist Party, Angolan, 232;
    European, 11; French, 196; South
    African, 158, 161, 165, 225, 243,
    245; Sudanese, 249
Compagnie française de l'Afrique Orientale,
    114
compradores, 46, 56–8, 64, 70, 80, 122,
    131, 212, 213
Confédération des Associations Tribales du
    Katanga (CONAKAT), 200
Conférence des forces vives, 262
Congo, Belgian, 102–3, 103–5, 109,
    117, 123–4, 130, 136, 138–9, 141,
    169, 174, 176, 178, 198–202, 207;
    Democratic Republic of, 201–2,
    231–3, 249; see also Zaïre; Free
    State, 82–3, 84, 90, 101–2; French
    (Republic of the Congo-

Brazzaville), 44, 101, 102, 141, 200, 232, 249, 253; -Océan Railway, 101, 141; river, 28, 38, 59, 64, 81–2, 84, 101
Congress of South African Trade Unions (COSATU), 243, 245
Congress of the People, 225
Conrad, Joseph, 101
Conservative Party (UK), 173, 193
Convention People's Party (Ghana), 181–2, 185–6, 214–15, 248
co-operatives, 172, 175, 182
copper, 20, 59, 103–5, 173, 206
Copperbelt, 104–5, 118, 133, 173, 177, 193
Coptic church, 24–5
Coquery-Vidrovitch, Catherine, 11, 22, 170
cotton, 41, 61, 83, 102, 114, 116–17, 123, 130, 135, 140, 141
'country wives', 46
Coussey Commission, 185
cowries, 44, 78
craft production, 20–1, 24, 26–7, 58, 140; organisation, 32; Portuguese, 37
credit, 47, 54, 130–1
Creoles, 57
Creswell, Frederick, 156
Cuba, 51, 54, 238, 241–2, 251
Cuito Canavale, 241
currency, 44, 54, 78, 255–7
Curtin, Philip, 8, 43
Curtis, Lionel, 152
customs, 47
Cyprus, 41

Dahomey, 45, 54, 57–8, 64, 84–5, 100, 124, 134, 143, 144, 218
dairy farming, 108
Dakar, 65, 80, 122, 168, 171, 266
dance, 133
Dar es Salaam, 9, 178, 233
Dar Fur, 61
Darwin, Charles, 76
Daura, 121
Davidson, Basil, 8, 9, 12–13
De Beers Corporation, 160, 253

de Gaulle, Charles, 176, 197
de Klerk, F. W., 243–4
De la Rey, J. H., 158
decolonisation, 173–5, 184–203, 210–11, 231–4, 238–9
Defiance Campaign, 225
Denmark, 79
dependency theory, xii, 9–10, 35, 40, 49–50, 98–9, 149–50, 182, 205–7, 212, 254
Depression, Great Nineteenth Century, 76; of 1929, 105, 107, 144, 161, 164, 168–9, 172, 254
Dergue, 250–1
Deutsch Ost-Afrika Gesellschaft, 103
development as ideology, 170–1, 185, 248
Diagne, Blaise, 143
diamonds, 87, 105, 160
Dike, K. O., 7
'divine kingship' in Africa, 21–2, 24
Doe, Samuel, 265
domaine de la couronne, 101
Douala, 168, 179
Drakensberg mountains, 29
drought, see famine
DuBois, W. E. B., 3
Durban, 161, 224, 237
Dutch East India Company, 47–9
dynamite, 89
Dyula, 91

earth cults, 19, 21
East Africa, 7, 16–18, 58–62, 85–7, 113, 133, 134, 140, 174, 178–80, 210; state formation, 28, 30; coast, 36–7; and the slave trade, 42; decolonisation, 189–93
East African Association, 145
East African Community, 207
ecology and settlers, 108
ECOWAS, 265
'educated elite', 7, 132
education, 132, 143, 162, 173, 175, 185, 187, 213, 215–16, 224, 237–8, 245, 258, 265
Egypt, xii, 18, 21, 25, 30, 35, 61, 83, 94, 184

Elder Dempster Line, 114
elders, 17, 19, 117, 136
Electricity Supply Corporation of
    South Africa (ESCOM), 160
Elisabethville, *see* Lubumbashi
Elmina, 37, 42
Emecheta, Buchi, 31
*Emerging Themes in African History*, 8–9
Eminent Persons' Group, 243
Engels, Friedrich, 22, 215
ensete, 18
Equatorial Guinea, 219, 259
Eritrea, 24, 87, 169, 184, 251, 260–1
Eritrean Peoples' Liberation Front
    (EPLF), 260
ESAP (Zimbabwe), 258
essentialism, 6, 266
Estado Novo, 238
Ethiopia, 15, 18, 24–5, 36–7, 42, 61–2,
    73, 83, 86–7, 92, 94–5, 126, 169,
    183–4, 250–2, 260–1, 264
Ethiopian churches, 138
Ethiopian People's Revolutionary
    Party, 251
Europe, 245, 259; anti-slavery
    movement, 51–3; decolonisation,
    176–7; and Egypt, 61; expansion,
    16, 34–5; ideology of imperialism,
    73–6; 'informal empire', 63–4;
    medieval and early modern,
    15–16; mode of production, 30;
    and the partition of Africa, 76–96;
    settlers in Africa, 47–9, 106–9,
    173–5, 178–80, 189, 200, 212,
    231, 244; and the slave trade,
    40–2; workers in Africa, 106
*evolués*, 199
Evora, Cesaria, 267
exploration, 64
Eyadema, Etienne, 218

Fagan Commission, 166
Faidherbe, Louis, 65
family relations, 17–18, 19–20, 112; *see
    also* lineage
famine, 18, 45, 126, 250, 252
Fanon, Frantz, 9
Fante Confederation, 79–80

Farouk, king of Egypt, 184
Fashoda, 86
Fasilidas, 37
Federale Mynbou, 229
Feierman, Steven, 8
Fernando Póo, 115
fertiliser, 171
feudalism, 95
Firestone, 109
fishing, 17, 20, 29
*Fonds des Investissements Economiques et
    Sociales*, 170
football, 133
foraging, 116–17, 8
Ford Foundation, 4
Fort Jameson (Chipata), 108
Forty Group, 191
franc, CFA, 212
France in Africa, 4, 7, 11, 35, 42, 48,
    51–4, 56, 62, 64–5, 79, 80–1,
    82–4, 84–6, 91–2, 94, 100, 102,
    112, 113–14, 121, 137, 139,
    143–4, 169, 170, 175, 177, 180,
    182–3, 195–8, 217, 238, 253,
    261–2
Frank, Andre Gunder, 10
Freetown, 57
French Equatorial Africa, 102–3, 106,
    123–4, 141, 196–7, 199
French Union, 176
French West Africa, 106, 114, 123,
    132, 143, 144, 169, 178, 195–7
*Frente de Libertaçaõ de Moçambique*
    (FRELIMO), 233–4, 238, 262
*Frente Nacional de Libertaçaõ de Angola*
    (FNLA), 232, 238
Frere, Sir Bartle, 87
Freyhold, Michaela von, 210
Frontline States, 239
Fulbe, 26–7
Fusion government, 161–2
Futa Djallon, 196
Futa Toro, 80

Gabon, 44, 65, 82, 139, 205, 236, 253
Galli, Rosemary and Jocelyn Jones, 259
Gama, Vasco da, 30, 36
Gambia, 55, 64, 85, 116, 189, 250

game reserves, 108
Gandhi, Mohandas, 155
Gandhi–Smuts Agreement, 155
Garvey, Marcus, 142, 182
German East Africa, *see* Tanganyika,
    Ruanda-Urundi
Germany in Africa, 48, 74, 77–8, 83–6,
    90, 96ff, 102–3, 112, 135, 136,
    137, 146, 155, 221
Gezira, 116–17
Ghana, ancient, 25–6; modern, 27,
    182, 186, 205, 214, 218, 236,
    248–9, 249–50, (*see also* Gold
    Coast), 255, 256–60, 263–4
Gizenga, Antoine, 202
Gladstone, W. E., 88
Glen Grey Act, 152
gold, 20, 25–6, 27, 29–30, 35, 37–8,
    88–9, 90, 142, 150–1, 156–7, 160,
    162, 163–4, 165, 228–9, 234,
    239–40, 257
Gold Coast, 37, 42–4, 54, 56, 58, 64,
    80–1, 85, 114–16, 121, 123, 126,
    127–8, 132, 142, 143, 172, 175,
    179, 180–2, 184–6 (*see also* Ghana)
Golden Stool, 121, 127
Goldie, Sir George, 81, 84, 97
Gondar, 36
Gordon, Charles, 83
Gorée, 56, 122
Government of National Unity (South
    Africa), 245
Grañ, Ahmed, 35–6
Grand Bassam, 65
Great Trek, 67–8, 89
Greeks in Africa, 25, 113
Griqualand West, 87
Ground-nut scheme, 171
ground-nuts, 54, 55, 80, 115–16, 124,
    143, 171, 252
Group Areas Act, 223
Guggisberg, Sir Gordon, 143
Guiné-Bissau (ex-Portuguese Guinea),
    122, 127, 234, 259, 265
Guinea, 84, 91, 116, 124, 127, 196–7,
    209, 248, 253
gum arabic, 42, 56
Gumede, James, 161

gun trade, 27, 44, 54, 59, 62, 63,
    71, 86
Gusii, 135–6
Guyana, 52

Hadza, 16
Haile Selassie, 183, 250
Haiti, 41, 53
Hamburg, 78
Hammarskjold, Dag, 201–2
Hausa, Hausaland, 26, 32, 44, 78, 126,
    134
Heddle, Charles, 56
Hehe, 100
Hemson, David, 165
Herbst, Jeffrey, 263
Herero, 95, 140
Herskovits, Melville, 8
Hertzog, Albert, 221
Hertzog, J. B. M., 153, 158–9, 164,
    166, 166ff, 221
*Het Volk*, 153
Himyarites, 24
Hispaniola, 53
*Historian in Tropical Africa*, 8
historiography, African, 1–13, 14–15,
    111–12, 139, 159
Hobson, John, 74–6
Hodgkin, Thomas, 8
Hofmeyr, Jan H., 165, 221
Hopkins, A. G., 78
horses, 22
Hottentot Proclamation (1809), 67
Houphouët-Boigny, Félix, 196, 197,
    262
*How Europe Underdeveloped Africa*, 10
hunting and gathering, 16–18, 19,
    67
Hutu, 28, 261

Ibadan, 134–5, 168, 188; school, 7;
    University, 131
Igbafe, Philip, 93
Igbo, 31–2, 46, 144, 187–8, 217
Igbo-Ukwu, 27
Ijebu, 44, 85, 93
Imbangala, 20, 46
Imerina (*see also* Merina), 62, 94, 180

Immorality Act (South Africa), 223, 240
imperialism; xi–xii, 6, 12, 71, 73–9, 207–8, 211–12; conquest of Africa, 79–96; and settlers, 106–7; in South Africa, 150–1, 153, 251
India, 15, 44, 60, 114, 130, 171, 177
Indian Ocean, 30, 36, 44, 60, 107
Indians in Africa, 38, 108, 113, 122, 130, 145, 172, 179, 190, 194, 257; in South Africa, 69, 155, 165, 222, 223, 224–5, 237, 240, 244
indirect rule, 69, 120–1, 127–8, 143, 186, 187–9, 209, 257
Indo-China, 196
Industrial and Commercial Workers' Union (ICU), 157–8, 161
Industrial Revolution, 34, 49–50, 52–3, 71; and slaving, 42; Second, 78; South African, 149–50
industry in Africa, 171, 205, 208, 212, 255, 258; in South Africa, 156, 160, 164, 228–9, 237
influx control, 223, 226, 228
'informal empire', 63
'informal sector', 265–6
Inkatha Freedom Party, 244
*Institut Solvay*, 198
Institute of Race Relations (South Africa), 165
International Association, 82, 101
International British East Africa Association, 86, 103
International Monetary Fund, 254
investment, foreign in Africa, 75, 76–7, 258; South African, 246
iron, 16–19, 20, 29, 44
Iron and Steel Corporation of South Africa (ISCOR), 160
Ironsi, Major-General, 216–17
Isandhlwana, 88
Islam, 1, 6, 16, 25–7, 30, 32, 36, 57, 59, 60, 65, 83, 85, 92, 116–17, 134, 139–40, 143, 188, 195, 265, 266
Israel, 205
Israelites (South Africa), 159

Italy in Africa, 83, 86–7, 92, 95, 100, 107, 169, 183
Iteso, 130
ivory, 53, 58, 61, 70
Ivory Coast, 44, 45, 65, 84, 91, 100, 115, 123–4, 170, 195–6, 210, 212–13, 217, 236, 253, 255, 262
Iyayi, Felix, 253

Ja Ja, 85
Jamaica, 41, 57, 142
Jameson Raid, 90
Janssens, General E., 201
Japan, 37, 94, 229
Jehovah's Witnesses, 146
Jesuits, 37
Jews, 24–5, 113
*jihads*, 16, 27, 63, 65, 135, 139
Jinja, 257
Johannesburg, 10, 88, 90, 220, 229
Johnson, Rev. Samuel, 3
Johnston, Sir Harry, 2
Johnstone, Frederick, 163
Jos Plateau, 103, 105

*kabaka* (of Buganda), 28, 63, 92, 110, 128, 194, 210
Kabaka Yekka Party, 194, 210
Kabarega, 92
Kadalie, Clements, 157–8
Kagnew base, 184
Kalahari, 17, 253
Kalondji, Albert, 201
Kamba, 59, 70
Kampala, 257
Kananga (Luluabourg), 199
Kandjadja, 265
Kanem, 26
Kano, 94, 116, 168
Kasai Province, Zaïre, 105, 199, 201
Kasavubu, Joseph, 200
Katanga Province, Congo, *see* Shaba
Kaunda, Kenneth, 215, 236, 248, 259
Kavirondo, Bantu, 134
Kazembe, 100
Keita, Modibo, 248
Keita, Salif, 267
Kennedy, John, 230

Kenya, 11, 36, 86, 103, 107–9, 113,
    117–18, 123–4, 126, 134, 135–6,
    138, 145, 155, 169, 174, 176,
    179–80, 190–2, 207, 210, 211,
    214, 218, 255, 262–3; Mount, 59
Kenya African National Union, 192,
    211
Kenya African Union, 190
Kenyatta, Jomo, 145, 182, 190–2
Kérékou, Matthieu, 218, 262
Khalifa, 92
Khama, Sir Seretse, 210
Khartoum, Khartoumers, 61, 80, 116
Khoi Khoi, 48
Kibachia, Chege, 190
Kikuyu, 59, 138, 145, 174, 180, 191
Kilimanjaro, Mount, 117
Kilwa, 30, 37, 42
Kimbangu, Simon, 138–9
Kimberley, 87, 89
Kindergarten, Milner's, 152–3
Kinjikitile, 135
Kinshasa (Léopoldville), 168, 171, 198,
    199–200, 232
kinship, see lineage
Kisangani (see Stanleyville), 200
Kisii, 136
Kliptown, 225
Klitgaard, Robert, 259
kola, 27, 55, 63
Kongo, 28, 38–40, 43, 45, 50, 139,
    200, 201, 231–3
Kordofan, 61
Krio, 57
Kru, 58
Kruger, Paul, 89
Kumasi, 80, 127
!Kung San, 17
Kwa Zulu Natal, 244
Kwilu, 249

La Baule, 262
labour and capitalism, 52–3; and
    colonialism, 99; in the Congo,
    102; forced, 100–2, 176, 196, 234;
    history, insurgency, 177–8;
    migrant, 104–6, 109, 115, 117–18,
    128, 137, 196, 213; mines, 89,

103–6; process, x,
    98–9; skilled, 129, 143; South
    African, 68, 70, 150–1, 156–8,
    160–1, 164–5; unions, 177–8, 182,
    187, 192, 193, 242, 250; wage, 59
Labour Party (South Africa), 156–7,
    159–60, 161, 221
Labour Party (UK), 173, 235
Lagos, 57, 63, 64, 85, 92, 131, 143,
    168, 171, 178, 187; Plan of
    Action, 255
Lake Province, Tanganyika, 178, 192
Land Act, (1913), 138, 154
Land Freedom Army, 180, 191
Landes, David, 78
Langa, 226
Lat Dyor, Damel Cayor, 81
Latin America, 10, 51, 209, 242
Leadership Code (Tanzania), 215
League of Nations, 112, 155, 183
Lebanese in Africa, 113, 122, 143
Lee, Richard, 17
Lembede, Anton, 165
Lenin, V. I., 74–6
Leopold II, King of the Belgians, 82,
    86, 90, 101–2, 201
Leopoldville, see Kinshasa
Lesotho, 70, 87, 92, 121, 164, 195, 210,
    229, 230, 236
Lever Brothers, 114
Leys, Colin, 211
Liberal Party (South Africa), 229
Liberal Party (UK), 88, 153
Liberia, 41, 58, 73, 109, 136, 236, 250,
    264–5
Libreville, 65
Libya, xii, 183
lineage organisation, 17, 19–21, 22, 24,
    28, 32
Lippert, Eduard, 89
Lisala, Zaïre, 216
literacy, 1, 25, 27, 39
Little Englanders, 88
litunga of Bulozi, 63, 209–10
Liverpool, 56, 78
Livingstone, William Jervis, 146
Loango, 44
Lobengula, 89, 100

Lomé Convention, 255
Lonsdale, John and Anthony Low, 170
Lourenço Marques, *see* Maputo
Lovedale, 68
Luanda, 41, 70, 168, 231
Luangwa, 108
Luba, 29, 200
Lubumbashi (Elisabethville), 104, 199–200, 202
Lugard, Lord, 94, 105, 120, 126
*luliiko*, 128
Lulua, 199
Luluabourg, *see* Kananga
Lumumba, Patrice, 200–3, 249
Luo, 191–2
Lusaka, 243
Luwero triangle, 256
Luxemburg, 189
Lyon, 78

Maal, Baba, 267
Maasai, 59, 107
Macauley, Herbert, 143, 187
Machel, Samora, 233, 241
Macias Nguema, 219
Macmillan, Sir Harold, 193, 230
Madagascar (Malagasy Republic), 48, 62, 94, 113, 136, 179–80, 197, 236, 249, 262
Madeira, 41
Madhvanis, 257
Maghreb, xii, 196
Mahdi, 83, 86, 92, 100, 140
Mahdiyya, 83
*mailo*, 110, 116, 128
maize (corn), 39, 151
Maji Maji, 95–6, 135, 136, 141, 231, 249
Majuba, 88
Makoko treaty, 82
Makonde, 233
Malan, Daniel François, 162, 166, 221
Malawi (Nyasaland), 29, 104, 108, 113, 118, 145–7, 164, 173, 193–4, 230, 236, 255, 262
Malawi, Lake (Lake Nyasa), 59, 85–6
Malaysia, 255

Mali (ancient), 26; Mali (modern; ex-French Sudan), 18, 81, 91, 116, 196, 197, 209, 248, 260, 262, 265
Mali Federation, 197
Malindi, 110
Malvern, Lord, 173
Mamdani, Mahmood, 69, 263
Manchester, 78
Mandela, Nelson, 227, 243–4, 245
manganese, 253
Mangope, Chief Lucas, 244
Maniema, 104
manillas, 44
Maoism, 12, 227, 249, 261
Maputo (Lourenço Marques), 89, 178
Marchand expedition, 86
Margai, Sir Milton, 189, 218
Maria's War, 231
maritime power, 35–6
Marketing Boards, 172, 175, 248, 256, 257
Marks, J. B., 165
Marks, Shula, 141
Maroons, 57
marriage, 20, 112
Marx, Karl, x–xi, 12, 30, 74, 76, 98, 215
Marxism, xii, 11–12, 30, 75–6, 99, 159, 249
Mashonaland, 141
Massamba-Débat, Jacques, 232
*masu sarauta*, 32
Matadi, 178
Matanzima, Kaiser, 227
materialist history, x–xi, 11–12, 30–1, 50
Mathu, Eliud, 176
matrilineality, 20, 131
Mau Mau, 179–80, 191–2
Mauritania, 25, 26, 42, 100, 252
Mauritius, 42, 52, 55, 195, 236
Mba, Léon, 205
*mbeni*, 133
Mboya, Tom, 191–2
Mbundu, 40, 46
Mecca, 94
medicine, 78, 162, 172–3, 213
Medina, battle of, 65

Mediterranean Sea, 36, 41, 169
*Meison*, 250
Mengistu, Lt-Col. Haile Mariam, 250, 260
Meqdela (Magdala), 61
mercantilism, 40, 76
mercenaries, 219
merchants (*see also* trade and merchant capital), 25, 32, 41–2, 47, 56–8, 60–1, 77–8, 92–3, 106, 113–14, 115, 131, 140, 182, 187, 188, 196, 259
Merina, 100
Meroë, 25
Merriman, John X., 68, 153
Meru, 179
Methodists, 56
methodology as mystique, 5
*Mfecane*, 16, 29, 33ff, 59, 67, 70, 86
*Mfengu*, 70
Middle East (*see also* Arabia, Arabs), 6, 15, 205
migration, 20; *see also* labour migration
militarism, 75–6
military and warfare in Africa, 36, 58, 59, 61, 62, 67, 78, 92–3, 118, 261; and slaving, 44–5, 55; resistance, 91, 93–4, 100; coups, 252, 256
millet, 18
Milner, Sir Alfred, 90, 151–3, 158–9
mines, mining, 20, 37, 78, 87, 88–9, 103–6, 127, 129, 142, 149, 150–2, 156–7, 160, 163–4, 165–6, 187, 234, 257, 259
Minilik (Menelik), 62, 86–7, 92, 93–5
Mirambo, 59, 62, 91
missionaries, 64, 70, 82, 85–6, 134, 136–8, 140, 217
Mitterrand, François, 196, 262
Mixed Marriages Act, 240
Mobutu Sese Seko (Joseph Desiré), 201, 218, 232, 249, 262
mode of production, 11, 22, 30–2; capitalist, 97–9
Moi, Daniel arap, 262
Mombasa, 36, 118, 133, 178, 190
Mome Gorge, 153
Mondlane, Eduardo, 233, 235

Monrovia, 58
monsoons, 29–30
Moodie, Dunbar, 222
Moors, 26, 65
Morocco, xii, 196
Moshweshwe, 92, 93
*Mouvement National Congolais* (MNC), 200–2
*Movimento Popular de Libertaçaõ de Angola* (MPLA), 232–3, 234, 238–9
Mozambique, 29, 37–8, 48, 50, 70, 89, 102–3, 109, 113, 118, 122, 146, 166ff, 169, 174, 178, 229, 233–4, 235, 238–9, 241, 245–6, 255, 262
Msiri, 59
Mugabe, Robert, 235, 239
Muhammad Ali, 61
mulattos, 40, 46, 70, 231
Muldergate, 240
Mulele, Pierre, 249
Mumbo cult, 135–6
Muriddiya (Murids), 116, 140, 252
Murtala Muhammad, 250
Museveni, Yoweri, 256, 264
muskets, 44
Mutesa, *kabaka*, 92
Muzorewa, Bishop Abel, 239
Mwana Lesa, 135
Mwanga, *kabaka*, 92

Naguib, Mohammed, 184
Nairobi, 145, 168, 171, 174, 190, 191–2, 207, 257
Nama, 159
Namibia, 242 (*see also* South West Africa)
Napier expedition, 61
Napoleon, 52, 65
Natal (*see also* Kwa Zulu Natal), 68–70, 87–8, 95, 141, 150, 152–3, 155, 225, 237
National Congress of British West Africa, 142, 143
National Congress of Nigeria and the Cameroons (NCNC), 182, 187–9
National Union of South African Students (NUSAS), 237

nationalism, African, 177; 3–5, 6–7, 10, 11, 14, 140–1, 180–203, 209, 225, 236, 238, 248–9, 255; Afrikaner (and National Party), 89, 158–62, 166, 173, 220–4, 229, 240, 244; in Ethiopia, 251; European, 75–6
Native Affairs Act (1920), 154
Native Affairs Commission (1905), 152
Native Authorities system, 105–6, 121, 132
Native Urban Areas Act (1923), 161
navétanes, 55, 116
Ndebele, 87, 89
Négritude ACC, 182
neo-colonialism, 10, 205, 207–8, 211, 254
Netherlands in Africa, 35, 37, 41, 42, 48–9, 51, 65–7, 79–80, 89
Neto, Agostinho, 232
New England, 41
New York City, 266
Ngoni, 86, 100, 108
Niamey, 252
Niger Company (Royal), 85, 103, 105, 114
Niger-Congo languages, 28
Niger republic, 196, 203ff, 252, 253, 262, 265
Niger river, delta, 43, 44, 46, 47, 54, 56, 64, 81, 85, 126; interior delta, 18, 27; river, 27, 64, 80, 84, 85; valley, 26, 80
Nigeria, xiii, 7, 11, 24, 26, 28, 57, 85, 100, 103, 105–6, 114, 115–16, 117–18, 120–1, 123–4, 126, 130, 131, 134, 135, 140, 143, 144, 169, 174, 175, 178, 186–9, 210, 211, 212, 214, 216–17, 218, 252, 253, 263, 267
Nike, 46
Nile river, 64, 83; valley, 15, 25, 61, 86, 116
Nimeiri, Gaafar, 217, 249
nizers, 210
Nkomati Accord, 241
Nkomo, Joshua, 235

Nkrumah, Kwame, 181–2, 185–6, 205–7, 214, 218, 248, 257
non-governmental organisations (NGOs), 258, 259, 265
North Africa, see Maghreb
Northern Elements' Progressive Union (NEPU), 188
Northern People's Congress (NPC), 188–9
Northwestern Univesity, 4
Nouakchott, 252
Nuba Hills, 100
Nujoma, Sam, 242
Nyamwezi, 59, 70, 134
Nyasa, Lake, see Lake Malawi
Nyasaland, see Malawi
Nyasaland African Congress, 194
Nyerere, Julius, 182, 192, 207, 214–15, 248, 257

oathing, 191
obas, 24, 93
Obasanjo, Olusegun, 211
Obote, Apollo Milton, 194–5, 205, 210, 215, 248, 256
Ochieng, William, 9
Ogot, Bethwell A., 7
Okonkwo, 147
Oman, 60
Omdurman, 86, 168, 181–2
Opobo, 85
Oppenheimer, Sir Ernest, 160
Oppenheimer, Harry, 230
oral tradition, 1
Orange Free State (Orange River Colony), 68, 87, 95, 152–3
Orange river, 87
Oranje Unie, 153
Ordinance 50, 67
Organisation for African Unity (OAU), 207, 219, 255
Orientale province, Congo, 202
Orientalism, 6
Oromo, 251
Osagyefo, 248
Ottoman Empire, 35–7
Ovambo, Ovamboland, 236, 237
Ovimbundu, 70

Oyo, 45, 63, 121, 137
Oyono, Ferdinand, 130

Pact government, 159–62, 163, 221
palm, coconut, 60; oil, 18, 53–4, 64, 78,
    81, 82, 85, 109, 124
Pan-Africanism, 3, 142, 181–2, 207,
    214
Pan-Africanist Congress (PAC), 226–7
Pangani river valley, 110
Pare, 179
Paris, 182
*Parti Démocratique du Côte d'Ivoire* (PCDI),
    195–6, 262
*Parti Démocratique du Guinée* (PDG), 196
*Partido Africano da Independencia da Guiné é*
    *Cabo Verde* (PAIGC), 234
pastoralism, 18, 28, 48, 67, 100, 117,
    252, 264
patrilineality, 20
Patriotic Front, 239
pawning, 115
Pax Britannica, 111
peanuts, *see* ground-nuts
Pearce Commission, 239
peasantisation, 126
peasantries, 25, 26, 68, 75, 95, 107,
    109–10, 126–8, 135, 137, 241,
    248–9, 250–3; and cash crops,
    111–18, 170–2, 191; insurgencies,
    178–80, 260
Pedi, 67, 70, 87, 93
Pemba, 193
Persia, 94
Person, Yves, 91
Peter the Great, 94
Petite Côte, 65
petroleum, 183, 251, 25, 263
Phillips, Anne, 98
phosphates, 253
Phungula, Zulu, 165
Pioneer Column, 89
Pirow, Oswald, 161
ploughs, 112, 130, 171
Poland, 213
polygamy, 20, 130, 138
*pombeiros*, 40
Pondoland, 226

*ponteiros*, 259
Ponty, Ecole William, 132
Popular Front, 177
population, 112–13, 127; and the slave
    trade, 43
porterage, 55, 59, 99, 101, 112
Porto Novo, 143
Portugal in Africa, 20, 35–40, 41, 42,
    44, 46, 60, 82, 84, 86, 89, 90, 96ff,
    102, 107, 112, 122, 137, 176, 178,
    217, 231, 234; liberation wars, 9,
    10, 231–4, 236, 238–9
Positive Action, 185
Post, K. W. J., 126
Poulantzas, Nicos, 10
*prazos*, 38, 55
pre-colonial Africa, 5, 14–71, 98–9
Pretoria, 90, 226
primitive accumulation, 98
privatisation, 245, 256
Progressive Party (later Progressive
    Federal, then Democratic Party),
    229–30
proletarianisation, 106, 118, 125–6,
    128–9, 241, 253
Protestants, 57, 62, 85–6, 137
Providence Industrial Mission, 145
Province of Freedom, 57

*quatre communes*, 122, 143, 175
*qat*, 264

race and racism, 4–5, 14–15, 28, 49,
    76, 107, 131, 137, 151, 175, 178,
    189, 190; 'race relations', 10, 153,
    165
Radama I, 62
railways (and roads), 81, 89, 99, 101,
    102, 105, 107, 111, 116, 118, 129,
    160, 170, 178, 234
Rand, *see* Witwatersrand
Rand Revolt, 157
Randlords, 89, 150–2, 160
Ranger, T. O., 5, 9, 11
*Rassemblement Democratique Africaine*
    (RDA), 195–6
Rawlings, Jerry, 249–50, 256, 263–4
recaptives, 57

reciprocity, social, 21–2, 32, 126
Red Sea, 18, 24, 36, 61, 83, 86
religion (*see also* Christianity, Islam), 19, 24–5, 32, 36, 46, 135–40, 264, 265, 266–7
Rembrandt Tobacco, 222
*Resistência Nacional Moçambicana* (RENAMO), 241, 262
Réunion, 42, 55
*Review of African Political Economy*, xii
Revolutionary Councils (Uganda), 264
Rhodes, Cecil, 86, 89–90, 103, 152
Rhodesia (*see also* Southern Rhodesia), 205, 210, 219ff, 234–5, 239, 241
Rhodesia, Northern, 103, 104–5, 108, 118, 121, 133, 136, 169, 173, 177, 193, 209–10 (*see also* Zambia)
Rhodesia, Southern, 88, 89, 103, 109, 111, 118, 124, 129, 136, 169, 174–5, 193
Rhodesian Front, 234–5
Rhodesian Railways, 105
Rhodesian Selection Trust, 104
rice, 18, 62, 116
rinderpest, 154
Rivonia, 227
Roberto, Holden, 232, 238–9
Roberts family, 46
Rodney, Walter, 10, 47
Roger, Baron, 65
*rois de la brousse*, 118
Rozvi, 38
Ruanda-Urundi (*see also* Burundi, Rwanda), 104, 109, 112, 116, 118
rubber, 53, 74, 101–2, 109
Rufisque, 122
Rupert, Anton, 222
Russia (*see also* Soviet Union), 94
Rwanda, 28, 210, 261, 262

Sá, Salvador da, 41
Sahara, xii, 15, 17, 25–6, 71, 81, 84, 100
Sahle Silassie, 62
Said, Edward, 6
Saint Domingue (Haiti), 41
Saint Louis, 46, 56, 65, 80, 122

Salazar, Antonio ACC, 231
Salisbury (Harare), 168, 171
salt trade, 20, 29, 44
Samori Toure, 77, 91, 93, 100, 139
San, 17
Sankara, Thomas, 268ff
Sanlam/Saambou, 221
Saõ Tomé, 40–1
*Saro*, 57, 63
Satiru, 135
Saul, John, 9
Savimbi, Jonas, 233, 239
*Sawaba*, 196, 203ff
Sayyid Muhammed Abdile Hassan, 139
Scandinavians in Africa, 48, 51, 255 (*see also* Denmark)
School of Oriental and African Studies, 4
Scotland, Scots, 86, 138
'second economy', 266
secret societies, 21, 46
segregation, 69, 137, 149, 152–4, 160–3, 221–3
Seme, Pixley, 161
Semitic languages, 14, 24
Senegal, 11, 26, 41, 55, 58, 65, 78, 80–1, 116, 117, 118, 124, 140, 143–4, 175, 182, 195, 197, 218, 250, 252, 265; river, 46, 80
Senegambia, 26, 42, 45, 54, 56, 65, 81
Senghor, Léopold Sédar, 182, 195, 218
Sennar, 25
separate development, 224, 229
Seychelles, 195
Seyyid Said, 60
Shaba Province, Zaïre (formerly Katanga), 29, 44, 59, 103–6, 136, 199–200, 202, 209
Shaka, 29
Shambaa, 179
Sharpeville, 225
sheep, 48, 66–7 (*see also* wool)
Shepstone, Theophilus, 69, 87
Shewa, 62
Shona, 29, 141, 235
Siam, 94
Sicily, 41

Sierra Leone, 46, 56–9, 64, 85, 124,
    136, 143, 186, 189, 218, 264
Sierra Leone Company, 57
Sierra Leone People's Party, 182, 189
*simbas*, 249
Simone, T. Abdou Maliqalim & Edgar
    Pieterse, 266
sisal, 109, 124
Sithole, Revd. Ndabiningi, 235
Slagters Nek, 67
slave trade, 9, 20, 27, 35, 39–40, 40–7,
    59–60, 61, 62, 63, 80, 82, 98, 101,
    115; abolition, 51–5, 57, 64
slavery in Africa, 22, 30, 32, 38, 42–3,
    45, 54–5, 63, 65, 70, 93, 104,
    109–11, 113, 115, 147, 196; Cape,
    48, 67; slavery in the New World,
    35, 41–2, 43, 48, 52–3
Smit Commission, 166
Smith, Ian, 235, 239
Smuts, Jan Christiaan, 2, 153,
    155–6, 158–61, 164–5, 166ff,
    221–2, 234
Sobukwe, Robert Mangaliso, 227
socialism, 157, 165, 177, 262, 264;
    African, 214–15
Société Commerciale de l'Ouest
    Africain (SCOA), 114
Société Générale, 102, 103
*Sociétés Indigènes de Prévoyance*, 172, 248
Sofala, 37
Sokoto, 55, 65, 85, 94, 121, 135, 188
*Solvay, Institut*, 198
Somalia, Somalis, 61, 83, 100, 139,
    183, 251, 264–5
Songhay, 26
Soninke, 25
sorghum, 18
South Africa, xiii, 2–3, 10–11, 29,
    47–9, 57, 65–71, 75, 78, 98,
    107–9, 112, 113, 130, 136, 138,
    149–66, 173, 183, 205, 209, 210,
    217, 220–31, 234–46, 262
South African Congress of Trade
    Unions, 227
South African Party, 156, 161
South African Republic (*see also*
    Transvaal ), 67, 69–70, 87–8

South African Reserve Bank, 160
South West Africa (*see also* Namibia),
    84, 95, 112, 118, 141, 155, 159,
    169, 223, 236, 237–8, 242
South West African People's
    Organisation (SWAPO), 236
Southern Africa, 17, 71, 113, 127, 135,
    220–46
Southern Rhodesia, *see also* Rhodesia,
    Southern
Southern Rivers, 46
Soviet Union (*see also* Russia), 3, 161,
    177, 201, 205–8, 213, 227, 239,
    242, 251, 254
Soweto, 10, 223, 228, 238
Spain, 51
spice trade, 35
sport, 267, *see also* football
squatting, 69, 126, 154, 174,
    179–80, 220, 223; urban, 165
stabilisation, labour, 104–5
Stanley, Henry Morton, 64, 82
Stanleyville, *see* Kisangani
state, pre-colonial, 4–5, 9, 21–32, 56,
    59, 77, 133; colonial, 77–9, 102–3,
    107, 118–22, 128, 181; post-
    colonial, 185, 210–13, 214–16,
    218–19, 247–8, 254, 259, 260–6
'stateless' societies, 23, 31, 100; and
    slave trade, 45
Stevens, Siaka, 189
Steyn, M. T., 153
'strange farmers', 55, 116
Strijdom, Johannes, 224
structural adjustment programmes
    (SAPs), 254–60, 261, 263–4
Sudan, xiii, 25, 61, 83, 92, 100,
    116–17, 140, 184, 199, 217,
    249, 267
Sudan, French, 116, 197
Suez Canal, 83
sugar, 41, 52, 55, 58, 69, 109, 257
Sukuma, 134
Sundkler, Bengt, 138
Susenyos, 37
Sutton, J. E. G., 17
Suzman, Helen, 229
Swahili, 30, 36, 205

Swainson, Nicola, 211
Swazi, Swaziland, 93, 121, 164, 195, 210, 229, 230, 245
Sweezy, Paul, 10
swollen shoot, 179, 181, 185
Swynnerton Plan, 191
syndicalism, 156

Table Bay, 47–8
Tabora, 59
*talakawa*, 32, 126
Tananarive (Antananarivo), 62, 168
Tanganyika, 84, 108, 109, 112, 113, 123–4, 132, 134, 135, 140, 155, 171, 172, 174, 178–9, 182, 190, 192; African Association, 132; (*see also* Tanzania)
Tanganyika African National Union (TANU), 182, 192, 214
Tanganyika Federation of Labour, 214
Tanganyika, Lake, 59
Tanzania (*see also* Tanganyika, Zanzibar), xiii, 9, 11, 29, 30, 36, 59, 96, 182, 193, 207, 209, 210, 214–18, 233, 239, 255
taxation, 25, 100, 109, 112, 132, 118, 119–21, 145, 179
teff, 18
Teke, 82
telegraph, telegraphists, 80, 178
Tema, 248
Terray, Emmanuel, 11, 27
Tete, 234, 235
Tewodros (Kassa, Theodore), 62
thaumaturgy, 21–2
Thiès, 118
'Third Force', 243
'Third World', 11, 245, 261
Thompson, Leonard, 8
Thuku, Harry, 145
Tigre, 24, 62, 251, 260–1
Tigrinya, 25
timber, 115, 212
tin, 20, 74, 105–6, 109
Tippu Tip, 59, 62, 77, 91
*tirailleurs sénégalais*, 58, 78
title societies, 21, 31
tobacco, 58, 124, 174, 222

Togo, 84, 112, 123–4, 197, 218, 253
Tomlinson Commission, 224
Touré, Sékou, 196–7, 248
tourism, 257
trade, long-distance, 5, 20–1, 22, 25–7, 55, 59, 64, 134; and class in nineteenth-century Africa, 71, 92–3, 98–9; export-import, 171–2, 246, 254, 256; gold, 37, 59; and imperialism, 76–7; 'legitimate', 54–5, 56, 132; nineteenth-century Cape, 67; ocean, 29–30, 48; and wage employment, 129–30, 266 (*see also* slave trade, merchants and capital, merchant)
Trades Union Congress (UK), 178
Transkei, 227
Transvaal, 89–90, 95, 150–2, 156–7, 221, 225–6, 237 (*see also* South African Republic)
Traore, Moussa, 260
Trapido, Stanley, 151
Treason trials, 227
*trekboers*, 67–8, 69
tribalism, 133–5, 188, 192, 199, 260, 264, 265
tribes, 5, 19, 23, 59, 133–5
tribute, 24, 27, 28, 36, 38, 69, 98, 100, 109
Trinidad, 52
Trotskyism, 12
True Whig Party, 250
trust, 47, 56
trypanosomiasis, 108
Tshombe, Moïse, 200–2, 209
*tsotsi*, 224
Tswana, 89, 93, 210
Tuareg, 26
Tunisia, xii, 196
Tukulor, 81
Tutsi, 28, 261
*tyeddo*, 45

Ubangi-Shari, *see* Central African Republic
Uganda, 28, 86, 103, 109, 110, 113, 119, 121, 123, 128, 130, 174, 189, 194–5, 199, 200, 205,

208, 210, 215, 218, 248, 256–60, 264–5
Uganda Agreement, 110, 128
Uganda People's Congress, 182, 194, 210
Uganda, Railway, 107
Uige, 231
uitlanders, 90
Umar, al Hajj, 65, 81
underdevelopment, see dependency theory
unemployment, 245
Uniaõ das Populaçaõs de Angola (UPA), 231–2
Uniaõ Nacional para a Independencia Total de Angola (UNITA), 233, 238, 241
Unilever, 109, 114, 131, 171, 207
Union des Populations du Cameroun (UPC), 179–80, 195
Union Minière du Haut-Katanga (UMHK) 103–4, 201
Union Soudanaise, 196
Unionist Party (South Africa), 156, 159
United Africa Company, 81, 131, 172, 185, 207
United Democratic Front (South Africa), 243
United Gold Coast Convention (UGCC), 181, 185
United National Independence Party (UNIP, Zambia), 209–10
United Nations Organisation, 183, 197, 201
United Party (South Africa), 161, 166, 221, 229, 240
United States of America, 4, 7, 41–2, 43, 51–3, 57, 58, 74, 76, 96ff, 137, 138, 142, 145–6, 177, 181–2, 187, 202, 205, 218, 228, 230–1, 232, 249, 262
Upper Volta (Burkina Faso), 268ff
'Urabi Pasha, 82
uranium, 253
urban society, 128, 133, 156, 160–1, 162, 165, 169–70, 181, 190–1, 198; urban bias, 254
Usuman dan Fodio, 135

Vaal river, 67
Vail, Leroy, 108
van Bilsen, J., 198
Vansina, Jan, 8
veeboers (see also trekboers ), 48
vent-for-surplus, 111
Vereeniging, 90, 226
verkramp, 240
verlig, 240
Verwoerd, Hendrik Frensch, 224, 226–7, 229
Vichy, 122, 169
Victoria Federation of Co-operative Unions, 172
Victoria Nyanza, lake, 28, 85, 107
Vietnam, 196
Vincent, Joan, 130
Volksraad, 89
Volta rivers, 248
Vorster, B. J., 226, 236, 240
Vridi canal, 170

Waalo, 65
Walata, 25
warrant chiefs, 119
Wehler, Hans-Ulrich, 75
Welensky, Sir Roy, 193
Welsh, David, 69
Wernher, Beit & Co., 90
West Africa, 7, 15, 16, 18, 22, 25–8, 29, 43–7, 53–8, 64–5, 71, 77–81, 105–6, 112–13, 114–16, 117–18, 122, 136, 140, 142, 175, 179, 184–9, 195–8, 200, 218
West African Frontier Force, 78
West Indies (see also Cuba, Haiti, Jamaica, Lesser Antilles, Trinidad), 9, 52–3, 58, 143
wheat, 48, 108
White Flag Rebellion, 184
White Highlands of Kenya, 107–8, 126, 174, 179, 192, 211
whites, see Europe/Europeans, racism
Williams, Eric, 52
Williams, Raymond, 12, 31
Wilson, Harold, 235
wine, 48, 66
witches, 136

Witwatersrand, 88, 90, 103, 156–7, 161, 165, 220–1, 234
Wolof, 139
women, 17, 18, 20, 32, 33ff, 38, 39, 45, 49, 54, 113, 115, 117, 129, 130–1, 133, 138, 144, 147, 160, 181
Women's War, 144
wool, 67, 68
World Bank, 254–5, 259–60
World War I, 76, 90, 100, 112, 156, 169
World War II, 164, 168–70, 177, 220–1
*Wretched of the Earth*, 9
Wrigley, C. C., 9

Xhosa, 67, 70
Xuma, Alfred, 165

yams, 18, 115
Yohannis IV (John), 62
Yoruba, Yorubaland, 19, 45, 57, 63, 64, 85, 92–3, 100, 121, 134–5, 188
Youlou, Fulbert, 249

Zaïre (*see also* Congo, Belgian), 28, 44, 206, 216, 252, 253, 261, 262, 266
Zaïre river (*see* Congo), 28
Zambesi river, 29, 38, 40, 58, 63, 86, 234, 235
Zambia, 29, 193–4, 206, 209–10, 215, 217, 219ff, 230, 232–3, 236, 239, 248, 259 (*see also* Northern Rhodesia)
Zanzibar, 42, 55, 59–60, 62, 63–4, 109, 174, 190, 192–3, 210
Zanzibar National Party, 192
Zikists, 187
Zimbabwe (*see also* Rhodesia and Rhodesia, Southern), 29, 30, 38, 95, 141, 239, 258
Zimbabwe African National Union (ZANU), 235–6, 239
Zimbabwe African People's Union (ZAPU), 235, 239
Zionist churches, 138, 145
Zoutpansberg, 67
Zulu, 29, 68, 70, 87–8, 93, 95, 141–2, 152–3, 224; Kwa Zulu, 243